WITHDRAWN

THAT'S NOT FUNNY, THAT'S SICK

THAT'S NOT FUNNY, THAT'S SICK

The *National Lampoon* and the Comedy Insurgents Who Captured the Mainstream

Ellin Stein

W. W. NORTON & COMPANY

NEW YORK   LONDON

For information about permission to reproduce selections from this book,
write to Permissions, W. W. Norton & Company, Inc.,
500 Fifth Avenue, New York, NY 10110

For information about special discounts for bulk purchases, please contact
W. W. Norton Special Sales at specialsales@wwnorton.com or 800-233-4830

Manufacturing by Courier Westford
Book design by Daniel Lagin
Production manager: Devon Zahn

Library of Congress Cataloging-in-Publication Data

Stein, Ellin.
That's not funny, that's sick : the National lampoon and the comedy insurgents
who captured the mainstream / Ellin Stein. — First edition.
pages cm
Includes bibliographical references and index.
ISBN 978-0-393-07409-3 (hardcover)
1. National lampoon—History. 2. American wit and humor—Periodicals—History.
I. Title.
PN4900.N324S74 2013
051—dc23

2013006174

W. W. Norton & Company, Inc.
500 Fifth Avenue, New York, N.Y. 10110
www.wwnorton.com

W. W. Norton & Company Ltd.
Castle House, 75/76 Wells Street, London W1T 3QT

1 2 3 4 5 6 7 8 9 0

To Enid, who isn't here to read this, and to Chris, who is

CONTENTS

CONTENTS

THAT'S NOT FUNNY, THAT'S SICK

1

LAMPY'S CASTLE

Immediately after the last Labor Day of the 1960s, two recent Harvard graduates moved to New York to work on a magazine called the *National Lampoon*. Unlike many recent graduates who start work on new magazines, Henry Beard and Doug Kenney came in as the chief editors. Unlike many magazines that have recent graduates as chief editors, the *Lampoon* had backers committed to the tune of $350,000 (about $2 million in today's money), a deal negotiated by a Harvard student who was still finishing up his last term. Six years later, the two editors would each be $2.5 million (nearly $11 million today) richer. Five years after that, one would have found a measure of equilibrium by keeping a low profile while the other, having blazed a comet-like trail of highly visible successes, would tumble to his death off a cliff in Hawaii.

Along the way, the *National Lampoon* helped trigger a chain reaction of groundbreaking projects that would spread to theater, records, radio, television, and movies, making satire and subversive humor a gateway to commercial success when the conventional wisdom had previously considered it to be an obstacle. It was a pebble thrown into a pond, with ripples ultimately including *The Simpsons*, *The Onion*, *This*

Is Spinal Tap, South Park, The Daily Show, 30 Rock, and *Superbad,* but its most significant and proximate influence was on *Saturday Night Live,* the breakthrough television show that for over thirty-five years has been the premiere launching pad for American comedy talent. Satirists and humorists emerged in amazing numbers to bounce off each other in ever-shifting groups and combinations, generating considerable heat, occasional light, and more than a few dramatic explosions. The *Lampoon* and its offspring reflected, defined, and enhanced an iconoclastic sensibility that would emerge as the dominant style of the '70s, a decade that otherwise often seemed like the hangover after the blowout of the '60s.

Huge pop culture successes are big rivers fed by many obscure streams. The tributaries feeding into the mighty *Lampoon* included improvisational comedy troupes such as Second City, early video production collectives like TVTV, underground comics, and, primarily, the *Harvard Lampoon (HL),* humor organ of the august university and, at the time, as unlikely a source for future television comedy writers as could be imagined. But in time, membership of the *HL* would change from being an excuse to hang out to being a coveted launch pad into the entertainment industry, all due to the unexpected success of Beard and Kenney's efforts.

Much as the *HL*'s frivolity departs from Harvard's overall serious-mindedness, so its home resembles an elaborate and charming joke, an unusually whimsical exception to the order and harmony of the university's architectural vernacular. Although called the Castle, the building is only three stories. However, it does have a tower with a pointed roof, atop which perches the Ibis, the organization's frequently stolen mascot. Vaguely medieval detailing such as emblazoned wooden doors and leaded glass windows add a certain baronial flair. Upstairs is the Great Hall, a big room that looks like a Hollywood version of something called "The Great Hall" down to its vaulted ceiling and magnificent sixteenth-century Elizabethan fireplace, suitable for smashing plates and glassware against (the building comes complete with a maintenance staff to clean it up). The walls along a winding staircase are covered with framed covers of *HL* projects dating back to the founding of the organization/publication by seven undergraduates in 1876.

"It's not clear whether the *Harvard Lampoon* is a social club or a humor magazine," observed Michael Frith, an *HL* veteran and later creative director of the Muppets. "At different points in its history, it's been one or the other and sometimes both. Most likely it's neither very successfully and probably a combination of the two."

The organization has a number of quaint traditions including weekly formal dinners that may involve the aforementioned smashing of plates and glassware. Most of the rest involve practical jokes. *HL* president George Plimpton ('48), for example, distinguished himself by putting a goat into Widener, the Harvard undergraduate library. One of the *HL*'s most daring pranks was inspired by an editorial written for its 1936 parody of wholesome general-interest magazine the *Saturday Evening Post*, which fulminated, "Some morning we may wake up to find a Communist flag waving from the staff of our greatest public buildings." Sure enough, shortly thereafter the Soviet hammer and sickle was discovered at dawn billowing from the flagpole of the Supreme Court in Washington DC, with a copy of the *HL* left near the scene of the crime, like the Mark of Zorro. This led the court's security chief to huff, "The Supreme Court of the United States is no place for Harvard Socialists to have fun."

Another cherished tradition is annoying the *Crimson*, the well-respected Harvard student newspaper, usually by publishing at least one *Crimson* parody annually. *Crimson* staffers would invariably retaliate by stealing the Ibis, but the institution was at a distinct disadvantage. The *Crimson* couldn't decide whether to get into the feud or remain above it, recalled 'Poonie Peter Gabel ('68), "because they were a serious organization of political expression and ideas whereas we were a bunch of assholes."

HL membership hovered around forty or fifty, although the number of those actually involved in putting out the magazine was usually fewer than ten. A student could attempt to join as a writer or, if not creatively inclined, as part of the business board. Admission to the editorial board was either by writing sample or by good social connections to existing editors. Earlier distinguished *HL* members included *New Yorker* humorist Robert Benchley, the philosopher George Santayana, and journalist John Reed (who salvaged, legend has it, the brassware that adorns the Great Hall's mantle from the 1917 storming of the Winter Palace in St. Petersburg during the Russian Revolution).

Ostensibly, the *HL* produced its own publication five times a year and, from 1917 until World War II, put out an additional magazine parody virtually every year. But by the time Michael Frith joined in 1959, the fortunes of the *HL* were in decline, with circulation having sunk to an all-time low of nine hundred. "The magazine had become ingrown and rife with debt," he recalled. "We were amazed to hear that other college humor magazines divided up their profits among the staff—we paid dues!" The dues mostly went toward the formal dinners, with publication costs funded solely from magazine sales. The malaise lifted in the early '60s, when the organization was revitalized by a remarkably energetic intake of members that put out an unprecedented nine issues a year.

With this newfound energy came a revival of the magazine parodies, triggered by a young staffer at *Mademoiselle*, a fashion and lifestyle magazine for young women, who in 1961 suggested to its august editor in chief, Betsy T. Blackwell, that it might be a good idea to give the magazine's traditionally low-circulation July issue the *Lampoon* treatment. Not only did Blackwell agree, she offered the amazed *Lampoon* editors an honorarium.

Far from feeling constrained by producing the *Mademoiselle* parody alongside the magazine's ladylike staff, the *HL* pranksters "really enjoyed them," Frith said. "What a bunch of eccentrics!" He remembered particularly Blackwell, a large woman given to terrible coughing spells that could throw editorial meetings into a state of suspended animation. During one such meeting, a new, very serious *HL* writer earnestly remarked that, in order to make the parody work, it would be essential to "get a real suppository of ideas," whereupon, recalled Frith, "I thought we'd lose Betsy T. Blackwell."

The *HL* suppository worked, and *Mademoiselle*'s July circulation shot up. The Harvardians were invited to edit the summer issue for the next two years running. By 1963, they were already bored with parodying *Mademoiselle* and amused themselves by using that year's July issue to parody the men's magazine *Esquire*, thus creating total confusion.

Besides increasing the *HL*'s own subscription list by several thousand names, the success of the *Mademoiselle* parodies made the 'Poonies reconsider the size of their potential audience. Access to professional production facilities and the ability to parody the target magazine's format exactly was a revelation to Frith's *HL* contemporary and future *Sesame Street* lyricist, Christopher Cerf. "All of a sudden we were putting out a national magazine and working with models and photographers," he said. "We didn't feel confined to only putting out the *Harvard Lampoon*."

After the second *Mademoiselle* parody in the summer of 1962, Cerf, a born instigator, teamed up with Frith to write a parody of the adventures of President John F. Kennedy's favorite fictional character, James Bond. Dubbed *Alligator*, the slim seventy-seven-page paperback was then slipped into all twenty thousand copies of the fall *HL*.

So accomplished was *Alligator* that it might easily have been mistaken for the real thing. The book's villain, one Lacertus Alligator, a short megalomaniac with "pointed teeth made of burnished steel," pet alligators, and a penchant for spraying everyone who comes within arm's reach with a purple aerosol spray, is only slightly more outlandish than the average Bond baddie; Bond's capacity for remaining unaffected by substance abuse ("he had quickly showered and dressed, tossed down seven double martinis") or physical pain ("the beast tore itself away from B*nd, bringing with it a substantial portion of his foreleg and, B*nd realized thankfully through senses clouded by agony, the ropes that bound his legs. He now was free to move about") only slightly exaggerated; and the hero's instructions for the preparation of food and drink ("'A bacon, lettuce and tomato sandwich,' he said. 'The bacon must be crisp, not, however, over-cooked. Lettuce from the inside please, but not the heart.'") only slightly more elaborate.

Cerf's father, Bennett, editorial director and cofounder of publisher Random House, took note of *Alligator*'s glowing reviews. He thought he could bring *Alligator* out in hardcover and, Frith recalled, "wrote Ian Fleming a nice letter that said, 'Dear Mr. Fleming, wouldn't it be wonderful if . . . ?'"

The urbane novelist replied to this suggestion with a furious letter heaping scorn on the *HL* parody. This reaction shocked the parody's authors, who had thought the Bond books were *supposed* to be funny. A nervous B. Cerf suggested the *HL* publish only an additional one hundred thousand copies and asked (unsuccessfully) that the rights then transfer to Fleming, who was about to do a children's book (*Chitty Chitty Bang Bang*) for Random House. The additional *Alligator* copies sold out immediately, and this windfall looked like it might only be the beginning. "We had movie offers, somebody wanted us to do a Broadway musical," Frith sighed, but the collegiate authors were legally unable to further exploit their notoriety.

Fleming's ire extended beyond the grave. After he died, the people who had obtained the rights to continue the series approached Frith and C. Cerf and asked them to write the further adventures of James Bond. The collaborators accepted, but a routine check revealed a codicil in the late author's will that prohibited in perpetuity Frith and Cerf specifically from writing any Bond books after Fleming's death. Not even over his dead body would the author let his hero fall into the parodists' clutches a second time.

When the *Esquire* parody appeared in July 1963, there was already a favorable climate for light satirical comedy. A record making good-natured fun of the Kennedy clan, the *First Family*, became a hit. A former ad man named Stan Freberg was exploring the possibilities of audio parody on radio and records, while a comedy team from Chicago, Mike Nichols (later the Oscar-winning director of *The Graduate* and *Working*

Girl, among many others) and Elaine May (who went on to write or direct well-regarded film comedies such as *The Heartbreak Kid* and *A New Leaf*), mined a rich vein in the new widespread interest in Freudian analysis. On television, Ernie Kovacs had already injected surreal comedy into prime time, and a cartoon show called *Rocky and His Friends*, which depicted the eternal struggle between an all-American squirrel and two Soviet agents, was grafting sophisticated adult humor onto a program ostensibly for children.

As well, in October 1962, three Cambridge University graduates—Peter Cook, Jonathan Miller, and Alan Bennett, along with Dudley Moore (from Oxford)—had brought their hit comedy sketch revue *Beyond the Fringe* from London to Broadway, where it received a rapturous reception and a yearlong run. Though *Beyond the Fringe* is credited with starting England's so-called satire boom of 1961–1963, the perpetrators were more inclined toward anarchy than satire, aiming at being funny rather than reforming. "None of us approached the world with a satirical indignation," Miller said. "We had no reason to. We were all very comfortably off and doing very nicely."

Nevertheless, *Beyond the Fringe* appeared radically innovative and shocking because it took previously sacred subjects such as religion, patriotism, and the royal family and treated them as suitable subjects for mockery. Evading all labels, the show did not take an easy politically liberal line. As one critic wrote, it was "anti-reactionary without being progressive," a description that could equally apply to the yet unborn *National Lampoon* and *Saturday Night Live*.

Recognizing kindred spirits after seeing *Beyond the Fringe*'s Boston preview, the 'Poonies invited Cook and Moore to the Castle, where, after some sustained socializing, the British team had to be given large amounts of coffee before they could leave to do their show. After *Alligator* appeared, a Broadway producer asked Frith and Cerf if they wanted to do an American *Beyond the Fringe*. Although Frith declined, it seemed to him "very natural" that they would get an offer. "As soon as I graduated from college in 1963, I was being interviewed for things like appearing on television panels," he said, "and my attitude was 'Oh, all right. I hope it doesn't take too long.'"

This insouciant expectation of a seamless transition to a pleasant postgraduation life belied the growing turmoil in the broader society outside the Castle's walls. In 1962, all fifty-three members of a little-known organization called the Students for a Democratic Society (SDS) had produced a statement setting forth guiding principles for something they called the New Left, a proclamation that went virtually unnoticed by the world at large. August 1963 brought two hundred thousand civil rights demonstrators to Washington DC, where they heard Martin Luther King dream of a fully integrated nation. Then in November 1963, President Kennedy was assassinated, and nothing would be quite so wholesome again.

Harvard, and the *HL* especially, were for the most part still unruffled by the gathering forces of change, but they would not remain so. When John Weidman, a future *National Lampoon* contributing editor, came to Harvard as a freshman in 1964, he found the campus "more like Harvard in 1944 than it would be like in 1968 when I left. The change in those four years was enormous." In 1963, when buses going down to Mississippi bearing the Harvard contingent of voter registration workers had departed from the Castle's doorstep, the 'Poonies came out in black tie to toast the departing Freedom Riders with champagne, behavior that did not go down well. When Weidman went on a campus tour shortly thereafter, the tour guide, he recalled, "made a point of stopping in front of the Castle and sneering."

However, by 1964, in its own detached way, the *HL* had started to reflect the oncoming metamorphosis, devoting its May '64 issue to civil rights. "How many of us really realize that the Negro is a sick man—that Negrosis is a disease like any other?" one writer argued. "If he begins ranting about 'equality' or 'our heritage,' the disease is in its terminal stage and the victim should be removed from society." This modest proposal, ostensibly by "D. Fritz Overholt Jones-Oglethorpe, of the Memorial Hospital, Birmingham," was in fact written by the almost as absurdly named

George William Swift Trow, then-president of the *HL*. Trow, another future *National Lampoon* contributing editor, was an *HL* anomaly in that he already had a conception of himself as a professional writer.

Trow also embodied a certain WASPy prep style that would become less and less typical of the *HL*. "Affect (oh go ahead) POVERTY!" Trow would write in a 1965 *HL* piece called "Igor Cassini's Christmas," little dreaming some of Harvard's most gilded youth would be taking his advice five years later. "While all your pedestrian middle-class friends scream and shout about the Waring Blender they're going to get for Christmas, you steal the show in eye-catching *rags*."

This prep school influence, however, did not loom nearly as large at the Castle as it did at other Harvard subsocieties. The university disdains fraternities but instead has final clubs, then peopled largely by boys similar to the protagonist of the Harvard-set *Love Story*; old money, old school, and old family preferred. Among the clubs itself there were further hierarchical distinctions, and decidedly not in the top drawer was the Spee, which had a distinct literary-intellectual tinge and valued brains over background. This was the final club to which many of the *HL* members belonged.

According to Peter Gabel, an *HL* contemporary of Weidman's, non-preppies viewed the 'Poonies as "elitist, artsy-fartsy types" and maintained "the slightly hostile distance characteristic of people's attitudes toward the clubs," but the *HL*'s exclusivity had a different cast to it. "The *Harvard Lampoon* was not as if you took five characters from *Brideshead Revisited* and dropped them onto the Harvard campus in the mid-60s, sort of detached and aristocratic, sipping sherries," Weidman said. "In the '60s, the *Lampoon* wasn't particularly elitist. However, people did think they were wittier and smarter and having a better time."

There were other crucial differences. For one thing, unlike the clubs, the *HL* had a project beyond reinforcing privilege and networking; this was to put out a magazine, however desultorily. For another, it had different role models. "You felt connected to the culture of satire, to people who did pranks and wrote funny things," Gabel said. "On the high culture side, you were connected to literary people like Santayana." These connections were more than in the mind. Chris Cerf was already an editor at Random House. Weidman's father, Jerome, was a playwright and *New Yorker* contributor, and Gabel's mother, Arlene Francis, had joined Cerf's father on the panel of a popular television quiz show called *What's My Line?*

Where the *HL* diverged most noticeably from the clubs was, by 1965, in the ethnic background of the membership. Several of the '60s 'Poonies had been non-Protestant preppies, an experience that informed the insider-outsider perspective characteristic that would come to define the *National Lampoon*. "We were almost all Jewish and Catholic," said Conn Nugent, another late-60s recruit to the *HL*. "It was a real urban melting pot—very New York influenced. Some members' parents were actually Democrats."

These distinctions loomed in the mind of Doug Kenney, a clever sophomore from Ohio who gave little indication of becoming one of the guiding forces behind the *National Lampoon* when he joined in the spring of '65. The subject of preppies propelled Kenney's *HL* debut, a parody musical libretto called *Backside Story* (the movie version of *West Side Story* having swept the previous year's Oscars), which chronicles the ongoing feud between the Preps and the Townies. It kicks off with Kenney's version of "When You're a Jet," as the Preps enter singing, "When you're a prep, you're a prep through and through / From your Brooks Brothers suit / To your Bass Wee-Jun shoes."

While Kenney may have arrived at Harvard prepped out to the max, that doesn't mean he was quite the real thing. According to Nugent, both he and Kenney were "Irish Catholics from social-climbing families who went to prep schools generally considered mediocre." But Kenney's pose was hardly seamless: "Doug could go out and buy a white linen suit and get his hair cut and look as preppy as anyone I'd ever known," a friend said, but, while Kenney might buy white linen suits, "then he'd sleep in them." Moreover, Kenney was hardly alone. "We all assumed the preppy persona in and out," Nugent recalled. "The *Harvard Lampoon* was a place where one developed one's poses—preppy, hippie, social activist, literary type—and sometimes they ran amok. We simultaneously thought that we were great stuff and that our essential fraudulent postures would be found out."

Gabel saw Kenney as "a combination of a boy from the Midwest and embryo preppy. He was elusive as a person, in some way always performing, trying things on all the time." But, Weidman maintained stoutly, "Doug didn't posture and he didn't pose. He went through a lot of evolutions. There were good Dougs and bad Dougs and stoned Dougs and all different kinds of Dougs, but there was nothing false or faddish about him."

Perhaps the distinction to make is that Kenney's identity itself was fluid and the style followed. Alex Garcia-Mata, a college girlfriend who subsequently became his wife for one year, compared Kenney to an onion. "You would get down to what you thought was the core and there would be another layer, like so many masks to take off," she said. Kenney may have been unable to pick a social persona—whether smooth preppy or creative bohemian or ambitious Midwesterner—and stick with it because he was always aware of the inherent ridiculousness of that particular image. If nothing else, his field trips into different social milieux enabled him to satirize them all the better for having been there. "In one way, he could be perceived as a social climber," an *HL* colleague said. "On the other hand, he very clearly expressed his contempt for the whole thing and was very funny about it."

These were not cries for reform but rather for admittance. "Any of us who joined a club were into social climbing," Nugent declared. "We cared about things like whether a tweed jacket was nice or hideous. If we were liberal it was mainly because liberal implied sophistication. There wasn't much sense of social mission at the *Harvard Lampoon*," he said. "We thought of admitting black people and so one got in [in 1969], but that's as far as our consciousness went at that time."

Nor were 'Poonies especially caught up in the other burning issue of the day since, thanks to student deferments, Harvard students were in no immediate danger of being called up to go to Vietnam, a war that had been intensifying since the early '60s. There was a general gentlemanly opposition to the war, but this was not put into action, at least on an organizational level. The *HL*, Weidman felt, "was neither political or aggressively nonpolitical or even apolitical. Individual members were involved or not."

The prevailing attitude toward politics around the Castle, said Nugent, was that "no sincerely stated statement should be safe for more than fifteen seconds and boundless enthusiasm was generally symptomatic of ignorance." Issues of major importance such as nuclear annihilation were not on the Castle table. "The *Lampoon* encouraged one form of rebellion only," he said: "thumbing your nose at propriety, establishment values, the whole Pollyanna *shtick*. There was no refuge from the high irony of the place," and so the most frequently heard adjectives were "boring" and "tedious." This applied not only to God, Motherhood, and the Flag, but also the Peace Corps, the War on Poverty, and other manifestations of mid-60s idealism.

The rebellion of the self-consciously disenchanted usually took the form of embarrassing people and a general prankish disrespect, like a plan to make off with some invaluable moon rocks from Harvard's geology department, which fortunately failed to come off. Some students, like Jim Rivaldo—a member of the business board, Weidman's roommate, and a scholarship student—had trouble entering into the proper spirit of irresponsibility. "When I think of having lobster food fights and filet mignon food fights . . ." he said, remembering the Thursday-night black-tie dinners. In time, the *HL* grew less tolerant, if anything, of such scruples. "We do get problems with new members from poor backgrounds," a 1986 member admitted. "But you just lift their wrists, force them to drop the plate, and they squeal with delight. Somebody's going to clean up anyway, so a couple more pieces of glass aren't going to matter."

The mid-60s crop was similar. "It wasn't mean-spirited or even unconscious," Rivaldo recalled. "Somehow it was just another absurd thing, part of being removed from what the rest of the world was experiencing. Everything you did as a member of the *Lampoon* was some kind of absurd statement in behavior or attitude. When you walked into that bizarre castle, you had a responsibility to act different and think different and be different." By the end of 1965, it was getting harder to keep up the pose: the US presence in Vietnam had increased by sixty-one thousand troops, and the first draft card had been burned. That August, the first of several urban riots had erupted in a clash between police and the residents of Los Angeles's Watts district that left thirty-four dead, four thousand arrested, and millions nervous.

By April 1966, the war and the official obfuscation surrounding it had come to even the Castle's attention, at least to the extent of providing grist for the mill in "The Great American Guinea Pig," a long essay by a junior from Connecticut, future *National Lampoon* editorial mainstay Henry Beard. "Whenever an American wishes to display to a foreigner the inherent rightness, goodness, or harmlessness of something he has done," Beard wrote, rather than resorting to "the messy statistics and confusing facts for which his country is so justly famous, he cuts through the web of ignorance and false knowledge . . . and offers himself as a guinea pig." Applying this principle to foreign policy, Beard suggested that the abortive Kennedy-era CIA-funded attempt to have anti-Castro Cubans invade their homeland "would have looked a great deal better if we had let the Cubans stage a Bay of Pigs of their own in the Chesapeake with exiled Republicans to prove that interventions of that sort are enjoyable."

If Kenney was an ersatz preppy, Beard, an ectomorph given to a professorially shabby image complete with pipe and tweedy suits (Beard would later describe himself as the owner of "a lint suit that picks up blue serge"), was the genuine article. He was known for the consistency of his persona, which Nugent described as "anachronistic, literary, ironic, and perpetually bored," and he soon became a Castle fixture. "Henry was the *Lampoon* guy," Weidman recalled. "Everyone else had girlfriends and was banging around, but you went to the Castle and Henry was there, or his extraordinary presence was." Consequently, Weidman said, Beard "was treated with a certain kind of deference. He could really do it. He could put paper in the typewriter and wail."

A capacity for hard work and a lack of extroversion also distinguished Rob Hoffman, a 1965 addition to the business board. "Everyone deferred to Rob's financial judgment while having a great affection for him," Rivaldo said. "It was clear from the beginning that he was going to be a multimillionaire entrepreneur," and indeed Hoffman would make his first million before he was twenty-four from engineering Kenney and Beard's *National Lampoon* deal.

Even so, the magazine's writers were ambivalent about Hoffman's expertise while appreciating his financial acumen. "Rob would get a lot of shit for being practical," Nugent recalled. "He was the thick-skinned, intelligent guy who could do the organizational work the poseurs didn't want to do." Despite assuming the pivotal role of treasurer, Hoffman never became a highly visible presence because, while he joined in singing around the piano, he did so quietly and the focus of the Castle's denizens stayed on the boisterous merry pranksters who claimed center stage.

Singing around the piano had become increasingly central to *HL* life. One of Nugent's fondest memories was of Kenney and ten other 'Poonies singing selections from the early '60s' bumper crop of great party songs like "Hang On Sloopy" and "Louie Louie" that cry out to be sung in a state of inebriated camaraderie.

These songs had a restless drive that fit the rhythm of the young men's experience far better than the string-laden sentimentality of popular favorites like Mitch Miller, Patti Page, and Perry Como. Swaddled by material prosperity and political stability, the 'Poonies had a passion for unmitigated experience that led them to embrace the raw, exciting sound produced by artists for whom a sheltered life was rarely an option. "It was not uncommon among members of my generation (the generation that grew up as wards of the meretricious adulthood of the 1950s) for one to feel one's first strong sense of reality through the agency of Negro music," Trow wrote in his 1980 *New Yorker* essay (later book) *Within the Context of No Context.*

The 'Poonies did not pretend to remain above this aspect of their generation's upheaval. At the start of the 1960s, the British had started producing a seemingly inexhaustible flow of great bands rooted firmly in American blues and R & B. But many contemporaneous US radio stations' playlists remained effectively segregated, with record labels reluctant to spend advertising dollars on "race" music. However, one by-product of the civil rights movement was greater cultural as well as political integration, and with a boost from Motown, this rich musical tradition finally went mainstream.

The Castle didn't get a stereo until '67, but the members listened to the Temptations and Smokey Robinson and the Miracles in their rooms and tried to recreate these groups' choreographed routines around the piano. Even more than the Motown groups, the names to drop were the true Soul Men like Sam and Dave and Otis Redding. "It was real important to my roommates and me to let people know we listened to black music so we were cool," Nugent said. "Otis Redding was *it* even though we secretly listened to the Lovin' Spoonful."

As America became the land of a thousand dances, white boys had to attempt to move their pelvises in public, a task many found mortifying and undignified. Girls, on the other hand, took to the Pony, the Jerk, and the Swim with enthusiasm. After years of having to appear ladylike, they were finally allowed to work up a sweat, and they started shaking their hips in all directions with enthusiasm.

Possibly girls were celebrating the fact that they were finally able to breathe normally. Panty hose had started hitting the market in the mid-60s, and while to many boys they seemed to be merely nylon chastity belts and no great step forward, to girls this was one less layer of rubber between their bodies and the world. Bras, too, lost their conical rigidity—one small step toward valuing the tactile if imperfect reality of women's bodies over the stiff illusion of perfection. As well, the Pill had become widely available. Harvard University Health Services began distributing contraceptives around this time and, Nugent observed, "something was definitely happening along those lines. It was clear you could get laid more easily than you could a few years before."

Added to this was the influence of hang-loose breezes blowing eastward from California. Like the Brits, the Californians had their own exotic argot, exciting musical sound, and distinctive image. Hedonists of all stripes flocked to the West Coast to find the "fun, fun, fun" the Beach Boys sang about. But even if the Californians were going casual, when Natalie Wood came to the Castle in 1966, the 'Poonies turned out to greet her in jackets and ties. If '50s standards of deportment and ironing did not disappear overnight, neither did '50s standards of morality, dance moves notwithstanding.

Until his junior year, Nugent, for example, went to Mass where he agonized over "the French kiss as mortal sin" and experienced "high nervousness about procuring condoms." Parietal rules were still in effect and coed dorms were undreamt of. Even though nice girls were starting to, most of the naked women the 'Poonies saw had staples in their navels. Not that they saw many women, naked or otherwise. Harvard was an all-male institution and so were its clubs, so officially, no women were allowed in the Castle, although by the mid-60s 'Poonies were sneaking women into the building for social functions.

The women were definitely there as adjuncts, not participants. Before female comedians like Sarah Silverman and Lena Dunham became visible enough to prove there's nothing inherently dainty about women's humor, there was a widespread view that, as Nugent said, "there is a kind of Bad Person humor that breaks taboos which comes from men and relatively few women shared the belittling, sexually demeaning, raucous, and unkind sense of humor which we found hilarious. A lot of us could have said, 'Chicks aren't funny,'" an observation attributed to Doug Kenney.

Despite their low opinion of female humor-generating capabilities and the exchange of much male-bonding genitalia-oriented banter, the 'Poonies were, relatively speaking, still your sensitive Harvard intellectuals more than your macho louts. The question of which pose to assume was exacerbated by the split emerging in their lives. By day the Harvard boys were immersed in the Judeo-Christian tradition, which counseled duty, responsibility, and rising above our animal nature. By night they danced to songs that urged them to, as one put it so well, "Sha na na na na na live for today."

So there they were in the spring of '66, maintaining a pose of ironic detachment but getting down around the piano and putting out a magazine that, as Rivaldo put it, "was a sleepy backwater for kind of irrelevant people who every now and then would make a splash here and there." Then at the beginning of the summer of 1966, *HL* president Walker Lewis suggested doing a *Playboy* parody. And everything changed.

2

REVENGE OF
THE LIBERAL
ARTS MAJORS

Collège humor magazines flourished during the '50s and '60s
(over in New Haven, undergraduate Garry Trudeau was shortly
to take the helm of the *Yale Record* in 1968, while future director Terry Gilliam was already editing Occidental College's *Fang*), and all
of them did a parody of *Playboy*. The attitude at the Castle, said Hoffman, was "we are the *Harvard Lampoon*, the greatest college humor
magazine in the world, and we're going to do our *Playboy* parody *right*,"
despite having only $4,000 in the checking account. However, they also
had well-heeled friends who kindly paid for printing an unprecedented
550,000 copies.

Other strings were pulled. A connection to a former Playmate led
to Hef himself, who proved a good sport, setting the parodists up with
his own printer and newsstand distributor. Then in April 1966, *HL*
editors blitzed the New York advertising agencies, selling ad space at
fairly nervy prices. However, they did not go unarmed. Hoffman carried
around with him an oil painting by an *HL* illustrator in the style of illustrator Antonio Vargas, whose depictions of ladies with not a lot covering their gravity-defying forms had been a staple of *Esquire* and *Playboy*

for generations. This particular pseudo-Vargas girl was depicted wearing nothing at all as she inquired, "Hi! How do you like my breasts?" The wit may not have been deathless, but the unsubtle visual aid was certainly enough to get the 'Poonies through the door.

HL artists were in much shorter supply than *HL* writers, so, although policy dictated only current undergraduates could work on the magazine itself, the rules were stretched for this side project, and Michael Frith was called up from the reserves to work on the *Playboy* parody, collaborating with Chris Cerf on *Little Orphan Bosom*, based on *Playboy*'s long-running comic strip *Little Annie Fanny* (itself a riff on sentimental newspaper comic strip *Little Orphan Annie*), the adventures of a sort of Candide-cum-Barbie doll.

Annie Fanny's creator was Harvey Kurtzman, legendary guiding genius behind the original *Mad* magazine. Born in 1952, *Mad* originally limited itself to parodying comic book genres such as horror, sci-fi, and Westerns. Visually, *Mad* was unlike anything else readily available. Its content didn't go much beyond lightly satirizing the consumer society and popular culture. Its real message lay in its cluttered panels teeming with images, suggesting any real culture was rapidly disappearing under a barrage of slogans, trademarks, logos, and jingles. Amid all the hygiene and moral uplift of the early '50s, *Mad* introduced a whole generation to the pleasures of trash recycled through a subversive sensibility, before subsiding into a gentle liberalism during the '60s.

The 'Poonies were Kurtzman admirers from way back. For the *Annie Fanny* parody, Frith created a tribute to leading *Mad* artist Wally Wood with a detail-cluttered version of Hefner's legendary circular bed complete with pipe rack, video monitors, automatic drink pourer, autographed Tony Curtis photo, and teddy bear. In a nod to Hef's tendency to present his "Playboy Philosophy" as a high moral crusade, an entourage of beaming young men equipped with *Playboy* cardigans and pipes applaud every word from the statuesque Orphan—who keeps tumbling over due to her top-heavy proportions—as a blow to hypocrisy and prudery. These insights are along the lines of "Gloriosky,

Mister Educator! Did you ever stop to think where the world would be today *without* bosoms?"

A better question might be where magazine publishers would be. Unlike more unassuming publishers of magazines in the same niche, Hefner promoted the idea that *Playboy* aspired to stimulate the brain as much as any other organ. The discerning *Playboy* reader demanded not only the finest women but also the best in consumer goods—his food, his liquor, his stereo system, his Jaguar XKE. Women were seduced not just by his animal magnetism but also by his savoir faire. He was, in fact, James Bond.

Despite all this sophistication, the jump between *Mad* and *Playboy* was less broad than might appear. In their own ways, both publications championed the right to refuse to grow up and accept responsibilities, at least the kind of responsibilities popularly associated with Mom or the Wife: work hard, come home at a decent hour, don't spend your money on expensive toys, don't drive so fast, stop fooling around. In a pre-Pill world where sex might well lead to pregnancy, or at any rate might entail a high degree of matrimonial expectations on the woman's part, the Playmates depicted in the magazine's centerfolds offered sex without strings. You wouldn't find her requiring souk-like haggling over sexual favors in exchange for pins, rings, or promises of commitment. Who knew if she could even speak? Those captions about her hobbies and so on were probably written for her by the editors.

Certainly they were in the case of the parody. The 'Poonies came up with the ideal Playmate, a sort of female Tarzan from a Carolina coastal island whose English is restricted to "My name is Oona. Mama and Papa dive into sea. Berries and herbs, herbs and berries," although a photo reveals that this child of nature's beach reading apparently includes *The New York Review of Books*. The 'Poonies had stumbled onto the trick that would be the financial cornerstone of their subsequent parodies and later the *National Lampoon*: because the naked ladies were presented in a joke context, the reader could feel superior to his sweaty-palmed brethren who genuinely sought out this kind of fantasy stimulant without having to deny himself any of their voyeuristic gratification.

The *Playboy* parody went on sale on Labor Day of 1966. Staying in the Beverly Hills Hotel, Rob Hoffman was delighted to see the parody on the hotel newsstand and even more delighted when a day later all the copies were gone. An impressive 450,000 mock *Playboy*s sold out nationally in less than a week. Back for the fall term, the returning 'Poonies realized the gamble had worked. After paying off its debts, the *HL* was left with a handsome profit of $91,000. "It was incredible," Hoffman said. "It changed everything."

The new affluence meant instead of serving just cheese and crackers at cocktail parties for *HL* candidates, the 'Poonies could serve cheese, crackers, *and* boiled shrimp. More significantly, the financial cushion enabled them to repair the Castle, which had been in a perpetual state of disrepair since it opened in 1910. The biggest change was in members' self-conception. "There we were," Gabel said, "these prep school kids let out of these incarceratorial institutions and given this incredible building for only fifteen dollars in dues, and then we made this money from *Playboy*—I don't think any of us even thought it was all that good—and we could make up anything we wanted and publish it and then succeed at it. It was very romantic." The 'Poonies decided to spend the loot on extravagant dinners, a pool table, and an expensive sound system, which led to lip-synched Motown routines replacing singing around the piano. It also led to civil war between the R & B and acid rock contingents.

Except for this playlist conflict, the *HL* was relatively quiescent during 1967, when the members were primarily absorbed in renovating the building and literally eating up the *Playboy* profits. The same could not be said of the country at large. The summer of 1967 is widely remembered as the Summer of Love, but everywhere you looked, conflict crackled. In Vietnam itself, the New Year had brought the Tet Offensive, which fueled both the perception that superior firepower would not win this war and a suspicion of technology in general. The spring saw approximately one hundred thousand antiwar demonstrators turn out on both the East and West Coasts as opposition grew along with mounting US casualties. Meanwhile, a new organization called the Black Panthers had been started in Oakland, California, by young African Americans fed up with the slow speed of change via the ballot box. Possibly reacting to the killing of twenty-six citizens in Newark, New Jersey, during one Summer of Love riot and a National Guard occupation of Detroit that left forty dead during another, the radical Panthers adopted a concept of active self-defense called "Black Power."

Another resistance struggle was gaining strength as potential draftees started destroying draft board files, trading avoidance tips, and visiting Canada in ever-increasing numbers. This movement had a sudden appeal for the previously apolitical 'Poonies as graduation drew near. "I don't think in '66 we ever believed we would actually have to go fight in Vietnam," said Gabel. But by the end of '67 this perception had changed, leading Kenney and Beard, two of the least gung ho people on earth, to join the ROTC (Reserve Officer Training Corps).

"Neither one of them had a deep concept of the injustice of the war or the concept of American military imperialism around the world and all that," Rivaldo recalled. Beard would "go on and on about the directives and the stupidity of the army in general, but it was just another absurd institution that provided fertile ground for satire." Students who join the ROTC looking for its ironic potential are unlikely to become model soldiers, and just as he was about to graduate, and thus lose his student deferment, Beard was not given a commission. He was suddenly left with nothing to do except avoid the draft, so he joined an army reserve unit and went off to boot camp in New Jersey.

Kenney, realizing an officer's uniform might make him all the more attractive to North Vietnamese snipers, was inspired to similarly get kicked out of the ROTC. He and Beard came up with a scheme that involved Kenney, who was acting as the defense attorney in a mock court martial, slipping a mock prosecution witness a real ten-dollar bill as an inducement to confess. This display of conduct unbecoming ensured that Kenney got his wish.

But leaving the ROTC meant that he could be drafted as a regular soldier and, entering his senior year in 1968, Kenney panicked. He discovered that, if you display the associated symptoms, there was no way to prove you didn't have epilepsy, so he spent the year faking faints and convulsions, resulting in frequent visits to the Cambridge ER. Finally, when he could no longer put off getting an army physical, he submitted to one, being sure to mention that he was "taking this medicine for my headaches." When the doctor asked him if he had epilepsy, Kenney said he really didn't know. "Well," said the doctor, "I'd be interested in finding out more about this, but your eyesight is so bad you're 4F," the designation given to candidates physically unfit for service.

In his first two years at Harvard, Kenney was perceived as a social butterfly, known for his inclination toward high-style girlfriends, garden parties, and spending more time at the Spee Club than at the Castle. But in his last two years, he shed much of his preppy incarnation and, when not having epileptic fits, took a more active role as an *HL* writer. Right before graduating in June 1968, he contributed *Cramalot*, a parody of the hit musical *Camelot*. It opens with a song that may have reflected his feelings about his first two years.

> *A law was made 300 years ago here*
> *For preppie, jock, or academic snot*
> *Let all your worst pretensions bravely show here*
> *Then Cramalot!*

went the first verse.

Another of Kenney's creations was the campus radical Lawrence Nightinjail. However, despite their draft fever, the 'Poonies had resisted the urge to join the Movement. It was more a problem of style than of substance, according to Rivaldo. "The campus radicals were too much Long Island High School Jewish troublemakers," he said, "so whatever the intellectual sympathies might have been, I don't think there was a great personal and social rapport."

It also went against the standard disengaged *HL* pose. "We were the only people who were cynical enough to make fun of the things that were really silly—nonnegotiable demands [of the kind issued by student radicals as a condition for vacating an occupied campus building], for example," said Hoffman, for whom the idea of *anything* being nonnegotiable may have been absurd. Despite a higher profile from the *Playboy* success, the 'Poonies still found themselves to be considered marginally important by their Harvard peers. As a phrase in currency at the time had it, "If you're not part of the solution, you're part of the problem," and the *HL* was definitely not part of the solution.

"College students became very serious and issue oriented," Hoffman observed sadly. "All those college humor magazines started going out of business," but not, thanks to its *Playboy* padding, the *HL*. While the *HL* officially kept its pose of amused detachment, it was increasingly difficult for individual members not to be swept up in the current of feeling.

But they found time for one last spectacularly successful prank. In March 1967, the 'Poonies had bought a thousand copies of the *New York Times* and put them in storage. A year later, they printed up a phony front page dated March 7, 1968, slipped it over the year-old *Times* inside pages, and dropped the hoaxes in bundles at Harvard Square newsstands before dawn.

In the original's own characteristic straight-faced style, the *HL NYT* covered stories such as a plan by then-governor Rockefeller to turn the New York State Thruway into a northbound one-way road, the seizure of the US naval base at Guantanamo by Cuban forces, and, most devastating of all, the reduction of the Parthenon to rubble by an earthquake. Gabel claimed that only a few people who bought the issue noticed that something was not as it should be. This strains belief considering a story that appeared in the lower left-hand corner headlined "Walrus in Central Park Zoo Speaks" ("all the more shocking after years of silence," was its keeper's comment), but the Harvard SDS met to prepare a statement supporting Castro's action at Guantanamo and the distressed senior tutor of Harvard's classics department cancelled his classes. Later, some disgruntled readers, doubtless frustrated by not being able to find out what the walrus said (his actual words were supposedly found in the continued story on an inside page), threatened lawsuits.

After two years' worth of renovations, acquiring new toys, and dinners, the *HL* was not really worth suing. At this point, Hoffman, Beard, and a couple of other hard workers decided the time had come to refill the coffers. They kicked around two schemes—starting a national spin-off of the *HL* or doing a parody of *Life*, at the time a hugely popular photo-driven general-interest magazine—and decided to go with the latter.

Released from boot camp, Beard had returned to Cambridge in the spring of '68 with time on his hands. Both he and Kenney had graduated and had no idea what they wanted to do except not leave the Castle. Beard now took on a leadership role editorially, while Kenney, too, came into the inner circle with the *Life* parody.

With Hoffman spending the summer serving in the Coast Guard, Rivaldo was made general manager. As such, he was in charge of the checkbook and had access to what remained of the *Playboy* cash. He frequently found himself taking his unemployed coworkers out to dinner, occasionally slipping a completely broke Kenney money for clothes and food. While admitting this might be "technically embezzlement," no one, he said, "got a color TV out of it. It was just enough to keep people working, whatever it took to keep Doug and the others perking along." Part of what it took, at the time, was drugs.

With only two years left in the decade, the '60s had come to the Castle at last. 'Poonies were already smoking marijuana but, until that summer of '68, never in the building. Pot fit right in with the *HL* spirit, promoting feelings of good fellowship and collective silliness. It was hard to take yourself or anything else too seriously when stoned.

However, it was possible to take this mellow detachment too far. Rivaldo shared an apartment with Beard, which they never used because they slept at the Castle, too tired to return after working on *Life* until the wee hours. This meant they remained blissfully unaware that their apartment had no lock on the front door until one day, two months after moving in, Rivaldo came home to discover that everything he owned had been cleared out.

There may have been such occasional lapses, but "the *Harvard Lampoon* was not a druggy experience, although people at the *Lampoon* did drugs," Weidman asserted. "The precision with which the material was written indicates this." Some people eschewed marijuana altogether. Beard, ever the traditionalist, stuck to getting drunk. But although pot may have been the most popular drug at the *HL*, some members were going further. "You'd be sitting on rugs worth thousands and thousands of dollars, drinking the most expensive alcohol and loaded on acid. It was part of the idea of parody," Rivaldo said, "especially for scholarship students like me. We were parodying rich people. Taking drugs was in keeping with our self-perception as pampered geniuses who were above the ordinary rules."

As well, psychedelic use was usually a more solitary, introspective experience than pot, fostering the detachment from conventional wisdom that informs the satiric perspective. As Rivaldo observed, "To be a professional absurdist means always looking for new angles to perceive everyday life. Drugs really unleashed a lot of things."

This proved especially true for Kenney. Experimenting with different social personas was nothing compared to experimenting with different modes of consciousness. A Letter to the Editor of the parody *Life*, headed "Drugs on Campus," provides some evidence. "Dear Sirs," it began. "I I thinc thad yuor stadement taht drucks are CHRIST IT'S TOOO HOTT harmbful iss a untru because taht that they have nott beeen pruved in aa labortoory," wrote one "Etaoin ShRlDlu" from "Harfard uniunivErsitY."

Like many of their contemporaries, the 'Poonies were struck by the way denunciations of drug-crazed youth appeared in media laden with ads that celebrated the joys of tobacco and alcohol consumption. "In a mad rush, men and women charge to the 'bar', clamoring to get their oily hands on a frightening array of off-color bottles containing that revolting poison—alcohol," revealed a mock *Life* special report entitled "Drink: Curse of the Thrill Crazy Middle-Aged."

To the 'Poonies, *Life* represented square Middle American culture as found in Chagrin Falls, Ohio (Kenney's all-American hometown), which had not yet accepted the pleasure principle. Hard as it is to remember now, in 1968 college students of the opposite sex living together still evoked outrage. The *HL Life*'s Letters page bristled with missives from indignant correspondents responding to a previous issue's exposé of male students sharing living quarters.

"I am a sharp-nosed, vulgar suburban wife who drops names, spreads rumors, and is possessed of an almost infinite capacity for hysterical indignation," wrote one Mrs. Meade E. Ochre from Larchmont, NY. "When I read that university students across the country were *forced* to cohabitate in dormitory rooms why you can just imagine the shrill whine of my consternation! I didn't spend 23 years social climbing to see my boy tampered with by some pervert."

"A lot of us here go out with girls and demonstrate our masculinity to them in a variety of ways, like drinking so much that we're sick . . . and then pestering them with our odious attentions," declared a similar letter from Yale man "Horace W. Getahead." If anything differentiated the 'Poonies from this "active contemporary student of meager intellect and middle-aged disposition," it was a willingness to put pleasure above responsibility and a reluctance to defer gratification.

As well, with the growing perception that several heretofore respectable jobs were somehow tied into despoiling or oppressing something or someone, some men were considering how to define the male role. They turned to Beat Generation heartthrob Neal Cassady as a model, the man rich in experience as opposed to mere money. "We were caught up in the aspect of the counterculture that was against the enforcement of stupid traditional values that were repressive to people's spirits," as Gabel said. However, if the 'Poonies had anything against corporate America, it was not that it was trashing the environment, practicing racial and sexual discrimination, exploiting cheap Third World labor, fueling the onrushing juggernaut of the war machine, or any of the other crimes it was commonly charged with by their more radical contemporaries; no, what they objected to was the regimentation and conformity of corporate life and the fact that if your boss said something incredibly stupid, you had to keep your mouth shut.

While the newly rebellious youth perceived the straight workaday world as soulless and stifling, only a few were alienated enough to think the problem lay in the structure of capitalism itself. "We were trying to satirize everything the mainstream wanted to impose on us for our life identities," Gabel said, "but we never consciously believed in a socialist state or anything like that." Most of the 'Poonies had nothing against accumulating private property. Indeed, during his poverty-stricken *Life* summer, Kenney declared that if he weren't totally convinced he'd be rich by the time he was thirty, he'd commit suicide right then.

The notion of vast numbers of late '60s graduates being disaffected enough to alter their career plans and go off script has always been an exaggeration. However, there was a palpable emphasis on intangible— as opposed to material—rewards. "There was no feeling of the big bad corporation," said Nugent. "At the same time, it wasn't quite cool to say you wanted to work for one. It was how smart and witty you were, not how much money you made." Former 'Poonies who had been among the wits around the Algonquin Round Table were more important role models than former 'Poonies who had made it on Wall Street. In any case, most of the vintage '68 'Poonies had not formulated their post-graduation ambitions beyond not visiting Vietnam, and if they had, they kept quiet about it. "You would have gotten your ass hooted out of the place if you had talked about your goals," Nugent said.

It did not escape the 'Poonies that some of the loudest denunciators of the Pig War economy were those whose families had already comfortably benefited from it. "The kids are telegraphing Westport poppas from the country over. 'We're tired of the same old $$$' they're screaming. 'We don't want your ******* trust funds, we don't want your ******* final clubs, you can keep your ******* junior year abroad!' " as Kenney reported in his *HL* 1966 Tom Wolfe parody, *The Wire-Rimmed Blue-Lensed Hard Rock Candy-Sucking Baby*.

Certainly one thing the 'Poonies found money could buy was a better-looking magazine. However, *Life*'s superior quality also meant higher production costs. When it sold less than half the number printed, the *HL* lost some $75,000. They blamed this on *Life*'s lack of newsstand appeal: the cover featured a broken egg painted like a globe to illustrate "The End of the World" instead of, like the *Playboy* parody, a scantily clad babe.

It may not have been just the cover that kept *Life* from selling. In April 1968, Martin Luther King had been assassinated and urban riots followed, leaving more fatalities in their wake. That same month, SDSers, Panthers, and approximately one thousand actual students occupied the administration buildings of Columbia University, ostensibly protesting against an on-campus think tank connected to the Defense Department. Inspired by the events at Columbia, antiwar demonstrations on two hundred college campuses followed. Then, in June, Robert Kennedy was shot. By the fall of '68, when the *Life* parody appeared, people were in no mood to laugh.

While the 'Poonies saw the media primarily as parody fodder, their more radical peers perceived it as a spineless tool of the established order. However, some representatives of even the most mainstream media were shocked during the 1968 Democratic National Convention, when they, along with ten thousand protestors, got roughed up by the authorities, "roughed up" meaning anything from a shove to being clubbed with a nightstick, teargassed, or thrown through a plate-glass window. Televised images of the convention chaos further electrified and polarized the country.

Even the *HL*, in its way, was moved to protest these events on its 1968 record, *The Surprising Sheep*, with a Cerf-penned tribute to the Windy City that began, "So long peace and quiet / It's really a riot / Yeah, the folks who know Chicago say it's really a gas."

This was not the *HL*'s first excursion onto vinyl. In 1962 they had produced a collection of largely forgettable songs called *The Harvard Lampoon Tabernacle Choir Sings at Leningrad Stadium*, possibly inspired by the fact that the sharpest musical satirist of the day was a homeboy, Tom Lehrer, moonlighting from studying at Harvard for a PhD in math. The *Sheep*'s sales were weak, but nevertheless subsequent 'Poonies started to feel that they could turn their *HL* experience into an actual career. "There was a sense that everyone thinks we're great and all we have to do is get it together and we'll make a lot of money," Rivaldo recalled.

Talk of starting a national humor magazine revived. But in the fall of 1968, Hoffman was in the Coast Guard, Beard back in the reserves, and Kenney busy being a pseudo-epileptic. It seemed unlikely that the trio would hold together long enough for Hoffman to return and mid-wife the national *Lampoon* into existence. To keep Beard and Kenney from getting other jobs until he finished his service, Hoffman decided the *HL* would pay the two writers to come up with a parody of J. R. R. Tolkien's *Lord of the Rings* (*LOTR*), at the time an unlikely best seller by a retiring Oxford University medievalist.

Celebrating the power of good vibes over brute force, *LOTR* was popular with the counterculture's large unicorn-and-rainbow contin-gent, and as such seemed to beg for the *HL* treatment. The result, *Bored of the Rings* (*BOTR*), is an epic full of unheroic deeds. Cowardice, con-fusion, and passing the buck are the order of the day. The furry protago-nists, the Boggies, are "an unattractive but annoying people . . . slow and sullen, and yet dull, they prefer to lead simple lives of pastoral squalor." In a literary equivalent of the *Mad* panel crowded with the flotsam of consumer culture, Beard and Kenney populated the imaginary world with other beings drawn from contemporary advertising mythology: Arrowroot, son of Arrowshirt; Orlon; and the green giant Birdseye, Lord of the Vee-Ates, who reduces the Boggies to whimpering jelly with lines like "Lettuce go and meet my subjects who live in the forest. They cannot be beet. Ho Ho Ho."

Beard and Kenney found that they had complementary strengths as collaborators. Beard's discipline and strong sense of structure provided a framework for Kenney's flashes of manic brilliance. Likewise, Beard's rather dry wit was fleshed out by Kenney's feel for popular culture. Together they forged the characteristic tone of the *National Lampoon*: assuming all actions are the result of greed, malice, or sheer stupidity; promiscuously interweaving icons from high and low culture; snobbery; and ironic distance from everything (including the work itself), all made palatable by sheer mastery of the traditional techniques of comic writing.

The *BOTR* team's progress by spring vacation of 1969 was unimpressive, so Hoffman, by now off boats and finishing up his senior year, offered a bribe: a trip to the US Virgin Islands to complete the manuscript. Meanwhile, Hoffman talked the parody's publishers into giving its authors two percentage points above the standard author's royalty deal. By the mid-80s, the $5,000 invested in Beard and Kenney's living expenses had already returned more than $100,000 to the Castle, and *BOTR* (reissued in 2001 as a movie tie-in) still provides the *HL* with substantial annual royalties.

As soon as the boys flew in from St. Croix in April 1969, they were greeted by the news that Harvard had succumbed to strike fever, and, as Gabel recalled, students who had taken over a university building were "getting their heads smashed in" by the police in Harvard Yard. The 'Poonies gave their version of the strike in a parody of *Time* they started working on immediately after *BOTR*. "Inside, the demonstrators wreaked havoc, lighting bonfires, ripping toilet paper off rolls, and defacing blackboards with slogans etched in chalk," a story in the *HL Time* began. "By early afternoon their numbers had soared to forty-two, including at least eleven registered students."

As the country became increasingly polarized, the *Time* parody showed the 'Poonies to be positively reveling in their distance from Middle America. For example, "Cloudy Days for Fair Harvard," a report compiled "after long minutes of research and objective interviews with Harvard rejects, drop-outs, and flunk outs," reveals "the University openly discriminates against 'good ol' red-blooded American kids who aren't suckered in by that old-world egghead baloney.'"

The magazine's capsule reviews provide a quick overview of late '60s culture. One Off-Broadway show, *Oh! Moolah!*, is a "daring experiment" by avant-garde ensemble the Living Theatre, in which "an all-nude cast rolls around in the gate receipts." The title is a nod to *Oh! Calcutta!*, one of the more commercial productions that seized upon the stage nudity pioneered by the experimental company, as no-clothes theater, originally intended to protest against the commercialization of art, became a highly commercial genre in itself.

The trend for theater-in-the-raw also provided the perfect excuse for a photo essay that would hopefully answer the question "Does Sex Sell Magazines?," the cover line shown on the parody's cover next to a semiundressed sultry blond model, Weidman's girlfriend at the time— the 'Poonies wouldn't make *Life*'s painted-egg mistake twice. Other *HL* girlfriends were game up to a point, portraying, along with the editors themselves, the cast of *Oh! Moolah!* holding straw boaters over their posteriors. They were not, however, willing to pose wearing nothing but garbage cans over their heads. For that shot, the 'Poonies had to enlist professional nude models.

Sexual frankness was suddenly acceptable. Sexuality was natural, it was argued; it was the war that was obscene. A purported *Time*/Harris poll in the magazine examined the widening disparity in values. "American youth is asking, for the first time in recorded history, whether some of the things long considered Good in this country are actually only Nice, or, more startlingly, even actually Bad," it revealed. "This turning away from the once accepted do's and don'ts . . . has not come from the lower classes, of whom one might naturally expect the worst because of the filth and squalor in which they choose to live," the pseudo-*Time* thundered. "Actually it is the college-educated upper middle-class individual who is responsible for an ethical atmosphere wherein, as Harris states, 'everybody thinks it's OK to live like pigs.'" To prove the point, an accompanying photo showed a dissolute-looking Rivaldo and Kenney sprawled on a couch portraying "college students smoking LSD."

Life, to some extent, imitated art. Several of the 'Poonies lived together during the parody's incubation, sharing two apartments paid for by the *HL*. "It was a very tense time," Hoffman recalled. "We had to produce and didn't have any money and we were all living very closely together." Others, however, had more festive memories. "It was wild," Rivaldo recalled. "Late hours, drugs, running around." One acquaintance, a student putting himself through Harvard by dealing drugs, would come by with recently invented mystery psychedelics and usually found a willing test subject in Kenney, whose productivity was once again spurred rather than hampered by drugs. He and Beard, Hoffman estimated, wrote two-thirds of the *Time* parody between them.

The real estate situation was also conducive to group living. University towns like Cambridge were full of multibedroom houses that had become too big and expensive for single families. Communal life became a testing ground for the emerging women's liberation movement when domestic duties like dishwashing, assigned in rotation, came to male members of the household. With eternal enmities founded on things like one party eating all the cottage cheese and never replacing it, it was in many ways like being married to eight people at once.

The 'Poonies may all have been under one roof, but they knew better than to style themselves a collective. Their system was simple but equitable: *nobody* cleaned up. "There was no organizing of food or housework," Gabel said. "In the context of our antiserious *Lampoon* culture, a chart on the refrigerator assigning household tasks would have been preposterous." There was, however, a chart of another sort in another apartment. Alex Garcia-Mata, Kenney's current and Gabel's ex, had a diagram on her wall depicting everybody's past and present romantic involvements with everybody else.

Needless to say, this may have contributed to the tension Hoffman recalled. But although being up front and sharing one's feelings was another tenet of the youth culture, it was not the style at the *HL*, where having deeply meaningful conversations was secondary to constantly trying to be funny.

This was particularly hard on Rivaldo, who that summer was wrestling with the first glimmerings about his sexual orientation. Although by 1969 homosexuals were starting to identify with minorities who were refusing to meekly accept second-class status, the idea that one might actually be unashamed about being gay was still in its infancy. For Harvard students, "homosexuality wasn't even an option to be considered. I remember we'd get drunk and at the peak of the night one or two of us would go home to a girlfriend and the rest of us would just poop out when ordinarily people would tear off their clothes and go wild," said Rivaldo, who clearly moved in exciting social circles. "Later on we discovered all kinds of people who had been on the *Lampoon* were gay and we thought, 'Oh, *that's* what was going on.'"

As the art director of the *Time* and *Life* parodies, Rivaldo was part of the group discussing a postgraduate national version of the *HL*. But after *Time* appeared, the others, in what Hoffman termed an "incredibly sad and difficult meeting," told him they didn't think he would work out. Even those 'Poonies who were not thinking about becoming professional humorists felt somewhat excluded and jealous, a conflict intensified by their faith in Kenney and Beard's ultimate success. This faith was shared by the principals themselves. "We had a lot of confidence that we knew how to do it even though we didn't know what 'it' was," Hoffman said. Armed with this combination of adult wiles and youthful self-belief, he went off in June 1969 to wrestle with the magazine's potential backers.

Facing Hoffman across the negotiating table were two seasoned businessmen with considerably more experience in magazine publishing. Len Mogel and Matty Simmons, partners in a company called 21st Century Communications, had first worked together in 1952 on a Diners Club newsletter. In 1967 they had started a magazine aimed at the emerging youth market, employing talented young journalists to report on the counterculture from the inside. The magazine was called *Chee-tah*, a spin-off from a network of successful clubs of the same name.

Four-color and slick, *Cheetah*'s production standards were high and so were its editorial standards. Unfortunately, just as *Cheetah*, the magazine, started to turn the corner, Cheetah, the club network, started to fade. The magazine followed, but the experience left Mogel and Simmons convinced that there was a market for a hip publication. In the summer of '68, Mogel was asked to help the *Life* parody's languishing ad sales and indeed, said Hoffman, he "basically pulled our cookies out of the fire." Discussions about a national *Lampoon* began soon after.

Simmons brought the same flair for promotion that had made him a successful publicist to his personal style, leading the 'Poonies to see him as something of an exotic. Beard and Kenney "thought there was an interesting contrast between this tweedy Ivy League stuff and these fast-talking New York operators," Rivaldo recalled. It would be a source of continuing irritation for Simmons that his editors would use words like *operator* to describe him.

According to Hoffman, Simmons's involvement in *Time* was limited to selling ads and helping the students find a printer. Simmons, however, had a different story. "I taught those kids the magazine business," he declared. "They were writing a pamphlet called the *Harvard Lampoon*. They didn't know how to put a magazine together."

When Hoffman started negotiations with Simmons and Mogel in June 1969, the initial concept was that the Harvard boys and 21st Century would form a new subsidiary company called National Lampoon Inc. The three 'Poonies would get one-third of the company for their expertise, 21st Century would get one-third for *their* expertise, and one-third would go to outside backers. 21st Century agreed to put up $350,000 (around $2 million in today's money), and the 'Poonies agreed to come up with a license for the *Lampoon* name. Then 21st Century wanted to change the deal and replace the outside backers' contribution in return for two-thirds of the new company.

"I thought we were going to end up being a minority interest in a subsidiary," Hoffman said, "and so we needed a way to sell out, which can be difficult as a subsidiary of someone else. I said, 'We have to negotiate our divorce at the same time as we negotiate our marriage.'" The contract remained unsigned until October 1969, at which point more than six hundred thousand copies of the *Time* parody had sold out in less than two weeks, strengthening Hoffman's hand. After an investment banking firm determined that publishing stocks were selling for sixteen to eighteen times earnings, Simmons and Mogel signed a prenuptial agreement promising to buy out Beard, Kenney, and Hoffman's one-third interest for that amount, a concession that would in later years prompt a rueful but admiring Simmons to describe Hoffman as "probably the only used car salesman ever to graduate *magna cum laude* from Harvard."

The three graduates feared the worst. "We thought they could manipulate the earnings figure and screw us," Hoffman recalled. Even so, with the contract still unsigned, Kenney and Beard finished the *Time* parody at the end of August, took a week off, and, on September 1, went to work in New York.

3

THERE BUT FOR ADVERTISERS...

Mogel, Simmons, and their Harvard editors were in total agreement on at least one point: no one had any intention of starting a magazine that would not make money. If some of their contemporaries were considering dropping out to farm mung beans, the 'Poonies were not among them. "We wanted to be successful," Hoffman said. "Our goal was to sell four hundred thousand copies a month."

The fates of two magazines both founded in 1957 on opposite ends of the taste spectrum suggested this goal was ambitious to the point of unrealistic *Monocle*, an irregular journal of thoughtful political satire that had been started by two Yale law students. Literate and witty, its contributors included *New Yorker* humorists, distinguished novelists, and other members of the liberal intelligentsia. Its small readership was engaged with the progressive end of traditional politics and loved Jack Kennedy for his flashes of irreverence as much as for his policies. Six years into its existence, the magazine finally obtained distribution on newsstands and on November 20, 1963, printed up seventy thousand copies (sixty-five thousand more than usual) of a special "CIA" issue full of Kennedy jokes. The president's assassination two days later meant it was never distributed, and shortly thereafter, *Monocle* folded.

If the *Monocle* audience still wore ties to work, and indeed had actual jobs, the alienated Beat contingent was claimed by the *Realist*, a publication that positively rejoiced in offending good taste. Like *Monocle*, making money was never the *Realist*'s top priority. Its founder, Paul Krassner, a truly puckish soul with an absurdist view of life, had started his magazine of "free thought, criticism, and satire" in order, he said, "to make waves and to serve as the First Amendment in action." Rather than worry about offending advertisers, he decided it was simpler to do without them. His determination to test the limits of public tolerance was exemplified by the magazine's most notorious article, the 1967 "Parts Left Out of the Kennedy Book," which mixes actual though at the time not-widely-known gossip such as the Marilyn Monroe–JFK affair with the Krassnerian invention of Jacqueline Kennedy witnessing Lyndon Johnson perform an unnatural act with the throat wound on her late husband's body. It proved difficult to find a printer willing to touch the issue, but some people liked it. The leader of the American Nazi Party, for example, applauded Krassner's "balls of steel."

The *Realist*'s other best-known piece was the 1967 *Disneyland Memorial Orgy*, a cartoon by *Mad*'s ace illustrator Wally Wood that depicts many of the Magic Kingdom's most beloved inhabitants engaging in some very adult pursuits while maintaining their characteristic cheerfulness. Amazingly, initially Disney did not sue because, Krassner speculated, "they hoped if they ignored it, it would go away." Their attitude changed after the illustration became a best-selling poster, often seen in college dorms.

The *Realist*'s reputation as a forum for controversial views led literary raging bull Norman Mailer to opine in a 1962 interview that "it's better to commit rape than to masturbate" (he did add a "maybe"), because "if one masturbates, everything that's beautiful and good in one goes up the hand, goes into the air, is *lost*." Somewhat more restrained contributors included Krassner's mentor, the hugely influential hipster comedian and satirist Lenny Bruce, and, another Bruce acolyte, the similarly self-destructive and brilliant Richard Pryor, then unknown outside the black community. In 1971 the future comedy legend contributed "Uncle Sam Wants You Dead, Nigger," a bleak miniscreenplay in which a high-school graduate ignores the advice of a Black Panther friend, joins the army "to be somebody," receives medals for killing some Vietnamese villagers, and is killed himself, only for his family in the United States to be told, "We don't bury no niggers in this graveyard."

Muckraking became a higher priority in the *Realist* in the '70s. Its biggest scoop came from the late Mae Brussell, a conspiracy buff who, in August 1972, when the mainstream press was still calling the Watergate burglary a "caper," asserted that the Watergate burglars were working for the CIA at the time of their arrest and that their actions were part of a larger scheme to throw the election. "Two governments have existed side by side, one visible and one invisible, for many years. . . . If the Watergate affair is exposed, you will see how invisible government agents go about their business," she predicted.

After her Watergate success, Brussell generated long screeds linking the Mafia, the Vatican, the Third Reich, drug kingpins, arms kingpins, assorted right-wing regimes, and, of course, the CIA, multinational corporations, and the US military. The *National Lampoon* found this kind of conspiracy theorizing that increasingly came to dominate the *Realist* risible, and there was no way Beard would approve of the loose editorial quality control, but the magazine owed much to the efforts of Krassner, and before him, Bruce, when it came to exploring how far the boundaries of taste could be stretched in the name of coruscating humor. "Sometimes the *National Lampoon* humor seemed cruel," Krassner later observed, "but as a First Amendment freak, it was irrelevant to me." However, he felt the *Lampoon* was more interested in being entertaining than in stirring things up and "cared about looks as much as content." His own indifference to production values meant the *Realist* resembled a newsletter more than a magazine, and this lack of slickness put off distributors almost as much as the content. In the sixteen years of the *Realist*'s existence, Krassner never received a salary, and by 1974 he was burned out and closed it down. He had run out of money, and, he said, "I had run out of taboos, so I guess my goal had been reached."

Krassner's burnout coincided with his increased involvement with a group of like-minded spirits loosely assembled as the Youth International Party, or Yippies, who shared his knack for combining political statement with outrageous gesture and similarly preferred ridicule to rhetoric. Basically anarchists, they were more concerned with altering the culture than gaining control of the political apparatus, which led more serious-minded activists to suspect them of being irresponsible lightweights.

But there was method in the mockery. The Yippies realized early on that in a three-minute clip, they would get more mileage from an outrageous sound bite and an effective visual than from a sober lecture about Vietnam. Any factual corrections would only make the inside back page of the next morning's paper. It may be that Michael Moore and Roger Ailes, then a young media consultant to Richard Nixon and later head of Fox News, learned from the Yippies' attention-getting techniques and their conflation of political commentary and entertainment.

Unable to buy media access, they realized they could substitute amusement value. "Media is free," wrote Yippie spokesman Abbie Hoffman in a 1968 *Realist* article. "Use it. Don't pay for it. Don't buy ads. Make news." The charismatic Hoffman had a superb instinct for mediagenic guerrilla theater. In one notable instance in 1967, he got together with members of the Diggers, an idealistic commune, and threw actual US currency onto the floor of the New York Stock Exchange, letting the subsequent undignified scramble speak for itself.

Then in October of that year, as approximately one hundred thousand people gathered in Washington for an antiwar march on the Pentagon, Hoffman and other members of what the *New York Times* dubbed a "militant minority" attacked the building with a formidable weapon: refusing to take it seriously. Demonstrators gathered to levitate the structure via psychic energy, chanting, "Out, demons, out." To those inside the Pentagon, their work seemed eminently rational; to the

Yippies, strategizing for a first-strike nuclear war was clearly the work of the devil. Like most Yippie actions and pronouncements, the "exorcism" was both media put-on and sincerely felt.

The Pentagon demonstrators got off easy with minor fines, but the Yippies would soon encounter someone it would take more than symbolic action to confront—Chicago mayor Richard Daley. In January 1968, the Yippies announced a "festival of youth, music, and theater" to be held during the August Democratic Convention. In fact, the Yippies brought relatively few people to Chicago, with the majority of demonstrators provided by more serious-minded protest groups.

In the wake of the Chicago confrontation, Hoffman did not get off with a fine. After the 1968 election put the Nixon administration in office, he was charged with conspiracy and crossing state lines with the intent to incite a riot. When not on this coast-to-coast rabble-rousing tour, Hoffman was a print provocateur and had already written three books for Random House, where his editor was Chris Cerf. "Chris and I were considered to be the people who looked after small weird projects," said Frith, who had also been hired by his friend's father.

Hoffman did a lot of his writing in his editor's office, a fact that the boss discovered in dramatic fashion. One day, Frith recalled, Bennett Cerf was giving "someone very famous and very pompous" the grand tour of Random House. "The door to Chris's office was closed," Frith said, "and Bennett—you know, the proud papa—said, 'This is my son's office,' threw open the door, and there was Abbie, no shirt on as usual, the place dense with dope. 'But that's not my son!' Bennett said in a horrified voice." Hoffman, of course, replied, "Hi, Dad!"

More impish than incendiary, Hoffman had always seen demonstrations as an all-American pastime. "Homecoming Day at the Pentagon and the cheerleaders chant 'Beat Army! Beat Army!' It's SDS at the 30-yard line and third down," he wrote in an account of the Pentagon exorcism. In the same spirit, Hoffman suggested to Cerf a mock football program might help defray the costs of the Chicago conspiracy trial, which began in September 1969 and lasted five turbulent months.

The government originally charged eight defendants, evenhandedly ensuring that all leading radical factions—Black Panthers, SDS, Yippies, and so on—were represented. "The joke was you couldn't tell the players without a program," Frith said, so he and Cerf decided to do one. As for why they would take time from their promising careers to support known troublemakers, "politics is what life was all about at the time," Frith said.

Hoffman had achieved celebrity dissident status not by being a leading artist and intellectual (like Czechoslovakia's Vaclav Havel) or an actual revolutionary (like Che Guevara) but through being a quick-witted satirist with a theatrical flair for media manipulation. As such, he would have been a beacon of hope for the project's lone non-Harvard recruit, Michael O'Donoghue, then trying to eke out a living on the fringes of New York's cultural underground by employing these same qualities.

But Hoffman's high profile came at a price. "Abbie's one of the great funny people of the world," Frith recalled, "so when he'd come up with these wild stories about the FBI tailing him and being beaten up in a dark alley at night, we'd say, 'Yeah, yeah, yeah—there he goes again.' You really couldn't give it credence then, the stuff was so bizarre," like wild-eyed stories of COINTELPRO, an FBI counterintelligence program that used disinformation, provocateurs, break-ins, and telephone taps against organizations it considered to be too far to the left, or of a list of twenty-six thousand dissidents to be detained in case of an unspecified national emergency, all of which turned out to be true.

Hoffman's stories became more credible when Cerf and Frith discovered their mock football program for "the Big One" between the Washington Kangaroos and the Conspiracy Albatrosses was attracting genuine official attention. "We really did have problems at the printers with people snooping. It ended up with the FBI going down and trashing the presses," Frith recalled. He and Cerf found it hard to believe that their little lark, typed on the same Random House typewriter used by Dr. Seuss, could be considered a threat to the American Way of Life.

"We thought, 'Talk about paranoid,'" he said. "It was so innocent. It was just college humor."

A jovial collegiality does in fact distinguish the program, or as the front cover calls it, the *Official Pogrom*, which deftly manages to puncture both the government's paranoid authoritarianism and the defendants' self-important posturing. Driven by Cerf's dedication to verisimilitude, the parody contains such hallmarks of college football programs as cheers ("Boom-a-lark-a! Chick-a-lark-a! Sis! Boom! Bah! / Outside Agitators! Rah! Rah! Rah!") and a plan of the playing field, in this case the Chicago federal courthouse, which shows that the majority of seats have been reserved for such Kangaroo supporters as the FBI, the CIA, Dow Chemical, and "Spontaneous Demonstrators for R. Daley." But the heart of the program is the thumbnail player profiles. With a fine grasp of just how much of a united front the Conspiracy really presented, each Albatross profiled concludes by expressing remarkably similar sentiments.

"There's always the temptation to look past this game to that Panther-Kangaroo contest coming up on the coast," says Black Panther defendant Bobby Seale, referring to a pending murder and kidnap charge. "But I know I can lead the Chicago conspiracy to victory anyway!" Likewise, "handsome 165-pound" SDS representative Tom Hayden (later a California state senator and Mr. Jane Fonda) declares, "There's no doubt in my mind that . . . I can take the 'Trosses all the way to the championship!"

The back cover of the program was given over to a recruitment ad for "today's 'groovy' new Action Army," featuring a photo of an extremely hip-looking Frith, complete with shades and joint, a call to arms written by O'Donoghue, whose first book, a slim nihilistic picture story called *The Incredible Thrilling Adventures of the Rock*, had been another of Cerf's small weird projects. "We were blown away by this guy," Frith recalled. "We weren't used to people of this kind of eccentricity."

The son of an industrial engineer, O'Donoghue came from a very different background than most 'Poonies, but he was at least as much of an anomaly among the kids at his high school in rural upstate New York. Under the influence of Franz Kafka, Nathanael West, Terry Southern, and other exponents of mordant humor, O'Donoghue had precociously developed an outsider's tendency to accentuate the negative.

The relatively more broad-minded atmosphere of the University of Rochester did nothing to improve his bad attitude. Antisocial behavior such as defacing campus property in a fraternity food fight and stealing a campus police car got O'Donoghue, then known as Michael Donohue, expelled in his junior year. But it wasn't all troublemaking; while at Rochester, he discovered an affinity for Zen Buddhism that led him to later observe, "Comedy collectives—like the *Lampoon* and *Saturday Night Live*—are very similar to Zen monasteries. Both deal with something that can't be explained: the moment of *satori* and laughter."

An interest in Zen inevitably led to an interest in the Beats, and by 1960, a twenty-year-old O'Donoghue was On the Road to San Francisco. There he managed to get a job as a trainee reporter on the *San Francisco Examiner* but was fired after getting into an altercation in the newsroom. Returning to Rochester, he paid the bills by selling *Life* subscriptions, shrubbery, and costume jewelry. He also got married and divorced in short order and became a DJ for a local station where, during newscasts, he would read accounts of sensational tragedies from the wires instead of the important stories. But nothing really panned out until he had a play accepted for publication by a literary magazine in New York called the *Evergreen Review*.

Another 1957 start-up, the *Evergreen Review* showcased work by Beat luminaries such as Allen Ginsberg and William Burroughs (an O'Donoghue favorite) when those writers had limited opportunities to publish. Moreover, coeditor Barney Rosset had provided the judicial system with some of its steamiest legal transcripts by publishing *Lady Chatterley's Lover* and Henry Miller's *Tropic of Cancer* under his Grove Press imprint, publications that led to landmark obscenity trials.

In this tradition of standing behind controversial work, Rosset ended up distributing the 1969 *Official Pogrom*. He also hired O'Donoghue to write an ongoing comic strip, *Phoebe Zeit-Geist* (the adventures of a frequently undressed sci-fi/fantasy heroine), and found other ways to support the fledgling writer, who had by then moved to New York and returned his name to the original Irish spelling. "Rosset couldn't pay Michael enough to live on just for *Phoebe Zeit-Geist*," Frith recalled, "so he would pay him to wander around New York checking up on all the newsstands to see how the *Evergreen Review* was doing, and of course Michael would never leave his loft. He'd sit there making up statistics and phone in these bizarre stories to Rosset, who knew they were all lies."

This was one of several marginal scams O'Donoghue put together to be able to fund his writing time. For a year he was the creative director of the Electric Circus, the original multimedia discotheque and the coolest scene around. It opened in a former Polish dance hall in the East Village just as the area was becoming New York's hippie central, a grungier and more druggy alternative to the genteel bohemianism of neighboring Greenwich Village. The house band was the Velvet Underground, then closely associated with Andy Warhol, who often frequented the club accompanied by early Factory stars and who made it a hangout for leading Pop artists.

Anticipating a later nightlife trend, the ambiance incorporated performance art pieces, especially the spontaneous variety then known as Happenings, that didn't compete with the music. "I tried shutting the music off a couple of times," O'Donoghue recalled, "and never tried it again. All these little hitters from Astoria [Queens] went nuts." Under duress, O'Donoghue developed nonverbal theatrical concepts, such as flooding the club with coconut-scented green fog while circulating, "dressed in a worshipping insect kind of garb, offering to pay people twenty dollars for their souls. They all wanted to do it," he said, "then later they'd read this scary document they had signed," said document being a "fairly binding" legal contract drawn up by a lawyer.

Having signed a scary document of his own, R. Hoffman began penetrating the power elite at the Harvard Business School as the decade turned. When he tried to merge his two lives by writing a case study on the founding of the *National Lampoon* and enlisting Kenney to come up and help with the presentation to the MBA class, "no one in the B School really got it," Hoffman said sadly. "They wondered why these college kids were messing around for twelve thousand dollars a year." Hoffman's family was among those unconvinced. When he told them what he was planning to do with his expensive education, "they thought I was nuts," he recalled. "Afterwards they thought I was crazy to sell out."

After the simultaneous success of *Time* and *Bored of the Rings*, Beard and Kenney were more relaxed. "When the thing started out, I don't think there was any clear notion of what they were doing at all," Frith said. "They just knew they wanted to create a humor magazine and it would be big and glossy and wonderful and they would have a great time doing it and it would be a great success." How exactly this was to be accomplished remained vague, so they asked *HL* elder statesmen Frith and Cerf to moonlight from their Random House jobs and act as advisors.

Frith, however, had reservations about the use of the *Lampoon* name, even though the Harvard version would get a 5 percent royalty on each copy sold. "I don't think there had been a board of the *Harvard Lampoon* in ten years that hadn't said, 'Wouldn't it be neat if we could all go to New York and put out something sort of like a . . . a national *Lampoon*,'" he said. But now that it was a reality, he felt it was problematic because "if it succeeded, it couldn't help but change the sense of identity for the kids in college."

Aside from O'Donoghue, who was vouched for by Frith and Cerf, it was also to fellow 'Poonies that Beard and Kenney turned for writers, first and foremost to George Trow, who, in Frith's view, was "meticulous, witty, abstract, and careful," providing a welcome counterbalance to what Frith perceived as Kenney's undisciplined style. Kenney also asked Weidman, then busy avoiding the draft by teaching school in Harlem, to contribute to the first issue, making the approach more in the spirit of offering an informal invitation than presenting a major career opportunity. It seemed to Weidman that the *Lampoon* "was something that was being made to happen by Doug and Henry, but was also sort of pulling them along with it." Or, as Hoffman said, "everything had just fallen into place for them."

Eventually the founders realized that there would have to be pictures to go along with the words and they might have to look beyond Harvard for talent. This realization brought them to Rick Meyerowitz, an ebullient commercial artist and caricaturist whose broad cartoony style reflected the influence of his "visual father," the seminal Harvey Kurtzman. Meyerowitz had first stumbled across Beard and Kenney's work in October 1969 when he picked up the *Time* parody on the way to a protest in New York's Bryant Park, where, he recalled, he "sat oblivious to the speeches, cackling out loud in this group of fervent antiwar demonstrators."

At first Meyerowitz tended to see the two graduates as a team but soon learned to sort them out. "Henry was kind of quiet and shy in that Eastern Establishment way," he observed. "He appeared to keep you at arm's length, but he could really be a friend." Kenney, on the other hand, was "more gregarious, and everybody liked him and wanted to be his friend, but he was always a little standoffish, ultimately more so than Henry," at least with those who were not his intimates.

Both editors struck him as a little wet behind the ears. Although only one year their senior, Meyerowitz was already earning a good living as an ad illustrator while they were living on a stipend from Simmons and were frequently short of cash. Consequently, it was the artist who paid for their dinners in Chinatown and gave Kenney money to go home in a cab. Beard and Kenney reciprocated by inviting Meyerowitz to join them at what became known as "celebrated dinners." Remembering the *HL* tradition of sending ideas and repartee flying around the table along with the odd drumstick or vegetable, the novice editors had their most productive brainstorming sessions in restaurants (more sober organizational meetings were held in Simmons's apartment). "Even though I couldn't get my mouth open before any one of them, I was accepted in that group and it gave me great pleasure," Meyerowitz said, "that group" being O'Donoghue, Trow, Cerf, Weidman, Beard, and Kenney, with other Harvard contemporaries like journalist Tim Crouse (who was then acting as a sort of Boswell-cum-babysitter chronicling Hunter S. Thompson's travels for *Rolling Stone*) occasionally sitting in. "When everyone went out to dinner, Doug paid for everything," Hoffman noted. "Except when he went out with Henry. Henry always paid for Doug and Henry."

Beard and Kenny were thus living the dream 1969 style. "It wasn't about selling a product," Trow said. "It was about being with brothers doing something new. We thought, 'We don't have to leave school; we can continue to play football,'" not that any of them ever had in the first place.

This reluctance to leave youthful hijinks behind was not, in Trow's view, peculiar to this particular circle of 'Poonies but endemic to their generation. "The culture, for reasons having to do with the working of the marketplace, did not make available any but the grimmest, most false-seeming adulthood," he wrote in *Context*. "An adolescence had to be improvised and that it *was* improvised—mostly out of Rock-and-Roll music—so astounded the people who pulled it off that they rightly considered it the important historical event of their time and have circled around it ever since." Trow found it inevitable that these perpetual adolescents, having grown up immersed in television commercials, should turn to parody, which he described as the natural art form for people who have been shaped by a meaningless iconography.

Besides possessing a sense of being bombarded by insignificant cultural artifacts and their high-domed foreheads more and more exposed to the elements with every passing year, the socially and financially secure Trow and the struggling bohemian O'Donoghue would seem to have had little in common. Trow struck Meyerowitz as "a very refined individual. He always dressed impeccably. No one else dressed like that."

O'Donoghue, by contrast, "was really scruffy in those days," Frith said. "The only suit he had was this gangster suit he found in a garbage can. He had no money at all," and there were months when his *Lampoon*

buddies had to pay his utility bills. When the lights were on, O'Donoghue's loft in SoHo (at the time a dreary industrial neighborhood within
the economic reach of a struggling writer) was known for its cleanliness,
despite a number of feline inhabitants, and its unique decor, which featured walls festooned with dead typewriters ("Whenever Michael would
wear out a typewriter, he'd nail it to the wall," Frith explained).

His reduced circumstances did not prevent O'Donoghue from
adopting an aristocratic haughtiness. "There were two of us in the *Lampoon* who were very high-handed—George and myself," he said with a
reminiscent chuckle. "We treated the others like they were workers in
the factory. They always resented us in a certain way and were semis-
cared of us—less so as time went by." One thing this unlikely pairing
did have in common was a belief in the importance of truth, artistically
speaking anyway, with Frith perceiving in O'Donoghue's work "a sear-
ing honesty he would be the last person to admit to."

What is not so readily apparent in much of his best-known work is
that O'Donoghue was a satirist in the classical sense, aiming to instruct
more than amuse. "I've always considered comedy what you use to get
people to swallow the pill," he pronounced, "not the pill itself. It's only a
device to be used to a greater end," this noble purpose being "basically
to give them a migraine headache," an ailment the writer frequently suffered himself, leading one of the writer's close friends to hypothesize
that all O'Donoghue tried to do was make others suffer the way he did.

Like Beard and Kenney, Trow and O'Donoghue found their differences complementary while sharing an interest in the tension between
civilized behavior and anarchistic impulses. O'Donoghue had a highly
developed sense of personal style and a taste for gracious, if unconventional, living he could not yet afford to fulfill but which Trow embodied.
Trow, meanwhile, beneath his demure WASP exterior, had disorderly
leanings that occasionally surfaced at the celebrated dinners in the form
of "Party Treats," a more sophisticated version of Castle food antics.

"If you were at a restaurant—and it worked particularly well at a
restaurant where you paid a lot for the food and weren't particularly

happy with it (the stuffier the restaurant the better)—George would take food from everyone else and make up a big plate, all arranged decoratively," O'Donoghue explained. "He'd use napkins and ashtrays and make a big concoction, all the time doing a Julia Child sort of chef rap. It was quite amusing." And, as at the Castle, cleaning up the mess could be left to someone else.

If Trow could break the rules of proper behavior because he knew them down to the last semicolon, O'Donoghue was seen as a child of nature to whom these rules did not apply. "They adopted him as this genius they'd found in the bush," said Sean Kelly, a Canadian academic who started writing for the magazine shortly after its inception. "'Imagine how wonderful he'd be if he'd had the benefit of a Harvard education!' They could patronize him while idolizing him."

"Patronize" may be too strong a word. O'Donoghue may have simply been the first actual bohemian the boys had come in contact with. "When I was growing up in Ohio," Kenney said in 1978, "I wrote stories about beatniks. I'd have them getting off the IRT at 68th and Bleecker [some sixty blocks away from where Bleecker Street actually is in Greenwich Village] and going into a coffeeshop. O'Donoghue had that kind of stuff with authority."

"Doug and Henry were fairly clean cut," recalled Anne Beatts, a friend of Kelly's who also started writing for the magazine in its early days. O'Donoghue, by contrast, "was an underground star at the time because of *Phoebe Zeit-Geist*. He probably appeared to them more worldly and sophisticated than he perhaps was." At any rate, he was perceived as having gone to the school of life rather than Harvard. As Trow said, "Michael suffered a lot before he got his chance. His view was wider. We were privileged."

O'Donoghue was inclined to agree, declaring, "Doug and Henry didn't have any ideas. Their best idea was meeting me, quite frankly." Actually, O'Donoghue was as likely to produce this kind of remark from a desire to shatter yet another tenet of accepted behavior as from sincere belief. In fact, he thought "Doug and Henry's ideas sounded good.

Henry was a little odd but funny. Doug was funny, too, but a little dorky if you didn't know him. They seemed in need of a severe psychic beating, but then most people are. The fact that George vouched for them lent to their credibility because George had lots of taste."

Nevertheless, O'Donoghue had doubts, based mostly on his dim view of other humor magazines. "I knew a lot of comedy magazines and I hated them all," he declared. "I hated fuckin' *Mad*. I thought it was clownish, rube-like, and unsophisticated. These guys started EC Comics [*Mad* publisher William Gaines inherited EC from his father, the founder] and the minute the Comics Commission [a self-regulating industry body that was actually called the Comics Code Authority] cracked down on them, they dropped to their knees and gave up." Nor did the more sophisticated *Monocle* appeal to him. "I wouldn't have *Monocle* in the house," he said scornfully. "That's people who would rather be intelligent than funny." One would think the outrageousness of the *Realist* might be more to his taste, but no. "It had its moments," he admitted, "but it was a little fey. Also it wasn't visually oriented. It had this kind of beatnik attitude towards graphics," a problem shared by his benefactor. "The *Evergreen Review* was stark, very literary-looking. And even though it was artistically free, there were still these kind of liberal sensibilities," he said.

Kenney and Beard were similarly without models in terms of magazines that came out regularly (as opposed to *HL* one-offs), though unencumbered by O'Donoghue's anarchic and Kenney's countercultural inclinations, the liberal, current affairs–minded Beard might have been inclined to emulate *Monocle*. "The *Harvard Lampoon* subscribed to the *Realist* and *Evergreen Review*," Rivaldo said, "but people didn't really read them, although Doug and Henry read a little of everything current or sexy. The Yippies didn't inspire anyone directly. Nothing out there was really quite *it* yet for Doug and Henry," not even *Private Eye*. The British satire magazine is very much tied to real events and real people while the *Lampoon* ended up being more a vehicle for the editors' creative expression. This reflected the publications' different orientations:

Private Eye is interested in slaughtering sacred cows and uses humor as a technique, while the *Lampoon* was intended to be funny and produced satire as a by-product. As for the *Realist*, while Kenney may have browsed through it, "he thought the *Realist* was vulgar," Gabel said. "He was shocked."

Another possible model for Beard that Kenney and O'Donoghue didn't share was *The New Yorker*, where Trow was employed writing unsigned Talk of the Town pieces. Trow himself felt the magazines shared some common ground, noting, "Generation after generation attempts some truth about what America is. *The New Yorker* arose out of an attempt by worldly people in the '30s. The *Lampoon* arose out of one by worldly people in the '70s." But times had changed. "*The New Yorker* world was primarily a world of people," he observed. "The *Lampoon* world was one of trends, entertainers, and products," and Beard and Kenney realized that a jazzier tone, style, and appearance would reflect this world better than *The New Yorker*'s austere elegance. As well, the *Lampoon*, a product of the prevailing youth culture, did not believe in doing things just because they had been done before. This absence of guidelines, and just possibly the prospect of a small but steady salary, finally brought O'Donoghue on board, drawn in by "this intoxicating freedom of being able to go in and do whatever I wanted."

What he wanted was "to mindlessly kick ass. I was extremely alienated when I joined the *National Lampoon*," he said. "Coming out of the '50s with its parking lot mentality, I just wanted to do some damage, search and destroy. 'Why wait for the law? Let's hang the son of a bitch now'—that's the kind of comedy I like." As might be imagined, O'Donoghue found the Ivy League sensibility somewhat sheltered. "I got so bored with Harvard stories about the night they got drunk and fired billiard balls from the standing ashtray into the Common, or something," he recalled. His reaction was to purchase a Harvard degree at Goodwill for two dollars and hang it up with the price tag still on it.

If the Harvard boys gave O'Donoghue access to commercial credibility, he had a contribution to make in return. "The Harvard people fought with the épée. They made little digs in the wrist, you know—'Ha ha! Have at you!' I taught them to fight with the truncheon," he said. "It was just a more brutal form of humor—less sport, more murder." It's quite possible, however, that even before meeting O'Donoghue, Beard and Kenney were capable of coming up with hard-edged material, as shown by their parody of *Life*'s last page, which usually featured a heart-warming photo. In the *HL* version, a young girl in white ankle socks, her hand over her eyes, her anguished expression revealing a missing front tooth, points a gun at a dead white cat lying in the road. The caption, "No Hard Felines," reveals nothing except the editors' rejection of sentimentality.

But O'Donoghue did not wield his truncheon indiscriminately. "Could this power be used for evil? No," he declared. "I always fought on the side of the angels. I have a little radio in my head from God, and He tells me what side to take." On the side of the angels or not, Beard was not about to start brandishing a club on O'Donoghue's say-so. The ever-plastic Kenney was another story. Frith felt that "Doug didn't know what he was trying to do until Michael came along. O'Donoghue gave Doug a voice." Under O'Donoghue's tutelage, Kenney shed the last vestiges of his preppy persona and became ever more the disheveled writer, perhaps his most authentic self. "It may well be that Michael turned Doug on to using four-letter words in print, but the potential," Hoffman asserted, "was always there."

As the turbulent late '60s drew to a close with guns blazing at home and abroad, the Gang of Four plotted the *Lampoon*, each bringing his particular talent to bear. "I knew about the past and thought about the future," Trow said. "Michael was our genius; his loft was the real office of the *Lampoon* that mattered. Henry was committed to keeping it going and knew how to do it. Doug was our *guy*." Four, as it turned out, were not nearly enough cooks to spoil the broth. But more were on the way.

4

BIG AND GLOSSY
AND WONDERFUL

The first issue of the *National Lampoon* appeared in April 1970 and sold fewer than half of the five hundred thousand copies printed. Some readers may have thought they were buying yet another *HL* magazine parody, understandably confused by a cover that was a variation on the *Time* parody; a dimly lit model in revealing costume posed against a muddy brown background with the caption "Sexy Cover Issue." Less predictably, next to the model was a grinning cartoon duck—a Kenney idea. "Henry would say, 'Wouldn't it be great to do an interview with [legendary *New Yorker* humorist] S. J. Perelman,' and Doug would say, 'We gotta get a duck for a mascot.' Doug would go on and on about jokes with this duck and more naked girls," said Frith, who was a little disturbed by the less mature aspects of Kenney's omnivorous cultural appetite. Kenney got his duck and with it the art directors he wanted to be in charge of the magazine's visual aspects—a victory he would later regret.

The look of the new magazine had been a source of strife. Keeping newsstand appeal in mind, Simmons wanted the national version to be slick like *Cheetah*, but his editors had other ideas. "Doug and Henry, mostly Doug, had this idea the magazine would be rough, in an underground vein," Meyerowitz recalled. Glossy was just not cool.

By the time the *National Lampoon* started, there were some three hundred underground newspapers in the United States. With an advertising base resting precariously on the counterculture trinity of sex (escort services and massage parlors), drugs (head shops, mail-order bongs, etc.), and rock 'n' roll (local music venues and record stores), many of the underground papers operated on smaller budgets than even the early '60s *HL*. Their appearance reflected this lack of resources, but these funky production values were seen by readers as a testament to the integrity of the editorial content. As well, low overhead meant low or nonexistent cover prices. Salaries, too, were low or nonexistent, and this led to constant staff turnover, resulting in contributors with widely varying degrees of ability.

Several of the undergrounds ran cartoon strips created by graphic artists who had been warped by the same influences as the *Lampoon* editors: Kurtzman's *Mad* and the fresh-from-the-crypt horror of EC Comics. Beginning in 1967, when the raunchy *Zap* No. 1 emerged from the pen of Robert Crumb—the artist most associated in the public mind with underground comics (or "comix" as they were sometimes called by the kind of people who spelled America with a *k*)—these predecessors of the graphic novel had filtered out into the world through head shops and progressive bookstores.

Despite their remoteness from the Harvard side of the *Lampoon*, "the undergrounders were by no means looked down on," according to Weidman. "Everyone I knew thought R. Crumb was wonderful," he said. "Shelton [Gilbert Shelton, creator of the *Fabulous Furry Freak Brothers*, a sort of dopester Three Stooges] was also highly appreciated." The *Lampoon* and the underground comics had much in common: an anarchistic viewpoint that made them willing to deride conservatives and self-righteous liberals alike; a love/hate relationship with anything covered by the label "bourgeois" (not least themselves); an interest in experimenting with format; and, above all, a delight in puncturing hypocrisy.

But Frith (whose shelves, he said, "once groaned with the *East Village Other*," the underground paper serving greater Lower Manhattan) felt that "most of those *Lampoon* guys were yuppie conservatives playing at being counterculture." If so, they may have seen the comics as communiqués from the genuine underground. "What Doug really liked was to hang out with the real counterculture '70s beatnik types," said an *East Village Other* writer. "People who were really avant-garde, who weren't in it for the money."

Back in late 1969, having just moved to New York, Kenney had come across the genuine underground cartoonists Peter Bramley and Bill Skurski, whose Cloud Studios was based in an East Village storefront. Although he also created magazine illustrations and book covers, cartoons were Bramley's true love. "Bramley lived and breathed cartoons. He drew cartoons all night and would always bring the conversation back to cartoons. Actually, he was a pretty one-dimensional guy," said Meyerowitz.

Appointed as the *Lampoon*'s first art directors thanks to Kenney, Cloud insisted on illustrating everything themselves, but when it came to administration, they knew less about standard art-directing practice than Beard and Kenney knew about professional magazine editing. It was learn while you earn for all concerned, and it showed. "The first issue was just ugly," Frith declared.

On the editorial side, things weren't so much ugly as out of focus. "The first six issues were kind of fumbling around," Weidman admitted. In these early days, the magazine sought to hire writers from the ranks of established humorists and cartoonists who would lend credibility to the *Lampoon*, but these outsiders' approach tended to be too genial. Hard-pressed to find writers with a suitably aggressive style, the editors instead drew on their own resources. A large proportion of the first issues were written by Kenney and Beard, though this was not always apparent. Once a writer exceeded a two-articles-per-issue quota, anything more had to run under a pen name. O'Donoghue, a.k.a. Commander Barkfeather, was another workhorse, while vivacious Tamara Gould, one of the *Lampoon*'s few regular women writers, was in fact Trow.

Trow, the only *NatLamp* writer with a real flair for gossip, was able to pick up *Vogue*'s breathless style. "People are talking about . . . crime, petite crime, street crime," wrote Tamara. She also contributed *True Finance* to the May 1970 Greed issue (each issue was built around a theme). "In a trice, my glamour issue lay on the floor around my feet and my tiny little cotton futures were all that stood between my domestic auto sales and his hard-core unemployment," panted Tamara.

In a subsequent (October 1970) Politics issue, Beard did for legislative procedure what Trow had done for finance. "With a sudden motion, he attached his riders to my omnibus bills and I felt a groundswell building up for ratification as his enormous package approached enactment in record time. 'I've got a quorum, I've got a quorum,' he suddenly cried and my lower chamber filled up with his supporters," Beard wrote in the steamy *True Politics*.

The first issue also contained Kenney's most successful assumption of a female persona. Modeled on the ongoing *Private Eye* feature Mrs. Wilson's Diary, which purported to be the intimate musings of the wife of the British prime minister, Kenney's Mrs. Agnew's Diary chronicled life in the shark tank of the Nixon inner circle through the ingenuous eyes of Judy Agnew, wife of saurian vice president Spiro "Spiggy" (a name borrowed from "Spiggy Topes," *Private Eye*'s John Lennon stand-in) Agnew.

Judy might have come across as merely an easily mocked bouffanted ditz, but behind the faux-naif voice was Kenney's genuine affinity for naive characters, and he endowed Judy with an inner life that made her sympathetic as well as ridiculous.

For example, after hearing a talk by "that Gloria Steinem girl," Judy develops a strange urge to express herself and by January 1971 she's stealing from the grocery money ("you know how Spiggy feels about a woman getting too much education, and where her place is anyway") to attend the Famous Writers School, an actual correspondence course whose titular head was Bennett Cerf. B. Cerf's death in 1971 provided an ongoing source of jokes about Judy's unawareness of this fact, jokes that Kenney was not about to forgo out of consideration for his contributing editor C. Cerf.

Soon Judy is receiving comments from "that nice Mr. Cerf" on poetic efforts such as this May 1971 tribute to President Nixon's daughter Julie:

> *Hail and welcome keen-eyed Julie!*
> *Nymph of charm and temper scalding*
> *Our troubled youth adores you truly*
> *Though cares of state have left you balding.*

Jokes about Julie's husband, David Eisenhower, grandson of the previous Republican president ("O spawn of saintly Eisenhower" in Judy's words), were a staple of the early *Lampoon*. He turns up again in a February 1974 Kenney parody of the then-popular romance-oriented comic books aimed at young girls (only instead of being called *First Love*, this one is aimed at young boys and so called *First Lay*) and in *White House Romance*, another Kenney love comic, which suggested that the marriage of the Republican dynastic offspring remained unconsummated. The *Lampoon* writers struck Beatts as "the kind of kids who had Ant Farms when they were younger," and the gawky Eisenhower may have been such an irresistible target not only because of his Republican connections but because he evoked the editors' road not taken—the privileged white boy who had not gotten hip and did not question authority.

The anxieties of sexually inexperienced adolescents still caught in pre–sexual revolution morality became Kenney's special purview, notably in *First Blowjob*, another tale of lost innocence. Perfectly capturing the style of magazines aimed at preteen girls in those more sheltered days ("Blotting her cherry-frost lipstick on a tissue and giving her pert, blonde curls one last flick with her brush, Connie sighed and stepped back from the mirror for final inspection"), this is a date story with a twist as dreamboat Jeff Madison, "co-captain of the Varsity Football

Team, chairman of the Student Senate and Hi-Tri-Y activities coordinator," turns out to be a raging psychopath who forces Connie to perform the title's sexual act, ties her wrists and ankles to the steering wheel, and lashes out "viciously at her unprotected body with a snapped-off car aerial," something he's been wanting to try ever since he "first heard Negro music."

Unlike many subsequent *Lampoon* writers, Kenney identifies with the vulnerable, and his humor is black instead of vicious, arising out of how the world hurts the innocent rather than mocking innocence itself. When Connie returns home, "her half-naked body crisscrossed with red welts," her kindly but firm dad punches her out. Connie's experience was the inevitable outcome of playing with fire, or so proclaims future first lady Nancy Reagan in her July 1971 *Guide to Dating Dos and Don'ts*, another demonstration of Kenney's affinity for Republican political wives. "Dating is like dynamite," she warned. "Used wisely, it can move mountains and change the course of mighty rivers. Used foolishly, it can blow your legs off."

While sensitive to the slightest wrinkle in the weave of the social fabric, "Doug didn't really grasp politics," as O'Donoghue said. Yet the events leading up to the magazine's launch were such as to politicize even the uninvolved. In the 1969–1970 school year, there had been nearly two hundred bombings on college campuses, mostly targeting ROTC and defense industry–related buildings. Then in a horrific and grimly ridiculous incident in March 1970, three members of radical group the Weathermen blew up both themselves and an elegant Greenwich Village town house that belonged to a member's parents where they were constructing a homemade bomb. Some homemade arsenals proved more effective. In December 1969, a Bank of America branch was bombed in the days following the conviction of five Chicago Albatrosses.

The increased militancy flowed in large part from the perception in more radical circles that the current administration was prepared to disregard peaceful antiwar protests, no matter how widespread. Indeed, it decided to expand the war and in April 1970, American troops crossed the border into Cambodia. Even Kenney was moved to write an editorial in July 1970 on the "liberation of a somewhat surprised and bewildered Cambodia," suggesting it would soon enjoy the same benefits as South Vietnam, which, "once an underdeveloped Asian sump full of mosquitoes, overcooked rice and foreigners has blossomed under our tutelage into a veritable Eden of rusted tanks, Coca-Cola bottles and highly decorative half-breeds."

The war at home was escalating as well. On May 4, members of the Ohio National Guard, faced with a group of Kent State University students hurling barbed words and the occasional stone, fired into the crowd, wounding nine and killing four. In the wake of Kent State, 437 schools went on strike and over seventy-five thousand people marched on Washington. And yet the father of one of the dead students received letters calling his daughter a "communist whore" and a poll in the May 18 issue of *Newsweek* showed that 58 percent of respondents blamed protestors for the deaths at Kent State. A week later, two more students were killed at Jackson State, a predominately black university in Mississippi, an event that drew less media attention.

When the small group of writers met between the Labor Day 1969 move to New York and the April 1970 launch to discuss what the new magazine should be, they were not opposed or even indifferent to the protestors' aims, but they were uncomfortable with the overheated rhetoric often used to express those aims. As Beatts said, "Conditions were so bad as to be absurd, so the only intelligent reaction was black humor."

Right from the start, the *Lampoon* approached efforts to change the existing power structure with a degree of fatalism. This arose less from allegiance to it than from the knowledge that it was too entrenched to dislodge. As the children of privilege, the Lampooners knew "what the men in power were thinking and ... what their strengths and weaknesses were, and also that they had virtues and were not easily to be dismissed," as Trow observed.

The Mafia, for example, was not seen as the enemy of the established order but as its dark twin. "The recent change in Administration brought with it a long-awaited reduction in Federal interference and destructive over-regulation and the welcome removal of several short-sighted and overzealous officials whose hostility toward free enterprise has been so harmful in the past," wrote one Nicholas Fish (a.k.a. Beard), author of the *CosNosCo Annual Report* in the May 1970 Greed issue.

In 1970, there was no shortage of publications ready to attack the Establishment. What distinguished the *Lampoon* was its lack of faith in a viable alternative. The politics of the editors themselves ran the gamut from noncombatants like Kenney to gonzo anarchists like O'Donoghue to more traditional liberal Democrats like Cerf and Weidman to Terry Catchpole, a self-professed Libertarian right-winger (despite being a Harvard alum), a frequent freelance contributor until 1973. According to Sean Kelly (a self-professed anarchist who became a frequent contributor in 1971), Beard also described himself as a Libertarian, although another genuinely right-wing *Lampoon* editor dismissed him as "just a *New York Times* liberal."

In Catchpole's view, "one of the *Lampoon*'s greatest accomplishments was that you never had to define yourself in any terms other than your capacity to be funny," and the writers were at their best when going after what they held most dear. Thus the liberal Weidman could take swipes at the welfare bureaucracy while Catchpole could go after the idea of peace through strength. He contributed a remarkably prescient piece along these lines in the May 1971 issue (with the appropriate theme of the Future) called "But You Hadn't Heard of Vietnam in 1957," describing the situation in the imaginary "oil-rich sheikdom" of Abaqa on the Persian Gulf, under increasing pressure from Arab militants to sever its Western ties. "It's no longer a question of what we're going to give them, or how much," says a Defense Department spokesman, "only when and how."

"There's a perception that the *National Lampoon* was left-wing, hippie, liberal," said Ed Bluestone, a stand-up comedian who started freelancing for the magazine in 1971, "but we had real right-wing followers." Although the *Lampoon* editors shared some conservatives' dim view of human nature, finding it unlikely that people would work as hard out of concern for the common good as when driven by the carrot of greed and the stick of fear, they also rejected the right wing's authoritarian tendencies. At the same time, the refusal of many self-styled radicals to recognize the shallowness of their commitment to change when it came down to personal sacrifice continued to provide an irresistible target. Worse, militancy of any stripe precluded insubordination and the Lampooners did not take to being given orders by the politically correct any more than they did from the ROTC.

"It says here you are starting a funny magazine," read a letter from an irate imaginary reader in the April 1970 premiere issue. "All I can say is you people have a lot of nerve. Haven't you looked outside your own selfish egos long enough to see that people are being wronged and oppressed all over the world? Take the fascist military regimes which grow in number every year . . . and you, with your funny magazine."

The editors were not refusing to look outside; they just had a different take on what they saw. "What was going on had a great effect," O'Donoghue said. "Society was depicted in black and white," white being "the hippies, the pure idealists who would put the flower in the barrel of the gun," and black, of course, being "the power brokers, Dow Chemical, the pigs. We could stand in the center with the sniperscope and take turns blowing the shit out of them. 'Kill them all. God will know his own,'" was O'Donoghue's motto, borrowed from the Green Berets. "It was a very easy game to play," he said, "because they were so sharply defined. Then in the mid-70s, the smoke cleared and we found it was a silly conceit we'd made up. There were these two schools, but essentially everybody was drinking Coca-Cola."

O'Donoghue took some of his best shots in an August 1970 parody of an underground paper, targeting excessively groovy flower people ("Dear Mr. Newspaperman—I just think there would be peace if everybody just got together and rapped with each other and we could smoke dope rolled in strawberry-flavored cigarette papers and make love in the park and listen to Buffy Sainte-Marie records," etc.), psychedelic band names such as "The Organic Egg Cream" and "The Stuffed Bedlington Terrier," and the constant staff turnover ("Staff: The real editor OD'd last week, so somebody else was filling in but he got busted for a bomb plot and the associate editor split for the Coast. . . . Maybe I'm the editor now"). Unlike the ridicule of hippies that appeared regularly in the mainstream press, the *Lampoon*'s satire had credibility in the same circles it tweaked. It was clearly from the inside; you wouldn't know what kind of person would voluntarily use strawberry-flavored papers unless you'd been there.

If O'Donoghue had a bead on hippies present, some unsigned author was gunning for hippies future. "Aquarian Entrepreneurs Cast Bread upon Waters, Returns on Investments," read a headline of the *Gall Street Journal* in the Greed issue. "'The economic philosophy that motivates these kids is light years away from Adam Smith's,' asserts Harvard economist John Kenneth Galbraith," the *Journal* says. "'While parents are only concerned with the money to buy food, clothing and shelter, the younger generation is more concerned about lifestyle. You know, better things to eat, expressive wearing apparel, comfortable, diverting places to live. Hey, wait a minute . . .'"

Those who were still simply living as opposed to having a lifestyle drew Trow's fire. "Why do you need Mediocrity?" he asked in the July 1970 Bad Taste issue. "The Wonderful World of Mediocrity," which starts out with a genuine quote from a genuine mediocre senator speaking up on behalf of a Nixon Supreme Court nominee. "Even if he were mediocre, there are a lot of mediocre judges and people and lawyers and they are entitled to a little representation, aren't they?" the senator asks plaintively. "We can't have all Brandeises, Frankfurters and Cardozos." Furthermore, the article advises, "mediocrity is a way of ridding yourself of the disastrous *highs* and *lows*, the unwanted excess that is destroying your fragile sanity."

"George's special target was the booboisie," said Kelly, who felt that Trow, whom he described as "a Tory radical, a left-leaning aristocrat," was the only Lampooner besides Weidman who had "any real passion about racism." At the same time, he said, "George was very antibour-geois in the Mencken tradition: the working class are OK, aristocrats are OK, it's the jerks in the middle you have to deplore. My argument was 'I'm one of those people. So are my parents. You can't write them off.'" These tender sentiments did not stop Kelly himself from writing "The Great Kitsch Conspiracy Trial," which went after middlebrow taste in the March 1971 issue. But Trow's objections were not based purely on snobbishness. It was the political expression of this yearning for bland-ness he minded, the constituency claimed by President Nixon as "the silent majority."

The Lampooners disdain for the Nixon administration exempli-fied exactly the kind of Ivy League East Coast snootiness the president resented, but it also reflected an uneasy realization that the principles they had been brought up with were increasingly irrelevant.

This change in values was reflected in a political shift identified in the early '70s by Carl Oglesby, a founder of SDS. Oglesby argued that power in the Republican party had moved from what he called "Wall Street"—East Coast–based, internationalist, and with a lingering sense of social responsibility—to the Sunbelt-based "Cowboys": isolationist, rabidly anti-Communist, and determined not to give a penny to anyone who lacked the gumption to make their own fortune.

The Cowboys first flexed their muscle by installing Arizona conser-vative Barry Goldwater as the 1964 Republican presidential candidate and consolidated their triumph with the election of Ronald Reagan. With the Republican center of gravity moving west, even born-and-bred Wall Streeter George H. W. Bush had to recast himself as a son of the Sunbelt. Both factions—Wall Street and Cowboys—were devoted to defending the interests of capital, but it was a classic clash of old money versus new money, and the *Lampoon* definitely resented a takeover by men sporting large diamond pinky rings and white belts.

The *Lampoon*'s aversion was based on substance as well as style, as illustrated by Beard's scathing November 1971 attack (modeled on an ad for Ultra-Brite toothpaste) on formerly liberal Republican New York governor Nelson Rockefeller's conversion to Cowboyism in the wake of losing the 1968 nomination to Nixon. "One day I overheard a top leader in my party (you wouldn't know his name in a million years, but he's on the board of 147 top corporations) say to a mediocre party war-horse (who runs a leading free-world democracy), 'Too bad Nelson's such a goddamn pinko. What do you say we give him that ole heave-ho?'" Rockefeller confessed. "He recommended Ultra-Right . . . all it is is a powerful mixture of blatant racism and crude fear-enhancers combined with simpleminded rhetoric. . . . In just weeks, convictions I had held for twenty years were gone, and with them that logy, washed-up feeling that can accompany defeat in a major election."

The acme of mediocrity in politics was personified, in 1970, by Judy Agnew's better half, Spiggy. He became the muse for one of the early *Lampoon*'s most inspired works, *Eight Days that Shook Wook, Iowa: The Assassination of Spiro T. Agnew* by the mysterious Punji (who was actually Tony Hendra, a new contributor from the British satire scene by way of Bruce-influenced stand-up and television comedy, writing in collaboration with Beard), that combined photos, fake newspaper clippings, and text to create a sort of scrapbook effect. One photograph shows the first few suspects all gleefully claiming responsibility, joined in subsequent photos by even more happy self-described assassins. An excerpt from the *Burger Commission Report* on the crime asserts that the hole in the vice-presidential skull "through which the fatal ice pick was introduced had been in his head for some years."

The article appeared in October 1970, a seventh issue that almost marked the *Lampoon*'s death as well. A meeting the previous month had considered whether to keep publishing the magazine in light of its poor sales. "I give you five issues, tops," one Hugh Hefner allegedly wrote in to the July 1970 Letters to the Editor (which were, naturally, all written *by* the editor). Even before the first issue appeared, *Newsweek* had prophesied in March 1970 that "putting out a monthly that will entertain the nearly-30s may make the three youthful editors old fast." The initial source of consternation was the art direction. Beard and

Kenney were falling out with Cloud fast while Simmons was already putting out feelers for a new art director. In the interim, he fell back on his own resources. "I was very unhappy with the covers, so with the September issue I said, '*I'm* going to do the cover,'" he recalled. The result, Minnie Mouse in pasties, brought the *Lampoon* its first lawsuit, from the no-longer acquiescent Disney organization, for $11 million. "I'd always warned them about being sued," Simmons chuckled, "and then my idea gets it."

Whoever came up with the cover concept (Meyerowitz also claimed responsibility), it marked the *Lampoon*'s first success. Then, three issues later, the magazine went into the black, "but," as Weidman said, "who cared? We didn't think twice about it. Into the black—big deal." All their other projects (except *Life*) had been successful. Why should this be any different? But Simmons, who knew a new magazine's break-even point is usually at least a year down the line, was happily surprised to get there only six months in. The vital ingredient was the new art director, a twenty-five-year-old named Michael Gross, whose highly developed visual sophistication departed from Cloud's funky approach. "When the commercial reality of the thing hit home," Beard told *Print* magazine in 1974, "we saw that what we really needed was a slick art director who knew magazines."

Besides organizing the art department to run efficiently and bringing coherence to what had been a hodgepodge of design elements, Gross "made the *Lampoon* special from a visual point of view," said David Kaestle, originally Gross's assistant and later art director for *NatLamp*'s nonmagazine output. The visual aspects of the magazine were divided into three components. One was the standing elements—the headings for regular features like Letters and the Diary. The second was simple illustration, which could be graphics, photographs, or lettering. The third, which the *Lampoon* became most associated with, was parody.

Articles parodying other magazines poured forth: *Pethouse* (soft-focus photos of totally nude furry animals in provocative poses); *Stupid News and World Report*; a 1940s' *Life*; *Gun Lust* magazine; *Popular Evolution*;

Third Base—the Dating Newspaper; and the aforementioned *True Politics* ("Dear God, Why Do I Want to Be Named to the Bureau of Indian Affairs?") were just some of the publications from the parody mill in the first three years. Then there were parodies of other types of publications—for example, the *Eddie Bean Down-Filled Catalog* that explored the new craze for functional yet expensive outdoor gear.

As with the *HL Time* parody, the *NatLamp* parodies were notable for their attention to detail, although the tedious task of making sure the parodies looked like the originals fell largely to the art assistants (all female) while Gross and Kaestle focused on concepts. It was rare for art directors to be involved in the conceptualization of imagery to the extent that the *Lampoon*'s were, and, said Kaestle, it spoiled them for life.

It also drew top illustrators to the *Lampoon* even though it didn't pay top rates, because, Kaestle recalled, "they were allowed a freedom of imagery they couldn't find anywhere else." Regular contributors like masters of the macabre Gahan Wilson and Edward Gorey were permitted a particular degree of autonomy. Still, not all illustrators were swayed. The much-admired Robert Crumb thought the context was too commercial, while the vitriolic caricaturist Ralph Steadman, who illustrated Hunter Thompson's odysseys for *Rolling Stone*, also resisted numerous overtures.

The hands-off attitude applied not only to Gross's relationship with the artists but also to the editors' relationship with Gross. This unsupervised approach usually worked because the art director tried to fully understand the writer's premise before commissioning the artwork—usually, but not always. In an editorial that appeared in the November 1972 Decadence issue, O'Donoghue had a simple explanation for why the cover of that issue, intended to be a parody of Sir Walter Scott's "The Lady of the Lake," showed a sword emerging from a bathtub clutched by a man's hand instead of a woman's: "Michael O'Donoghue, who came up with the idea, turned the entire project over to Art Director Michael Gross. O'Donoghue didn't bother to go over every detail with Gross because he figured any schoolboy has read *King Arthur*, not realizing

Gross, who's still trying to finish a *Blackhawk* comic he began some months ago, thinks King Arthur is a seaport in Texas."

Gross retaliated in the January 1973 issue's editorial. "Do you think the editors who insist, month after month, that I am the cause of all our cover problems, can possibly be right? This month's brilliant cover [a photograph of a revolver being pointed at the head of a very apprehensive-looking dog with the caption "If You Don't Buy This Magazine, We'll Kill This Dog"] is a success primarily because of one element—a *joke*," he wrote. "The problem around here lately is that the combined efforts of the entire editorial staff have not resulted in a single funny cover in four months." Gross was later vindicated when the cover won an Illustrators' Guild Award to add to the eighteen design awards the *Lampoon* had already collected in its brief existence.

In contrast to most magazines where writers and artists are rarely in contact, at the *Lampoon* they often collaborated on the concept for an article. For example, Gross was able to finish illustrating a movie poster—part of an imaginary publicity package for *Right On!*, a purported Hollywood attempt to cater to Revolting Youth—even before Catchpole's copy came in. Gross's poster features an illustrated image of Jane Fonda wearing a skintight T-shirt and jeans in character as an "Aquarian Age activist whose sexploits rocked a nation!" while Catchpole's accompanying synopsis informs us that she is "Jan Henry," an actress who "abandons her makeup case and *haute couture* wardrobe and, throwing away her bras, dons the severely simple—but revealing, male readers!—garb of the committed activist!"

All the press kit's graphics are, like Catchpole's prose, dead on. "Parody has to be accurate," Gross said. "If you're imitating schlock, you have to know what makes it schlock. A parody should be so like the original that one has to look closely to see the difference." Consequently, the happiest collaborations were with artists who let the material carry the joke. Frank Springer, the illustrator of *Phoebe Zeit-Geist* whose muscular super-heroic illustration style particularly suited action stories, was especially in demand. "When we knew Springer would be drawing it, all we needed to do was think of every possible joke on the subject," Cerf said. For example, when he, Beard, and Kelly created *Prison Farm*, a saga about a convicted Watergate burglar doing hard time at a "country club" light security prison, they met over drinks to brainstorm prison farm jokes. "We had list after list of these things," Cerf recalled, "and Frank got every single one of them into that strip somewhere," including the moment when the prisoners, pushed beyond endurance by a selection of inferior vintages, bang their tin cups and call for "Montrachet!"

Springer also worked with Kenney, who was still immersed in '50s obsessions, on April 1972's *Commie Plot Comics*, which depicts the Russian takeover of a small Midwestern town. Renamed Stalinville, its Howard Johnson's is reduced to serving only one flavor of ice cream— "Red Raspberry, and we are out of that too, little comrade. Ha! Ha! Ha!" Kenney also collaborated with artist Daniel Maffia in March 1971 on *The Undiscovered Notebooks of Leonardo da Vinci*, in which Maffia's delicate pen-and-ink drawings, very much in the style of the originals, illustrate further evidence of da Vinci's uncanny ability to anticipate modern inventions. These include "la Personalle Vibratoria—una Christamma presente per Il Papa Innocente III, ha ha," and the "Rota-Riducione? Circula Magica? Hulus Hoopus?"

Some of the most striking examples of artist-writer collaboration, and certainly of the latitude the magazine was willing to allow both, were surreal photo collages, like Trow's *Bland Hotel* in the September 1972 issue, illustrated with Jim Hans's wonderful facsimiles of '30s hand-tinted postcards. "The fashion now is for twin hotels joined by a marble subway," Trow wrote. "The Bland Hotel suffers. Recently, Parlour Pimps have appeared in the lobby. Nothing can be done to dislodge them." However, all this obscurity wasn't quite as left field as it might seem. Surrealism had become less niche as college audiences, already enticed by the surrealists' pastimes of drugs and subversion, flocked to the films of Luis Buñuel and the Marx Brothers, which, like the *Lampoon*, combined black humor, ridicule, blasphemy, anarchy, silliness, and cruelty in varying amounts.

The magazine's willingness to bend its format attracted artist-writer hybrids whose work transcended categories. One of these was Bruce McCall, who discovered the *Lampoon* in 1971 after his brother sent him a copy. It was a revelatory experience at a transitional point in his life. "I thought, 'This is what I've been doing all my life,' but I never believed there might be a mass media outlet for it," he recalled. For the April 1972 issue, he wrote and illustrated a six-page brochure on the '58 Bulgemobile ("too great not to be changed, too changed not to be great!"). This ode to the great American automotive romance describes "scrumptious extras like Full-Vu glass and new Ejecta-matic ashtrays" and backseats of "richly simulated Wonda-Weev fabric-like material," depicted in the accompanying illustration as being big enough for at least seven people, a nostalgic thrill for passengers crammed into the backseats of the newly popular Japanese imports. Such hyperbole came naturally to McCall, whose day job for many years (as European creative director for the Ogilvy & Mather agency and later another agency) was concocting Mercedes-Benz ads. "After working as a commercial artist," he said, "this was my revenge."

Glowing descriptions of unbelievably enormous, impossibly luxurious modes of transportation became McCall's specialty, and he took snob appeal to gargantuan extremes. The first-class boat deck on McCall's April 1974 RMS *Tyrannic* is a vast expanse dotted with a few well-dressed figures in polo coats. "The Right crowd, and no crowding," reads the caption, while the heading urges, "Pray, Gambol Tyrannically! Gentlemen are requested to refrain from riding ponies through the Steerage after 8:00 P.M."

McCall wasn't the only artist to poke fun at his livelihood in the *Lampoon*'s pages. Kelly Freas, who regularly drew *Mad* covers, produced one of the *Lampoon*'s most notorious images when he presented *Mad* mascot Alfred E. Neuman as accused atrocity perpetrator Lt. William Calley asking "What, My Lai?" on the cover of the July 1971 Bummers issue. However, it seemed to an uneasy Frith that some artists were parodying themselves. "If Gross wanted the look of a third-rate pulp artist, instead of getting somebody really good to work a little cleverer change on it, he would hire the most famous third-rate pulp artist. You never knew whether it was a letting go and having great fun with something or whether there was an innate cruelty." This perceived cruelty was one of the reasons Frith became disenchanted with the magazine before the end of 1971, even though his name stayed on the masthead for another year. The *Lampoon* was drifting ever further from Harvard.

5

TWENTY-FOUR HOURS A DAY

Perceived cruelty was only one of the reasons for Frith's disenchantment with the *Lampoon*. He also felt the general tone of the magazine was being set by Kenney rather than by the more intellectually oriented Beard. As a result, the *Lampoon* was becoming, in his estimation, "an excuse to be as puerile as possible and to be rewarded for it enormously. It was beautifully, professionally packaged sleaze." His old collaborator and fellow *NatLamp* contributing editor, Cerf, took a more tolerant view; without the sleaze factor, Cerf felt, "the magazine would not have worked, because no one would have paid any attention at all."

Right before the third issue in June 1970, the tension between Frith and Kenney exploded. According to Frith, "Doug came by my office in a terrible state of jitters. He couldn't sit down. 'First of all,' Doug said, 'Henry isn't running this magazine—I am! You keep talking about Henry as if he were the editor in chief. That's me. I do that.'" Further, Frith recalled, Kenney added that he couldn't work with Frith anymore because "it's like working with my father!"

Kenney's unusual outburst was an indication of the strain he and

Beard were under, producing monthly issues in five weeks instead of the standard three months. Then, as if writing most of the magazine was not enough, Beard and Kenney often rewrote other writers' articles, though the original author's name usually stayed on the byline. "Henry was really the coauthor of my first piece," Bluestone acknowledged, "but he didn't take any credit—not like some people at the *Lampoon*, who if they put in a comma would try to take coauthor status and 90 percent of the money. If Henry got credit for everything he wrote in the first thirty-six issues, the quantity would turn out to be 1,000 percent more than he got credit for," Bluestone said, maintaining that several contributors would never have lasted past two or three issues if Beard hadn't rewritten their pieces. Moreover, the editors managed to do it in such a way that their interference was appreciated rather than resented, with O'Donoghue describing Kenney as "the master safecracker. He left no fingerprints."

With so much to be done, the two editors saw anyone who wanted to take on added responsibility as a godsend, not a threat. Despite Kenney's outburst to Frith, they didn't have much time to fret about titles, job descriptions, or status, even had they been so inclined. The Lampooners preferred a more fluid management style that prioritized developing and executing ideas rather than approval hierarchies.

No one doubted who was really making the magazine work. "Henry and Doug were the creative assets in addition to being minority stockholders," Catchpole said. "They had enormous authority and basically determined what would be in the magazine," with O'Donoghue behind the throne as, in Beatts's words, "the Cardinal Richelieu of the *National Lampoon*." Throwing their weight around was not the chief editors' style. "It was very casual," Beatts recalled. "Doug and Henry were there every day and everyone else would drop in and out. You didn't go to a receptionist. You went right to Doug's office and say, 'I have to see you,' and he'd go, 'In five minutes' or 'What about?' or 'Not now.'"

"Nobody used rank, and if there was an organizational chart, I never saw it," McCall agreed. "Everyone was in these ratty offices without names on them, and they all looked the same—messy. It was hard to tell who did what around there. It seemed to be full of kids about twenty-one years old, a sort of floating dorm party all the time." When he first started dropping by, all McCall could deduce was that "Matty was the owner and Henry was sort of the nominal editor and everyone else sort of swam around in a state of controlled anarchy and did what they wanted to do. And by some miracle of arguing back and forth, they would come up with the next issue."

Controlled anarchy might describe many writers' natural environments, but it does not make the job of editors and publishers any easier. According to Simmons, his staff "didn't meet a deadline for the first five years." Not that an occasional effort wasn't made, usually at Beard's instigation, which led to periodic departures from the overall collegial approach. In Catchpole's view, "the editorial process at the *Lampoon* was not any more democratic than at other magazines. There's always a time when it's one big happy family. There's another time when we're a magazine factory and we're all on the assembly line."

At least the assembly line had long lunch breaks. And cocktail hours. And dinners. The usual steakhouse gatherings expanded and became mobile—from a Japanese restaurant down the street to Little Italy to, when they wanted to see what the expense account would bear, the Plaza. Often Beard and Kenney would take the contributing editors to, said Beatts, "relatively cheesy places," where they would commandeer several tables and conduct what McCall termed "great communal kind of brainstorming sessions where we'd blab for hours," sometimes starting in the early evenings and not finishing up until around midnight.

"A lot of stuff got written on napkins—that's the way it really did work for a while," said Gerry Sussman, an advertising copywriter who started freelancing for the *Lampoon* in 1971 and continued to write for it for the next eighteen years. The first thing to be noted on the napkins was the issue's theme, and who would get stuck with executing it. Anyone—anyone who was a staffer or an inner-circle freelancer like Cerf or McCall—could put in a bid to edit an issue at which point, Kaestle said, following "a number of cocktail party sessions and lunches and a lot of sitting around offices, Henry would say, 'You've got to come up with a list of contents and it's got to fill sixty-two pages.'" Armed with a list of proposed articles and people to write them, the issue editor then acted as a sort of foreman, responsible for making sure the writers delivered on time and taking first crack at editing copy.

While hardly likely to adopt the fair but glacial collective decision-making process favored by more politically correct organizations, the Lampooners came up with their own equable solution: trial by fire. "There was a savage kind of editing value system," McCall said. "You could clearly tell whether the other guys thought this was a boring idea. They'd go, 'That's not funny enough.' Everybody would put in his oar in this informal voting on pieces," especially Cardinal Richelieu, who was feared but respected.

Still, McCall insisted, such severity was a form of tough love, not an attempt to force writers into a particular style. On the contrary, he felt that the *Lampoon* editors "trusted the people they invited to contribute to be their own editors in terms of suggesting what was good enough to be in the magazine. Also, there was an allowance for noble failures." For newcomers, the trick lay in breaking into that inner circle of credibility. "You had a bunch of very intelligent, overeducated, witty men 'running the dozens' [an African-American term for trading ever more baroque insults about each others' mothers], so there was a lot of fancy footwork and fencing to see who would get off the *bon mot* of the evening," Beatts said. Her own footwork had to be especially deft as she was often the only woman present among six or seven men.

On these occasions, Beatts got the distinct impression that "neither Henry or Doug particularly wanted me to be there. Girls weren't very much a part of their lives." However, because the editors had been brought up to be polite, "they weren't about to run to Michel [Choquette, a *Lampoon* contributor and her boyfriend at the time] and say, 'Can't you just leave her at home?'" She served notice that she was more than a social appendage one night when, at O'Donoghue's urging, the group had gone to a restaurant called Sayat Nova that turned out to be terrible. "Everyone was chaffing Michael because its appeal for him was clearly the romantic associations—the music, the garden—more than the food," Beatts recalled, "and when someone said, 'What does Sayat Nova mean anyway?' I said, 'Hello, Sucker.' People were as startled as if the rug had spoken."

These gatherings were less enjoyable if you weren't at the center of things. "In 1971 they used to have dinner together every night when they were closing an issue. They liked them, but it was really boring for non-*NatLamp* people," said a woman who at that time was a close personal friend of O'Donoghue's and a marginal contributor to the magazine. Similarly Bluestone, who wasn't particularly interested in becoming an insider, felt that while "if you have five funny guys at a small dinner, people will say funny things," he didn't think he was witnessing "any new version of the Algonquin Round Table. Those theme meetings were never very funny, 'All these themes suck—which should we choose?' being a typical remark."

With the bulk of important decisions made after working hours, freelancers who were not on the cocktail circuit were at a disadvantage. The window between article assignment and completion was ordinarily around a month, but if the issue didn't seem to be jelling, a writer might be told the theme had been changed and he had to start over only days before deadline.

The only way the *Lampoon* process functioned at all was because it involved such a tight group. "The *National Lampoon* was always written by a very small number of people—six to ten on an issue," Beatts said, "and some of those people were also editors. I don't know how receptive they were to people who weren't at those dinners."

Nevertheless, Canadian Sean Kelly managed to be adopted and contribute frequently despite being unable to socialize due to living in Montreal, where he had a job as an English teacher, until the end of 1972. He had been drawn into the *Lampoon* orbit by Choquette, a French-

Canadian who had been exposed to US showbiz culture as half of a two-man music-comedy act. Just as the act was breaking up, Choquette wrote a letter to the *Lampoon* in 1970 that was actually printed. By early 1971 he was a contributing editor. His most famous coup was discovering a Hitler look-alike and persuading Simmons to send himself, the look-alike, and a photographer to a Caribbean island for a story on the former dictator's life in retirement, a four-day assignment that somehow took weeks to complete.

A prolific contributor in the magazine's first two years, Choquette began to collaborate with Kelly as early as July 1970. The next month, their "The World: A Paranoid Projection" dispensed prejudice even-handedly, labeling LA as being filled with "hebes, plastic, queers, phonies, atheists and other religious fanatics, sun, carrot and devil worshippers," Canada with "inferiority complexes, fixed hockey, Royalist WASPs," and the Midwest with "campus bums, black firebugs, panicked National Guardsmen, squares, hicks, Teamsters." It also fingered Switzerland as the headquarters of the "Wide-Eyed One-Worlder Conspiracy," India as the HQ of the "Undeserving Poor Conspiracy," and New York as the HQ of, naturally, the "International Jewish Conspiracy."

This was right up the *Lampoon* alley, as was "Guilt Test" in the August 1970 issue, which asked, "Which groups do you associate with the following: garlic; greasy hair; sweat; flashy clothes; gold Cadillacs; barefoot and smelly; love grass, high all the time; lisping and mincing?" (The answers: "vampires; garage mechanics; athletes; clowns; wealthy sheiks; goats; mountain goats; Castilian butchers.")

At first, Kelly's name never appeared on a byline without Choquette's. Consequently, he recalled, "there were rumors among the editors that I didn't exist except as a figment of Michel's imagination." He soon became known for his erudition, or, in a crowd whose heads were stuffed full of miscellany ranging from what Beard termed "bubblegum cards to the Edict of Nantes," for a higher grade of miscellany. His particular expertise was parodying poets ranging from T. S. Eliot ("I grow old . . . I grow old / Some who I sent up for life have been paroled" in

August 1972's "The Love Song of J. Edgar Hoover") to Robert Browning ("Fags! They edited the fashion mags / Had strongholds on arts and letters / Wrote TV dramas, ads and gags" in "The Pied Piper of Burbank," a March 1971 collaboration with Choquette).

Determined to see how much obscurity the *Lampoon* would bear, Kelly wrote a dense parody of *Finnegans Wake* that required an editorial label warning, "Attention, College Kids." Unsurprisingly, this highbrow approach left several readers cold. "I found it difficult to hook into a lot of the stuff Sean wrote because frankly I'm not as educated as he is," Bluestone said, "and when he did a word-for-word parody of *The Waste Land*, the whole thing would just miss me."

Kelly was also fond of skewering campus enthusiasms. He mocked four of the most in-vogue theoreticians in a superhero comic strip called *The Utopia Four*. It features the exploits of "Super Bucky" Buckminster Fuller, who has successfully harnessed biology and technology to create an energy-efficient Spaceship Earth; "Media Man" Marshall McLuhan, who promotes (in 1971) a world brought together by decentralized communications technology; "Mr. Mulch" Charles Reich, who suggests consciousness is slowly evolving from a mechanized model of the universe to a more organic postindustrial one; and "Karate Kate" Millett, who proposes a world unified by the absence of men. The plot of the comic involves our four heroes being called in to stop a ghetto riot and unable to come up with any practical way of doing so despite their best theorizing.

Kelly's next contribution, an August 1971 collaboration with Beatts and Choquette, was "Right On! The Campus War Game" (unrelated to Catchpole's movie of the same name), an elaborate board game that pits Longhairs (English and sociology majors "who give the V-sign at Baez concerts, worked for [Democratic dove candidate] Gene McCarthy and are opposed to meaningless violence") against Straights (fratmen, ROTC types, business students, and engineers, who "can be distinguished by their crew neck sweaters, slide rules and attendance at various sporting events"). Then there's the Womens' Lib contingent, the support of which "will invariably be lost if The Leader asks them to rustle up some sandwiches."

Choquette frequently made the editorial version of this request, off-loading the tedious task of finding appropriate photos to accompany his articles onto his girlfriend, Beatts. In one instance, she handled the photo research for a "Canada Supplement" to the August 1971 Bummers issue. Her efforts drew a response from a Canadian reader who pointed out that a photograph allegedly of contemporary Toronto "was obviously ten years old," though it was, in fact, a picture of Cleveland in the '30s. Beatts and Choquette may have been inspired to collaborate on this salute, entitled *The Retarded Giant on Your Doorstep*, by their recent relocation from the serenity of Canada to the rowdy East Village, a neighborhood so filled with excitement that their building's janitor had to post a sign in the hallway requesting visitors to "vomit outside, not in here."

The supplement's collection of Canadiana included Canadian bumper stickers like "My Country, Correct or Misinformed," translations into the Canadian ("Up against the wall you mutherfuckingpig" turns into "Now wait a minute officer, let's be reasonable"), and a "Canadian cwiz" ("What's the capital of Canada? Mostly American; What wars did Canada take part in? Oh, the same ones"). Canadian McCall had his own explanation for the large number of fellow countrymen on the *Lampoon*. "Canada," he said, "is very bland and controlled. They wait for red lights. This creates a climate where anybody who has any kind of rebellious feeling and creative sensibility probably turns to some kind of satire since parody is one of the few forms of aggression tolerated."

If there was one subset of *Lampoon* writers larger than Harvard grads or Canadians, it was refugees from the world of advertising. Some of the same tools—conceptualization, verbal facility, thriving under pressure—came in useful. But at the *Lampoon*, these skills were used to undermine the consumer culture they had helped create.

Gerry Sussman, like McCall, was a little older and had been a successful copywriter when he decided to go into humor writing full time, a move he described as "kind of a foolhardy thing to do." One day he got a call from a *Lampoon* editor who had read one of his pieces in a humor anthology. Writing for the existing humor market made Sussman an anomaly among the *Lampoon* inner circle. "They sneered at the *Playboy* contributors, commercial humorists," McCall said. "They didn't want to buy any of the established ones" once they had their own stable and no longer needed the professionals.

Sussman not only was unusual, he felt unusual. For one thing, he came out of the Catskills tradition that pronounces the first letter in *humor* as a *y*. For another, he said, the Lampooners were "really into all that counterculture stuff and I wasn't." However, he noted, while his colleagues might have been "into drugs and sex and rebellion, they weren't into that brown rice stuff at all. Some of them were totally involved in building their image and didn't make any pretense about it. Others might have hidden it behind a fuck-you attitude toward the world, but they were all," he asserted, "very, very ambitious."

It seemed the same to Dean Latimer, a writer for counterculture staple the *East Village Other* who became a frequent *Lampoon* contributor. The *Lampoon*, to his mind, "was not a happy-go-lucky counterculture operation. The motive was to make money, not to change the world." Or as Weidman put it, "It was a commercial venture from the start, and subversion was the product being sold."

Kenney had originally contacted Latimer in 1970 on O'Donoghue's recommendation. "O'Donoghue loved Latimer," Kelly recalled. "He was O'Donoghue's Wild Child. He wears rags, smells bad, and reads eighteen languages. He's a genuine wandering scholar. There's nothing fake or self-conscious about him." Latimer's fellow wanderer at the time was the *East Village Other*'s movie reviewer, one P. J. O'Rourke from Ohio by way of Baltimore, where he had edited an underground paper called *Hairy* after getting an MA from Johns Hopkins's writing program. "We trolled all the bars on the West Side, went through chorus lines of women. We went out, got drunk, got laid," Latimer recalled. He main-tained, however, that illegal drugs were not among the substances he and O'Rourke abused. "That was one thing we liked about hanging out with each other," he said. "Neither of us even did pot by that time. It was nice going to parties together, to have that support when you turned down that line of coke or joint. We *were* into beer, my God."

O'Rourke, in those days, had embraced a fashionable countercul-ture accessory: Marxist rhetoric. "When I first met him, he was espous-ing radical this, radical that," Latimer said, "but I always thought he was doing it to be In in that scene. I think it came as a relief to him to find out he didn't have to espouse all that bullshit and people would still accept him. It was certainly fine by me."

"That bullshit" provided the springboard for Latimer's August 1972 picture story, "Tommy Tucker: A Reactionary Hero's Glorious Chal-lenge to the Forces of Arrogant Progressivism," a Libertarian tract mod-eled on the kind of hectoring Maoist propaganda brandished to confer revolutionary credibility in radical circles.

"'Why can't I do my own part,'" Tommy wonders, "'to collabo-rate in the arrogant American project of rapine and plunder of third-world countries? Am I impeding the progress of American imperialism by doing nothing?' As he thus yearns to participate in the righteous enslavement of suppressed peoples a vehicle approaches." It is a bus, "an integrated progressivist imposition on right-thinking segregationist American education," that runs over Tommy. But the story has a happy ending when three General Motors stock certificates Tommy swallowed as a baby are revealed during his resulting operation. "'Through close study of President Nixon's repressive thought, I have treacherously furthered the enslavement of all peoples and made myself a bundle!'" exclaims Tommy, hailed as "a true exponent of glorious monopoly capitalism."

O'Rourke himself underwent a similar conversion. After a year of pub-crawling, he grew tired of being broke and began an unsuccessful hunt for a major agency copywriting job. By Christmas 1971, he was on the verge of writing copy for a direct-mail firm when he accompanied Latimer to the *Lampoon* offices, where Kenney commissioned one of their story ideas.

The breakthrough idea was a July 1972 comic strip called *Third World Thrills*, based on the (actual) mysterious disappearance of Nelson Rockefeller's son Michael in "the slumbering enigma which is New Guinea." The strip posits that the younger Rockefeller had gone there to supervise the development of a sickle-cell anemia virus as part of a plot to appropriate Africa's natural resources. Far from having died, as was supposed, he lives on a plantation in pre–Civil War splendor, having trained the natives to be suitably subservient, with the plantation school teaching simple English phrases like "Yas, Boss, dat sho'am some fine waddy-melon!" The last panel depicts a Republican Convention, where the president proclaims "a secret formula for ending racial strife, crime in the streets, bussing, riots, drug addiction" as conventioneers hoist signs bearing the logos of 3M, IBM, DuPont, Texaco, and other party stalwarts.

It was with some trepidation that Latimer went uptown to the *Lampoon*'s office on Madison Avenue, "the belly of the beast" from his East Village perspective. But he was pleasantly surprised to find "a sort of hippie commune, except everybody had money. You could wear a tie or you could go around barefoot. There were girls all over the place," some of whom may have even worked there.

On the other side of the stylistic coin from the shambolic Latimer was Brian McConnachie. Tall, well groomed, and steadily married, McConnachie had passed for normal successfully enough to have been employed at CBS and a large ad agency. But behind a horn-rimmed exterior lay profound eccentricity. McConnachie was the one editor whose sensibility the others found difficult to categorize. The best they could do was to suggest that he was Not of This Earth. The June 1972 issue offered a "Brian McConnachie Grab Bag" containing a "complete Book with all the info—where BRIAN's idea of what's funny comes from—how to adjust YOUR feelers to the same sector of the night sky!"

The package could be ordered from "Atomic Mole People, 11 Grove St., Pleasantville, Planet Mole-Dar." McConnachie *was* from a different planet in the sense that he was known for a certain sweetness of temperament, proving, as Sussman said, that "you didn't have to have a vicious antiestablishment, antihuman nature, like some of them did."

McConnachie's creations included ineffable comics such as *Amish in Space* and *The Attack of the Sizeable Beasts*, an account of a town terrorized by large squirrels, as well as renditions of the national anthems of countries like Chad, Liechtenstein, and Bermuda, but all resist excerption. For a little over a year, he turned out Tell Debbie, an agony column in which correspondents requesting guidance in dealing with deep personal problems were given advice such as "How very unfortunate."

"Brian's issues were very particularly Brian," Weidman said. "He had a very specific view of what he wanted, and frequently, only Brian understood what it was." One such McConnachie issue had the theme Sweetness and Light, not the *Lampoon*'s usual cup of tea, "all so Brian McConnachie can have something to show his mother," the March 1973 editorial stated. This doesn't mean that McConnachie was vapid—only that he favored the zany over the scathing.

Possibly this was due to a happier childhood. To McCall, it seemed that his colleagues "were all settling scores, all angry adolescents who didn't get enough sex in their teens or somehow felt left out." But alienation and exclusion was not McConnachie's youthful experience, or so he told the *New York Times* in 1972, recalling that he "summered at the shore and went on dates and bought wrist corsages."

If McConnachie and McCall, to whom lapses of taste did not come naturally, represented the whimsical end of the *Lampoon* spectrum, another defector from advertising arrived to bolster Kenney's teenage-kicks contingent. More than any other writer, Chris Miller was responsible for the sci-fi–laced adolescent male sexual fantasies that in time became the genre most associated with the *National Lampoon*. In stories like "Groin Larceny," "Remembering Mama," and "Invisible Robkin in the Girls' Locker Room," Miller explored the dilemmas of men who were, respectively, missing their members, delivered by time machine to an Oedipal episode in the parental bed, and no explanation needed. Like some of the underground comic books, Miller's work was heavy with raw id, but his genial angst-less style made it familiar and cheerful rather than dark and disturbing.

Miller had been working as a copywriter when he started writing short stories for porno tabloids, exploding out of a "relatively controlled life into one filled with sex, drugs, and rock and roll, and I was glorying in it," he said. As Miller got more caught up in the burgeoning hedonism of New York in the early '70s, he found it difficult to keep going into work and devoted more time to freelance writing, unsuccessfully sending stories "to everybody in the world," including the *Lampoon*. He was, he recalled, on the verge of going back to advertising when, having found the enticingly titled "Caked Joy Rag" in the files, "Doug called to say, 'I think you're our discovery of the year.'"

Having hung out in raunchier scenes, Miller found the *Lampoon* editors to be somewhat lacking in street sense. "O'Donoghue had some," he said, "but by and large, these were people coming from things they had thought up in their heads rather than experienced." Like the gentlemanly McConnachie, Miller was at ease with the opposite sex, though wrist corsages were not exactly his style. Matty Simmons's son Michael, then seventeen, remembered him as being "a very flamboyant character. He had real long hair, smoked little cigars, and was very charming and likeable. He also had a million broads."

Miller's easygoing, open personality was in distinct contrast to another recruit to the inner circle, Tony Hendra, who had come to the *Lampoon* with a varied background that included stints as a novice monk, appearing with future Monty Pythoners Graham Chapman and John Cleese in a 1962 Cambridge University undergraduate revue, and writing dialogue for television variety shows fronted by, respectively, singer Andy Williams and Hugh Hefner (who, after Hendra's arrival, became frequent contributors to the *Lampoon* Letters column.)

Hendra, however, would say he was more in the vein of the Lenny Bruce, dark, nightclub comedian than the Oxbridge–*Private Eye* satire mafia, and indeed when he first arrived in the United States in 1964, he had appeared on the same bill as Bruce in nightclubs and on television variety shows as part of the two-man comedy team Hendra and Ullett. Having been a rare working-class boy at an elite British prep school, he also identified strongly with a British cultural movement known as the Angry Young Men, who examined working-class life and added an element of class analysis to the Beats' general alienation. "One of the things Tony and I brought to the *Lampoon* was that we had grown up in a different political system where socialism is a viable position," Kelly observed. "We would have said the Republicans and Democrats are in the same house. We were talking about the other house—the one that isn't supposed to exist in this country."

Hendra at one time took his principles very seriously in contrast to the Harvardians' posture of disengagement. At one point, he refused to write for a television comedy show sponsored by General Motors and took out an ad in trade papers to clarify the antipollution stance behind his action. Because they believed in the existence of a viable political alternative, Hendra and Kelly were more susceptible to disillusion than their colleagues, who had never entertained serious hope. Kelly responded by growing melancholy, but Hendra became angry. A reporter who profiled the *NatLamp* gang felt that Hendra was the only one "who wrote out of some kind of bitterness."

"Tony was always fighting a class war," Meyerowitz said, recalling how Hendra had once told him, "You just don't understand how I feel about those people," those people being the British upper class. Besides class warfare, Hendra brought the rather more practical contribution of strong editing skills to the *Lampoon*, and his rise up the masthead was rapid. By April 1972 he was managing editor, although it is generally agreed that *Lampoon* titles were meaningless.

Most of Hendra's pieces were written collaboratively, although if a photomontage had some kind of meat in it, chances were it was a man-ifestation of Hendra's obsession (meat, not photomontages). His most frequent partner was Kelly, again working with half of a former two-man comedy team. Physical opposites—Kelly was dark and slight while Hendra was large and fair—the collaborators found they had, as Kelly said, "a lot of shared prejudices—like anyone who couldn't read Latin was probably functionally not worth talking to." Doubtless in an effort to identify just which readers were worth keeping, Hendra created an illuminated manuscript depicting the Virgin Mary supporting the Holy US Space Effort written entirely in Latin. The two shared deeper bonds than classical educations and leftist leanings: they both had children, troubled marriages, and a complicated but intense relationship with their Catholic backgrounds.

The new recruits had differing views on whether the national *Lampoon* was still a Harvard offshoot, and whether this influence was benign or harmful. Latimer, for one, welcomed a residual Harvard influence. He thought it gave the *Lampoon* a historical perspective in contrast to the underground press, which, he said, "was convinced that what they were doing was unique and had never been done before."

Kelly, by contrast, felt that the Harvard perspective limited the *Lampoon* editors' perceptions and held them mired in the recent past. "In some ways, Frith and Cerf were more cosmically important to the *Lampoon* than those of us who actually worked there. The Harvard bunch had a tendency to mythologize one another the way guys who've been in the army do. It's quite natural," he said tolerantly. In this pan-theon, he felt, Henry Beard became "the smartest human being God ever made, Mike Frith the greatest artist, unquestionably." As for Ken-ney, "he was always the golden boy to the Harvard guys, their Huck Finn, unbelievably brilliant and American and everything. One did finally feel," said Kelly, "that if you hadn't gone to Harvard with those guys, you weren't making the cut." But Kaestle thought that any Har-vard influence, good or bad, was minimal. "I think Doug and Henry saw themselves as outcasts from Harvard," he said. "They didn't talk about the good ol' college days. That isn't to say the good ol' boy network wasn't functioning full tilt."

Contributors who resisted the prevailing tendency to bond through witty insults found the magazine's offices a dangerous place. It seemed to Miller that "you really had to have your helmet on when you went up there," especially as O'Donoghue could be counted on to "always shoot a few bullets at your feet every time you came into the room." Fortunately, not everyone was on military alert. "Henry was very amiable. John Weidman and McCall were good guys, and Doug was a prince," Miller recalled. But beyond that, "you didn't feel welcomed. You felt like you had to engage in a sword fight."

Miller had seen enough similar skirmishing at the ad agency, where he had "been involved in a lot of office politics and cliques and little vendettas. I hated it," he said, "so to the extent the same was true at the *Lampoon*, I just wasn't interested." The struggle was for attention, not power. "They were all class comedians, and when they got in the same place, they were very competitive with each other. When I was hanging around the *Lampoon* and getting drunk with those guys, I often felt I was back at the frat," Miller recalled. But it was, as Bluestone said, "like a mean frat," with the *Lampoon* adopting the old frat tradition of seeing if aspiring members were tough enough to take it. "The initiation ceremonies were truly horrendous," O'Rourke declared. "The magazine had an almost tribal men's clubbiness to it."

However, having been admitted to the club, it became the most important thing in their lives. "A *Lampoon* editor was a *Lampoon* editor twenty-four hours a day," Kelly noted, "hence, our very successful marriages." As well, domestic commitments in general were going out of fashion. As celebrated in contemporary song, guys were always putting on their thirsty boots and heading down that long lonesome road because they heard the highway calling and were born a ramblin' man. They aspired not to be in a nuclear family with one woman but in a rock band, which would, ideally, provide access to lots of women. The idea that women might want to form their own bands was just emerging;

most girls still accepted being herded into the sandwich-making ladies' auxiliary, though not without a certain restlessness.

"To much of the public (especially that large and active part of the public born during the 1940s and 1950s)," Trow wrote, "the mode that deals with real experience is the adolescent mode—the mode of exploration, becoming, growth and pain. The adolescent mode is the mode of the music business," and the rock band provided adult privileges without adult responsibilities. The band had to be held together by a self-chosen, not imposed, purpose. The most important thing was that the tribe lived by its own rules, as at the *Lampoon*, and the freedom to be their true selves at work increased the overlap between job and social life.

Not that the Lampooners (with the possible exception of Beard) were insatiable workaholics; rather, despite interoffice competition and tension, being together was big fun. For people trying to write humor, having kindred spirits to bounce off of increases their powers. "Comedy requires peer support to establish standards, to manufacture a vision," Beard declared. "Three or four people working together can do as much as ten working alone." The *Lampoon* writers had found more than drinking buddies: they had joined a sort of gym for the intellect, where their creativity could be stimulated and stretched. McCall, for example, felt that he had finally found a group where his "heretofore private and somewhat odd view of the universe was reciprocated."

The Lampooners were, in their minds if not outwardly, the outcast, the mutant, the weird, and they had found each other. "We were like Sgt. Rock's platoon," Weidman said, "a fighting unit." Together they developed the characteristic *Lampoon* voice: from Britain via Harvard, they imported a strain of humor which, as O'Rourke described it, "puts people in their place and cuts them down," combined it with a Canadian stance of amused detachment, and laced them both with an Irish banshee wail of avenging fury, all resting on a base of traditional American Elks Club smoker humor.

Excitement over their creation inevitably morphed into self-congratulation. "They were very cliquish and very excited about themselves, this group," said Sussman. "They knew they were the hot game in town." And why not? After all, they had it made: earning decent money without having to cut their hair, partying on the expense account without having to be at work early, thumbing their noses at authority and being applauded for it. Most of all, they spent their time producing something they cared about—passionately, if the truth be known. And for the moment, the unit was kept busy fighting hypocrisy and fatuity, not each other.

6

THE BREAKING
OF THE TABLE

By mid-1971, Kenney had tired of the role of editorial honcho. "The first year it was fun," he said in 1978. "I thought I could make it three years the first time out." But by the end of that first year, the strain was mounting. Invited to lecture a New York University class on the role of an editor, Kenney behaved in a manner consistent with his editorial style, which Mogel, the course instructor, described as "enigmatic, to say the least."

Kenney kicked off the class by locking himself in a closet. Finally persuaded to emerge, the editor proclaimed, "I always wanted to be a tap dancer," and proceeded to pursue this vocation on the desk. Then, Mogel recalled, "he said, 'OK, we're going to get very serious. My assignment is to fill eighty pages. First thing we do is get Chris Miller. He's always good for five or six pages of sexy text. Then there's the masthead. That's one page. Then we get something from Hendra or Kelly. Then I'll call Gahan Wilson, whose stuff is always great and gives the magazine some class. Then there's Beard, O'Donoghue, Weidman, and P. J. Then I write maybe ten pages. Then we do letters to the editor. Some way we fill the other forty pages.'"

To the students, this unorthodox approach may have been just what they expected from a *Lampoon* editor. His coworkers knew better: Kenney's drinking and pot smoking had become less an adjunct of sociability than a crutch. He was alarmingly manic, driving himself unrelentingly at work. To his coeditor, it seemed like "Doug was coming unglued."

Besides working together constantly, the two editors shared a brownstone for a short time, though they lived on different floors. Despite this, they were not intimates. "Doug and Henry were good partners," Hoffman said, "but not especially good friends." The third member of the household was Kenney's wife, his sophisticated college girlfriend Alex Garcia-Mata, whom he had married to the surprise of his associates shortly after the *Lampoon*'s launch. Meyerowitz went so far as to tell the prospective bridegroom that the marriage was a bad idea "because the only reason Doug could give me for going ahead was that 'it seems like the right thing to do.'"

"For Doug, Alex was very much a transitional personality between the Spee Club and Michael O'Donoghue," Weidman said. However, within a year, Kenney had shed his Ivy League persona behind and the marriage was unraveling. In July, he decided he had had enough of adult responsibilities and used the *Lampoon* American Express card to head off to LA. He left behind a note saying "he had to go find the meaning of life and had seen the great cosmic eye in the sky or something," Kelly recalled. "Then he vanished without a trace."

The mark of an artist, one definition goes, involves the ability to entertain two conflicting ideas simultaneously. This was Kenney's natural state—a *Lampoon* editor described him as being able to argue with himself—and he was as ambivalent about becoming a professional as he was about any other major decision. In late 1969, when editorial meetings were still being held at Simmons's home, he used to leave the conferences and wander into the den where a teenage Michael Simmons was purportedly doing his homework and talk to the boy until the elder Simmons came in hours later, demanding, "What the hell are you doing?"

"He bounced things off me as a potential reader, but mostly I think Doug related to fifteen-year-olds more easily than he related to adults," the younger Simmons said. If Kenney was a boy at heart, he was a Lost Boy. "Doug had an aura of being lost and bewildered most of the time. He seemed terribly unsure of himself considering the amount of success that he'd had," said Emily Prager, an occasional *Lampoon* contributor, novelist, and subsequent girlfriend. "He could never quite figure out how it happened nor if he wanted it to happen, so the more that happened to him the more unsure he would become about whether he actually wanted it to and whether he didn't want to run away with Peter Pan someplace."

In disappearing to the West Coast, Kenney had run away, not with Peter Pan but with Peter Ivers, his best friend from college. Like Kenney, Ivers was mercurial, creative, and undirected except when it came to expressing that creativity. Also like Kenney, he was profoundly ambivalent about the possibly dampening effects of a steady job on his creative spirit. "A lot of people were looking at the time for two-way bangers," said a mutual friend, "something that would reward them with money and fame for being exactly what a father might regard as a bum. Rock was the avenue Peter took." When Kenney arrived, Ivers was casting about the LA music scene looking for a record contract, so they were both at liberty to run around the Hollywood Hills firing toy cap guns at each other.

Two months later, Kenney was back in New York and going through a divorce. Unlike some of his *Lampoon* colleagues, however, he never took out his problems on others. Bluestone, who first met Kenney after his return, recalled him as being "very approachable and helpful, even though he was losing interest in the magazine by the time I came around." Meanwhile, he said, "Matty was running around screaming, 'Where is he? Why doesn't he ever *do* anything? Why does he still get paid?'"

No sooner had Kenney returned from the West Coast than the *Lampoon* sent him out on a grueling schedule of college speaking tours.

Though Kenney later described them as a series of "unmentionable places, unspeakable hosts," his theatrical side welcomed the chance to be in the spotlight. "Doug loved the college tours," Kelly said. "He *very* much wanted to be a star." At any rate, he undoubtedly loved the chance to return to Harvard in triumph and be feted at the Castle. But while Kenney enjoyed the attention, it took its toll, and a year after his first bolt, he disappeared again—this time to Martha's Vineyard. Michael Simmons had a half-serious theory that Kenney chose the Vineyard "because he wanted to hook up with James Taylor," one of the few white musicians Kenney truly admired. It was Simmons's feeling that Kenney saw a lot of himself in Taylor, particularly with regard to a tenuous grip on emotional stability that was the downside of heightened sensitivity (the singer-songwriter had been in and out of a prestigious psychiatric hospital near Boston).

Recreating their *Harvard Lampoon* pattern, Kenney came and went, attending what Latimer called "every party under the sun—show openings, disco openings, rock parties," while Beard remained the office rock, often spending fourteen hours a day there. Similarly, Kenney's writing method relied on attacks of sudden inspiration while Beard preferred the strategic campaign of craft. "It's almost as if Henry made a judicious decision to learn comedy as a discipline," O'Donoghue speculated. "Like he said, 'I *could* go to Wall Street, but there's money to be made in this damn comedy.'"

The contrast extended to the founders' personal styles. Kenney was perpetually in transition, growing his hair or beard, then shaving, then gaining weight or losing it. One never knew what to expect, though his trusty bomber jacket from his prep school, Gilmour Academy, and tattered sneakers remained constants. Beard, on the other hand, had one look only. "We always thought Henry wore the same turtleneck sweater to work every day," Hoffman recalled, "but one day he said, 'Oh no—I have five sweaters exactly the same.'"

It was a manifestation of his general constancy. "The *Lampoon* was a chaotic place, and there were a lot of fairly wild people," Cerf recalled, "but Henry managed to get along with everyone and could calm them down."

If Beard were considered merely some sort of reliable drudge, he never would have commanded enough respect to effectively defuse potential explosions. But as Meyerowitz realized in 1975, when he went to a two-hour editorial meeting to discuss (a year early) a proposed *Lampoon* Bicentennial Book where the "lines were flying so fast it was incredible," it was Beard who had "the quickest brain-to-mouth speed of all fourteen people there. He was like a gunslinger, and everyone deferred to him."

Beard also possessed a secret weapon: he alone had some idea at any given time of how close the issue was to coming together and what remained to be done. In theory, he and Kenney were equal partners, but Kenney's indecisiveness meant editorial responsibilities invariably fell to Beard. His technique for expressing any negative assessment was well known: rather than actually saying no, Meyerowitz recalled, "he'd puff on his pipe and go, 'Tempting.'" But the magnitude of Beard's contribution was not fully appreciated until Kenney's departure for the Vineyard in 1972, when it became clear who was really steering the ship.

With Beard at the helm, the *Lampoon*'s financial picture grew ever rosier. Over the course of 1972, the per-page ad rate nearly doubled. However, this was only an adjunct to the main revenue stream. Having realized that readers would be more loyal to a boundary-stretching satire magazine than easily offended advertisers, the publishers had geared their business model toward circulation. By the end of 1972, this stood at over half a million (the kill-the-dog cover of January 1973 sold over 600,000 copies), up from just 165,000 in 1970. Circulation was climbing by nearly 200,000 every six months, which was like a child growing several feet over the same period rather than several inches. By the end of 1973, circulation had risen to 700,000, and advertising revenues to $1.2 million ($6.3 million in 2012 dollars).

Starting in 1971, 21st Century was showing a substantial annual profit from the *Lampoon*. The rapidly mushrooming ancillary product line—which included anthologies, posters, and T-shirts—provided another sizeable income stream. As a result, in the first six months of 1972, NatLampCo made more than $250,000 ($1.4 million in 2012 dollars). When the bonus negotiated by Hoffman was added to Beard's annual salary, it turned out that he made $50,000 that year (equivalent to more than $250,000 today). Kenney would have made this amount as well, but he had given up his 1972 bonus in return for his yearlong trip to the Vineyard, and instead it was divided among the staff.

Staffers and contributors had an opportunity to further share in the good times when they were offered first dibs on 21st Century stock after the company went public in 1972. Yet aside from this offer, the magazine was not a financial bonanza for its writers and artists, or staffers, even after payment rates went up. "I remember taking the subway home from the *National Lampoon* at two o'clock in the morning because I couldn't afford a taxi," Beatts said, and when cash flow was really bad, she and Choquette were reduced to pawning their television.

The person credited with bringing the same professional attitude to the *Lampoon*'s ad sales that Michael Gross had to the magazine's appearance was a young whiz named Jerry Taylor. Like Gross, Taylor was highly professional but hip enough to relate to the *Lampoon*'s iconoclastic spirit. By the time Taylor arrived in 1971, the magazine had already run through three advertising managers.

Taylor's predecessors may have been defeated by the thanklessness of drumming up advertising for a publication that subverted consumerism and exposed advertisers' strategies for what they were. For example, with cigarette ads recently banned from television, tobacco companies were turning to magazines, especially those aimed at young people. But in the *Lampoon*, their ads risked running alongside a piece like the 1971 column by the *Realist*'s Paul Krassner. "I wrote, 'I don't feel guilty. Anyone who buys cigarettes because they saw an ad in the *National Lampoon* deserves to die of cancer,'" Krassner said, "except the *Lampoon* took out 'of cancer.'"

Although advised by Beard "not to get up on a soapbox," Krassner never managed to sound sufficiently detached and was a regular columnist for only a year. In fairness, it's possible Krassner's piece was probably edited for reasons of space or style rather than fear of offending advertisers. "We constantly lost advertisers because of content," Simmons said, estimating that the magazine lost as much as $10 million in cancelled contracts over the years.

Taylor's brain wave was to embrace what the core *Lampoon* audience, college-age males, liked best. Consequently, like the undergrounds, the *Lampoon*'s economic base was drugs (beer and cigarettes), sex (posters, condoms, and endless editions of *How to Pick Up Girls*), and rock 'n' roll (records and sound systems)—plus jeans. His other big idea was to convince advertisers that they didn't have to actually like the magazine to advertise in it.

Taylor also sent the magazine to everyone he could think of in the music industry. The plan worked, and record companies used the *Lampoon* to promote their more acerbic, esoteric artists like Randy Newman and Frank Zappa. It was inevitable that the Lampooners would want to make their own record and see it advertised in the magazine's pages. "It was obvious," said Kelly, "that what was hot was to have an album. I remember Brian McConnachie once pounding his fist on the table and saying 'I want to *be* an album!'"

The rise of the long-playing album was made possible in part by the emergence in the late '60s of FM radio—previously regarded as suitable only for classical music and college baseball broadcasts—as an alternative to the dominant AM's screaming DJs and Top 40–dominated playlists. Like the *Lampoon*, "free form" FM stations were guided by personal enthusiasms, not perceived audience taste.

Laid-back to the point of being comatose, the cool FM stations were the hip community's jungle tom-tom, keeping listeners abreast of rideshare switchboards, drug emergency hotlines (for overdose aid, not emergency supplies of more drugs), upcoming concerts and political actions, and news that was more than a rehash of wire reports.

On the really hip stations you could also hear comedy ensembles whose routines, designed specifically for radio as opposed to live performance, made sound effects and total freedom from visual representation central to their work. The best known and certainly the zaniest of these groups was the Firesign Theatre, whose wildly associative surrealism got them labeled psychedelic but whose dense wordplay and punning revealed a debt to the Marx Brothers. The titles of their *Lampoon*-advertised albums—*Waiting for the Electrician or Someone like Him*; *Don't Crush That Dwarf, Hand Me the Pliers*; and *I Think We're All Bozos on This Bus*—suggest the appeal of their oblique brand of humor. Like the *Lampoon*, the creators of Firesign were drawn to genre parodies, using them as points from which to leap into the imaginative ether. Another four-man group called the Credibility Gap focused on topical humor, creating a daily satirical news show for a Los Angeles hip FM station in a mere six hours. Their work was compiled in albums that were, of course, advertised in the *Lampoon*.

In 1972, the Lampooners landed a record contract of their own with RCA records. Hendra and O'Donoghue, the *Lampoon*'s two veteran (relatively speaking) dramatists, acted as the album's equivalent of issue editors. They were determined to have the record be as exact in its audio recreations as the magazine was in its visual parodies, enlisting a musician/actor/writer named Chris Guest as musical director. At twenty-four, the multifaceted Guest had already been directed by the country's leading interpreter of Samuel Beckett and appeared on Broadway as well as in a long-running soap. Through Guest they found Bob Tischler, an audio producer whose day job was producing movie trailers. This meant that, just as the *Lampoon*'s magazine parodies had an authentic look, Tischler's access to the same voice-over artists who usually narrated the real thing meant that the record's audio parodies would have an authentic sound.

O'Donoghue and Hendra claimed not to be influenced by the Firesign Theatre. "They wanted to have more of a satirical hard edge. Frankly," Tischler observed, "the *Lampoon* writers at the time had incredible egos, and they really didn't want to be compared to anybody else," even though Beatts remembers "getting really stoned" with O'Donoghue and Kelly "and listening to the Firesign Theatre and going, 'This is great!' But," she added, "there was no conscious attempt to copy them. It just all went into the hopper."

The final product, *Radio Dinner*, assembles unrelated bits of variable quality that might have benefitted from a bit of the Firesign's overarching conceptual brilliance. The adolescent humor, gathered under the rubric "Phono Phunnies," includes a scene in a urinal (the sound effects give it away), a panting sex scene punctuated by a stupid joke, and "'Quinas 'n' 'Rasmus," a philosophical discussion in Negro dialect that perfectly illustrates the *Lampoon* tendency to confuse mocking a stereotype with reinforcing it. This was not Hendra and O'Donoghue's natural turf, as it would have been for Miller and Kenney, and the result is an unhappy combination of burlesque and condescension. Far better are useful public service announcements such as "Light your faith and you can light the world. Set fire to the church of your choice."

The most memorable pieces are three out-and-out parodies. One was a take on John Lennon's primal scream / public psychoanalysis phase that also offered a tribute of sorts. As portrayed by a raging Hendra, Lennon gets a lot off his chest: "Yoko is a supreme artist! I'm sensitive as shit! I wasn't the walrus! Paul was the walrus!" all culminating in the chorus "genius is pain."

Radio Dinner then tackled "Desiderata," a collection of maxims ostensibly written in 1693 that had been transformed into an unaccountably popular contemporary poster typified by sentiments like "Speak your truth quietly and clearly; and listen to others, even the dull and ignorant; they too have their story," and expressions of connectedness like "You are a child of the universe . . . you have a right to be here." Hendra's version, "Deteriorata," offers guidance like "Know what to kiss, and when" as a chorus croons "You are a fluke of the universe. You have no right to be here," before concluding "Give up."

Hendra also worked Tom Wolfe's Radical Chic turf, aiming right at the jugular of holier-than-thou liberals in the person of folksinger Joan

Baez ("I'm the world's Madonna / dona dona dona don . . . / So many grievous wrongs / For me to right with tedious songs"). Exalting the failed 1971 San Quentin escape attempt that transformed George Jackson and other Black Panthers from live activists into dead martyrs, Baez urges her would-be soul brothers to "pull the triggers, niggers, we're with you all the way / Just across the Bay" in prosperous San Francisco.

Bourgeois liberals trying on one trendy cause after another feature in a running joke created by Guest. His too-cool teenager and girlfriend are overheard in a restaurant, a bowling alley, a shower, and other date locations discussing the philosophical significance of George Harrison's *Concert for Bangladesh* album, the prototype for solving world problems by record purchase. "Like, bombing North Vietnam more than we ever have isn't as important because everyone is sort of bored with that—total, total, *total* bummer," says the teen sage. Now, he thinks, "like, Bangladesh is the most important thing and it's really great George sort of fixed up that you can take care of it just by buying the album. 'Cause that's where the '70s are *at*, I think, you know?"

All of Guest's characters on *Radio Dinner* emerged out of his remarkable ability to improvise, except for one Beatts-scripted piece in which he portrays Bob Dylan pitching a *Remember Those Fabulous Sixties?* album, a joke that packed more punch in 1972 when the commercialization of protest songs seemed highly unlikely. Guest could not only do a dead-on Dylan, he could do the different ages of Dylan. "He was truly the man of a thousand voices," Beatts said. "He once told me and Michael that sometimes when he was making a hamburger, he would find himself doing the voice of the hamburger and wonder if he was flipping out."

Ultimately, much of the album emerged from Guest-improvised material edited down by Tischler. The actual recording was completed in less than three days, just as a culture clash threatened to break into open conflict in RCA's New York studio. "The RCA engineers hated our guts," O'Donoghue said happily. "They despised us for this pornography we were polluting the vinyl with. They could barely work with us, these old lard-ass techies." The technicians' disapproval alone could not impede the project, but unfortunately, the RCA management shared their opinion. The final straw was some sketches featuring that *Lampoon* standby, David Eisenhower, who turned up throughout the record in different sex scenes with his legal spouse. At this point, Tischler recalled, "RCA just went crazy and said, 'We're not putting it out.'"

David and Julie ended up being cut, but by then *Radio Dinner* had been contracted to a somewhat smaller company called Blue Thumb ("Someone said there was a Black Hand at the end of the Blue Thumb," Beatts noted), which released the record in September 1972. It sold well, was nominated for a Grammy as best comedy album, and actually won one for its deco-ish cover art. Although, as with all *Lampoon* record projects, *Radio Dinner* contributed only a small proportion of *NatLamp*'s total revenues, it proved that the magazine's sensibility could translate into another medium.

Initially, the collaboration between the two producers was a happy one. Both had a flair for the dramatic and a capacity for anger that, when directed against the status quo, yielded creative results. At other times, it was used less constructively to fuel personal animosity. O'Donoghue's rages were legendary, and he knew it. One such legend involves him phoning the Columbia Record Club (a frequent *Lampoon* advertiser), which had sent him the wrong order. Screaming at the top of his lungs, O'Donoghue threatened to send the club forty pounds of bricks COD, whereupon he slammed down the phone and tore it out of the wall for good measure as the magazine staff listened raptly outside his office. "Then," Michael Simmons recalled, "this little face peered out with a big smile."

Given his low tolerance for human failing, O'Donoghue did not often risk exposing himself to the inanities of others. Latimer described him as being "primarily reclusive. He didn't hang out and schmooze with the guys after work. We were always going out and stuffing our faces on the company tab, but you never saw him doing that," with exceptions like the ill-fated expedition to Sayat Nova. "He was reclusive," Latimer continued, "except when it was time for him to be *on*, at meetings and so on. What Michael really wanted to do was be on stage," and indeed O'Donoghue had given himself a short monologue on *Radio Dinner*.

Without an actual stage to perform on as yet, he was limited to developing a "Michael O'Donoghue" persona. As part of this character's evolution, O'Donoghue's image changed drastically. When he appeared as "YumYum" O'Donoghue, the centerfold of a January 1970 *NatLamp* parody of *Cosmopolitan* clad only in a strategically placed garland of daisies, he had been a chubby, open-faced fellow with a moustache and scraggly shoulder-length hair. Two years later, he had slimmed down to an ascetic but dandified figure with a wary expression and neatly trimmed hair and beard, given to wearing white caps, white suits, and floral Hawaiian shirts.

The disproportionate fury was another part of this worldly figure's mystique. "You have to put up with a lot to deal with Michael O'Donoghue," said Catchpole. "You don't just indulge his humor but also his personality. . . . You make your pact and he produces great stuff," such as the *Vietnamese Baby Book*, the January 1972 article Lampooners cite most frequently when they want to illustrate how hard-hitting the magazine could be. Adorned with pictures of amputee toddlers and big-eyed storks carrying little coffins, the "book" records Baby's weight chart (from 8 lbs. 2 oz. at birth down to 5 lbs. 12 oz. at one year), Baby's progress report ("Four weeks old: able to whimper; Six months old: first nightmares; Two years old: knows bombing raids without being warned; Four years old: able to pimp"), and Baby's first word ("Medic"). There is also room for a sample of Baby's first dressing and a photo of Baby's grave.

It was important, O'Donoghue felt, that bad taste be used not simply for shock value. "There has to be a base of integrity you work off of," he declared at the time. "It's not like we poke fun at everybody," though of course several other editors claim making fun of everybody was the distinguishing feature of the *Lampoon*. Even O'Donoghue admitted that "most *NL* people didn't share this idea of a base of integrity."

"O'Donoghue was probably the most moral of them all—that's what made him such a good critic," McCall observed. "He was so firm in his standards of what's right and what's wrong." O'Donoghue himself would have been the first to agree. "Certain satirists will include a good man to give perspective to the rest of the grotesquerie," he said. "I assume that I myself am that good man, and from that standard we judge these other ludicrous things. There has to be some standard that says this is good, this is to be fought for. When it's really good, it's rage." However, he observed, apparently willing to accept the value of moderation in art if not in life, "rage is only interesting when it's controlled. When you repress those emotions, you always get something artistic and interesting." Alas, he felt, "most of the *National Lampoon* and *Saturday Night Live* people didn't rage. They were just peevish."

Not everyone was prepared to have their standards of integrity set by O'Donoghue; Hendra certainly was able to summon up a different sort of righteous anger on his own. If O'Donoghue's rage was the sudden violence of a summer downpour, accompanied by considerable thunder, Hendra's anger was the cold, interminable rain of an English winter. It was also more diffuse. It is hard to know what to make of "The Story of Jessica Christ," an illustrated Bible story "Fr. Tony Hendra" contributed to the December 1971 issue. Jessica, a voluptuous Messiah in provocatively low-cut robes, performs assorted miracles: "She cured all the icky lepers. She kissed people's dead relatives and made them better." The female savior also offers words of wisdom: "The poor you have with you always but I can only stay a minute . . . what does it profit a woman if she gain the world and lose her figure?" Was Hendra seeking to undermine Bible stories? Stereotypes of women? Attempts to smash stereotypes of women? The whole idea of a Messiah? Or was he simply contemplating career opportunities available to his young daughter, Jessica? Similar confusion surrounds his November 1971 comic strip, *Dragula, Queen of Darkness*. After Dragula attacks unsuspecting victims at a hockey game, remarks like "Sunnuvabitch," "Gimme a brew," and "Punch press" are replaced by "Bauhaus!" "Brancusi!" and "Gimme that puck, you bitch!"

Likewise, a black militant charges toward Dragula shouting, "Die, running dog honky neo-colonialist faggot dupe!" only to return declaring, "I have this dynamite recipe for hamhock soufflé!"

The mincing vampire then encounters a well-endowed female *Esquire* reporter disguised as a man, who whips off her raincoat challenging him to "gnaw on these, caped cruiser!" Dragula takes flight, first as a French poodle, then as a pink flamingo. When it is struck by sunlight, "the City is released from its infernal bondage," while in the *Esquire* offices, fully clothed men paw nude women proclaiming, "Terrific headlights!" and so on as things return to normal.

It's not clear whether Hendra was mocking or celebrating macho attitudes, since the gay stereotype presented in Dragula was on the wane at the time. The gay community knew, if Hendra did not, that the new archetype was more likely to involve lumberjack shirts or leather cowboy chaps and savored the irony of taking these butch images to the extreme. At the same time, straight men were looking more femme, or at least pop stars were, as exemplified by Lou Reed, David Bowie (in his Ziggy Stardust phase), Mick Jagger (in his trailing-scarf-and-eyeliner phase), the New York Dolls, and other glittered-up androgynes.

The *Lampoon* editors made an unconvincing attempt to acknowledge the fashion for fey in a photo taken for a Stones' album cover parody. It treated readers to the sight of Hendra in a maid's uniform, O'Rourke in a short-skirted parochial schoolgirl's outfit, and O'Donoghue in a feather boa and bouffant wig, but on the whole, this was one cutting edge they stayed well back from. With the exception of O'Donoghue, Beatts, and Trow, the Lampooners failed to grasp the humor potential of zebra-striped upholstery or cha-cha heels. The same could not be said of John Waters, a Baltimore-based director of low-budget films that were gathering a large cult following on the midnight movie circuit. Like Krassner, Waters combined funky production values with a willingness to push the envelope of taste even further than the *Lampoon*.

The *Lampoon* was not afraid to tell people to eat shit, but in Waters's

1972 trash classic, *Pink Flamingos*, the three-hundred-pound transvestite, Divine, who later reached the mainstream as the star of Waters's *Hairspray*, actually did so, smiling with malicious glee. Waters also shared with the *Lampoon* an inclination to go after the groovy. In 1974's *Female Trouble*, Divine, playing a juvenile delinquent who has become a bitter ex-model and celebrity criminal after her face is scarred by acid, performs a nightclub act in which she bounds on a trampoline while boasting about her sexual experiences with well-known mass murderers and firing a rifle into an audience of horrified nonviolent hippies. So while Middle America may have found O'Donoghue's black humor shocking, he would have been aware that Waters was going even further in attacking what they both perceived as current morality, presenting egomania, viciousness, and greed as the keys to modern success.

According to a woman who knew both O'Donoghue and Hendra, this moral dimension was the crucial distinction between the two editors. "Despite the chair-throwing and everything else that went on, there was an underlying sense of ethics and morality O'Donoghue had that I never found with Tony," she said. "Tony was ruthless, but Michael didn't go insane unless someone had wronged him," and his anger turned from the general to the particular only with provocation. O'Donoghue's attitude toward Hendra darkened after a breakdown in the *Radio Dinner* collaboration. A collaboration in many ways resembles a marriage, and as in a marriage, bargains are struck. However, trouble in collaborations usually arises when one party does too much rather than not enough. After *Radio Dinner* was recorded, Tischler and Hendra were spending every day in the studio editing, which made O'Donoghue feel excluded. On top of this, said Simmons, "there was an 'incident.' Michael was crushed by it and became a wild man after that."

Tensions came to a head when Hendra, then married with small children, cancelled dinner plans with his fellow producer, ostensibly to spend the evening at home. In fact, he went out to dinner with a young protégée of O'Donoghue's and then ensured that his rival discovered this. O'Donoghue's fury was stoked by the feeling that not only had he been betrayed, he'd been made to look foolish. "I was the last domino," said the woman in question.

Not that girlfriend rustling was anything new at the *Lampoon*. The few women who worked at the magazine "tended to have several different *Lampoon* boyfriends, which caused a lot of trouble," as one *Lampoon* editor observed. Choquette, for example, returned from his Hitler-in-the-Caribbean junket to discover that a girlfriend—not Beatts, who was still in Montreal and ignorance—had been intimate with several other staffers in his absence. This freewheeling atmosphere was a sore point with O'Donoghue even before the Hendra incident. "Michael," Kelly recalled, "had a little joke: 'Michael, we're starting a magazine. You bring the girls,' because he thought the only dates the other *Lampoon* editors ever got were with his girlfriends."

"I had a fight with Doug Kenney over this sultry Italian girl, and I didn't talk to him for a year because of her. That slut," said O'Donoghue, chuckling. He patched up the fight with Kenney, but Hendra was another story. The original disagreement may have had its roots in the personal, but given the magazine's blurring of professional and social life, that distinction was nearly meaningless. Soon O'Donoghue had installed a dartboard in his office, telling colleagues he was practicing to put out Hendra's good eye (one is glass). O'Donoghue also insisted Simmons get down on the floor with a tape measure to ensure that his office was not, as he suspected, three inches smaller than Hendra's.

This behavior did not make for a happy ship. Moreover, if Captain Beard was hardworking, pipe-smoking Dad, Kenney, with his capacity for empathy, had ended up being Mom-like, settling fights between the kids. In the early days, it was Kenney, Miller said, who "went across the board, like Type O blood." But once Kenney departed for LA and later the Vineyard, petty squabbles festered and grew into feuds, in part because Beard did not have time to soothe ruffled egos unless the blowup threatened the magazine's actual functioning. The "hideous battle which O'Donoghue carried on publicly and ostentatiously was the beginning of the 'breaking of the table,' as Malory might have it," said the hopelessly allusive Kelly, referring to the fifteenth-century author's tales of King Arthur's knights, another band of brothers fractured by a love triangle.

For his part, Hendra just got even. Right after the conquest of the young protégée, he started seeing another O'Donoghue girlfriend, albeit a former one. Furthermore, he was given a live theater project that was originally supposed to have been created by both *Radio Dinner* producers. "No one felt Tony was getting a plum," Kelly said, but it turned out to be one, and it stuck in O'Donoghue's craw.

7

OK, NOW JUMP

After the relative success of *Radio Dinner*, Simmons decided to back a follow-up album based on the concept of the "Woodchuck Festival of Peace, Love, and Death." It was felt that this album, called *Lemmings*, would benefit from actual, not recorded, laughter. This meant the material would be performed live. A Greenwich Village venue, the Village Gate, was booked for a limited run, and Hendra was tapped to direct.

Hendra knew from the start that Guest would be in the show. Guest brought in Paul Jacobs, a Juilliard graduate whom he had met at a country-and-western recording session (Guest also played bluegrass guitar), to cowrite the music with him. Meanwhile, Kelly, whose gift for parodying poetry found the perfect context in writing parody lyrics, collaborated with Hendra on the songs by phone from Montreal. Hendra then called Alice Playten, who had played Baby Louise in the original production of *Gypsy* and, though only in her early twenties, was already a Broadway veteran. The *Lemmings* team struck her as inexperienced and disorganized, but Playten nevertheless agreed because she "wanted to perform for an audience I thought I might be in" for a change.

Further auditions were held to fill out the cast, with a stalwart Guest improvising with each new hopeful. Prospective cast members who flinched at the *Lampoon*'s no-holds-barred approach were easy to weed out. Even an old friend of Hendra's, Garry Goodrow, had a few qualms about the proposed "Pull the Trigger, Niggers." While appreciating the song's humor, he was bothered by the fact that, "like most of the Left, they spent more time attacking each other than the opposition." These scruples aside, he got the part because, he said, "Tony was sleeping on my couch at the time."

Finding actors who did not require their roles to reflect their personal philosophies was not, in 1972, all that easy. For many of the most committed performers, theater was a way of life, if not an actual religion. Mobile ensembles such as the Bread and Puppet Theater founded in 1963 on New York's Lower East Side traveled about like medieval mystery troupes, performing political instead of religious parables for the edification of the folk. These experimental companies were directly influenced by the leading German playwright of the pre-Nazi years, Bertolt Brecht, with his unsparing political analysis and distrust of bourgeois sentimentality, and his French contemporary, poet-playwright Antonin Artaud, a prime exponent of blurring the lines between life and art (and art and madness), whose linkage of politics and spectacle led Abbie Hoffman to declare, "Artaud is alive at the walls of the Pentagon." Artaud had a vision of a vital, almost savage art form that would be central to society, not at its fringes—a theater that would "give us everything that is in crime, love, war or madness" created "in order to restore a passionate and convulsive conception of life."

Goodrow himself was a veteran of a particularly passionate and convulsive ensemble, *Time*-parody target the Living Theatre, which, he declared, "was in attack upon the culture. We broke barriers." Founded in New York in 1947 and still going, the Living Theatre was also incorrigibly serious, leading Goodrow to defect to comedy in the mid-60s by joining The Committee, a politically oriented satire ensemble that specialized in improvised topical humor.

One of The Committee's biggest fans was Peter Elbling, who had been Choquette's partner in the two-man music-comedy act and had known Hendra since the days when they had played the same clubs. Elbling declined Hendra's invitation to join *Lemmings*, instead suggesting that Hendra contact John Belushi, a dynamic twenty-two-year-old then working with the Chicago-based improvisational comedy troupe Second City.

Second City's roots went back to 1955, when a group of University of Chicago alumni including Mike Nichols had formed a theater company called the Compass Players. The company soon split up, but at the end of the decade a cell of Compass alumni founded a new group: the Second City (a name drawn from a condescending reference to Chicago coined by *The New Yorker*). At first, Second City included improvised sketches based on suggestions from the audience only at the end of a performance. The ones that worked were often refined and then incorporated into the regular show.

In contrast to the Compass Players' intellectual but static slant (sketches about analysts, for example, were popular), Second City's style embraced the physical and became more rooted in objects and reality, reflecting the influence of theater games developed by Viola Spolin, the mother of the company's director.

Belushi's first director at Second City was Del Close, a hard-living hipster who became something of a role model for the young actor. Close imparted to Belushi his belief in choosing deeds over words on stage. Consequently, "Belushi always made active choices rather than word game choices," said Bill Murray, another Second City member, in a 1986 interview. "He would make such strong moves that the entire scene would shift in that direction. It was almost like martial art."

Spolin theorized that by concentrating on playing a game instead of "acting," a performer could minimize self-consciousness and enhance spontaneity. Her games emphasized group interaction as opposed to technique. Actors with this training were oriented very differently from the reality of commercial theater, where the actor fills (as opposed to creates) a role and has an incentive to stand out from the group in order to secure a larger part in the next show.

In Second City, the actor developed a role from scratch, tailoring it to his or her unique strengths. However, especially successful bits were often passed down. For example, Belushi took on a samurai character that had previously been done by his immediate predecessor, who himself had inherited it from a previous Second City member.

Operating on the assumption that the ensemble was what's important, Second City was not the place for star turns. "You can always get all the attention, you can always steal the focus and be the funny one. Just stick your finger in your nose," said Gilda Radner, who joined the Toronto branch of Second City in the early '70s. "But," she added, "to equal the other people on stage, to give them their moment and then take yours and go back and forth—that was the much more difficult and greater thing."

An improv ensemble has to be able to anticipate each other's moves, and true improvisation, like a trapeze act, only works if the performer knows the others are there to catch him. "One of the most important things to succeed as a performer is to lose the fear of failure," Goodrow said. "You have to be prepared to step off the cliff. Second City improv training's very good for this, so people with it work better under pressure."

The company's direction changed yet again with the blossoming of the counterculture, a shift that was not entirely Belushi's doing despite his brother Jim's assertion that "John changed Second City. He cut through the academic stuff. They used to talk about Descartes, Kant, moral philosophy. John would play a hippie who had lost his memory from pot."

Belushi had already specialized in similar roles as part of the West Compass Players, a company he had formed in the late '60s with two friends that performed in hippie cafés. However, even before Belushi dropped out of college to join Second City in 1971, the troupe was already introducing an element of "head" humor. He *was* a new departure in the sense that he didn't come from the same middle-class, professional background as the other Second Citizens (his father, an Albanian immigrant, owned two restaurants in Wheaton, a conservative Chicago suburb), and that in itself introduced a different perspective.

According to Simmons, Hendra came back from scouting Second City raving about "this great kid" he'd seen, but Elbling remembers lightning striking more slowly, with Belushi sending Hendra an audition tape, which he had apparently made "when he was drunk or something, and it was awful." Nevertheless, the young actor was allowed to send a second tape and this time projected the feeling of "a homicidal maniac," Hendra recalled in 1978. "Watching him act, you were always glad he hadn't taken up something more dangerous. He was always threatening to go over the edge, and the more dangerous the situation, the funnier."

Since the actors were expected to double as the show's band, all the performers (at least all the male performers, as women were not expected to excel on anything beyond acoustic guitar and tambourine) had to have rudimentary musical skills at a minimum. This led to an acquaintance of Guest's from artsy Bard College getting a role despite having no stage experience. "As I remember, I was awful," Chevy Chase said, but luckily for him, he was pretty good on the drums.

Chase and Guest had more in common than having gone to Bard and dimples in their chins. They both came from social yet cultured New York circles (both had fathers in publishing), were natural athletes, and had great musical facility. Given his lack of experience, this stood Chase in good stead when rehearsals began. "Chevy had the best ear as far as picking up musical things," Jacobs said. "He was a really bright guy, very quick. He didn't have the acting skills of John or Chris, but he learned a lot from them."

"From working with John, I learned how to listen, how to play off another person," Chase admitted. But he also felt that he made his own contribution to the production in being "probably the only one there who was willing to fall down and really wanted to do that kind of stuff."

Falling down for a laugh was definitely not Guest's style. For all the similarity between their talents and backgrounds, the two Bard grads had very different personalities. The reserved and cerebral Guest was "very, very careful in his work," Goodrow said. "He's a perfectionist and tends to get angry if you fuck up." Chase, on the other hand, was "a loose and silly guy" who tended to plunge in and worry later. "He had a natural kind of preppy insouciance, an 'I don't give a fuck' quality. It works in all kinds of situations because you have to be prepared to fail." While Guest was more a character actor, submerging himself totally in a persona, be it Dylan or a hamburger, Chase was always a star, portraying the same nonchalant persona in a variety of contexts.

In life as in art, Guest was intense and directed while Chase took the casual approach. Chase did not have Guest's impressive list of stage credits, but his postcollege career included stints as a film soundman, truck driver, camp counselor, and studio musician. He had also spent two years working with Channel One, a small group of Bard grads who created their own comedy videos that were eventually noticed by the editors of *Mad*. This led to Chase writing a couple of pieces for *Mad*, which in turn brought him to the attention of Kenney and Beard, who called him in 1970 about writing for their new magazine.

When he went over to the brownstone to meet the two editors, Beard struck him as "very studious and depressed," while Kenney seemed "more like me—more out there." Although a big fan of the *Time* parody, Chase had decided against contributing to the *Lampoon*. For one thing, the sedentary, solitary life of a writer did not appeal to him. "I was much more spontaneous and wanted to be outside. I'd rather drive a truck. Plus," he said, "I just didn't think I was capable of writing prose as good as the *Lampoon*'s."

As well, the *Lampoon* offered him $100 a page, "but there were lots of words on a page, whereas I could get $200 for eight frames of cartoon dialogue at *Mad*," he said, and since he was holding down several gigs simultaneously, the time-money ratio won. Despite his relative penury, the part in *Lemmings* appeared to him as just another twist in the road—not a big break. "I had no goal in mind," he said. "*Lemmings* was all grist for the mill to me, and I wasn't sure what the mill was or where it was going. I never knew, really. I just knew it was fun and I was making enough money to live on."

There remained one slot for an actress, but Hendra had trouble finding one who was not put off by the material. In the end, he ended up hiring a close personal friend, Mary-Jennifer Mitchell. Hendra knew that the material wouldn't be a problem for Mitchell, who did a mean Joan Baez, as she had already collaborated with O'Donoghue, another close personal friend, on *Frederick's of Toyland*, a *Lampoon* catalogue purveying dominatrix outfits for toddlers. Having gathered his cast, Hendra had to gain their confidence and turn them into a team, but he was hampered by the fact that when the show went into rehearsal, the first act was still unwritten.

"It was like a blob in rehearsals," Alice Playten recalled. "There was a sense of wonderful pieces—the cast and the music—but no glue." In the spirit of the print *Lampoon*, the actors were expected to provide their own glue, improvising ideas for sketches. "I believe there were people at rehearsals, watching, writing, taking ideas from us," Chase said. Those "people" were *Lampoon* writers trying to shape the first act. The method particularly favored writer-performer hybrids like Guest and Chase who were able to create much of their own material.

Hendra also turned to non-*Lampoon* writers with more theatrical expertise than his magazine colleagues, among them David Axelrod, another old friend, who had written for the sophisticated, successful Julius Monk satirical revues of the early '60s. Axelrod found that while "you had to know a lot for Monk, for *Lemmings* you had to know a lot about music and drugs." Perhaps because these two subjects were outside of his expertise, he had a hard time creating suitably youth-oriented material for *Lemmings*.

The creativity of performers and writers alike was stimulated by the compensation structure: they were paid per minute of material used. Even Kenney, attracted by the bright lights, made an excursion down from the Vineyard and contributed a sketch based on Mrs. Agnew's

Diary that ended up being cut (it consisted, Playten recalled, mostly of "various Greek euphemisms for being fucked up the ass"). Another submission "required several members of the cast to fall on their backs and masturbate, and apparently they refused," said its author, Miller.

Form did not start to emerge out of chaos until Kelly came down from Montreal during Christmas vacation, but he was more interested in writing for act 2's rock festival parody than for the hodgepodge act 1, which he described as "stuck together with tape and gum. I had no interest in it."

The actors were also largely on their own when it came to developing characters. "Direction," said Elbling, "was not Tony's forte. But in any case, it wasn't like they were doing *Long Day's Journey into Night*." The two cast members with the most professional experience, Guest and Playten, were more discomfited by the lack of structure than were improv veterans like Goodrow and Belushi. Adding to the tension was the friction between Hendra and Guest. The latter had less than complete confidence in Hendra's relaxed directing style, while Hendra's latent class resentment was exacerbated by the fact that Guest's father was a British baron. Hendra, Kelly said, "hated Chris because Chris will have a title."

Trusting the actors to find their own way produced an uneven performance standard. Like some of the magazine's writers, a few cast members overestimated the power of sudden inspiration to make up for lack of preparation. "There was a tremendous cockiness on all the guys' parts," Playten recalled. "They felt they could just get up there and do it."

"Alice's concerns about acting and so on were things I didn't care about one way or the other. I was just a '60s pothead having a good time," Chase admitted. "I was never tense. I didn't take anything too seriously, including my own performance." This is not to say that Chase lacked ambition. "I wanted to make a mark," he said, "but in a different sense. I really just wanted to get laughs."

Moreover, Chase's previous experience was in video, where any business he threw in would not distract a live audience's focus from another actor. This unfamiliarity with sharing the spotlight may have accounted for his display of what Playten called "bad table manners. He loved to tell you if you were off-key in the middle of a run-through, when sometimes in rehearsal the point is just to get through it. I got no respect from Chevy," she said. "I'm sure I was doing irrelevant nose picking and things, but there was no ill intent. I was just inexperienced," Chase explained.

Nor did she get much from the director, who failed to restrain his more bumptious male performers. "Sometimes it would be the [two] girls against the guys as to what was funny, what was tasteless, what was stupid. But it was hard to get a word in as a girl because," she asserted, "Tony didn't think it was right that a woman should have a funnier line. One could never be appreciated as an equal," even if one had the strongest professional credentials among the cast and had been hired to lend the production credibility. Playten felt that she was "expected to be submissive. Tony would say, 'Let's talk about the sketch,' and I'd start to say, 'I have a problem with . . .' and Chevy would interrupt."

Belushi, on the other hand, was not about to let Chase get the upper hand. "John and Chevy were intensely competitive," said Michael Simmons, who took tickets and shepherded the cast to radio interviews. Every night new business would be added to the Chase-Belushi sketches as the two actors tried to catch each other off guard. For example, the script had Chase, portraying a drug dealer, suggest that Belushi, playing a dissatisfied customer, bend over to test the efficacy of some peyote buttons. Then one night Chase ad-libbed, "May I have the Vaseline, please?" Despite dueling egos, a phenomenon hardly unique to this cast, the *Lemmings* company started to coalesce. "If it was not one big happy ensemble, it was very much a company," Kelly said, so much so that after rehearsing together all day, the cast still wanted to see each other after work. Playten, who lived near the Village Gate, often found herself playing hostess to the cast, crew, and *Lampoon* writers connected to the show until four in the morning, with Hendra, O'Rourke, and Kelly proving even more difficult to dislodge than the actors.

"There was a lot of everyone going out on the town together," said Michael Simmons, recalling in particular an excursion that he, Jacobs, Belushi, and Chase—at least three of them on mescaline—made to see the Grateful Dead at Long Island's Nassau Coliseum. As Simmons was wandering around the Coliseum's ramps, he looked up to find Belushi deep in conversation with five New York policemen. "I know he's tripping his brains out," Simmons said, "but obviously the cops don't know it. He looks down and sees me and gives that eyebrow arch and smile as if to say, 'You and I have a secret.'"

Belushi's appetite for performing, as for many things, was apparently without limit. After finishing two performances of *Lemmings* per night that concluded with his epic takeoff on the soulful British rocker Joe Cocker, Belushi would head off to the comedy clubs at the end of the night "and get on stage and imitate Joe Cocker for an hour," said Ed Bluestone. This was all the more impressive considering the physical demands of *Lemmings* itself. "The thing I remember more than anything else was the amount of hard physical work they had to do," Axelrod said, "and they had to do it twice a night, and it was extremely difficult—a lot of running around and yelling and changing costumes—and they were exhausted almost all the time."

However, the youthful cast felt up to the challenge. "In your 20s, you feel like you're indestructible, that nothing can kill you and you laugh at death. Just try to kill me, you know," Belushi said in 1982. "You stay up for days and do as many drugs as you can and then in your 30s you think well, maybe I'll be around a little longer." *Lemmings* could be seen as the show's writers, whose average age was higher than the actors', adjusting to this new awareness of their mortality. As Playten said, "death was always the point of the show."

"We came here to off ourselves," proclaimed Belushi as the MC of act 2's Woodchuck Festival of Peace, Love, and Death. "All you people into macrobiotics, off yourselves in the Top 40 so you can be used as organic fertilizer," he suggested, adding, "This is for all you speed freaks in the tower—OK, now jump!" The festival's musical acts were similarly morbid, like the All-Star Dead Band, who staggered out onto the stage and, one by one, slowly keeled over. Heavy metal was just starting to emerge as a distinct musical genre, but Guest was already donning a curly blonde wig, painting his face, and screaming, "Dyin' is a high / Die, baby, die" as the lead singer of the metal band Megadeath (not to be confused with the later, actual metal band, Megadeth).

In a quieter vein, he parodied a popular singer-songwriter known to live on Martha's Vineyard, singing, "Shootin' up the highway on the road map of my wrist / Baby, I've just scratched you off my list," a tribute that moved the parody's subject to bury his head in his then-wife Carly Simon's lap when they came to see the show.

Like the magazine, *Lemmings* was able to cut deepest those it knew best. To some extent, the show was fueled by survivor's anger directed toward recently deceased Jimi Hendrix and Jim Morrison, blaming the musical icons for leaving too soon. "*Lemmings* was a very moral show," Axelrod said. "It was all about how people are killing themselves with drugs."

"I think *Lemmings* will bring a sense of relief to a lot of people and make them admit to a lot of mistakes, specifically about drugs and radical politics," Belushi told *Newsday* nine months into the run. "It's a positive show. We didn't all die. We didn't all overdose." In 1973, Belushi was still in his indestructible twenties, and though he may have seen *Lemmings* as a cautionary tale, he did not heed its message. He would sometimes show up for a performance having taken too many Quaaludes, a popular recreational sedative, and ask Goodrow to punch him in the kidneys before he went on. The pain would clear his head and allow him to deliver lines like, "The blue belladonna has been tested and it's real killer stuff, so get into it." Fortunately, for the most part drug consumption did not affect his performance. "John had a great deal of concentration," Jacobs recalled. "We probably did five hundred shows and he always came up with new things that were funny and good."

Even more than expressing a fan's disappointment in rock idols for burning themselves out so senselessly, *Lemmings* reflected the *Lampoon's* pessimistic outlook. A lot of the magazine's gross-out humor—the jokes about the lame, the halt, and the blind—reflected the prevailing near-medieval perception of the body as an ever-present reminder of mortality. Uncontrollable natural eruptions such as pimples, unwanted erections, and flatulence suggested the gap between man's immortal soul and the decaying temple in which it was housed. Awareness of this gap between the human and the sublime particularly informed the writing of one-time aspirant Benedictine monk Hendra and Jesuit-trained Kelly, whose outlook was in distinct contrast to the counterculture's welcoming acceptance of natural functions—including sexual urges, hair growth, and unadulterated body odor—as manifestations of the life force.

"It is not wrong to see a sense in which the *National Lampoon* was Christ-haunted," said Trow. "It wasn't a matter of choosing sides or coming up with an alternative or pointing out one or two things that were wrong. None of it was right." Or, as O'Donoghue put it, "everything was compared to the Grail and found wanting." Given what they perceived as the basic imperfectability of man, there was no point expecting anyone to improve. To those like Frith, who thought humor should be used to expand consciousness, the *Lampoon's* output, with exceptions like McConnachie and McCall's work, seemed despairing and negative. "It was never a magazine where the people felt comfortable enough with themselves to elevate, ever," he said.

Likewise, Goodrow—whose ideas about humor's potential to stimulate positive change led him to declare, "The purpose of poetry and satire is illumination as opposed to mere shock value"—had trouble with the *Lampoon's* omnivorous approach. This sensitivity did not stop him from making a brief appeal during a set change for an end to discrimination against "our nation's largest minority: dead Americans," initially in the person of a deceased senator and later as Lyndon Johnson, an alteration he introduced in a preview the night the former president died on January 22, three days before *Lemmings* opened. "There was complete silence," he recalled. "It took seven days; then they were falling out of their seats." In any case, Goodrow felt, the gap between the world of the *Lampoon* and the world at large was shrinking fast. "The whole culture is in love with death," he said, "either in love with death or with things going 'Boom!'"

Goodrow's contention was on display in full during the 1972 presidential election, which coincided with the *Lemmings* auditions. The *Lampoon* described the winning Republican candidate (Nixon) as a man who would "finish packing the Supreme Court with narrow-minded nebbishes, repeal the rest of the Bill of Rights, and make Indochina look like the bottom of a Shake 'n Bake bag," and the doomed progressive Democrat George McGovern as one who had "the economic know-how of a Bulgarian shoe-factory manager, the grasp of world affairs of a Bolivian civics teacher, and the decisiveness of a bed of kelp."

If there was anyone left who still believed that, as the Beatles sang, all you needed was love, the 1972 election offered proof of the extent to which money still talked. "Unless you have a hundred grand (minimum) to back up your opinion, there is only one other way to get your feelings across with impact. Just make sure the fuse is long enough," the *Lampoon* advised recently enfranchised eighteen- to twenty-one-year-olds in the editorial of its November 1972 issue, which further suggested that political statement buttons like "All Power to the People!" and "Peace Now!" be replaced by the more pragmatic "My vote is up for grabs. Make an offer," and "I work for the side that pays the most."

The question for dissident middle-class youth, who had options, was whether to retreat into the hills before what was perceived as a dinosaur-like postindustrial civilization unaware of its own imminent extinction collapsed into a morass of poisoned air and water ("We ran out of things to smoke / And say and eat and wear" was the *Lemmings* view of the back-to-the-land alternative) or to start climbing the greasy pole now that President Johnson's Great Society welfare program that had made dropping out less risky was drying up.

Even the genuine quest for spiritual growth that had led many youthful Westerners to study Eastern religions was now sending droves in search of quick Enlightenment (the old-fashioned method took so *long*) into the arms of incense-scented snake oil purveyors like the "boy guru" Maharaji. The Who's "Won't Get Fooled Again" was a popular anthem, and *Lemmings* was right in tune, as music writers knew. "Its strength is in a bitter refusal of any feeling that might promise some hope," wrote one, while in *Rolling Stone* Stephen Holden declared, "Though some find the humor cruel and morbid, in laughing at *Lemmings* we are all laughing at ourselves for having succumbed to the simplistic illusion that there ever was or could be a rock culture separate from and superior to the rest of humanity. And if there is anyone who still believes in that illusion, an evening with *Lemmings* should dispel it once and for all."

Critics who had never been part of the rock culture were less attuned to the show's undertone of bleakness. "The young in recent years have seemed so angry, serious, self-absorbed and just plain blue that one could scarcely guess that they had it in them to produce an uproariously funny spoof of the rock scene and its counterculture heroes," enthused *Time*. Perhaps now they would go back to uproarious panty raids instead of self-absorbed protest marches.

8

A DISGUSTING
IMPULSE TO
PERFORM

As a matter of fact, the young did stop marching, because January 1973 saw the signing of the Paris Peace Accords, the beginning of the end of America's Vietnam involvement. That same month, the *Lemmings* cast had more immediate cause for celebration: the show was a success, although the ninety-minute act 1, which remained a grab bag of unrelated sketches, still needed work. As he had so often for the *Lampoon*, President Nixon came to the rescue. "The first act finally had a reason when Watergate happened," as Playten said. "The whole show changed because we had a target."

Though none of the Watergate burglars, as far as is known, dropped by to see the show, other *Lemmings* targets were, like James Taylor, braver (or more masochistic), though not necessarily as able to take a joke. One night, Yippie cofounder Jerry Rubin and folksinger Phil Ochs came backstage after the show to object to Goodrow's portrayal of a ranting Weatherman, to which the actor replied, "I saw raving assholes like him at thousands of demonstrations."

Some members of Monty Python were also definitely not amused, at least by one sketch they thought had an overly familiar ring to it.

This was a hilarious mock academic lecture originally written by future Python Terry Jones for the *Cambridge Circus*, a show based on Oxford and Cambridge undergraduate revues that had come to Broadway in 1964 (later, a Canadian friend of Kelly's would report that a Python stage show in Toronto was stealing *Lemmings* material word for word).

The Pythons sued and Hendra ultimately removed the offending sketch. However, he may well have felt more sinned against than sinning. When the *Cambridge Circus* was rewritten to make it more comprehensible to Americans before the Broadway run, the troupe "dredged up a few numbers that were old things we'd forgotten about and certainly weren't in the original *Cambridge Circus*," said its director, "like a number Tony Hendra wrote."

One can imagine the glee with which the news of the Python lawsuit was received by O'Donoghue, still smarting from Hendra's second triumph in a row. Even before the lawsuit, Hendra's reputation around the *Lampoon* "for creating all of his material out of his own head was not great," as Kelly put it, which created a certain amount of bad feeling. In any case, a supportive attitude toward *Lemmings* would have been a stretch even for those editors who did not hold a personal grudge. "Satire. Isn't satire what closes in New Haven on Saturday night?" read a plug for the magazine on the *Lemmings* program's back cover, with a note at the bottom adding, "Only kidding, Tony. Heehee. The Gang."

As Chase and Belushi took to dropping by the *Lampoon* office, the writers were forced to confront this alien life-form, theater people. In Latimer's view, "there were these performing people around who were always on and always weird. Belushi seemed like the nicest guy in the world when you sat down with him and talked, but then he'd get this disgusting impulse to *perform*."

The enthusiastic response to *Lemmings* affected even those writers who were not naturally drawn to the spotlight. "I think everyone got a little struck by the showbiz bug," said Louise Gikow, who was alternating between working as an editorial assistant at the magazine and as a production assistant on the show (for one salary). The *Lampoon* had been in existence for two years, but the editors never received any direct feedback, other than letters from the public the staff rarely bothered to read, whereas suddenly *Lemmings* was being showered with immediate acclaim from audiences and critics. "It was very heady stuff," Gikow recalled, "and it gave a lot of people a sense of how far this thing could go."

Beard, however, was not about to be seduced by the promise of greater celebrity. According to Simmons, Beard "resented *Lemmings*. He didn't think we should be in showbiz," especially when it lured some of his editors into neglecting the magazine. But Simmons loved both his offspring equally. When *Lemmings* grossed $11,000 in its opening week at the end of January 1973 (over $57,000 in 2012 dollars), he reconsidered the limited-run idea and extended the show beyond its original eight-week engagement. For one thing, Weight Watchers had just bought out 21st Century's interest in their magazine for a seven-figure sum (and thrown in tickets for the entire *Lemmings* cast to a Broadway show called *My Fat Friend*). For another, *Lemmings'* overhead was so low it would have been profitable without the full houses the show was attracting, with production costs amounting to only 25 percent of its weekly gross.

Apparently, relatively little of the profits ended up in the writers' pockets. Kelly asserted he got a mere $1,000 for writing much of the first act and a large proportion of the lyrics. The actors fared somewhat better. "By the end of the run, I was making $1,000 a week," Chase recalled. "That was big money back then." Still, the cast had trouble understanding why all the favorable reviews, enthusiastic audiences, and sizeable box-office take weren't translating into more cash for them.

Rumors swirled of offers from Broadway producers, and in fact, said Simmons, producer James Nederlander wanted to bring *Lemmings* uptown, an option Simmons dismissed as "ridiculous." On Broadway, the overhead would have been much higher because the producers would be obligated to pay the cast and crew full union wages.

Nor was it likely that these increased costs could be made up for by higher ticket prices. The secret of *Lemmings'* success was that it was one of only two theatrical experiences that appealed to that mammoth but elusive rock audience (the other was the *Rocky Horror Show*, another show full of rock music and perverse attitude, albeit with a more camp sensibility) and this audience avoided Broadway prices and formality.

The Village Gate's club-like atmosphere was far better suited to *Lemmings'* revue format and bitter humor. But some of the cast felt the producers weren't fully exploiting the show's potential. Of course, with *Lemmings* predating cable, video on demand, DVDs, and digital downloads, the avenues were limited. Instead, acting on advice that a *Lemmings* tour could bring in $25,000 a night, Simmons decided to send a touring company to hotbeds of potential *Lampoon* readers, thus also swelling circulation. In the fall of 1973, Belushi and Chase hit the road while the rest of the cast stayed on in New York.

Instead of the intimate Gate, the touring cast found themselves booked into 2,500-seat venues, "and maybe seven hundred people would show up," Chase recalled. "It was tough." Also, he said, "any subtleties— not that there were a lot, but there were some—were gone, and there was a lot of physical stuff you just couldn't play any broader than it already was." Chase and Belushi were made even more unhappy by the news that the so-called national tour was not going to include California because, according to Simmons's explanation, the price of gas ruled out taking the show there.

Two people really came into their own with *Lemmings*: one was Kelly; the other was Simmons, who discovered that showbiz, where creativity meets hype, was his natural element. Like some of his editors, he had an expansive theatrical side that felt confined in the relatively low-profile world of print.

Simmons, however, declared that his true passion was for the written word, saying, "I wrote most of the humor for *Cheetah*, and for a long time, I was the only one associated with this company who ever wrote a book." Indeed, early issues of the *Lampoon* carried ads for Simmons's novel, a mass-market paperback called *The Card Castle*. According to the ad copy blurb, *The Card Castle* "rips the lid" off the credit card business, "the razzle-dazzle world of broads on the make . . . of Manhattan penthouses and Miami nightclubs . . . of the games business tycoons play in the boardroom—and the bedroom." On the same page as a genuine ad for *The Card Castle*, the *Lampoon* editors ran a blurb for *The Auditors*, an alleged best seller that "rips the tie clips and pen holsters off the booming accounting profession" via the saga of one "Arnold Brack, a ruthless human calculator with an eye for figures, whether they be on balance sheets or bedsheets."

Simmons was not about to attach any great importance to his inexperienced editors' views of his work. "I was a writer," he declared. "They weren't. Michael O'Donoghue had never even made a living at it. The year before he joined the *National Lampoon*, he made $2,000." Unlike O'Donoghue, Simmons believed that success in the marketplace was the truest indicator of value. "Everything I do is for money," he said in 1983. "I won't be hypocritical and say I've set my course to make this a funnier world. It's great to do well at something people enjoy, but I'm here to build my company, of which I am the principal stockholder."

As a businessman, Simmons's goal was to develop a formula for repeatable success, a Coke of comedy that would compel a similar customer loyalty ("Is any man as well loved as this soft drink is?" wondered Trow). These priorities were very different from those of his writers. Even though his commercial instincts may have been all that stood between them and the breadline, they nevertheless felt the creative tail should wag the business dog.

"Everybody had a little bit of a problem with money," Gikow said. "There was definitely some embarrassment about it." Such embarrassment was not apparent in a 1973 *Newsweek* article that reported, "Small wonder that the magazine's staffers, who share in the profits, are laughing all the way to their bankers. 'Maybe we should call it the *National Millionaire*' chuckles writer Sean Kelly," an observation that prompted a purported letter to the *Lampoon* editor: "I see here in *Newsweek* Magazine where Sean Kelly is quoted as quipping 'soon we'll be called The *National Millionaire*'. My God, that's clever. This could be the new Oscar

Wilde. It amazes me that a person could come up with a quip like that, right off the top of his head," read the letter ostensibly from "His Mom, Owen Sound, Ontario."

Kelly subsequently changed his tune. "For most of us, it didn't pay off financially," he said in 1987. "But only one definition of success is by the numbers. The other is, is it worthwhile? The *National Lampoon* was being done because it was fun and because we thought it was worth doing." At the same time, he felt, "It's easy to say we don't need that much money when there's a nice war rolling along keeping the economy going. All of us who spent our young adulthood in the '60s lived as if we were guys with inheritances," able to indulge in luxuries such as refusing to compromise for the sake of mere money.

"You *do* have to suffer for your art," O'Donoghue declared. His models were writers "like Bill Burroughs, who have held onto their integrity," though Burroughs, who enjoyed a large private income from an adding-machine fortune, may not have been overly tempted to sell out. But even though several *Lampoon* contributors—certainly those who had worked in advertising—were prepared to take a pay cut, they would have preferred to be in Burroughs's position: keeping their artistic integrity while enjoying the material comforts afforded by a large inheritance.

"The truth is, you did want to make money but not in a middle-of-the-road way," Gikow said. "It was the moral truth of what you were doing that was important and the commercial aspects were secondary, except that they were very important, but you didn't want to look at that." You may not have wanted to look at that, but there, reminding you, was Simmons.

This did not mean the Lampooners had a knee-jerk antibusiness bias (Hoffman, a businessman to his fingertips, was highly regarded, as was Taylor). But they did have a major problem with authority figures. "Matty used to get nowhere trying to curtail how wild it was," Bluestone recalled. "He would say, 'Do you have to say f-u-c-k? Do we have to lose this advertiser?' and people would say, 'Yes, we do—get out of here!' You never heard people talk to their boss the way Matty was spoken to."

One might wonder why Simmons put up with such insubordination, but he may have felt like *Mad*'s William Gaines, who, when asked if he was tempted to change editorial horses in midstream, replied, "Not when the horse has a rocket up its ass." Nor was Simmons entirely unappreciated. "You have to give Matty credit for giving them their chance," Gikow said. "I don't think he did it for the glory of it or because it was the morally right choice. He did it because he knows how to make money. But it took guts."

Simmons was regarded with less goodwill when he attempted to move beyond his accepted role of piggy bank. "Matty always had opinions, always had ideas, always put his two cents in," Weidman recalled. "You went in and sat and listened or didn't listen . . . and went ahead and did what you were going to do anyway." This does not mean that Simmons's ideas were never worth listening to. Kenney, for example, was at first vehemently opposed to recycling the "Does Sex Sell Magazines?" cover idea for the first issue but later admitted that Simmons was right to insist on it. "The hardest person to argue with is one who's a little bit right," Hoffman observed. "Matty was often a little bit right."

It was Simmons's style more than his substance that the writers objected to. "Matty rubbed people the wrong way," O'Rourke said. "People had problems with Matty's personality more than his point of view," a personality O'Rourke described as "abrasive and egotistical in a group of big egos."

In more bottom-line-oriented enterprises, this egotism might have been perceived as simply dynamic know-how. What Simmons was not was hedonistic and hip. "This was the adults and the children," as Bluestone said. At a time when men older than Simmons (forty-six in 1973) were loading on gold chains and making attempts at "swinging," Simmons remained a devoted family man.

Within his immediate family, Simmons's paternal interest was valued and his loyalty reciprocated. Outside of it was another matter. "Matty thought he was taking a fatherly attitude, but many people rejected that," Meyerowitz said. "The more he got involved, the less they were able to create. They wanted him to stay out of the way and didn't need his fathering." Moreover, Simmons offered this guidance at a time when the authority of patriarchal figures from God on down was being questioned, and this fed into the *Lampoon*'s embrace of postadolescent rebellion. "Matty was the father everyone was rebelling against," Gikow said. "There were all the boys doing bad things in the bathroom, and there was Dad, sort of blustery."

Nowhere was this dynamic more apparent than in Simmons's relationship with Kenney. Emily Prager, Kenney's girlfriend in the mid-70s, felt that "there was a bond between Doug and Matty. Matty had a great love for Doug, I think." One night, Kenney took advantage of this affection to ask Michael Simmons, who was alone in the family apartment while his parents were out of town, if he could come by with a romantic interest because he didn't have anywhere else to take her, and the boy generously offered his absent father's bedroom. Afterward, Kenney could not resist bragging about his exploits in the surrogate parental bed. "He thought that was a major accomplishment, and he made sure Matty knew," the younger Simmons recalled. Far from being upset, the publisher took a boys-will-be-boys attitude.

As is so often the case with father figures, the flip side of Simmons's support was control—particularly financial control. "Matty had an interesting management style," Hoffman recalled. "On the one hand, he'd be buddy-buddy with Doug. On the other, he'd kick him in the ass. He had a paternalistic love-hate relationship with him."

Surprisingly, there was also a special bond between Simmons and the obstreperous O'Donoghue, who presented him with a sled (bearing the legend "Rosebud") that the publisher kept in his office for many years. The gift exchange went two ways. "Matty was impressed by Michael and Michael had a tendency to get things he wanted. He was very indulged," as Beatts said, and in 1973 O'Donoghue asked for a plum of his own to counter Hendra's *Lemmings*.

Now, three years into its existence, the *Lampoon* was putting out an annual special issue, a more hefty affair containing totally original material, and O'Donoghue was given the chance to mastermind one, *"The National Lampoon Encyclopedia of Humor*, edited by Michael O'Donoghue"—the first time an editor's name had appeared on a cover. Compiling the equivalent of three magazine issues kept O'Donoghue occupied and out of trouble for five months. It might have taken even longer except that Simmons also put O'Rourke on the case. "Michael was a very fastidious and not very rapid worker. Since I was a friend of his and pretty organized, I was made managing editor of the *Encyclopedia* just to get things together," O'Rourke explained.

Contrary to what one might expect, O'Donoghue saw O'Rourke's contribution as welcome assistance, not interference. Indeed, a listing in the *Encyclopedia* for "Lads, Two Swell" celebrates "P. J. O'Rourke, through whose unflagging and tiresome [surely O'Donoghue meant tireless] efforts the *National Lampoon Encyclopedia of Humor* actually got done."

"P. J.'s a very good magazine editor, very professional. I always liked working with him," O'Donoghue said. Of course, there was no love lost between Hendra and O'Rourke, and the enemy of his enemy was O'Donoghue's friend. O'Rourke was essentially just as angry as the two feuding editors, but unlike them, he had no problem with either authority figures or capitalists; far from wanting to undermine the latter, he aspired to join their ranks. Recognizing a potential ally, Simmons had brought O'Rourke on staff in early 1973, half to work on the *Lampoon* and half to be his assistant.

After six months, O'Rourke was put on the *Encyclopedia* and "after that I never went back to the corporate stuff," he said, "although I always kept my interest in business." Because of his hybrid status, some other *Lampoon* writers saw O'Rourke as a sort of hall monitor sent to keep an eye on them. What kind of writer, some of his colleagues wondered, would be willing to assist Simmons? Perhaps someone who did not cling to the romantic idea of the artist as outsider, who saw no conflict between money and creativity. As Kelly said, "P. J. always knew which way the wind was blowing."

"As for being caught between management and labor, there was that element the whole time I was up there to a certain extent, but it was never a big deal," O'Rourke maintained, while acknowledging that "sure, it put me in an uncomfortable position. But it wasn't the world's most comfortable place anyway."

O'Rourke was certainly a harbinger of things to come. He felt comfortable in the workaday world of balance sheets and deadlines, but he embraced the quest for pleasure previously associated with the bohemian lifestyle. It wasn't as if he was perceived as a stiff. Instead, the main problem his colleagues had with him was that he let his ambition and pragmatism show rather too nakedly. Beard, Kelly asserted, "saw P. J. as a clear and obvious climber, a nice American boy on the make."

Or Kelly may have been attributing his own view to Beard, though the Canadian maintained that he simply felt O'Rourke "wasn't good for the editorial team." However, a determined O'Rourke put up with whatever was thrown at him in order to reach his goal. "P. J. wanted desperately to work there," said the Young Protégée, "and beat on the door. He wasn't in any club when he got on staff. Nobody even liked him. They gave him a hard time because no one thought his work was quite up to the standard of the magazine, and they were right."

What's more, O'Rourke shared this assessment. "I couldn't write well enough to do as much as I would have liked, and it was really a long time at the *Lampoon* before I felt I could," he said. "I didn't feel fully confident about my abilities until Doug and I did the *High School Yearbook*" the following year. He attributed this relative lack of craft to being "a product of the American public school system, while a lot of these guys had excellent secondary-school educations."

Unlike some of his coworkers, O'Rourke was willing to admit that he didn't already know everything and was eager to learn more. "P. J.'s a very fast study," said Beatts. "An amalgam of Henry, Doug, and O'Donoghue became his style, and he could do it quite well," or, in Kelly's more waspish assessment, "he learned to be bad tempered from O'Donoghue, learned to use big words from Henry, and learned to say, 'I'm just an American shit kicker, but . . .' from Doug."

Perhaps under the influence of his *Encyclopedia* senior partner, O'Rourke put his Establishment sympathies to one side long enough to savage the O'Donoghue-esque target of official hypocrisy in the face of individual suffering. "Q: What's it called when you give a Negro syphilis? A: Research!" went one of the science-minded jokes in O'Rourke's "Lab Riot" (listed under D for some reason).

O'Donoghue's influence was also apparent in another O'Rourke *Encyclopedia* entry called *Deco Desperados*, a stylishly drawn comic about a gang feud between the tasteful Deco Desperados and a tacky group of chunky transvestites called the Glitter Gangsters. It was so steeped in the deco aesthetic—a particular enthusiasm of O'Donoghue's at the time—that one practically needs to be a licensed interior decorator to get the jokes. For example, surveying the carnage wrought by the Gangsters on a villa belonging to yet another gang, the Bauhaus Bandits, one Desperado exclaims, "God! They painted big red lips on the Coldspot refrigerator designed by Raymond Loewy!"

It is a measure of how much Simmons was willing to indulge O'Donoghue that he would permit valuable page space, not to mention use expensive matte silver ink for the comic's elegant borders, to be devoted to such obscure humor. O'Donoghue was as unapologetic about his predilection for the aesthetic as Simmons was about his for commerce, declaring, "I brought all this avant-garde crap. I always considered what I was doing art, not wallpaper."

Beard, meanwhile, created a lexicographic tour de force, a list of 256 invented but real-sounding components of a tall ship's rigging ranging from lazzards and peggetts to bulk-snudgers and cadge-muffins, while Kenney emerged from seclusion on the Vineyard long enough to contribute the poignant *First Blowjob*.

Former copywriter Beatts—the *Lampoon* writer other than the two coeditors who appears most frequently in the *Encyclopedia*, assuming a far higher profile than she did in the magazine itself—was responsible for a fake ad that proved to be more costly than any other entry in the *Encyclopedia*. "If Ted Kennedy drove a Volkswagen he'd be President today" read the copy under a simple photo of a floating VW Bug. The *Lampoon* art department's consuming passion for accuracy meant that the typeface and trademark were exact replicas of the real thing, so technically Beatts's little joke *was* a Volkswagen ad. Consequently, a justifiably confused public—with the Chappaquiddick incident (in which the serving Massachusetts senator had been involved in an under-investigated fatal car accident) still fresh in their minds—accused the auto company of poor taste. Volkswagen filed suit, claiming with presumably unintentional humor that the *Lampoon* was using the company as "a vehicle for its political commentary." The suit was settled when 21st Century agreed to remove the offending page from all copies of the *Encyclopedia* sold after November 1973.

Besides writing *for* the *Encyclopedia*, Beatts found her love life written *about* in it, under the heading, "Limericks about Michael O'Donoghue." But why about O'Donoghue? Tired of having his girlfriends stolen by his coworkers, O'Donoghue had turned the tables and done some girlfriend rustling himself. According to Beatts, it was all quite spontaneous. During a spell of working late on the magazine, she recalled, she "was having dinner with Henry every night, and basically I thought, 'I can't take another dinner with Henry.'" For a change of pace, she had dinner with O'Donoghue instead and "ended up having a fling with him that turned into a three-year relationship."

Perhaps she felt those volcanic displays of temper suggested a passionate nature, but O'Donoghue also had something more compelling to offer. In contrast to Choquette, who was "very threatened by my ideas," Beatts said, "Michael was very receptive to them. It wasn't, 'I really like your mind—let's talk about it over breakfast,' as he once said jokingly."

Together the couple developed a certain retro mystique. O'Donoghue began carrying a walking stick to go with his white suits while

Beatts took to wearing hats, gloves, and '20s frocks. They became, as *Rolling Stone* observed in 1983, "known around Manhattan for their Gatsby-like attire." Their fellow Lampooners, naturally, took a dim view of all this stylishness. "If F. Scott and Zelda are Class," began another *Encyclopedia* limerick about O'Donoghue, "Cellini made things out of brass / And Dacron is fur / Air-Wick smells like Myrrh / And plastic's as good as stained glass!" Nor would they let O'Donoghue forget they knew him when. "A fat kid from upstate New York / (Not McCall, Kelly, Beard, or O'Rourke) / Developed a passion / For taste, style and fashion / And has learned to eat peas with a fork" went yet another limerick.

O'Donoghue was unfazed by his colleagues' mockery. "I was always conscious of style," he asserted, "but they're usually a dreary bunch, writers. Comedy writers are trained to attack styles and are jittery about having one of their own because they know what a fragile and vulnerable thing it is."

The couple were not so much eccentrics as in the vanguard, as fashionable young adults began abandoning jeans for pre–Second World War vintage. Even the economy started to embrace the vogue for the 1930s and began spiraling downward. It was a reaching back not just for a look but also for a code of behavior, a way of washing off the mud of Woodstock without adopting the stiff formality of polite society. One could return to elegance if, with the first stirrings of postmodernism, one did so ironically. "During the early 70s, a number of historic adult modes had begun to pall. A large number of over-experienced people, chronologically ready for adulthood, were without a next step to take," Trow wrote. "Under cover of irony, some of these people began to cultivate an interest in dated adult manners," and, despite their "unremarkable middle-class backgrounds" cultivated "an aesthetic (eclectic, appreciative, amused, fickle, perverse) that had in the past belonged to a few privileged people."

"At some point in your life, you decide to either grow up or to look like a grownup," O'Donoghue told *Time* in 1976. "We've chosen the latter." The writer decided to model himself on Baudelaire's boulevardier, the sophisticated, detached observer of urban life and forensic dissector of style whose dandyism arose from an acute awareness of how to use personal appearance as a form of self-expression.

The *Encyclopedia* had not really satisfied O'Donoghue's yearning for a project that would fully express that sense of style because what he really wanted was to continue the excursion into other media begun with *Radio Dinner*. Instead, there he was, "trapped in print again." But as the *Encyclopedia* wrapped in the summer of 1973, he finally received what he considered an appropriate reward for *Radio Dinner*.

9

MEANWHILE, BACK AT THE RADIO RANCH . . .

O'Donoghue had managed to persuade Simmons that the *Lampoon* should adopt the Credibility Gap model and produce a syndicated weekly radio show, of which he would be the creative director. "I was given the *Radio Hour* as a plum," he said, "because I was on the verge of fuckin' walking."

Released from his duties on the magazine to devote all of his time to the new project, he plunged in with typically perfectionist zeal. The first thing he did was ask *Radio Dinner*'s Tischler to work up a budget. The producer came to the conclusion that doing a weekly radio show to O'Donoghue's demanding standards would require a custom-built studio. "Also," Tischler said, "if we had our own studio, we could waste some time in improv." To his surprise, 21st Century agreed. "We thought we'd get our ten or twelve writers in a room and just say funny things," said Mogel. "We found out it doesn't work that way and ended up building a state-of-the-art studio."

The first four shows were recorded while the studio was still being built seven floors above the magazine's offices. So high was O'Donoghue's stock with Simmons at the time that he was able to engage

Charles White III, who had done the Grammy-winning *Radio Dinner* cover, to decorate the studio's lounge in a singing cowboy motif with cacti-patterned rug and couches and a big red-and-yellow desk shaped like a '30s radio. As if all this were not expensive enough, one day a man showed up to paint trompe l'oeil shadows of every object in the room on the walls, as if the setting southwestern sun were coming through the Madison Avenue windows.

Supervising all this gestation meant that O'Donoghue was kept busy on the eleventh floor instead of causing trouble in the editorial offices, which may have been one factor in Simmons's backing the project. O'Donoghue was frequently joined by Kenney, who took a proud uncle's interest in the studio's progress. Yes, by fall 1973 Kenney was back but had slipped down the masthead to senior editor while a Gang of Five (Beard, O'Donoghue, Hendra, McConnachie, and Kelly) held the position formerly occupied by him and Beard. "I don't remember his editing an issue, although he might have. He was keeping a fairly low profile," Gikow recalled.

When asked what he had been doing out on the Vineyard, Kenney replied, "Having a nervous breakdown." The main source of his unhappiness was the novel he had been writing during his sabbatical. It had not gone well. "Doug wigged out writing it. He choked," said O'Donoghue, who described the novel as "ungodly bad, although there was one great phrase in it about aliens: 'Their language sounded like a gunfight in a bell factory.'" Weidman, however, disagreed. "It wasn't bad—just scattered. It was," he said, "very much Doug." In any case, Kenney's opinion of the manuscript was such that he threw it out.

What Kenney had wanted to write was the contemporary equivalent of an Evelyn Waugh novel (although it is highly unlikely that Waugh would have embarked on a book called *Teenage Commies from Outer Space*). However, the open-minded and populist Kenney had little in common with the innately conservative Waugh beyond their both being upwardly mobile Catholics and sharp observers of social distinctions. A more appropriate model might have been F. Scott Fitzgerald, that other expansive Irish-Catholic boy from the Midwest who became fascinated by gilded youth at an Ivy League university and whose early success could not assuage a core of self-doubt or arrest a slide into addiction.

After his return to New York, Kenney moved out of the brownstone and into the Chelsea Hotel, site of numerous rock 'n' roll ODs and suicides—not exactly the ideal location in which to regain one's mental equilibrium. But the time for being roomies with Beard had passed. More and more, the two founders were going their separate ways. Beard had been left to put out the magazine by himself, and he would have been a saint not to resent it. "I knew I couldn't count on Doug anymore," he said, and Kenney, knowing he had let the team down, had lost some of his ebullience. He struck Gikow, who hadn't known him before the Vineyard sabbatical, as "a very sweet, generous, sometimes sad and troubled guy. He would be very bright and high energy one minute and very quiet the next. I never saw him yell at anyone." This alone would have put him in a distinct minority around the *Lampoon* office.

Kenney wasn't the only writer who found the eleventh-floor studio a sort of haven. "There's something about radio that's very intimate and comfortable because you spend a lot of time just sitting around in a dark womb-like studio," Beatts observed. "It was a pretty mellow atmosphere as opposed to the magazine's, which was getting nasty." By comparison, McCall agreed, the *Radio Hour* was "a breath of fresh air."

McCall himself became a frequent contributor to the *Radio Hour* and a special favorite of Tischler's because of his ability to write scripts that translated into what the producer called "incredible sound images." This talent was especially evident in the audio version of a piece McCall had originally written for the *Encyclopedia* called "The Romance of Creosote" ("man's silent ally in the urgent fight to stem the tide of wood rot"). The format is every educational film about an industrial process ever made during the writers' childhoods, and the narrator, who stirringly intones lines like "A coal tar cocktail—drink on, giant hoses!" while appropriate suction noises glorp in the background, is the same voice as issued from every school projector.

McConnachie was another frequent *Radio Hour* contributor. "Don't send money to so-called starving families in Europe," he urged in a public service announcement. "They're not starving at all. Can *you* afford to visit Europe?" Writers took every opportunity to perform their own *Radio Hour* scripts because this meant they got paid the AFTRA union minimum, a distinct improvement over what they got paid for merely creating them as nonunion writers. Beatts found the experience a liberating one. "It was very educational," she recalled, "to see how exciting it could be to just come up with something on the spur of the moment." Trow, too, became a regular, with a radio version of his recurring *Lampoon* gossip column, Mr. Chatterbox. Armed with a Morse code button to provide the audio equivalent of ellipses, he informed listeners what was "In" that week, such as little metal spiders, or what was, like toaster racks, "Out."

Not all the *Lampoon* writers had either the ability or the interest to take to the airwaves. Tischler's opinion was that "most of the *Lampoon* writers weren't good at writing *Radio Hour* stuff." Beard tried his hand with intermittent success, but O'Rourke remained dedicated to prose, declaring, "These side projects had no impact beyond robbing the magazine of writing talent." Nor, of course, was Hendra to be found at the *Radio Hour* studios. Kelly was, although Hendra would have preferred that his pal did not collaborate with the enemy, going so far as to order him not to write for the *Radio Hour*. "That's the only time I've ever walked out of a restaurant," Kelly recalled.

In fact, said Latimer, "Sean went head over heels into the *Radio Hour* and shamefully neglected the magazine," finding it impossible to pass up the opportunity to do more parody lyrics, such as the Pete Seegeresque number he wrote in collaboration with Guest, which the latter performed with his usual dead-on accuracy: "I wish I was a Negro / With lots of funky soul / Then I could stay true to my ethnic roots / And still play rock and roll / I wouldn't have to sing the middle-class liberal well-intentioned blues" went the wistful lament. Guest also collaborated with Kenney on microepisodes of "Flash Bazbo," which featured dialogue possibly salvaged from Kenney's *Teenage Commies*, like "The Incredulous was making good its escape from the Brain Gobblers from the planet Stinky."

Initially, there was no cast as such—only a pool of willing *Lampoon* acquaintances in addition to the writers. This included the actors drawn from Tischler's address book who actually did newsreels or industrials (advertorial films produced by businesses) and special guests such as Peter Cook and Dudley Moore, who came by during the run of their two-man show on Broadway. Lesser-known performers came in through the grapevine, including a young Billy Crystal, a friend of Guest's. One day, Kenney got a call from Emily Prager, then appearing regularly on the soap opera *Edge of Night*. An Afghan Harvard classmate of Kenney and Beard's told her about the *Lampoon*, and soon, she said, she was "sitting in the makeup room reading it and thinking, 'I love these people. They are so funny!'" It was the realization of a *Lampoon* editor's fantasy, where good-looking women would read the magazine and want to meet its creators. Prager ended up not only acting on the *Radio Hour* but also working on postproduction in the studio.

The *Lemmings* actors would seem to be a natural source of more acting talent, but with the exception of Guest, whom he knew from *Radio Dinner*, O'Donoghue viewed the cast with a wary eye. "I didn't trust those *Lemmings* people because of my falling out with Hendra," he admitted, "but I finally came to, one by one." There were some awkward moments in the interim, like the first encounter with Belushi, who had been instructed not to mention that he was in *Lemmings*. Initially O'Donoghue liked the energetic actor until Belushi let the secret slip. "We were out to dinner in a party of eight and I was sitting next to him, but I just crossed my legs, turned away, and didn't say another word to him for the rest of the evening," O'Donoghue recalled cheerily.

O'Donoghue was more willing to overlook Chase's association with *Lemmings* since the actor had once turned up to contribute a late-night drum session for the *Radio Hour*, a gesture that struck O'Donoghue as "a very classy thing to have done since he had just finished two shows."

Having gained O'Donoghue's approval, Belushi and Chase spent September 1973 shuttling back and forth between the Village Gate and the *Lampoon* studio prior to going on the *Lemmings* tour. "All those future stars of America running around asking for work because they needed the money," McCall said wistfully, while Beatts reminisced in a similar vein about the good old days when "the writers were in control" and the actors were "young, starving, and cooperative."

Chase was happy to return to the familiarity of the studio after performing for a live audience. "I loved it," he said. "Sometimes Michael would call and say, 'I need five minutes,' and I'd go in and do it," like the night when he "winged five minutes talking about how tight we were on the show and how we got letters saying we weren't tight and how I took offense at that. 'I want you to know we never wing anything here,'" he assured the listeners extemporaneously.

As with *Radio Dinner*, much of the *Radio Hour*'s material was created by Tischler editing down improvised material, this time in consultation with O'Donoghue instead of Hendra. O'Donoghue continued to write sketches himself in addition to editing other contributors' work. He found the great advantage of writing for the *Radio Hour* was that he could create fresh-from-the-headlines sketches like "El Allende—the Dead One," a parody of a popular commercial for Colombian Coffee adapted to reflect the September 1973 overthrow of Chile's democratically elected socialist president, a coup that was accompanied by rumors of support from the CIA and a leading telecommunications company. "The peasants are happy because their copper has been purchased by a large American telephone company," the Latin-accented narrator says over sounds of ethnic music and celebrations that are abruptly interrupted by machine-gun fire.

Beard addressed these same events in print, with a dialogue balloon superimposed on a news photograph of the Chilean presidential palace under siege. "Eet ees muy tragico! Our beloved President is dead, the victim of a self-inflicted air strike. Also, he shot himself 27 times in the back with a machine gun from thirty feet away, pausing only once to reload," it proclaimed.

The next month, Beard tackled Allende's successor. "In a further effort to get things back to normal, the head of the junta, Gen. Pinochet Ugarte . . . reduced the severe Chilean poetry glut by ordering the burning of a number of unpublished manuscripts by the leftist poet Pablo Neruda, whose death a few hours before the coup took place is generally thought to have been a pure coincidence by fair-minded observers in Chile who believe in El Lapino dos Noches (the Easter Bunny)."

Despite the creative rewards, up on the eleventh floor the strain of putting together an hour of original programming every week quickly began to tell on Tischler and O'Donoghue. After thirteen weeks, they decided to reduce the workload by cutting each program in half. They would, however, still call it the *Radio "Hour."*

"When we went from an hour to a half hour, we claimed we had donated the remaining half hour to the United Council of Churches. 'Since we tear down, it's only fair to give it to someone who builds up,' we said. On the first half-hour show, we did twenty-six minutes and then started the United Council of Churches broadcast. There was a deliberate sense of sabotaging the radio stations because we knew they'd get a lot of calls," O'Donoghue said with a mischievous little smile. In fact, the audience was never told the show had been shortened. Instead, the episodes ended as if they had suddenly been cut off until, after three weeks, they concluded the March 2 show with an announcement saying, "We understand that some of our stations have been cutting the show to half an hour. Please call your radio station and complain." The producers kept this up until the stations, deluged by unhappy listeners, begged them to end the joke.

Pranks such as this had a predictable effect on the efforts of the sales staff who were trying to get stations to carry the (half) *Hour.* Eventually the show was syndicated to some five hundred outlets—commercial stations plus commercial-free college stations. But although the *Radio*

Hour was popular, it was never a moneymaker because of high production costs and the reluctance of national sponsors to support it with ads.

"A lot of advertisers were afraid of us," said Simmons, and if any had the temerity to remain unbowed, O'Donoghue soon taught them a lesson. In its early days, the *Radio Hour* did have one national sponsor: 7UP. But then, Tischler recalled, "we went to a 7UP commercial after saying, 'The *National Lampoon Radio Hour* will return after this word from some insincere Nazis who are just trying to steal your parents' money.' Doug wrote that." The company pulled their ads.

Luckily for O'Donoghue, this was not a fatal blow. His employers' view was that, like the *Lemmings* tour, the *Radio Hour* would make up in publicity for the magazine what it lacked in actual revenues, and on this level, the show was deemed a success. As well, the company offered cassettes of the show for purchase.

Even if the *Radio Hour* audience was able to hear their voices, those writers who aspired to be as visible as the *Lemmings*' cast faced an uphill battle. "Being a writer was not the way to be a star in the mid-70s," Kelly pointed out. Undeterred, O'Donoghue and Kenney in particular made an effort to familiarize readers with the face behind the byline. Besides posing for the "YumYum" centerfold, a still somewhat chubby O'Donoghue had turned up in cartoon form in the March 1971 issue to illustrate the principles of "Michael O'Donoghue's How to Write Good": for example, pulling down a generator handle while urging the aspiring writer to "Jolt the reader!" O'Donoghue offers several other useful hints, such as the Ten Magic Phrases of Journalism (which include "violence flared," "according to informed sources," and "roving bands of Negro youths") and a never-fail ending for any kind of story. "There are many more writing tips I could share with you," the expert concludes, "but suddenly I am run over by a truck."

Similarly, a regular promotion in late 1970 issues featured a photo of a barefoot and unshaven Kenney clutching a stuffed animal and a tin cup above a caption reading "Little Doug Kenney will go to bed hungry tonight . . . unless you help. Raised in a small village called by the native 'Ohio' . . . he was almost 20 before he had his first ride in a Lincoln Continental, and his parents were too poor to send him to a fancy Swiss private school like his playmates. He has never tasted caviar . . . ," a poignant plea in aid of encouraging *Lampoon* subscriptions.

Even without visual aids, the *Lampoon* made readers aware of the personalities behind the prose to an unusual degree. Primarily this sprang from self-mythologizing, but it also reflected an emerging trend toward the demystification of media process. Revealing a few carefully chosen seams was supposed to confer that aura of authenticity, and the magazine offered readers flirtatious glimpses of its dirty laundry, mostly in the Letters column. The *National Lampoon* continued the *Harvard Lampoon* tradition of running letters to the editor that were patently false and self-referential, combining it with the *HL*'s Common Book. This large volume had served as a communal diary, bulletin board, and bathroom wall, where members wrote actual messages (mostly sexual, scatological, or insulting) to each other.

Kenney, for instance, addressed an irritable message to the assistant art director in the January 1972 issue. "Ellen," it read, "look, I'm sick and tired of you leaving letters out of this column, so make sure that you don't cut anything this time just so Gross can toss in some faggot artwork. Omit my stuff once more, and you'll be out of here quicker than you can say 'help wanted'. I've got to stop writing and go see my folks in Jersey, so tell Henry to finish this column. I know I can always count on him in a pinch." The next letter began "Sirs:" with the remainder consisting entirely of blank space.

Perhaps as a result of this episode, Kenney's ability to generate material for the column was dismissed by an anonymous correspondent two issues later, who noted that the writer of the Letters column was compounding "this limp and sophomoric jape by endeavoring to 'set up' the final letter so that it must end in the middle of a sentence" before concluding, "The 'writer' then proceeds to effect the aforementioned terminus by calling Jerry Tibbit, the linotypist who ultimately sets these lines, a series of obscenities beginning with" (for some reason, the rest of the letter remained unprinted).

This diatribe was followed by a letter in reply: "Jesus Christ, Doug, this last letter about the linotypist is *really* a piece of shit. Why don't you call O'Donoghue and see if he can't think of something a little less lame for the last letter? Henry."

At this point, McConnachie apparently decided to exploit Beard's dissatisfaction. "Sirs: I was reading your June 'Science Fiction' issue recently," he wrote in to the June 1972 Science Fiction issue, "and I noticed that Kenney is doing the 'Letters' column again, and while I don't like to say it's lame or anything like that, I just wanted to let you know I'm still available," to which a letter from one "D. Kenney, Chagrin Falls, Ohio" replied, "Over my dead body." (A McConnachie letter printed the previous month had complained, "Sirs: I can't go on writing Doug's column much longer unless you pay me for it.")

Sometimes the in-jokes were more upfront about personalities, especially when house-gossip Trow was in charge of the editorial page. "I had a terrible *heart-breaking* fight with Michael O'Donoghue for awhile but it got patched up beautifully. Now we *like* and *respect* each other even more than before and have begun to learn the meaning of the words *restraint* and *adult responsibility*. . . . Henry is in a *foul mood* but won't admit it. . . . Sean says it's a secret life that's the problem; I say it's *no secret life* that's the problem," he revealed in the September 1973 issue. Three months later, Trow provided further insight into *Lampoon* interoffice dynamics when Mr. Chatterbox took over the space that had been occupied by Mrs. Agnew's Diary.

"That FABULOUS STOMACH P.J. has been trying to keep to himself belongs to LANI [a female *Lampoon* employee]. . . . MICHAEL has a cane with a little ivory polar bear on top. . . . Michael's duet with snappy ANNE nearly came to a screeching halt when Anne knocked the cane (and the little ivory polar bear) off the table at a village eatery. . . . HENRY doesn't fool Mr. Chatterbox. Mr. Chatterbox knows for a fact that he keeps a CLEAN WHITE SHIRT and TIE in his right hand bottom drawer."

If other issues afforded glimpses of dirty laundry, this December 1973 issue, with the apt theme of Self-Indulgence, hung it out for all to see. The self-indulgence began on the editorial page, where the art department set their names in type four times larger than everybody else's. Taylor, by this time the publisher, claimed part of the editorial page to complain about the "elitist, self-serving, egomaniacal, and I might add, greedy editorial clique—the same bastards who keep stealing my office copies, insulting advertisers, and alienating stockholders."

It was just to tell them what kind of people they really were "in front of all your readers—the people who you secretly think are your fans and thrill to your *bon mots*" that Taylor "bought this page (and sold 2/3 of it to a friend)," the friend being Simmons, who used his share for a cartoon panel modeled on a pandemonium-filled newspaper cartoon called *They'll Do It Every Time*. Entitled *They'll Do It Every Deadline*, Simmons's version shows Beard (in characteristic turtleneck and dark jacket) walking into Simmons's office with a huge stack of paper saying cheerily, "I wrote this this morning before breakfast. We might use it as filler," while O'Donoghue, in cap and diapers, throws a tantrum on the floor screaming, "Somebody touched my door! There's a fingerprint on my door!" O'Rourke sits in front of Simmons's desk with a book entitled *Corporate Finance*, snapping his fingers in a managerial fashion and saying, "Okay, let's stop kidding around. We have a page and a half in for January. All we need is eighty more pages of copy." A busty phone-bearing secretary (the only woman in the room) informs Simmons that "Chris Guest's agent is on Line One. Chris Guest's lawyer is on Line Two. Chris Guest's manager is on Line Three and Chris Guest is on Line Four," while Kelly, who had finally relocated to New York during the *Lemmings* run, tells him that "if they build the Alaskan pipeline thru Canada my 11 kids can commute to New York daily. It'll only cost the company eight hundred a week." Meanwhile, notes from Kenney saying,

"Trying to put my head together. See you in '74" or "'76" or whenever lie scattered around the room.

The writers got cartoons of their own in a section called "Our Sunday Comics," parodies of existing comics that replicate each strip's illustration style with the *Lampoon*'s usual meticulous attention to verisimilitude. O'Donoghue, for example, was represented by a strip called *Poon-Wise!*, a parody of a dry educational strip called *Teen-Wise* that featured a sanctimonious owl providing ethical commentary on a teen dilemma each week. The *Lampoon* edition's problem is "Mike blows his stack at the slightest provocation!" Observing a white-suited figure hurling a "goddamn stupid telephone" against the wall, the owl points out that "Mike hasn't learned that you catch more flies with honey than you do with vinegar," whereupon an infuriated O'Donoghue interrupts his abuse of a phone company representative to grab the "goddamn stupid owl" and pound it to a bloody pulp with a hammer.

Meanwhile, O'Rourke's comic, based on the action adventure strip *Terry and the Pirates*, is set in exotic South America where, "on an airstrip high in the Chilean Andes, 'PJ' O'Rourke and his sidekick Al Rose [an artist friend of O'Rourke's from Baltimore particularly adept at an art deco illustration style] work feverishly—loading their plane with a vital crystalline extract of the rare Araucanian coca shrub while capitalist insurgents close in on every side!"

"Golly PJ, if we don't get this important cargo to highly-placed executives in the American record industry, how will the democratic government of Chile ever have the funds to battle the Anaconda lady and her hordes of ruthless copper pirates?" asks Rose. PJ's solution is to "(sniff) . . . just toss in three or four hundred shovelfuls before they get within range." The most self-indulgent of the Self-Indulgence articles was indisputably "Lampoon Girls Admit: If I Could Fuck Any Editor in the World It Would Be . . . ," said Lampoon Girls photographed in provocative poses and eschewing office wear for hot pants, miniskirts, and other revealing outfits. Trow is one of Gikow's choices because he is "the only guy who would take you to the Knickerbocker Club and the Cotton Club in one night." Her other choice is McConnachie, whose "authoritative wandering about the office makes him seem like an exciting bedroom partner."

O'Rourke, meanwhile, is Art Director Sonja Douglas's choice. "What girl wouldn't want to make it with someone who looks like Ringo Starr AND Rod Stewart?" she asks, while Judy Jacklin (Belushi's high school sweetheart, by then employed as the magazine's assistant art director) goes for "Groovy Tony. . . . I love the suicidal genius type, and I always like the attention he draws in public. . . . My fantasy is that someday *I'll* be the one in his office when he locks the door."

To be fair, these confessions were not included entirely gratuitously but were part of *Poonbeat*, "Humor's Official Teen Fan Mag," a parody of the teenage fanzines of the time. If *Poonbeat*'s contents—written by Kenney—would have been familiar to a readership of tween girls, the photos of these editorial heartthrobs on the table of contents page over captions like "Which editor's girlfriend pisses me off most? Page 180!" (Kelly) and "Find out who isn't talking to me this week! Pages 141, 142, 143, 144, and 145!" (Hendra) would have been a distinct and probably unpleasant surprise. As well, all the photos are interspersed with informative boldface headings like "Pathetic Would-Be Novelists!" "Washed-Up Execs!!" and "Hardly Any Jews!"

Poonbeat's exciting cover stories include "Will Doug Kenney Claw His Way Back up the Masthead?," "Is Henry Beard Almost Out of SJ Perelman's Jokes?," "PJ Confesses: I Was a Male Chauvinist Pig but Now I'm Just a Boar!," and "The Michael O'Donoghue Story: From Rags to Bitches."

The editors were fully aware that they were asking the readers to pay good money for a collection of internecine grievances, innuendoes, and grudge settling. "*Poonbeat*," noted the fine print at the bottom of the contents page, "is a wholly-owned subsidiary of the *National Lampoon* which, with a circulation of over one million, actually had the nerve to fill an entire issue with crap about the emotional retards and hack writers who make up its editorial staff. . . . But the NatLamp editors had fun doing the Self-Indulgence issue. Right? Bullshit! Grown fucking men screaming and yelling and threatening to kill each other over who goes on the asshole cover of goddamned *Poonbeat*, for Christ's sake."

But by perverse *Lampoon* logic, the amount of space *Poonbeat* devoted to ridiculing or casting aspersions on a writer was a reflection of that writer's status. Thus, a great deal of space was devoted to the relatively unabrasive and well-respected Beard. "Can You Love the New Henry Beard?" asked a feature devoted to the chief editor. " 'Not in that filthy turtleneck sweater, that's for sure' say all his old friends."

Rather more provocative interests were hinted at in *Poonbeat*'s "Phab Photo" section. For example, one photo shows O'Donoghue sitting in a low-slung bamboo chair while Beatts, in a handsome '30s suit and hat with veil, kneels beside him as they roll a stocking up the leg of a woman in a maid's costume. "Is this maid in Heaven? No, she's at Mike and Anne's house as they help dress her before she begins her day's chores," says the caption.

These triangular proclivities are further hinted at in Lampoon Girl Jane's preference. "Oh, to share a precious moment with these intoxicating post-Raphaelites," she sighed. "With all the zany things they do, we'd be one crazy *ménage à trois*. I've never been into turkeys, garter belts, or the Ritz, but then there's more to sex than organs." Were these and other references to the editors' personal lives based on actual incidents, were they merely jokes and rumors that were blown out of proportion to make the magazine contributors sound more sophisticated and interesting than they actually were, or, most probably, were they somewhere between the two?

Rather more sinister is the alleged O'Rourke leaning alluded to in *Poonbeat*'s "Humor Rumors": "RUMOR . . . P.J. O'Rourke hates WOMEN! Some gals are spreading the word that P.J. has a grudge against the entire feminine sex . . . FACT: Actually, he likes women very much. He's just waiting for the right one to come along so that he can teach her to sit, fetch, beg, roll over, and play dead." Then again, such behavior could easily be a side effect of the Araucanian coca shrub extract.

Not all the gossip was of a sexual nature. "RUMOR . . . TONY HEN-DRA IS LOSING ALL HIS FRIENDS!" alleges another Humor Rumor. "People are talking about the fact that this super-groovy Britisher seems to lose his friends soon after he makes them . . . a fact which brings tears to his eye. Is it true that terrific Tony's a failure at Anglo-American rela-tions? FACT . . . Tony has nothing against his old friends . . . he just finds it more stimulating to keep on meeting new people. Besides, if he gets lonely he can always call on chums Peter Cook, Dudley Moore . . . all the crew at Monty Python's Flying Circus" and several other British com-edy stars "with whom Tony once shared a lot in common including the same Queen, climate, and long-distance area code (01)." That Hendra needed to mend some fences around the office was further evidenced by the plug for *Poonbeat*'s " 'Tony Only', an entire magazine devoted to the 'English Sound!' " Among "all the pix and fax" supposedly found in this publication were "Last Joke Stolen!" plus "OVER 200 FOTOZ of Tony's pupils after he has some of his fave nasal decongestant!"

The coy references to cocaine were a way of both reflecting the *Lampoon*'s recreational habits and raising the hipness ante by show-ing that the editors were still one step ahead of their readers as pot use became commonplace. "The emergence of grass as a recreational drug and the rise of the *Lampoon* were strongly linked, both in terms of the editorship and the readership," Beatts said. "There was a definite connection. The fact that people were committing a crime made them subversive and gave perhaps a false subversive patina to the *Lampoon*. It was like, 'I'm hip—I smoke grass. I'm hip—I read this magazine. I'm hip—I wear aviator glasses.' After a while you started to see that the messengers [not to mention Simmons] were wearing aviator glasses, and you went, 'Whoa!' "

As an illicit thrill, grass was just too democratic. Not so cocaine: if one were into self-indulgence, one could hardly do better than throwing away large amounts of money on such an evanescent high. The cover of the Self-Indulgence issue showed a genuine $100 bill being genuinely burned up, but it might just as well have shown $100 worth of cocaine going up someone's nose. As well, in drug-sophisticated *Lampoon* circles, cocaine was known to be as addictive as heroin, psychologically if not physiologically. But unlike heroin, it was associated not with dingy tenement doorways but with the backseats of limousines. Using it was another expression of that "amused, fickle, perverse" attitude.

In terms of the tendencies it encouraged, cocaine was just what the *Lampoon* didn't need. If psychedelics encouraged viewing the individual ego in a cosmic perspective, cocaine restored the individual ego to its original place as the center and hub of all being, and restored it in a new, improved jumbo size. Continued consumption eventually resulted in paranoid and megalomaniac behavior, but in early days it could facilitate the kind of quick comeback and fast-flowing flood of ideas that put one at the top of one's *Lampoon* game.

Increased cocaine use was perhaps not ultimately at the root of the growing fractiousness at the magazine, but it didn't improve the situation any. Similarly, it may have been a symptom but not the cause of a larger generational retreat from communal activities into individualism. With the end of the draft, the urge for self-preservation, always an effective organizing tool, lost its power as a mobilizing force, and with the 1972 Nixon reelection, it seemed as if a lot of activism and consciousness-raising had been for nothing.

In the waning days of the Nixon administration, idealists who had not managed to make their lifestyle financially viable as well as alternative realized that, unless they were independently wealthy, they were going to have to drop back in, and they started wondering if there wasn't some way to have one's cake and eat it, too, to enjoy the material rewards of American life without becoming a total sellout. The Self-Indulgence issue proposes a possible solution in "When It Comes to Revolution . . . ," a two-page article by O'Rourke and Kelly. One page consists of "where are they now" photos of assorted '60s incendiary icons—for example, "Bob Dylan—Self-made millionaire; George Jackson—Dead;

Malcolm X—Dead." The second page offers a poster that depicts (in the distinctive super-heroic style of underground cartoonist Spain's radical *Trashman* comic) an illustrated O'Rourke (brandishing a pop rifle), O'Donoghue (in a Hawaiian shirt), Hendra (bearing a pie), Beard, Kenney, McCall, McConnachie, Kelly, and Trow (but not Beatts) under the rubric "We're All You've Got Left." If you can't beat 'em, was the idea, join 'em, but ironically. Any serious challenges to or hopes of substantially altering the status quo had been quashed, but mockery remained.

10

REAL BALLS

Loss of innocence, both personal and historical, fueled the *Lampoon*. It was, as Trow said, "a reaction to disinheritance, the shock of discovering that life did not conform to Harvard." Hardheaded pragmatists might have no trouble accepting that the United States was a world power like any other, prepared to convince by force when moral authority failed, but the Lampooners' generation had been sold on the Cold War public relations campaign for the American Way of Life. When they were in school in the '50s and early '60s at the height of the American Century, it was easy to believe that America was the last and best defense against the forces of tyranny.

But then fighting the draft had led to teach-ins about Vietnam, which in turn had led students to discover that the United States was not above using bullets instead of ballots to install leaders who would keep down the price of raw materials, local labor movements, and attempts to restrict the market for US goods. The unrest of the '60s was in part the political equivalent of adolescents realizing their parents were only human, or, as Trow put it, "getting to the center and discovering an ashtray instead of the king." In response to this, he said, "Most people shut up—some don't. We found that by telling the truth about this, you could get to be a star."

The truth the *Lampoon* had to tell was that the United States was not necessarily exceptional. The dollar was buying less, amber waves of grain were covered in pesticides, and the wide-open spaces were shrinking fast. As early as August 1970, Kenney had contributed "America as a Second Rate Power," which kicked off with a genuine quote from President Nixon, who declared, "I would rather be a one-term president than to see America become a second-rate power and see this nation accept the first defeat in its proud 190-year history." Even then it was apparent to Kenney that there would be no victory in Vietnam, and he had some ideas on how the country's new status might be reflected: a dollar bill with TV host Merv Griffin's picture on it, patriotic songs like "It's Quite An Adequate Old Flag," and a flaccid Washington Monument.

When the Paris peace talks began at the end of 1972 and defeat started looking more like a reality, Beard, Hendra, and Kelly marked the occasion with a "Special Defeat Day Sellout-Pullout Section" in the November issue featuring a tabloid called the *Daily Examiner*. The paper's headline screams "DEFEAT!" over a photo of an empty Times Square. "It's official. . . . And what's in it for us? Well may you ask," grumbles the *Examiner*'s editorial writer. "No guarantees, no free elections, no oil leases, no mineral rights, no trade agreements, no glory. Nothing. Just 'peace with honor.' "

When the tides of history start to turn and an empire begins losing its power, the tough get going and order the tide to turn back while the more philosophical lower their expectations and try to go with the flow, a response that made the *Examiner*'s fictional editorialist apoplectic. "Know what's wrong with this country? The whole Kit 'n' Caboodle's a stacked deck, with all the aces dealt to those squawking liberal-schmiberal Peace Corp-rupted Nader-type doves who . . . ramrod through creeping Socialist shenanigans that tighten the taxpayer's belt while paying welfare mothers to have junkies faster than we can shoot 'em," the enraged journalist spluttered.

In the grand *Lampoon* tradition of kicking them when they're down, the American grunt took a few more lumps in Kelly's reworking of the well-known prose poem "I Am the Infantry" in the same issue.

"I am the infantry, Closet Queen of Battle!" it began. "Both easy victories and well-covered up defeats I have known. Frankly, I owe a lot to friendly historians." Considering the *Lampoon* editors' service record, not to mention the unlikelihood of resident aliens Hendra and Kelly being called for active duty, it would be nice to think that this was more an attack on the tendency to glorify war itself than on the soldiers who fought it.

At least Kelly also sniped at profiteers in "The Peace Hymn of the Military Industrial Complex" ("We shall export wheat and hardware / We shall sell them DDT / Make loans at 95 percent in perpetuity / As we spent to keep them fighting / We shall get now they are free / We are splitting two-for-one!") and at those who didn't go in "The Brittle Hymn of the Draft Dodgers" ("From the hills of Nova Scotia / To the shoreline of B.C. / We avoid our country's battles very conscientiously"). The ferocity directed toward both those who served and those who avoided service suggests some ambivalence on the part of the native-born Lampooners about their own noncombatant status, but Kelly demurs. "The Americans I taught with in Canada were all draft dodgers," he recalled, "and they were very ambivalent. They felt their manhood had been called into question. No one at the *Lampoon* felt that way at all."

The Lampooners were aware, however, that large segments of the population might think otherwise. "I wouldn't expect a bunch of phony Ivy League intellectual assholes like you to know a goddamn thing about football," read a Letter in the October 1971 issue purportedly sent by a member of the Oakland Raiders (and indeed when Sussman edited a Sports issue, he had to write practically the whole thing himself). "The way you four-eyed smart-assed mental cripples dump all over our most sacred institutions is enough to make me want to puke, and is probably traderous [*sic*] to our country, too," the athlete wrote. But now that sensitive artists and iconoclastic troublemakers were in the ascendant, the four-eyed smart-asses were out for revenge.

Over and over again they exorcised the specter of the Real Man, most notably in April 1971's *Real Balls Adventure* magazine, a collaboration between Kenney, O'Donoghue, Catchpole, and John Boni. Headlines such as "'Eggheads Are Lousy Lovers!' Yawn Ivy League Call Girls," "Stalking the Fleet-Footed Homo," and "Automotive Experts Warn that Crackpot 'Ecologists' Crying 'Pollution' and 'Overpopulation' Want to Castrate You and Your Car Too!" scream from its cover.

One of *Real Balls*' timely exposés, "Know Your Enemy, No. 37: 'Party Girl,'" provides an excuse for several seminude photos of the voluptuous threat. "'No bra for me!' squeals this curvy Commie. 'I also believe in free love, nobody having private property, people of different races marrying each other, shooting our President and nobody bothering to build a bomb shelter,'" she says, surrounded by jars labeled "Fluoridated water" and "mariwana." For those seeking an alternative to these "pampered American girls," *Real Balls* offers an ad for imports from "Tijuana, centuries famous for its remarkable niteclub entertainments involving BEAUTIFUL SPANISH MEXICAN GIRLS and purebred intelligent German Shepherds. . . . The abandoned unclaimed offspring of these novel unions can make loving, docile and obedient life companions. All the benefits of a devoted spouse without the muss and fuss." Clearly the *Real Balls* man had no use for a relationship of equals, but then a man who had a different worldview than dominate or be dominated was no man at all, or so implies a letter to the "Real Balls Male Bag," which notes that "speaking of homos, a reliable source claims to have 'absolutely irrefutable statistical proof' that over 64% of last year's 'peace' candidates were 'definitely fags' or 'would be if they had half a chance.'"

It's not as if the Lampooners themselves played with dolls instead of guns when they were growing up. Like most boys, they played at being cowboys, soldiers, and so on, and their later mockery of these figures was so effective because it was fueled by their intimate knowledge of these archetypes. Their scorn was directed partially at the archetype itself, but also toward a world in which the heroic warrior images of their boyhood were less and less relevant. O'Rourke recognized this in his *Real Balls* ad for a boy's doll called T.G.I.F. Joe, an "Action Assistant Sales Supervisor™" who can be put "into hundreds of different exciting positions of duty and responsibility—sitting behind my T.G.I.F. Joe Action Desk™ ... searching for things in the T.G.I.F. Joe Action File Cabinet™ ... or riding on the T.G.I.F. Joe Action Commuter Bus™!" To the extent that the man of action was still operational, somehow he had gone from being Robin Hood or Superman to becoming a bully as much in love with death as the targets of *Lemmings*, who at least were only into self-destruction, not killing anyone else. Instead of developing his mental and physical personal strength to fight injustice, he relied on superior technology to assert dominance over the weak. He served the powerful, not those who needed protection from the abuse of power, and in so doing lost his heroic stature.

How could the John Wayne model of rugged male virtue have come to be perceived as a distasteful package of racism, sexism, and militarism? For one thing, as people of color, people of femaleness, and other members of what were condescendingly termed "special interest groups" began to speak up, the 30 percent of the population whose interests were not considered special but universal discovered that what they had seen as a largely benevolent paternalism could be considered oppression. Moreover, it began to look like the non–special interest group would have to fight dirty to retain its privileges, a prospect that threw the more sensitive members of its ranks into confusion.

The *National Lampoon* boys, like their *HL* forerunners, were constantly looking back to that more innocent age when their privileges could be taken for granted. This was McCall's special turf, nowhere more so than in a period piece (from July 1972) called "Colonel Teddy Jingo's Sketch."

"Answer, America," the colonel demanded. "Will it be groveling to an eight-armed idol in temples dense with the reek of incense, or will it be worship of an American Almighty? Will it be rats at Sunday table, or will it be apple pie? Will it be the harsh code of the coolie, the way of the jinriksha [*sic*] and the chopstick, or will it be Old Glory and Civilization?" Celebrating equal opportunity, Colonel Jingo reports that "the draft lets even Rastus don khaki and defend the American Way of Life. . . . 'I is fightin' mad!' says the simple Negro boy."

In the May 1971 "1906 *National Lampoon*," a compendium of "droll caprice" and "saucy wit," Kenney mocked his own publication's tendency toward elitist attitudes. The 1906 edition's editorial page includes a reaction to the idea of allowing African-Americans to join the local Democratic club: "Perhaps they should join the Knickerbocker Club as well. And let us not omit Paddy, Mario, and Mr. Chinaman while we're about it," the writer opines.

But being aware of their own exclusionary attitudes did not translate into doing anything to curb them. To the extent that minorities appeared in the *Lampoon* at all, it was to satirize white boys' images of them, not the real experience of being a minority. Something like the *Lampoon* Surprise Poster showing a white man holding a very small banana and a smirking black man holding a very large one may have been meant to send up the stereotype, but it ends up reinforcing it. Without black writers, images of African-Americans could not be explored with the depth and subtlety that the Lampooners brought to considering their own position as the inheritors of a privileged tradition.

A list of "depressing thoughts" Kelly compiled for the editorial of the August 1971 Bummers issue culminated in the observation that "surveys show that the typical reader of this magazine is a member of the species, the race, the sex, the nation, and the social class responsible for almost all of the world's misery," and while guilt was a word that did not appear in the *NatLamp* lexicon, the editors dealt with the grain of truth in this hyperbolic statement by concealing their true feelings behind veils of irony that both defended and mocked their situation.

House blue bloods Beard and Trow were often found on this marshy ground, for example in September 1972's "Our White Heritage," collaborating with token ethnic O'Donoghue. Shedding some light on the often-overlooked WASP contribution to America's history, the article offers a partial list of "organizations, foundations, and other groups dedicated to the advancement and betterment of uncolored people," among them "the Republican Party, the AFL-CIO, the United States Navy, the Supreme Court of the United States (since 1972) and Australia," as well as a list of some businesses that "an Involved White Person" might wish to support. These include General Motors, U.S. Steel, RCA, IBM, Monsanto, and several other white-owned concerns.

The authors fearlessly debunk demeaning stereotypes and myths surrounding those of Anglo-American ancestry, such as "Whites have 'natural reason', or extra lobes in their brains, which makes them good aesthetes"; "they smell good, talk too softly, and can't dance"; and "they go around reflectively rubbing their chins and saying 'Slide rule do your stuff' or 'Brains don't fail me now.'" Finally, the authors wrestle with the question "Are Jews White People?" to which they answer, "Technically yes, but . . ."

However, there was a price to pay for belonging to the privileged class, or such was the moral of Trow's "Anglo-Saxon Yuletide Tale" in the December 1973 issue, a Sendak-style illustrated story. When little C. V. Spoon III, clutching a Hotchkiss pennant and sporting a badge reading "Keep Your Distance" on his blazer, comes home to the family Locust Valley mansion (where even the mailbox bears the legend "Keep Your Distance"), he finds his parents engaged in a game of crazy eights, "and the loser gets the kid for Christmas." Wandering the streets, lonely C. V. is kidnapped by "unscrupulous postal workers looking for extra help over the holiday rush" and put into postal prison, where he makes friends with a poor youth named Pablo Spinoza. Pablo helps C. V. escape and takes the rich boy to his home where, clutched to Mrs. Spinoza's ample breast, C. V. thinks, "This is the first real love I have ever known." Meanwhile, at great sacrifice, Mr. Spinoza buys Pablo his heart's desire: a pair of scissors. Noticing there is no Christmas present for C. V., Pablo nobly leaves his new scissors beside his guest's bed with a note: "With love from Pablo."

"You call this a present? You've got to be joking" is little C. V.'s reaction, whereupon he instructs the Spinozas to keep their distance and find him a taxi. Returning home, he finds that "the shards and fragments of his mother's mind have scattered forever and spends a rather pleasant Christmas with a man from the trust department of the Anglo-Saxon National Bank." A soft heart was for losers, a liability on the path to power.

From this side of the *Real Balls* divide, the more compassionate model of manhood was seen as a shirking of responsibility, a failure to bend nature, whether internal or external, to one's will. As usual, the *Lampoon* editors stood in the middle of the dichotomy, taking shots at both sides. While they appreciated that expecting a man to be emotionally hard at all times was as unrealistic as expecting him to be constantly hard in any other sense (a July 1971 parody of *Everything You Always Wanted to Know about Sex* by John Boni and Beard offered such information as "the average penis, when erect, should measure approximately 12 inches, should keep erections after intercourse and should be able to have intercourse a minimum of 5 or 6 times a day"), sensitivity and compassion were another two words not found in the *Lampoon* lexicon.

Though individual *Lampoon* editors may have been kind, warm, and sympathetic human beings, the official *Lampoon* stance of disengagement had no use for such qualities. While they regarded the image of the Real Man with irony, they had still been brought up to be him. Keeping a facade of coolness and control at all times remained crucial. "I think we have a bunch of children up there—gifted but warped, baring all their neuroses," said Miller. "No one wanted to show his feelings. You didn't reveal your vulnerability because if you did someone would throw a spear in it." The only emotion that could be displayed was anger, and therefore sometimes feelings of caring, which could not be expressed, got all tangled up and emerged as hostility.

This hostility was often expressed in a very traditional form. Judging from the in-house messages in the Letters and Editorials, the Lampooners were real men enough to be attached to the classic male bonding ritual of perpetually asserting one's heterosexual prowess while perpetually intimating homosexual tendencies in one's fellows.

At least the Lampooners were self-aware enough to be able to take a couple of jabs at homophobia. "Are Queers Keeping You Up All Night?" asked an ad created by Beatts and Bluestone for the inside cover of "Norman [Mailer] the Barbarian," a "Macho Comics Group" publication that formed part of the May 1972 Men! issue. "Are you losing sleep due to constant fear of homosexual attack?" asked the ad for the "Rockwell Home Orifice Protection System." If so, you could secure peace of mind by ordering the "Big Bertha (oral-anal); Old Faithful (oral-anal-nasal); and Doc (eye-ear-nose, and throat)."

"I hear it was up in every men's room in every gay bar in the city," Bluestone reported. And back in July 1971, Weidman had created a quiz to answer the burning question "Are You a Homo?," so designed that if you were a sentient human being it was hard not to qualify.

If the Lampooners had no problem with homosexuality in the abstract but were perhaps uncomfortable with it on a personal basis, the situation with Jews was just the opposite. While several were close personal friends with and indeed actual members of the *Lampoon* creative inner circle, they did not number among the senior editors in the early years. This did not prevent the editors from receiving actual swastika-festooned letters from actual readers that started, "Listen, you Jew bastards." But contrary to what these correspondents thought, Jews do not have a monopoly on bad attitude, and in fact, "there were no Jews," as Weidman (of all people) said. "This was occasionally discussed."

One thing that emerged in these discussions was that "they were proud of not being particularly Semitic. It was probably something in the fact that a lot of humor had become Jewish and they were one of the first things that wasn't Jewish humor," Prager suggested.

"It was a reaction against *Mad* and that warm 'me like a schmuck' kind of comedy," O'Donoghue explained. "The *Lampoon* was more 'you like a schmuck.' It was always very arrogant white-person comedy." Just as guilt, that bedrock of Jewish humor, was not found in the *Lampoon* lexicon, neither was self-deprecation. "There are two kinds of humor: offensive and defensive," O'Rourke observed. "The *Lampoon* humor was offensive, and as a rule, we disliked the other. We used humor as a weapon rather than a shield."

However, the spirit of *shpritz* persisted in the person of Sussman, who felt he was single-handedly carrying on the tradition of Jewish comedian-humorists at the magazine. In his "Sunday Comics" strip, Sussman portrays himself as "world-famous aviator Smilin' Ger," who drops by the *Lampoon* office to find O'Donoghue exclaiming, "Donald Barthelme promised us a 'Fragment!'" Smilin' Ger sees the hand of the evil genius Von Fagg (nothing like a member of one excluded group going for someone even further down the totem pole) behind this sudden turn to the highbrow. Incensed, he seizes Von Fagg and extracts the antidote (Gentile Chicken Soup), thus saving *NatLamp* from a cruel fate before offering some parting advice: "Just keep 'em laughing, men." Clearly Sussman believed some down-to-earth Catskills humor would keep the magazine from getting too highfalutin and losing its audience.

Sussman's early pieces for the magazine were Jewish-oriented because, he said, "it was easy and comfortable." But often the satiric point of some of his Semitically slanted pieces is diffuse. For example, in Sussman's "Profiles in Chopped Liver: Our Greatest Jewish Presidents," it is hard to see how the presidents' Jewishness manifests itself other than in a propensity for throwing in some Yiddish, a language the magazine usually avoided. Far more devastating is the accompanying illustration by Sam Gross (who changed his name from Grosso under the impression that a Jewish-sounding name would do him more good in the magazine business), which shows scaffolding erected on Mount Rushmore to support the sculptured presidents' newly enlarged noses.

Just as Kelly and Hendra usually handled papal matters and Trow and Beard the more socially acceptable Protestant denominations, so Sussman "had first crack at being anti-Semitic. We were anti-everything. We treated Jews with the same satiric edge as we treated everybody else," he said. He conclusively proved that the *Lampoon* was an equal-opportunity offender in December 1974 with the creation of Bernie X, a self-aggrandizing, crude, obtuse, racist, paranoid, motormouth New York cabdriver who became possibly the magazine's longest-running recurring character and certainly one of the most popular. Bernie's shtick was regaling his captive passenger with far-fetched anecdotes and insights like, "What's the sense of talking about Spades and PRs? I never pick them up. I don't care how respectable they look. I figure I'm still too young to die. . . . Those fucking Gentile cunts are really working for their husbands all along! They know that Jews can fuck all day and all night so they seduce us and make us fuck our brains out until we're all going to get heart attacks!"

Non-Jews were also occasionally motivated to exploit Jewish stereotypes. *The Ventures of Zimmerman*, a publication of "International Jewish Comics" by Hendra and Kelly ("for you, $1.95" reads a sticker on the cover), suggests that "idealistic committed little folk singer Bobby Dylan" is in fact "The Amazing Zimmerman—faster than a proxy ballot, more powerful than an ulterior motive, and able to buy tall buildings with a single bond!" Zimmerman's potential is apparent even as a child when he refuses to sing "Happy Boithday" to his mother, remarking, "Listen, I get *paid* to sing!"

Twenty years later, Dylan is among the rock stars backstage at Woodstock panicking after the MC has announced that the concert will be free (the comic, which appeared in October 1972, would have been written as *Lemmings* was being developed). Crying "Up, up, and oy vey!" the mild-mannered folksinger is transformed into the hard-headed Zimmerman to save his fellow musicians from financial ruin. He hits the phones to Warner Bros., which soon realizes it "ain't seen nothing like the mighty Zimm," and returns to Woodstock, scattering record contracts and movie deals to the relieved stars.

Not only were Jews themselves fair game, but by extension, so was the state of Israel. "TORAH! TORAH! TORAH! Israel celebrates Bomb Kippur!" was the headline of the December 1973 "News on the March" section over a photo of tanks rolling into the Gaza Strip while a dialogue balloon, apparently coming from On High, booms, "Medammit, I said Promised Land, not Promised Continent!" Such criticism of Israeli military action was rarely found in the American press and in itself was liable to be considered evidence of anti-Semitism, as was a jibe at Israeli hero Moshe Dayan, shown announcing, "I'm a defense minister," in a plea for the "Middle East Appeal."

"Do you have any idea how hard it is to push people around for twenty years and still come off as the underdog?" Dayan asks. "Even with careful hoarding of World War II guilt, even taking advantage of the stupidity of our neighbors, this year self-righteous fervor may not be enough." But once again demonstrating the *Lampoon*'s evenhandedness, the preceding page carries a similar appeal from King Saud. "I'm a sheik," he says. "I know that without the Middle East Appeal there wouldn't be money for the inflammatory rhetoric, ludicrous weapons purchases, and pathetic bluffs that characterize our particular stage of mental development."

Inevitably, objections to Jewish schmaltz on principle spilled over, in some quarters, into objections to Jewish individuals in particular. Despite the fact that several of Hendra's long-standing friends and collaborators were technical white people, Kelly's view was that "Tony and P. J. were card-carrying anti-Semites for sure, as opposed to the Harvard gentlemen's agreement kind. They said horrible things to their faces, let alone behind their backs." Their primary target was Simmons, whom Kelly described as providing the magazine with "a general dose of Jewishness." But the *Lampoon* code dictated being able to take it as well as dish it out, so Kelly would retort, "P. J., you have to give the Jews credit. When Christ came along, they killed the stupid faggot." This, Kelly recalled, "would strike Matty as a terrible thing to say. But I told him, 'I studied under Jesuits. I'm allowed to say that. But P. J.'s not allowed to say that about Jews, is he?'"

Meyerowitz found the little remarks harder to shrug off even when they came from those like Hendra, whom he knew to be his friends. "I do get a little nervous when Tony starts making anti-Semitic remarks because I know he means them," the artist admitted. But Meyerowitz also felt that "part of Tony's charm was that he was such an angry guy and he could channel it into humor, which made him formidable. He wasn't just angry at Jews—he hated everybody."

"There was probably some personal anti-Semitic feeling from some people," Sussman admitted. Still, as far as he was concerned, the ecumenicalism of the hostility justified all. "The important thing was that everybody was a target. I have absolutely no complaints," he said. Indeed, Sussman felt that in the *Lampoon*, he found for the first time "my own sort of Lindy's [a showbiz hangout near Broadway where old-school comedians held their equivalent of the *Lampoon*'s 'celebrated dinners']. You know, the group," although he still got the impression that there were always parties going on that he wasn't being invited to ("*Everybody* felt that way," Gikow noted). However, in terms of fitting in, Sussman could have been at an even greater disadvantage—he could have been a woman.

11

GIRLZ

I f the *Lampoon* had a problem with less-assimilated Jews because they might be too emotional, too physical, too sympathetic to underdogs, women as a group seemed to display these tendencies to an even greater degree. If you said something cutting to them, instead of slashing you back they might burst into tears.

This is in fact what happened, no doubt realizing his worst nightmares, when Beard told it like it was to Beatts. It was no secret (indeed, it was a *Poonbeat* Humor Rumor) that Beatts, who had edited the May 1972 Men! issue, wanted to be an issue editor again. Finally, eighteen months later, Beatts invited Beard to lunch "and asked him how come I wasn't getting the kind of treatment I should get after three years of writing for the magazine," she recalled, to which Beard replied, devastatingly, "I just don't think what you do is funny." It was at this point that Beatts lost her composure and, to add insult to injury, a contact lens in her soup. "If I'd been a guy, I probably would have punched him," she hypothesized. As it was, she never wrote anything for the magazine again.

The idea of Beatts reduced to tears would have astonished several of her *Lampoon* colleagues, since the lone female contributing editor, like many women who are the first to muscle their way into a male preserve, had always given the impression of being Ms. Rhinohide. As O'Donoghue said, "she really fought her way onto that masthead."

"O'Donoghue once said if you accuse me of being afraid of mice, I'll eat the mouse. Well," Beatts said, "you had to be tough just to be there, and I was taught by masters." This struggle to be accepted provided the basis for *her* "Sunday Comics" strip, in which she depicts herself as bespectacled Little Beattsy trying to get into the boys' clubhouse, which has "Nashunal Lampoon—no girlz allowed" written on the outside. Inside, a group of boys chortle wildly at such story ideas as "Masturbation Self-Taught!" "Deadly Dump Trucks of World War Two!" and, from a little boy in a Harvard shirt, "The Whole Zits Catalogue!" When Little Beattsy knocks on the door, the boys tell her to go away. But then she calls through the window, "Hey guys—how about this? First base! Peel out! Round heels! Pizza face! On the rag!" while thinking, "They'll never see through my clever disguise." Sure enough, the boys reconsider. "She's only a girl but she acts like one of us guys!" one says while another adds, "Maybe she'll make us some sandwiches."

Once in the clubhouse, Little Beattsy asks, "Why don't we do something on guys who always want to show pictures of naked women and write stories about trying to get laid and masturbation and cocks falling off and think just the mention of the word 'zits' or 'homo' is hilarious and do parodies of war comics and science fiction and toy train catalogues and sex manuals and model airplane kits and stamp albums and the Hardy Boys as though every reader was a white middle-class American male who grew up in the Midwest and dreamed of the day when he could go to Harvard and learn some smart remarks to use on the yokels back home." The boys' reaction to this is to grumble, "Girls—no sense of humor!" while a quiet fellow in glasses kicks Little Beattsy out saying, "Tempting!" Then they go back to kicking around more story ideas like "Attack of the Ninety-Foot Homos!" "Funny Names for Different Parts of Naked Women!" and "Sgt. Rock's Stamp Album!"

Unlike some of her male colleagues, Beatts kept her head down and approached the *Lampoon* as a job, not an adventure. As in the *Lemmings* cast, the girl relied on preparation while the boys were happy to wing it. "Anne was prepared to put up with the hard-slogging organizational process because she had a strong sense of reality and purpose. She was really committed to her craft, to making it work on a career basis," said Terry Catchpole, whereas "other people were more boys' night out, just on a lark before going on to something real, like showbiz or movies."

Kelly, too, was struck by Beatts's professionalism. "Anne is not a humor writer," he declared. "Anne is a very brilliant person who can write whatever there is to write, and in this case she fell among humorists." This craftsperson-like approach made Beatts more akin to Beard and O'Rourke—who were able to write in whatever voice a piece demanded—than to others like McCall, Miller, and McConnachie, whose work always bore their own stamp. Beard's ability to submerge himself in a stylistic persona was brilliantly illustrated by May 1972's "My Gun Is Cute," a variation on the hard-boiled dick genre (allegedly from the pen of female crime novelist Germaine Spillane) that appeared in the Men! issue and brilliantly, if inadvertently, illustrated feminist points about the power of language to shape attitudes.

"Everyone thinks the life of a private eyelash is all glamour and handsome bulls," asserts detective Meg Hammer, "but take it from me, it isn't." However, Meg has some assistance from Patty, "a captain in Femicide. . . . You don't get too many cops passing the time of day in Kaffeeklatsches with private clits, but Patty wasn't like a lot of gum-pumps who never got over making it past metermaid and wore their badges as if they were a brass rag . . . and I knew without her I had about as much chance of getting anywhere with the NYPD as a good-looking rape victim who hasn't got a judge for a witness."

If Beard or Kenney wrote from the other sex's perspective, it was taken as evidence of their versatility, but if Beatts did, it was evidence of her limitations. "Her pieces gave me the impression they were done by the numbers," Kelly said, "as if she said, 'I know what they want and they want it done by a woman so I'll substitute period for wet dream.' I didn't see a different sensibility." There is some truth in this assessment, but at least one of Beatts's articles, a February 1973 "self-abuse pamphlet" called "Mother's Little Helper," could only have been written by a woman, which may be why it is more inspired and less workmanlike than much of her *Lampoon* output.

A compendium of excerpts from female-oriented porn, it offers something for everyone: Bestiality ("Ellen looked down at his sleeping form . . . suddenly she felt him stirring. He raised his head, nuzzled her cheek, and whinnied."), Masochism (listings for television soap operas), Sublimation (a notice from upscale department store Bonwit Teller's credit department stamped "Unlimited Credit"), and even Heterosexuality ("the silken curtains surrounding the bed fell away at a touch, and she was revealed to his gaze . . . he bent to kiss her rose-leaf lips. On the instant . . . everyone in the palace woke up and went on with their tasks, exactly as if they had not been sleeping for the past hundred years").

But even if Beatts had proposed more articles that reflected a female sensibility, they probably would have been shot down. "Our humor is white, middle and upper-class, male-oriented and effete," Beard told *Print* magazine with disarming frankness. "It's based on a personal nostalgia we all have in common." But the lack of female participation meant that, with the exception of Kenney, the *Lampoon* editors failed to exploit the humor potential of being raised as a girl.

This cultural divide was evident in the responses evoked by one of the few pieces Emily Prager wrote for the magazine, an October 1974 parody of a Tampax instruction manual. Like the original, the parody gives first-time users the impression that inserting a tampon is as difficult and dangerous a feat of engineering as building a bridge across the Rhine under fire during World War II. "NOTE" it warns: "The Clampax pontoon must be aimed in the right direction. This is important to avoid internal hemorrhaging and the ever-present possibility you may never be able to have children. . . . When you can feel units 1, 2, 3, 4, 5, 7 and 11 up inside you and the silken tickle of unit 6 against your thigh, the pontoon is in the correct position. You must remove all units except 1, 2, and 6 before you can leave the area."

While female readers of the magazine often cite this as one of the most memorably hilarious *Lampoon* articles, its appeal escaped several of the *Lampoon* editors who, being boys, had not been indoctrinated with the possible dire results of inserting anything Down There. "I suppose the *Lampoon* was pretty macho, but in those days, everything was," Prager observed, asserting that the only real problems she had were with *Lampoon* writers who didn't get her work. Such writers might not have hidden their view that the reason Prager succeeded Beatts in 1974 as the lone girl in the clubhouse was not because of what was between her ears. While agreeing with Beatts that "the only way women writers got in was by being involved with the men," Prager did not think it was a simple matter of trading sex for bylines; instead, she said, "generally speaking they wouldn't go out with you unless they thought you were funny," a theory that suggests *Lampoon* editors assessed a woman's attractiveness on the basis of whether she could be a potential contributor.

Whatever a *Lampoon* editor may have whispered in the way of pillow talk, there were no guarantees that going to bed with him would help a female writer get into the magazine. However, there were several women willing to test the theory, if Latimer is to be believed. "Christ, there were a lot of groupies in those days," he said, much as he disliked using "the term *groupies*—it's so demeaning. And they weren't like rock groupies. A lot of them, it wasn't like their whole life was to fuck somebody who got his name in the paper. Some of them were extremely intelligent."

As the midpoint of the '70s approached, many women believed they had the same innate talents and abilities as men but still felt they had to accomplish their goals through a man, or at the very least with his blessing. "Women actually had things that they'd written and would show to you in the afterglow and you'd think, 'Oh, this isn't professional.' How do you tell them that?" Latimer wondered. "It was kind of heartbreaking."

The most heartbreaking thing of all was that they didn't realize they were up against a basic biological fact of life. "When Doug said, 'I just don't think chicks are funny," it was an accepted idea, not an inflammatory statement," Beatts said. "There was no kind of 'let's have a token.' It never occurred to them. They just absolutely didn't think women had senses of humor," despite the fact that in 1972, the *HL* had finally admitted a woman (Patty Marx, later a writer for *Saturday Night Live*) to the editorial board. As for exceptions like Beatts or Prager, presumably it was thought that they had acquired some humor-creating capacity through physical intimacy with a *Lampoon* editor.

Moreover, the Lampooners were proclaiming the nonexistence of female satirists even though every week a young woman named Fran Lebowitz was emphatically proving them wrong in her column for Andy Warhol's *Interview* magazine. Equally inclined to be distrusting of nature and natural man and derisive of idealism and romance, she had a mastery of the acerbic epigram even Beard couldn't match. "The three questions of greatest concern are: Is it attractive? Is it amusing? Does it know its place?" she wrote, neatly encapsulating the *Lampoon*'s relationship priorities.

As with all prejudices, this theory of female humorlessness sprang from emotion, not reason. Bad enough when your *NatLamp* buddies used their intimate knowledge of your sore spots to assert their mastery through mockery; imagine if your girlfriend started doing it, too. You could never let down your guard. Tonight's whispered confession might fuel tomorrow's sarcastic remark. With wit your primary weapon, if your girlfriend got good at wielding it, you would lose a major advantage in the battle of the sexes. Humor *had* to be a language only men could speak. "Saying women aren't funny was a justification of those close masculine ties," Louise Gikow said. "They wanted to keep the fraternity isolated."

According to other *Lampoon* editors, it wasn't that they were opposed to publishing funny women—they just didn't get submissions from any. "My only criteria was what made me laugh," Sussman said. "I would get contributions from women occasionally and I just couldn't see it. It wasn't an antiwoman thing; it was just rare in general."

However, on her sole outing as issue editor, Beatts had no trouble finding women writers and brought in female contributors such as Amy Ephron (younger sister of noted humorist Nora), who moved in the *Lampoon* social orbit. But so pervasive was the *Lampoon* attitude that even those women who did gain access thought of themselves as anomalies. Ephron, for example, felt that "it wasn't a club that excluded women. Women weren't banging on the door to get in."

As a matter of fact, there were some aspiring female writers doing just that. Latimer described a friend of Beatts's, writer Deanne Stillman, as "carnivorous—she was really looking for a place," and remembers wondering, "Why isn't she coming to the after-work meetings and finding herself a slot?" For a woman, of course, casually socializing with a group of men usually did nothing to enhance her career prospects. "If you were a woman who wanted to write for the *National Lampoon*, it might have behooved you to hang out at the Bells of Hell and go over and have a beer with a *NatLamp* editor," said cartoonist Shary Flenniken, who became a *Lampoon* editor in the late '70s. "Except if you're a woman and you do that, it's taken the wrong way."

To be fair, the idea that no funny women made themselves known to the *Lampoon* is not entirely spurious. Women who were capable of making witty remarks were still cautious about revealing this penchant to men. Advice columns of the time counseled women to laugh at his jokes but never said anything about coming up with their own. In comedy mythology, women's ability to tell jokes was par with their driving skills: poor, due to a tendency to get flustered. Such few female comedians as existed, notably Phyllis Diller and a young Joan Rivers, specialized in the self-deprecating "me like a schmuck" brand of humor.

Furthermore, at the time few women were willing to admit they had the sexual knowledge, let alone experience, to make raunchy *Lampoon*-like jokes. Only Bad Girls had such knowledge, and their role was to be the butt of jokes. The role of Nice Girls was to be offended; and neither kind of girl was presumed to have the reservoir of aggression that fuels the professional humorist. As well, even if a woman were willing to put herself out there, she might look for a more hospitable environment than the testosterone-laden *Lampoon*, where any chink in her self-confidence would be ruthlessly exploited. Nevertheless, several women who weren't editorial girlfriends had their work deemed worthy to appear in the magazine on a regular basis—female artists and cartoonists. What mental gymnastics the *Lampoon* editors performed to allow this while still maintaining that women weren't funny can only be guessed at. Cartoonists in general were permitted more leeway from the standard *Lampoon* persona. Ed Subitzky, one of the most frequent contributors, often put a self-deprecating slant on his strips, and Gahan Wilson, while best known as a master of the macabre, contributed a long-running strip called *Nuts* in which childhood crises like a bad report card or a first funeral were treated not only with humor but also with un-*Lampoon*-ish empathy.

Likewise, Flenniken's strip *Trots and Bonnie* is simultaneously knowing and sweet. The central figure, Bonnie, a girl just entering adolescence, is naive and romantic while her pal, the worldly Pepsi, has a less sentimental "masculine" approach to love (when Bonnie sees the object of her unrequited affections, she says moonily, "Oh, isn't he dreamy?" to which Pepsi replies, "Well, Gary's not too bright but he's a great lay"). The joke is that Pepsi, in pinafore and pigtails, evokes the traditional picture of innocent girlhood. Like other writers for the magazine, Flenniken dealt with the tension between innocence and experience, but unlike other *Lampoon* articles, her work does not deride the former (Bonnie's dog Trots can talk, though only to her). Initially the editors found *Trots and Bonnie* a bit too naive. "The third strip I did for them was kind of goony," Flenniken admitted, "and they rejected it. So in the next one I took her clothes off." Even so, Flenniken's strip would not be confused with some other regular *Lampoon* strips—like Jeff Jones's long-running *Idyl*, for which the editors presumably put up with lots of mystical-hippie claptrap because of Jones's numerous depictions of undraped voluptuous ladies.

On the other hand, both male and female readers could appreciate

Byron Preiss and Ralph Reese's excellent love comic update *One Year Affair*, a fifty-two-episode strip about the minefield of modern dating that ran from 1973 to 1975, combining various states of undress with believable emotional reality and sharp dialogue.

Another female cartoonist who became a favorite contributor was the gentle-tempered, whimsical M. K. Brown. Like McConnachie (her editor at the magazine), Brown was tuned in to her own particular frequency. With farm or ranch romances set in the wide open spaces featuring human characters who looked just this side of mutant, lots of animals given to humming and buzzing, and like McConnachie, a narrative structure that ambled along rather than built, Brown's work was otherworldly but not alienated. As the artist herself described it, the strip was "down-home but at the same time very strange," as if drawn by a Martian with a great affection for Earth's fauna.

"I felt like the *Lampoon* was coming from a different place than me," Brown said, "but it feels like that wherever I work, and they were certainly the closest. They seemed open to anything, which so many magazines aren't. You could just be yourself." At the time Brown started contributing to the *Lampoon*, she was already signed to *Playboy*, while Beatts was supplementing her *Lampoon* income by writing for *Playboy*-wannabe *Oui*. Since it was assumed that there was no female audience for humor, magazines oriented toward men provided the market for the work of humorists of either sex, and it was perhaps inevitable that the *Lampoon* would fall ever deeper into this seemingly symbiotic publishing relationship between humor writing and naked ladies, extending the flirtation that had begun with the *Time* parody in 1969.

Most of the unclothed women who appeared in the *Lampoon's* pages were illustrated rather than photographed, heavily concentrated in the comic book parodies and in the "Comics" section at the back of the magazine. Finding editorial pretexts for photographs of actual nude women presented a bigger challenge, since they couldn't reflect the kind of blatant commercial exploitation the rest of editorial consistently undercut. The Lampooners fell back on the old *HL* solution of *ironic* commercial exploitation and, when all else failed, trotted out yet another *Playboy* parody in the form of January 1973's *Playdead*, which included a "pictorial essay" on the dead but definitely not yet decayed "Stiffs of Sweden" and a look at the "Playboy Fallout Shelter," which comes complete with "air raid sirens Carol and Vicki" so that "while it's Nagasaki outside, it's sakanookie inside."

The most reliable vehicle for ensuring that at least one pair of note-worthy breasts would be exposed in each issue was the Foto Funnies, the magazine's regular mini photo novellas. To the magazine's credit (or possibly due to its unwillingness to pay for professional models), the women in the early Foto Funnies look like real people and are no more glamorous than the editors themselves. But just as the baggy-pants comedians of burlesque needed a statuesque foil, so too the *Lampoon* was not complete without a resident sex bomb.

Miller found her in the person of Danielle Baron, a friend of his from sex-tabloid circles, who, in addition to being a fantasy figure for *Lampoon* readers, was also a real-life mom with a down-to-earth presence that suggested comfort as well as sex. This grounded quality enabled her to not appear ridiculous despite the many ridiculous situations the Lampooners photographed her in, such as having O'Rourke listen to her breasts for messages (as if they were seashells) or putting her breasts over Miller's eyes while he guesses which historical figure she is (Eleanor Roosevelt).

More often, she is shown amidst tousled sheets having postco-ital conversations, usually with Miller, whether enacting that old joke "Do you smoke after intercourse?" or falling asleep while he ponders exactly what fruit to compare her breasts to. As always, the Lampooners mocked their obsessions even while indulging them. "Do you realize each of these things weighs about 9 pounds? What's more in another few years they'll probably hang down to my navel," Baron informs an increasingly distressed Subitzky in another between-the-sheets conver-sation. "You men are so weird. All this excitement over a pair of big sweatglands," she sighs.

"As the years went by, tits and ass definitely held more sway in the publication. It was principally a publishing decision, and the editors rebelled a tremendous amount. Well," Gikow said, "not all of them rebelled." This is not to suggest that the Lampooners, several of whom had married and made babies, after all, were exactly of the same mind as adolescents sniggering at dirty pictures.

Nevertheless, a general distrust of unmediated nature and the physical body couldn't help but spill over into a lingering discomfort with the mysteries of sex in general and the female of the species in particular. Also, as if sex and love weren't dangerous ground to begin with, all the traditional guidelines were shifting, thus making the whole business even more fraught with peril. Instead of the carefully calibrated linkage of physical liberties to levels of commitment, suddenly it seemed as if everyone was leaping into bed with people they'd just met, knowing little more about them than their astrological sign. As well, in the past a girl with sexual experience could be relied on to keep it to herself for fear of being labeled a slut. But now, further pressure was put on men by the likelihood that even a young woman had had previous lovers to be measured up to, and no doubt she would regale her girlfriends with unflattering comparisons. The question of what women wanted was more impenetrable than ever. Did they still expect one to get on top or what? And if you did, would they think you a pig, and if you didn't, would they think you a wimp? Would they still respect you in the morning?

"I think a lot of the writing expressed fear and discomfort and hostility toward women," said Miller, who felt that his colleagues were "more macho and more into showing off their witty machohood," than he. "My writing may have sometimes reflected a little fear, because my characters were usually young," he said, "but basically my attitude was that women were just wonderful and sex was great."

Miller's sympathy took a tongue-in-cheek turn in his "Stacked Like Me," an account in the Men! issue of a man who, with the aid of implants, passes as a woman in order to experience "male sexist oppression" firsthand. Before long, he's trying to figure out the meaning of the word *hypoallergenic* and being made to feel embarrassed when purchasing tampons in a drugstore. So far so good.

However, gaps in Miller's understanding of the female experience become apparent when his unnamed transsexual offers a sexual favor to a man in return for his driving her to Los Angeles. "There it was," she observes. "All the while I thought men were the oppressors. But that couldn't be—not if I could make them do anything I wanted merely by inhaling. . . . While men strode about doing the work and thinking they ran things, the women sat back and coolly ran the men, controlling them like laboratory animals with electric-pleasure promises from the grottos of their vulvae."

Apparently, even the female-friendly Miller half seriously believed that women could cloud men's minds simply by judicious use of their physical attributes and that they had more to gain by going after power this way than directly. Certainly, if the status of the female staffers on the magazine who were never romantically involved with an editor is any indication, the forthright nonsexual approach did not get a woman very far. The masthead was top-heavy with men being all conceptual and brilliant and creative. Meanwhile, women clustered at the bottom, taking care of tedious details like correct comma placement and meeting the printing schedule.

This does not mean that the *Lampoon* was a hotbed of potential workplace discrimination lawsuits. While the support staff did not undervalue their contribution and was hardly unaware of the discrepancy in jobs, nevertheless, said Gikow, "no one really dealt with it. The women on staff didn't grumble, or not in the sense that we wanted to take over." The editors' opinion of possible female staff grievances was reflected in a January 1971 editorial written by Kenney. "In response to demands by female staffers for 1) all female staff members' salaries to be paid in real money or its equivalent, 2) a permanent cessation of corporal punishment for lateness or general editorial pique, and 3) exemption from the National Lampoon's weekly purification and fertility ritual," he writes, "after long sessions a compromise was finally hammered out, and we are pleased, ladies, that we have arrived at a happy solution. You're fired."

In her six years as copy editor, Gikow never aspired to become a senior editor and was not frustrated by a perceived lack of opportunity. "There was no time at which if I had gone to one of those guys and said, 'I want to write for the magazine' they would have said, 'You can't do that.' I would guarantee you anyone would have encouraged me to do anything," she declared. The only reason she didn't pursue this opportunity was because, she said, "they were incredibly brilliant and wonderful writers and I felt unbelievably intimidated."

Another member of the support staff, Janis Hirsch—who had begun working, virtually unpaid, for the *Lampoon* straight out of college, selling *Lemmings* group sales and *Radio Hour* ads—also felt that it was her own decision not to go for it. She singled out McConnachie, Kenney, O'Rourke, and Kelly as "wonderful teachers, very encouraging, and very, very generous." It wasn't that these editors made a point of offering Humor Writing 101 but that, said Hirsch, "they would look up and say just little things like, 'Never go for a joke name.'" Despite this evident approachability, Hirsch is convinced she "didn't say a word to any of those guys for the first year. I would have been way too intimidated."

Perhaps the senior editors felt more comfortable extending a helping hand to the support staff because they thought that these women, who had no opportunities to infiltrate the social-cum-brainstorming gatherings even in a girlfriend capacity, would remain supportive and not seriously expect to join the gang. "We wouldn't go have lunch with them," Hirsch recalled, "but then, the guys were working together." And if the editors sometimes let fly with that famous barbed wit in their direction, they "didn't take it personally. They treated everybody shitty," said an understanding Hirsch. In any case, she thought it was all worth it because she "was surrounded by smart men, which is pretty wonderful. They were basically a very nice group of guys."

That Hirsch's perspective may have become more starry-eyed in retrospect is made clear by a comic strip she wrote for *Titters*, an anthology of women's humor edited by Beatts and Deanne Stillman that appeared in 1976 (another contributor was one Arianna Stassinopoulos). "Somewhere I had read the most important thing to look for in a man was a sense of humor, so I looked," she wrote. Her first crush is on the grade school wit, at least until one day when she wonders, "What's that all over my gymsuit and my shoelaces and why are your pants . . . oh my God!" Her next crush is on the boy who crossed his eyes in their sixth-grade graduation picture because "Hippee," his hippopotamus-shaped eraser, told him to. In eighth grade, there's a boy with No. 2 pencils stuck up his nose who licks the teacher's knees as she sits down. Reaching college, Hirsch muses, "What kind of people laugh 'Ha!Ha! Ho!Ho!'?" as she sees a bunch of fraternity brothers chugging beer and chortling, "I was so drunk last night I totaled my Porsche! Ha!Ha!" and "I was so drunk last night I threw up on my date! Ho!Ho!" Miraculously undeterred, Hirsch retains her attraction to humorists, and one day, "my dreams came true. I got a job at a men's humor magazine," where she is shown sitting at a conference table while a man with pencils up his nose licks her knees, another tells her, "I took Ex-Lax and threw up all over my Porsche," another confesses that "Hippee" made him write an article, and a fourth urinates down her back.

Titters also featured some very *Lampoon*-ish magazine parodies such as *Slammer*, a magazine for reform school girls, and *Miz* ("Do you know the women's movement has no sense of humor?" "Yes," reads the parody's cover). Although as monosexual as the *Lampoon*, *Titters'* approach was far more ecumenical, with contributors ranging from the folksy Erma Bombeck to the ultrahip Lebowitz, as well as a large *Saturday Night Live* contingent.

The reason Beatts and her coeditor were able to uncover these allegedly nonexistent women humor writers was, she felt, because they "made an effort to find those women, to give them the kind of support that was only possible at the *National Lampoon* with a sexual contact. No one at the *Lampoon* had done that for women, and no one wanted to." Moreover, Beatts maintained, the *Lampoon* was not unaware of these female writers' existence. Many of them had already submitted work to the magazine. But the *Lampoon* view was that their submissions just weren't good enough. "I personally didn't think that many people who contributed to *Titters* were all that funny," said Sussman, echoing the view of several of his colleagues. Then again, it is easy to see why a group of less-than-secure men might not appreciate something like Prager's quaint sampler embroidered with the maxim "If God had meant women to give blow jobs She wouldn't have given them teeth."

However, *Titters* contributors shared with the Lampooners an appreciation of the discrepancy between what they had been raised to be and what now seemed appropriate, a gap that provided an equally rich mine of irony. Another of Prager's pieces for *Titters*, *The Girl Sprout Handbook*, lists the survival skills one must be proficient in to obtain Wily Arts badges, beginning with Daddy's Girl ("Know how to do four of the following: wink, giggle, blush, cuddle, fawn, plead, wheedle, whine") and moving on to Faking Orgasm ("Learn the words 'I never knew it could be like this'. Use them convincingly in a discussion with a friend") and Mommy ("Make up a story showing how a person ruined her life. Illustrate, using three of the following: soiled white gloves, a Negro, a public display of affection, an actor, too much makeup, New York City, bad posture . . . shoes without stockings, not learning to type, raising your voice, your own apartment").

It did not occur to the Lampooners that a whole field of satire was going uncultivated because, as usual, the experience of men was presumed to be universal while the experience of women was presumed to be specific. As Gikow said, "I can guarantee you the guys would think that men may be the ones who are funny but that the *National Lampoon* was a humor magazine for men and women while *Titters* was for women only and therefore an aberration."

The publishing world initially shared the *NatLamp* editors' view. "An anthology of women's humor—what's that? The world's shortest book?" was a common reaction, although ultimately *Titters* sold some one hundred thousand copies. Unfortunately, almost all of the editors' royalties went to legal fees (after an actual person, who discovered he shared a name with a fictitious person characterized in the book as a child molester, sued for libel), leaving them with little financial return on three years of work. Had Beatts known this in 1974 when she began developing the book, she probably wouldn't have bothered, especially since she and O'Donoghue had just quit / been fired from the *Lampoon* and neither one of them was in a position to take on a labor of love.

12
ALIENATION INC.

Simmons and his editors may have held different views on a number of subjects, but the appropriate role for women at a humor magazine was not one of them. "Matty was always saying to Anne, 'Would you get the phone, honey?'" O'Donoghue recalled, while Honey herself remembered the publisher replying to a request for a payment authorization with the question, "Why do you need money? I just gave your boyfriend $1,000." She was the only regular contributor who did not have an office of her own at the magazine. In 1974 she finally got at least a desk, but one spring day she returned from a trip to discover it now contained someone else's things.

O'Donoghue called Simmons to protest, and before long, the publisher was adding that if the two writers were unhappy, they knew what they could do. O'Donoghue, naturally, rose to the bait. "I told him, 'I'm out of here,'" he recalled. "I was making $350 a week, and I was just waiting for someone to give me shit." In fact, O'Donoghue was making $750 a week and, with stock options, was pulling down close to $50,000 a year (over $200,000 in today's money). Unbeknownst to O'Donoghue, Simmons was also about to cut him into the lucrative buyout deal awaiting Kenney, Beard, and Hoffman, leading the latter to observe, "O'Donoghue had the worst timing for his moves I ever saw."

A burned-out O'Donoghue may have felt getting himself fired was the only way to escape the pressure of producing the weekly *Radio Hour* without losing face. "There was friction with the print people because they didn't understand the technical demands," he said. "Tischler and I were killing ourselves and not being appreciated." Nevertheless, shortly before the fateful phone call, a blocked and exhausted O'Donoghue invited several print people up to the eleventh-floor studio "to do a big ad-lib about the comedy shortage. Beard and Trow were staggeringly good. It was," he recalled, "the last time we all really spoke to each other."

"Relations had been steadily worsening between Matty and Henry and Henry and O'Donoghue, but it was inevitable Michael O'Donoghue would blow no matter what the specific reason," McCall observed. The only surprising thing about O'Donoghue's departure was that it hadn't come sooner. Despite what Beatts called "penitential visits from Henry and Doug during the week, in which they bemoaned the situation but claimed there was nothing they could do," it was soon clear that this time O'Donoghue had quit once too often. Within days, a minion from the *Lampoon* mailroom was sent to repossess one of his *Radio Hour* perks, an expensive stereo system that the magazine had bought for him. The sun set on the Radio Ranch even before it was finished, and the fabulous furniture was sold, with the radio-shaped desk ultimately ending up with Beatts.

With its creative director gone, the sun almost set on the *Radio Hour* as well. But then Simmons decided it was time for a sequel to *Lemmings* and that he could have regular performers on the *Radio Hour* do double duty as the cast of the new stage show.

Simmons could afford to be in an expansive mood. Ad sales from the music sector alone rose by 35 percent in 1974, and in October of that year circulation passed the one million mark, making the *Lampoon* second only to *Playboy* on college campuses. Large corporate advertisers, however, were still resistant, and by the time *Lampoon* advertising sales peaked at $3.5 million in 1975, support was still based on sex, drugs (booze and tobacco), and rock and roll, even though market research showed that the average reader age was going up.

Some advertisers departed under pressure from religious groups. The December 1974 Judeo-Christian Tradition issue was particularly costly in this regard, as it inspired the Vatican-connected Catholic League for Religious and Civil Rights to remind music industry heavyweight RCA, a major *Lampoon* advertiser until that point, how much company stock the church owned. RCA found other ways of reaching the college market.

What could have roused the papal ire so? Could it have been the stained glass window depicting St. Onan, "patron saint of small families"? Or could it have been Hendra's "Catholic Sex Index" in which, under the heading "homosexuality," he reveals that "all indications . . . are that Christ practiced and intended his disciples—and, of course, their successors through Apostolic succession—to practice a physical as well as spiritual love for mankind"? The Mother Church was hardly the only religion mocked in the issue. O'Rourke drew on his Midwest background to create different Denominational Hells: in the Methodists' Hell, "for allowing the crabgrass to seed," a balding Everyman sits helplessly in an easy chair as the tab breaks off his beer can, his television goes on the eternal blink, and little boy demons put screwdrivers in electric sockets; in the Baptists' Hell, "for use of the flag as bunting," devils scream, "Neck! Neck! Or I'll make you pet!"; and the Episcopalians' Hell is a restaurant where the air-conditioning is broken, the wine list is limited to the likes of Thunderbird, and the service, provided by demon waiters, is terrible. Then there was Meyerowitz's less subtle religious commentary, "Martin Luther nails his ninety-five feces to the church door in Wittenberg, 1517."

Like O'Donoghue's departure, the only surprising thing was that the Vatican hadn't taken offense sooner. They overlooked Kelly and Choquette's *Son-o'-God Comics* in the same issue, in which the Divine Superhero battles the Antichrist. Deep in the bowels of the Pontifical

Palace, cardinals shoot craps chanting, "VII come XI!" as the Antichrist, who wears an archbishop's miter, plots the conquest of America while cackling, "The Boston police force awaits my signal! The Knights of Columbus are armed and ready!"

Meanwhile, disgusted by the sight of a Middle America addicted to bingo, "little Brooklyn nudnik" Bennie David is transfigured into the blond, muscular Son-o'-God and walks across the East River after summoning the twelve apostles, a dozen other skinny nudniks with thick glasses. Reaching St. Patrick's Cathedral on Fifth Avenue, Son-o'-God tangles with Satan, who warns, "Give up, you little kike! You are powerless in the grip of my Jesuit logic!"

Similarly, Bluestone's *Sermonette*, a recurring comic strip that began around the same time, escaped the Vatican's notice despite depicting a small crucified Jesus who appears as a regular guest on a radio program hosted by a priest. One week, the tiny Jesus offers to detach himself from the cross in order to prove that his suffering is voluntary but insists on being concealed with a small piece of cloth during the process. Draped by the priest's handkerchief, the Christ mentions, "If anyone is interested, this is what the Holy Ghost looks like, except then I have openings for my eyes."

While such articles were obviously intended to provoke, sometimes even milder material could cause trouble. In the course of coming up with a parody of hate-group newsletters, Beard and Cerf tried to think of the most innocuous ethnic group possible to serve as its target. The result, *Americans United to Beat the Dutch*, warns the reader to look for telltale florid faces, beer and/or cheese breath, and chocolate under their fingernails. The April 1973 newsletter also offers mail-order copies of such publications as *The Protocols of the Learned Elders of The Hague* ("minutes of a secret meeting of Dutch leaders to plot control of the Benelux countries") and *None Dare Call It Gouda*, "the shocking facts about what really lies beneath that innocent-looking outer layer of red wax."

The expensive part of the joke proved to be a caption under a photo of the royal family of the Netherlands, identifying them as "the Bandit Prince and his evil Queen, the Grand Dike Juliana," shown as they "enlist more dupes into their vicious drainage schemes." Unfortunately, *Time*'s media buyer turned out to be Dutch and objected to his queen being called a dike. He cancelled the news magazine's ads in the *Lampoon*, which immediately responded with a second *Americans United to Beat the Dutch* newsletter.

Some advertisers, on the other hand, were so enthusiastic they tried to make their ads resemble editorial, like the mail-order hi-fi supplier who advertised its wares by placing four sound systems in front of a recumbent naked lady on a fur rug under the heading "Five Great Reproduction Systems." Fortunately, most respected Taylor's injunction "You sell the products and we'll do the jokes," and the line between editorial and advertising remained largely distinct.

The only egregious example of the *Lampoon* giving it up to a potential advertiser was when John Lennon and Yoko Ono appeared in a March 1972 Foto Funny written by Yoko. It shows the famous couple wondering what has become of the rainbow. "See, there's one in my hat," says Yoko. "And in mine too, luv. Let's multiply and send it to all people," John replies. The inclusion of this cheerful fey conceit, so out of keeping with the magazine's usual wry dystopianism, doubtless had less to do with the fact that the couple had purchased a full-page ad on the next issue's back cover to announce "War Is Over (If You Want It)" than with the fact that it was, after all, *John Lennon*.

Who exactly were these readers advertisers sought to reach? Paul Krassner thought that the *Lampoon* audience was likely to be a mixture of college students, junior executives, and hip housewives, plus some blue-collar workers with a taste for irreverence. More quantitative demographic research initially showed the average reader to be about twenty-one, either in college or just getting out, and with a high household income—"high" in the early '70s meaning around $16,000. The chances were 80/20 that the *Lampoon* reader was male, and the chances were equally good that he was white. Whoever the typical reader may have been, the *Lampoon* writers didn't know much about him beyond that they didn't particularly want to know more.

"I was on a train trip to Canada with O'Donoghue when we were joined in the dining car by kids going on ski weekends or something," Beatts recalled, "and Michael said, 'It would be death if these people find out who we are, because they're going to come talk to us.'" The couple believed that *National Lampoon* readers were, as Beatts said, "people you wouldn't want to know, basically nerdy kids with too many pens and pencils in their pockets," people perhaps too reminiscent of the editors' own younger selves. O'Donoghue, however, denied that he felt superior to his readers. "Who's to write down to someone else?" he asked. "I don't have to write down because I'm a jerk from upstate New York. Maybe if I'd gone to exclusive Swiss finishing schools it would be different, but who am I going to write down to? Mr. Dog? Mr. Cat? Mr. Sheep?"

Kelly, too, claimed to have a more empathetic view. "The *Lampoon* always reached out to nerds and made them think they weren't alone," he said. "It was OK to be a nerd because there're nerds in New York making a living." This typical reader was not thought to be a modern tech geek so much as an old-fashioned bookworm, "kids who cared about reading but thought that meant they had to be boring assholes. I said I care about it and I'm a cool *National Lampoon* guy. One thing I hope I taught is that you can care very deeply about literature and not be a bonehead."

Kelly may have believed that he was addressing an audience of aspiring litterateurs, but his fellow editors thought otherwise, at least judging from the letters to the editor represented as coming from typical readers (though invariably written by Kenney). "The *National Lampoon* sucks dead boogers!" began a letter allegedly from one "Buster Hymen" of the Tappa Kegga Bru fraternity. "All kidding aside, the guys in the dorm . . . have been dumping on me for not writing you about a summer job (maybe you've seen my strip in the St. Tunafish University News. I bet you'd really dig the one where Blow-job Man jerks off the Pope on a pile of dead nuns)."

Similarly, a letter from the "Far Out Heads in Room 23 B" of Ohio State University reports that they "were sitting around the dorm really zonked . . . and Dave, who was getting behind some DMT, said wouldn't it be incredible like if Nixon comes on TV, like for a press conference or some jive like that, and . . . just bent over and *mooned the camera*!! I mean, drop trou and the whole bit!" It was already clear to the Lampooners that the lasting political legacy of the upheavals of the early '70s would be a determination to fight for the right to party. Actual correspondence from readers did not do much to discourage this dim view. "Everything you wrote was completely misunderstood by the people who wrote in. They were completely missing the point," said Bluestone. Not that the Lampooners minded inciting outrage in the reading public; on the contrary, it was a badge of honor. They would compare letters and the more upset the correspondent, the better. The largest outraged response was generated by the same O'Donoghue-devised contest that had proved too much for Garry Goodrow, which offered a prize for accurately predicting when former first lady Mamie Eisenhower would die. "People went bananas," Bluestone recalled. "A psychiatrist who was writing a book on criminal psychotics wanted to interview Michael and suggested the publisher get him treatment."

This was mild compared to a reaction elicited by the kill-the-dog cover. Shortly after the issue hit the newsstands, O'Donoghue was sent a package that contained what appeared to be sticks of dynamite and a note saying, "I hope you guys get a bang out of this." It was signed, "A Dog Lover."

According to Bluestone, O'Donoghue was proudly showing his gift around the office "saying, 'Look what we got. Boy, it looks real,' when somebody from the mailroom who'd been in Vietnam explained that a lot of the dynamite was already old and had turned to nitroglycerine and could blow up the place." In another version of the story, O'Donoghue was advised to look for leaking nitroglycerine by no less an explosives expert than *Paris Review* editor and fireworks enthusiast George Plimpton. In any case, the premises were evacuated and the bomb squad summoned, but not before Simmons, ever alert to a publicity opportunity, phoned the media. A local TV reporter arrived to find O'Donoghue lying in front of her feigning death and, to his deep disappointment, coolly stepped over him.

The *Lampoon* was not alone in its pursuit of young white male consumers of music and beer. "Our competition was *Rolling Stone*," Mogel said flatly. But, O'Rourke contended, *Rolling Stone*'s impact on the *Lampoon* was negligible, with one exception. "Hunter Thompson," he said, "was a personal influence on me, Doug, and Chris Miller." Thompson's brand of "gonzo" journalism was known for upending the distinction between fiction and nonfiction, with his perception of reality as much a part of the story as the actual events. His style was simultaneously two-fisted and pyrotechnically flashy, macho but not afraid of metaphor.

However, unlike some of his admirers at the *Lampoon* and later at *Saturday Night Live*, Thompson did not pursue outrageousness for its own sake. His wild-man persona was intended to hold up a mirror to what he saw as the accepted violence, excess, and out-of-control lunacy that passed for business as usual in '70s America. For once, familiarity did not breed contempt. Thompson remained one of the few cultural icons to go un-mocked in the *Lampoon*'s pages, although he did inspire the *Radio Hour* to make "The California Show" in October 1974, a Thompsonesque odyssey to the Golden State that reflected Belushi's affinity for the journalist's larger-than-life persona, fearless embrace of excess, and disdain for ordinary limits.

But in the summer of 1974, Belushi, having succeeded O'Donoghue as creative director of the *Radio Hour*, proved to be a model of dutiful application when he was sent out to find a new cast. One of his first recruits was Harold Ramis, a native Chicagoan who had started taking Second City workshops in 1968 (when the company turned their beer garden into a temporary hospital during the Democratic Convention). At the time, Ramis was working as *Playboy*'s party joke editor. He soon joined Second City's touring company and then, in 1970, the resident company, leaving the Hefner empire six months later.

Ramis was still around when the *Playboy* staff got their first look at the *Lampoon*. "My editor at *Playboy* showed me the first couple of issues and said, 'We want to start doing some comedy in this style,' an idea," Ramis said, "I resisted," even though he thought the magazine was "brilliant. They were writing for themselves. They were clearly not writing for the audience. They had picked up a kind of 'let the reader be damned' feeling from *Mad*—you could call the reader a clod and the reader would actually enjoy it."

Tall and somewhat reserved, Ramis did not fit the stereotype of either a swinging *Playboy* editor (he got married shortly after graduating from college and stayed that way) or a rambunctious, attention-grabbing comedian. Even in college, a friend said, Ramis had all kinds of colorful acquaintances given to nervous breakdowns or extravagant artistic visions for whom he became a sort of counselor they could come to for advice, thus assuming the Beard-like role as the calm center of a storm of more flamboyant personalities.

It was perhaps this apparent stability that led to Ramis being put into positions of responsibility. When Belushi called, he was already producing a Second City special for a Chicago TV station. Belushi also approached a member of the special's cast, a writer-performer named Brian Doyle-Murray (born just Murray but adding Doyle to avoid being confused with a British actor) whom he already knew from Second City's touring company.

The touring company "was sort of snot-nosed and naive," said Gerrit Graham, another member, "but it was much more abrasive politically than the resident company at the time." Graham himself had already been branded a political troublemaker, a reputation he maintained was based purely on appearances. "I had developed in the minds of the attorney general's office and the FBI an extremely dangerous record," he said, "based on the fact that I had been in *Greetings* and *Hi, Mom!*, two subversive features" that were director Brian De Palma's first films.

In fact, Graham was about as likely a firebrand as George Trow, whom he had met while summering on the Hudson with mutual friends when he was still in prep school and Trow at Harvard. Given his background, it is hardly surprising that Graham should have felt an affinity with the early *Lampoon*'s brand of humor. "One way in which one ensures one's standing at boarding school, the principal defense for many who have no physical prowess, is by being able to savage either the faculty or classmate or everybody with brilliant satirical humor, so you develop a knack," he said.

After his recruiting drive at the Chicago Second City, Belushi set off to raid the company's Toronto offshoot. He, Doyle-Murray, and Ramis had been in the touring company Second City sent up north as an advance party prior to a Canadian resident company being established in 1973. Their show had impressed a young actress in the audience. "I still remember everything they did and everyone who was in it. My only aspiration in show business was to be in Second City," said Gilda Radner, Belushi's primary reason for the trip to Toronto. "Gilda," Bob Tischler recalled, "was the big one to catch."

Like Beatts, Radner was an American who had moved to Canada for love. Like Belushi, she had started performing improvisational comedy in a coffeehouse while still in college, in her case the University of Michigan. Ann Arbor in 1968 was one of the nation's more highly politicized campuses, but Radner preferred stardust to teargas. "My friends would try to get me into political things and I'd say no, I have to do this play," she recalled.

By the time Belushi returned to Toronto, Radner had achieved her ambition and was a member of the Canadian edition of Second City—along with Eugene Levy, John Candy, and Joe Flaherty—performing sketches like one in which she gets hit by a car and an initially helpful crowd turns away in disgust after observing she's wearing dirty underwear.

Radner formed an especially supportive and creative stage relationship with Flaherty. "One thing about working at Second City," she recalled, "is that there would be nights when this magical, chemical, extra-sensory thing would happen between you and the others, and something incredible would occur onstage. . . . This connection was so strong working with Joe Flaherty that when he set me up, sometimes I believed he knew what he wanted me to say and that he'd actually put it into my mind." Like Radner, Flaherty was more interested in acting than activism, and the tastes of both ran more to gentler, character-based humor than to the *Lampoon* style of hard-edged, concept-based material.

"There was an old Second City cliché that when someone offers an idea, you're supposed to say, 'Yes and' as opposed to 'No but,'" Ramis recalled. "You create something better than either individual would come up with on their own. You find out what game is being played and help it along." The *Lampoon* impulse, of course, would be to find out what game was being played and then break the rules.

When Ramis, Doyle-Murray, Radner, and Flaherty accepted Belushi's offer to come to the dirty sauna that is New York in August, they found themselves in an alien environment. "I thought the magazine was funny, but it was too often shocking for my taste," said Flaherty, who "liked that *Harvard Lampoon* smart parody stuff. It was that other 'how do you make a dead baby float' stuff that crept in I didn't like. It's like, 'We don't want to make you laugh, we want to make you throw up.'"

Similarly, Ramis felt that "there was something misanthropic about many of the *Lampoon* editors that our company didn't have." Like many before him, he was made to feel "like a second-class citizen, not having gone to Harvard. They seemed to flaunt their sophistication and education." On the other hand, he added, "I didn't feel like a complete slouch. I seemed to get some respect, and generally I would say they did respect us and appreciate our company." As always, the editors were harder on each other than on outsiders.

For the most part, the actors were amused rather than intimidated by the Lampooners' sophisticated airs. "There was all this aggressive erudition, one-upsmanship, and pedantry flying around," Ramis said. "It was fun to watch. But the *Lampoon* writers almost never contributed to the *Radio Hour*. There was a kind of schism. I don't think the editors felt comfortable on our floor. Except Doug. He was pretty much around, but not really as a participant." Tischler, however, had a different view.

"Those *National Lampoon* writers who wrote for the *Radio Hour* and the actors loved each other," he said. "Doug and Brian McConnachie liked to come up to the eleventh floor and spend a good deal of the day there. Everybody socialized. It was like a family."

As often happens when a show is getting off the ground, the cast banded together in a kind of "first colonists of outer space mentality" that was enhanced by the fact that the Second City transfers did not know many people in New York and had little opportunity to meet anyone. In their few nonworking hours, they socialized mostly with each other, watching television at Belushi's place.

"All of us look back on it as a great period in our lives because we weren't doing it for the money," said Tischler. "There were no censors, no ratings pressure, so we could try very experimental things and if it was bad, it was bad. We were allowed to fail." But for Flaherty, who had previously lived in New York as an underpaid actor, the money was a big part of it. The actors were making more than they had at Second City. "After jobs like working in the stockroom of Saks Fifth Avenue, to come in and go to work doing a radio show that was fun to do—it was great, it was amazing," he recalled. Belushi appreciated both the freedom to experiment and the money, but it also made him nervous. "Good money, a lot of freedom, they let you write your shows and put them on with no hassles or producers or red tape, they spend as much as you need—it's a security trap. It gets so you can't escape," he said warily in 1975.

One reason the newcomers enjoyed creating the radio show so much was because it helped them avoid writing Son of *Lemmings*. Plus, as Ramis said, they had "the novelty of playing with our own radio studio," a facility that aroused envy in Harry Shearer, a member of radio improv group the Credibility Gap, occasional *Radio Hour* performer, and later bassist for Spinal Tap and the voice of *The Simpsons'* Mr. Burns. "We had been doing radio shows in these Spartan surroundings," he said, "and they had this elegant studio bought and paid for." Despite these technical resources, "technique was always secondary to believable characters and situations," Flaherty said. "The bottom line for us was, 'Is it funny? Does it work?'"

A piece like "The Immigrants" suggests that the new *Radio Hour* crew was willing to resort to easy stereotypes in pursuit of this goal. This saga of the "wretched refuse who came like mosquitoes to the yellow porch light of freedom" starts in the Old World, where "discontented hillbillies voice their discontent." Soon they set sail for the New World, recounting their hopes ("They've got lots of old refrigerators for the kids to play in") and dreams ("I'm just goin' to hang around bus stations, spittin' and pickin' my nose").

Later, the rather upper-class-sounding narrator lists hillbilly contributions to American culture, which include hush puppies, rickets, incest, and rotten teeth (though it's unlikely that the liberal comedians would have considered the legacy of poverty suitable humor fodder if the piece had been set in an inner-city ghetto). As with *Dragula*, a fuzzy satiric aim leaves the piece open to misinterpretation, and it is not clear if humor is being used as a shield to defend the powerless or a sword with which to beat them up.

As well, Belushi and Doyle-Murray came up with several short, unrelated sketches, mostly hockey based, that seem to embrace cruelty for its own sake. But two of the sketches comment on, rather than simply epitomize, the tough approach. The first features Belushi as an interviewer exploring the educational philosophy of "Dr. Howard 'Bear' Barnes," who runs an alternative child-care center for the under-fives that promotes constant training in "football, basketball, swimming, Kung Fu, and Thai boxing. At age 4, each child must pass a survival test." Barnes introduces one of his best-conditioned charges, three-year-old Jimmy Dugan, who, despite 105 recent stitches across his face from a hockey injury, is in top physical condition. "Go ahead, punch him in the stomach—he can take it!" Barnes urges the reluctant interviewer. When the child starts to cry, Barnes turns on him. "C'mon, get up!" he yells. "C'mon crybaby, stand up!"

Then in "The Jimmy Dugan Story," a narrator out of an old sports bio intones, "Jimmy Dugan—a great child, a great athlete, a great human being. Our story begins when he's three years old," and we hear Barnes urging the interviewer to hit Jimmy in the stomach. The blows are followed by two additional lines not in the first sketch: "He's dead. You've killed him."

Although Simmons maintained that the *Radio Hour* remained the same after Belushi took over, according to Tischler it changed drastically. Fully scripted pieces were abandoned in favor of edited improv sessions, a style that had been used before but now had more natural-sounding and funnier dialogue. Presiding over it all, after a fashion, was Belushi. If later in life his gonzo tendencies would give his employers headaches, at this point they had no complaints. "Belushi was a nice hardworking guy in those days," Mogel testified. "Then he began to change."

As a leader Belushi was more of an inspirational catalyst than executive organizer. "I wouldn't say John took it *that* seriously," Flaherty suggested. "But when you get a group of people together who are fairly talented and have worked together, you can trust them to get it done. John was just kind of overseeing everything." At most, Belushi was first among equals. "It was a real ensemble," Tischler said. "Nobody was a star. There wasn't that kind of ego the whole time the *Radio Hour* was on," although McCall believed that Belushi was always "an egotist, always acted like he was already the king."

A more centralized process might have made production more efficient but would have gone against the group-oriented Second City tradition. "For us, the *Radio Hour* was a fusion of the Second City working style with the *Lampoon* attitude," Ramis recalled, though Flaherty "never could figure out what the *Lampoon* was," beyond being "similar to us but on the page." It was this "on the page" idea that Ramis identified as the big problem. "There was nothing inherently theatrical about the *Lampoon*," he said. "There was something so literary about the writing in the magazine that it didn't easily translate."

Although Belushi and Doyle-Murray apparently believed the *Lam-*

poon sensibility meant focusing on death and violence, some of the lighter aspects of the magazine's attitude emerged in October 1974 when the troupe collaborated with Beard and Cerf on a radio version of their "Prison Farm" comic. Taking the form of a trailer for a forthcoming film, it opens with clanging music and hard-edged narration that immediately evoke every prison potboiler ever made. "Prison Farm—where Nixon's men and the nation's most desirable criminals are sent away for hard middle management for as long as they like! Watch men endure brutal beatings," the narrator proclaims as low-key cries of "down six, doubled and vulnerable! Geez, I'm down 500 points!" and "Guess bridge just isn't your game, Jim" fill the air. The narrator invites us to "hear the screams of agony in the hot box!"—screams like, "Boy, this steam is hot! Think I'll take a dip in the pool."

The revelation of President Nixon's taped conversations during the Watergate investigations had also inspired *The Missing White House Tapes*, an album based on some December 1973 *Radio Hour* pieces created by some of the more politically minded Lampooners—primarily Beard, Kelly, Guest, and Chase—in the interregnum between the O'Donoghue and Belushi eras. In one wordy segment, taken virtually verbatim from the magazine, Chase provides the tape-recorded voice of the mysterious "Mission: Impeachable" contact. "Several high-ranking members of the Democratic party are attempting to seize control of the government of the United States by legitimate means," he says as the recorder clicks on. "Should they succeed, all our attempts to repeal the Bill of Rights, pack the Supreme Court with right-wing morons, suppress dissent, intimidate the media, halt social progress, promote big business, and crush the Congress will be destroyed." Unfortunately, topical satire has never been a major audience-grabber, and the album, released in 1974, was not a big seller, although it was nominated for a Grammy.

Chase had already left for California by the time the Chicagoans arrived in August 1974, but Guest was around long enough to work with the new cast on the *Radio Hour* before he, too, headed west. As plummy-voiced BBC announcer Roger de Swans introducing a reading of Dostoyevsky's *The Idiot* ("We are proud, and yet, in a way, humble, to present . . ."), Guest has a wonderful time pronouncing the Russian names with excruciating correctness. After this highly dignified intro-duction, on comes the Idiot himself. "Everybody get out of here—there's lobster loose!" he warns. "Holy Cow . . . he's vengeful . . . Everybody get out of here quickly—there's going to be a tragedy! Oh God! Hah!" This inspired lunacy was improvised by another new recruit, Doyle-Murray's younger brother Bill.

13

THE AUDIENCE IS SNARLING

I f the *Lampoon* staff harbored a large contingent of malcontents reacting against the discipline of a Catholic education, Murray fit right in, having gone to parochial school and then a Jesuit college as a premed student. His medical career suffered a setback in 1972 when, while checking in for a flight on his twenty-first birthday, he was unable to produce an ID to prove that he was under twenty-one and thus eligible for a discount airfare. "That's too bad," Murray quipped. "I wanted to get on because I got two bombs in my suitcase." The resulting bag search led to the discovery of eight and a half pounds of pot, a brief visit to a Chicago jail, and a period on probation.

The likelihood of his becoming a doctor diminished even further when, having won a scholarship to attend some Second City workshops, he was offered Doyle-Murray's roles with the touring company when his brother left for New York. Shortly thereafter, Murray was enlisted to join the *Radio Hour* while serving as understudy for the live sequel to *Lemmings*. "Billy came on, tried to write, couldn't write a thing. Then he started to improvise, and he was wonderful," said Tischler, who considers Murray and Guest to be the most creative improvisational actors he's ever worked with. Murray had other useful talents as well, becoming the chief pitching asset of the *Lampoon's* crack softball team.

In October of 1974, after two months of working on the *Radio Hour* by day and writing the stage production by night, Belushi and the Second City defectors took the live show—now with the prosaic title *The National Lampoon Show*—on the road for a series of one- or two-night stands, leaving Bill Murray behind to pinch-hit on the *Radio Hour* with Tischler, the *Lampoon* writers, and other actors. After the cocoon of the studio, facing an actual, snarling audience came as a shock. "We toured some colleges, then some bars in Canada. It was terrible," Flaherty recalled. The problem of blending the raw, hard-edged *Lampoon* sensibility with the softer, more polite Second City approach had never really been solved, and the performers lacked confidence in their material.

Beard and Kenney had been brought in as consultants but, according to Ramis, "they had very little to add." Perhaps they had kept their mouths shut recognizing another tight-knit group when they saw one. Weidman remembered "going to a bunch of meetings with Doug, Ramis, Gilda, and those people. They had been operating as a group very comfortably creating their own material, and they were really into doing their own thing."

In retrospect, Ramis felt that the show would have benefitted from more fourth-floor input. "The key was we didn't have any help from the *Lampoon* editors," he asserted. Without the benefit of the editors' sophisticated irony and unable to use the usual Second City approach, which Ramis described as having "some political or social ax to grind"— the sound of grinding axes being anathema to the *Lampoon* spirit—the troupe, as they had on the *Radio Hour*, embraced the most aggressive and cynical aspects of the *Lampoon* style. "*The National Lampoon Show* didn't have a point of view, really, and we ended up with a vicious Second City show," Ramis said, recalling a scene in which Doyle-Murray tortured a live plant as particularly inflammatory to audience sensibilities. Flaherty didn't like it much either, asserting, "Brian wasn't trying to make a point; it was just for shock."

In fact, Flaherty didn't like "a lot of the stuff we did even though none of us took it seriously. It wasn't like we were trying to show people something new through black humor. It was like, 'Let's see how far we can go.' Belushi was sort of behind that." Belushi, always ready to test the limits, didn't want to make the audience feel good so much as blow them away. Flaherty remembered that at one point the company veered into a "let's get so and so" phase, and he and Belushi decided to go after Lenny Bruce, whose biography they had just finished reading. As the Ur-transgressive comedian who pushed the boundaries of conventional taste in the name of truth whatever the cost, Bruce would have been the template for Belushi as for so many others. But Belushi had trouble forgiving his heroes for their human failings. He wanted to "get" Bruce because, he told Flaherty, "he died a fat junkie and people are treating him like a saint."

Belushi-as-Bruce made his appearance in October 1974 in "The Dead Sullivan Show," a sketch created in honor of recently deceased television variety show host Ed Sullivan. When Belushi came on in Philadelphia as Bruce, "there was a sort of gasp," Flaherty recalled. "It didn't get a laugh or even an 'Aw, come on.' John liked that reaction, but I thought, 'I'm not in comedy for that.' I like a good laugh and applause." He wasn't alone in these sentiments. According to Michael Simmons, who had joined the company as road manager, "a lot of people around the show felt uncomfortable with the *National Lampoon* mean streak." Oddly enough, the sunny-spirited Radner was apparently unaffected by the dark *Lampoon* view. "Gilda didn't seem to mind the aggressive stuff," her pal Flaherty observed. "She wouldn't come up with it herself, but we could give her the blackest thing to do and she'd do it." "The Dead Sullivan Show," for example, began with a literal bang as Radner, portraying Jackie Kennedy complete with trademark pink pillbox hat, ducked under a desk at the sound of a starting gun.

In contrast to Beatts, who dealt with being the only woman by trying to be tougher than the men, Radner took the more traditional route of being supportive and winsome. "On the *Radio Hour*, she would joke about it and say, 'I'll make the coffee, fellas,'" Flaherty said, "but she would work closely on the things she was in and help make those characters she played as funny as possible." Small boned and large eyed, Radner had a waiflike vulnerability and openness that her coworkers found endearing. Afraid of flying, she had planned on traveling to the Toronto leg of the tour by train, but her cast mates convinced her to take the plane with them the next day and stayed up with her during a sleepless night, giving her Valiums at intervals. "The next morning she's downed out of her skull. Not," Michael Simmons was quick to point out, "that she did drugs usually—it was just for the flight. Anyway, she made a little sign for herself that said 'Hi. My name is Gilda, I'm not afraid of flying' and wore it on the plane."

If Radner was what several people described as "neurotic," she was not the kind of neurotic who makes life miserable for everybody else. Even if confrontational feminism was not her style, Radner appreciated the value of female solidarity. She became friendly with the *Lampoon*'s female staffers, telling them, "And I play The Girl." With The Girl comes, inevitably, The Love Trouble, and halfway into the tour Doyle-Murray asked if he could return to New York to work on the *Radio Hour*. His romance with Radner had cooled, and he was finding it difficult to concentrate among the embers. This gave Bill Murray the opportunity to join the company in time for the low point of the tour, assuming his brother's roles. "Here these people were, getting drunk and expecting to see a band. John's attitude was, 'Call the audience assholes. They love it.' I think," Flaherty speculated, "he was thinking of those New York crowds that go in for self-flagellation. You don't go into a bar in London, Ontario, where a bunch of bikers come and call them assholes."

The police in London had censorship power, so the cast had to substitute innocuous words like "lightbulb" for the usual expletives to avoid being closed down. Worst of all, the audience proved to be recidivists. "Matty had warned us we'd better have two shows' worth of material because in some of these small clubs we'd have the same audience for the second show," Ramis said, "but we had so much trouble getting material for one show, no way could we have enough for a second set." Then in London, the cast found, as Murray said, "there was only one audience's worth of people in the whole town. And they hated us."

Escaping from London, the cast moved on to a rock club called the El Mocambo in Toronto, where at least they could tap the Second City following. Nevertheless, they were still in a club and, not being stand-up comedians, were not used to competing with the beverage service for the audience's attention. Second City may have been improvisational theater but it was still *theater*, and actors came out of it expecting to be listened to. "I hate clubs. The noise of the bar, the talking," said Belushi in 1975. When Belushi introduced himself to the comedian and Second City alum Shelley Berman on an airplane, "Berman looked at me for a moment and said 'Stay out of the clubs,'" Belushi recalled. "That's all. Then he said it again: 'Stay out of the clubs.'"

After playing one club, Belushi would recover from the experience in another, an after-hours joint called the 505 run by Dan Aykroyd and his younger brother. Aykroyd was proud of his establishment even though, in the proprietor's words, it "bordered on serious squalor at times," like when he heard scrabbling in the bottom of the toilet bowl and looked down to discover an intrepid rat heading for the family jewels.

At least one person in the Toronto audience was paying attention to the show. This was Ivan Reitman, a twenty-seven-year-old film producer and fan of Radner's from her Second City days. "Ivan saw an unusual thing," Ramis recalled. "The audience didn't leave, and when we came to do a second show that started exactly like the first, they started booing. But we'd developed a technique of instantly improvising a second show. It didn't work too well in London, but our first night in Toronto, Ivan saw us starting to make these adjustments, and he was tremendously impressed."

According to Simmons, Reitman was so impressed "he told my son, 'I would do anything to be involved with the *Lampoon.*' He kept calling me and calling me. And one day, after he'd been calling me once a week for three months, everything hit the fan and I said to him, 'How'd you like to come to New York and produce *The National Lampoon Show*?' I needed somebody to watch it, and I was just too busy. And Ivan said, 'I'd cut off my right arm to do that.' He almost passed out he was so excited."

Reitman, who admits to thinking "the Canadian supplement to the *National Lampoon* was the greatest thing that ever happened," had a somewhat less dramatic version of events. "I was a big fan of the *National Lampoon* during its golden years," he said, "and I thought someone should make a *Lampoon* movie. There didn't seem to be anyone making comedy movies for my generation, not antiestablishment movies," if he doesn't count such films as De Palma's *Greetings*, Robert Downey Sr.'s *Putney Swope*, *A Hard Day's Night*, or John Waters's already considerable output, to name just a few.

Having perceived a market vacuum, Reitman "looked up who the publisher was, got the phone number from information, and just called him up. I introduced myself and said, 'I'm a film producer. Let's make a movie.' Matty said, 'I get calls about making movies every day of the week. But how about doing a stage show seeing as how you're an experienced theatrical producer?' "—a reputation Reitman had earned by coproducing *The Magic Show*, a Broadway hit of the time.

But first, Reitman had to get the performers to trust him. "I remember after I had made the deal with Matty walking into a room in New York with all these people and it was like, 'Who is this weird Canadian?' They were a formidable group," he recalled. Like a new lion tamer getting to know his charges, Reitman took it one step at a time. "I said, 'I want to take the show to New York. We have to develop it much further and polish it and focus it, and I'd like to help you do it.' Then there was just silence in the room. It's not that they said anything nasty. They didn't say anything at all. But I just braved it out."

"Ivan dressed like a nerd, a dork," said *Lemmings*' Paul Jacobs, who was on *The National Lampoon Show* tour as musical director. There was a certain formality in Reitman's demeanor that the cast may have mistaken for Canadian dorkiness, but it was in fact an Eastern European gravity. Reitman had learned early that life was a serious business. His mother was an Auschwitz survivor, and his father had fought with the resistance during World War II. The whole family, including the four-year-old boy, had fled Czechoslovakia in 1951, hiding under the floor-boards of a tugboat for five days. Another product of a parochial school (in his case Hebrew school), Reitman began his film career at college in Ontario with a $1,800 short called "Orientation," a comedy about the grim college rite of the same name. Remarkably, 20th Century Fox bought the short and distributed it to Canadian movie theaters.

After his first and only full-time job, a brief stint producing a children's TV show called *Coming Up Rosie* that featured Dan Aykroyd as a surly janitor, Reitman directed *Cannibal Girls*, a horror-movie parody. It was bought by Roger Corman's American International Pictures, which specialized in low-budget genre-exploitation films, and Reitman was launched as a producer of same.

These included the first two features by director David Cronenberg (who can forget the immortal *Orgy of the Blood Parasites*?) as well as a film called *The Columbus of Sex*. The latter led to the mild-mannered, clean-living Reitman incurring a fine making an obscene film. This brush with sleaze undoubtedly would have gained him points in the eyes of *The National Lampoon Show* cast, but by the time he hooked up with them, Reitman was better known for his association with the wholesome and toothy Canadian magician Doug Henning, a college friend. Henning's show *Spellbound*, produced by Reitman in Canada, was picked up by the same James Nederlander who had wanted to move *Lemmings* uptown. Under the title *The Magic Show*, it ran on Broadway for five years.

The excursion into theater was basically a detour for Reitman. His primary goal remained movies, and his agreeing to produce *The National Lampoon Show* in New York was a theatrical means to a filmic end. "The combination of talent was so astounding it was like an inspirational shower for me," he recalled. "It just opened my eyes in terms of what the possibilities were in film, and I immediately knew I would have to make movies with them, that they would all be famous, that this was where comedy was going."

While *The National Lampoon Show* may have been where comedy was going, some members of the cast weren't sure they wanted to go with it. Flaherty had decided to leave the show after going to see a Second City show in Toronto where "the audience was paying attention. But," he said, "I was getting depressed anyway. I think that's when the *Lampoon* humor finally wore me down, playing those audiences, looking at life from the black side." Belushi tried to dissuade Flaherty, telling him, "Boy, it's good to be a hit in New York. You don't know . . . it's the best feeling in the world." But Flaherty remained unconvinced and, with Doyle-Murray stepping back in to replace him, went off to join a new Second City offshoot in sedate Pasadena. By the time *The National Lampoon Show* opened in New York two months later, Flaherty was "sort of wishing I was back with it. I thought, 'This is taking it to the extreme,'" he said, "going from people throwing things and booing to [mystified Pasadeneans] scratching their heads."

Ramis had his own reservations and put a two-month cap on his contract for the New York run. "The strength of *Lemmings* for me was the excellent song parodies and the tightness of the music. We had nothing like that. That's one reason I was skeptical about the show myself," he said. In other words, without an overarching concept like the Woodstock parody to give it shape, the show most closely resembled the unfocused first act of *Lemmings*.

Meanwhile, in the run-up to the New York opening, the last *Radio Hour* went out the week of Christmas 1974, with Bill Murray playing a mean Santa. "For John Belushi I have nothing! Hah!" he snarls. Then, after replying to all of trusting little Gilda's timid requests for presents with "No, you can't have it," he dumps her off of his lap and tells her, "There's no more *Lampoon* radio show! We're taking it away!"

"When it was over," Tischler recalled, "everyone was both relieved and sad." But there was a new job to do and a new producer determined to whip the show into shape. "After a month or two, they came to trust me in a wary sort of way," Reitman recalled. "I think they realized that

I was a good guy as opposed to a bad guy—they divided the world into those categories."

Reitman assigned Ramis the task of imposing order on the morass of material. Although Ramis did appear on stage, his tendency to prioritize the show as a whole—as opposed to being primarily concerned with how many lines he had—marked him as essentially a writer rather than a performer. "I'd think in broad strokes and conceptual ways partly because I didn't dwell on what it was I would be doing in a scene or a show," he admitted. "Somehow because of my own need for structure, I naturally wanted to help everyone else structure what they were doing, and it seemed to help. Then I'd wonder what I was going to do."

When it came to translating the script to the stage, the responsibility fell, in a vague way, to Belushi, probably as much from force of personality as anything else. "Belushi was the main creative force," Reitman recalled. "He was the one who in the end said, 'Nah, nah, nah, we're going to do it like this' and people listened to him." But Belushi's membership in the group meant that he could be swayed, unable to view the show with the cool ruthlessness required to create a suitably professional polish. Reitman "sort of panicked" and, three weeks into rehearsal, decided to bring in an outside director.

Finding someone the cast would listen to was a challenge. "No one came to New York a humble amateur. We all felt like we were stars in our hometown," as Ramis said. "We were pretty cocky and arrogant in general and weren't impressed by too much in comedy." He suggested Charles Ludlam, playwright, star, and moving force behind the Ridiculous Theatrical Company, an Off-Off-Broadway ensemble. Ludlam's late-60s roots were in late-night seat-of-the-pants genre parodies with titles like *Eunuchs of the Forbidden City* and *When Queens Collide*, which drew heavily on the lamé-glitter aesthetic of drag revues. The plots were melodramatic, the music hokey, and the style of acting over-the-top, but Ludlam became an increasingly accomplished writer of farces that combined sophisticated in-jokes and broad slapstick. Like the *Lampoon*, his work was simultaneously refined and raunchy.

Ramis took Belushi to see a Ridiculous adaptation of *Camille*. It was built around Ludlam's tour de force performance as the eponymous heroine, and Belushi, though no fan of high camp, may have recognized an actor who was as risk taking and dynamic as he was. But Ludlam wanted to pursue his own work, and instead of an inspired original with an off-the-wall comic sensibility, ultimately the cast found itself with a safe, known quantity who had strong professional credentials and mainstream credibility.

This was Martin Charnin, who had directed the polished and long-running Julius Monk Upstairs at the Downstairs revues, a sophisticated entertainment very different from *The National Lampoon Show*'s reckless charge into bad taste. With only three weeks remaining until the opening, Reitman put Charnin in charge. "Frankly, the cast didn't like him," Reitman admitted. "His sensibility was a little too blow-dried, too ad world for them. But he did sharpen the show and make it slicker."

"All we knew," Ramis recalled, "was he was a Broadway guy who would come in and say, 'OK—applause, applause, applause' [director shorthand for 'Let's keep things moving here']. I think we were all skeptical of those Broadway licks he had, but he knew something about showmanship and found the best in what we were doing." When the show opened at the beginning of March 1975 at the New Palladium, a cabaret in the bowels of the Time-Life Building in the heart of midtown, what remained included Belushi checking the audience for potentially exportable illegal aliens, Murray impersonating chain-smoking talk show host Tom Snyder, and a parody of America's current TV sweetheart featuring Radner as Rhoda Tyler Moore, a spunky blind girl trying to make it in New York. Belushi played her boyfriend who would try to make himself appear a hero in her eyes, as it were, by altering his voice and attacking her, then chasing the "mugger" off using his normal voice (according to Belushi, sightless audience members would come backstage and relate even better blind jokes). In case anyone was left unoffended by the end of the evening, the cast serenaded the audience at the show's conclusion with a parody of "You're the Top" called "You're the Pits" (at least until the Cole Porter estate threatened to sue a month into the New York run).

The New York audience didn't take to the material any better than the Ontario bikers had. "It's one thing to write with hostility," Ramis observed, "but it's another thing to stand on stage and put it out there. The show was hostile and abusive to the audience, and it was a very rowdy crowd," a crowd he described as "probably the first audience that tried to bring their own liquor into the Time-Life Building," a high-rise corporate office tower.

The reviews didn't make the cast feel any better. Some were good, but more typical was this one from *Cue* magazine: "There's obviously a large market for this sort of disrespectful slop-jar humor. If you can laugh at the physically handicapped, the mentally retarded or—perhaps the single most odious moment in the show—[First Lady] Mrs. Ford's mastectomy, you'll enjoy it." Charnin had clearly not chosen to impose too much legitimacy and tastefulness. But not everyone was negative. "The revue is super—no bricks or bats, just good clever fun," wrote one Doug Henning in *Playbill*.

By the time Ramis left in April (to be replaced by future *Law & Order* stalwart Richard Belzer), the rowdy audiences and nihilistic material were getting to the cast. One night comedian Martin Mull came to see the show and "sat at a table down in front and yakked it up with some friends all through the show," said Gerrit Graham, who also happened to be in the audience. When Mull then had the temerity to go backstage to tell the cast how fabulous they were, Murray went for him. "Bill had to be restrained," said Graham. "Then he chased Martin all the way down the street with shouts of 'You're a medium talent, Mull! A *medium* talent!'" (Other accounts have Murray hurling this charge at Chase instead after a backstage fight at *Saturday Night Live*.)

Less dramatically but rather more poignantly, Belushi was found crying backstage one night after being heckled about his weight. Radner, meanwhile, "kept on threatening to give up on showbiz and was very depressed on a regular basis," said Reitman, who gave her periodic pep talks, telling her "You're going to be on some television show and you're going to be one of the great comediennes in America."

The troupe had another firm supporter in Kenney. "Doug's focus definitely shifted away from the magazine, and he plugged in very comfortably with the actors in *The National Lampoon Show*," Weidman said, adding, "He wasn't starstruck; he was just very turned on by what the group was doing."

"Doug would come by every day and just watch," Ramis recalled, and when Belushi's younger brother Jim went to the show, Kenney went with him, giving his expert assessment of each cast member: "Gilda—everybody loves her; Bill—he'll work a lot; John—he'll be a big star," the editor predicted. Kelly was another frequent visitor to rehearsals and even O'Donoghue dropped by occasionally to see what his *Radio Hour* successors were up to. As for the rest of the staff, "most of them turned up at the show bringing friends and guests," Ramis said. "They seemed to enjoy having someplace to go besides the *Lampoon*."

This camaraderie was reflected in a photo that appears on the back of the *Lampoon*'s fourth album, *Gold Turkey*, a 1975 "best of" collection from the radio shows. Nearly the whole *Radio Hour* crew past and present—writers, actors, musicians, and production people—are represented. Guest and McConnachie are incongruously clean-cut in suits and ties, while McCall and a couple of the older actors from Tischler's Rolodex wear turtlenecks and sport jackets. Most of the other men are dressed down in workshirts, T-shirts, and lumberjack shirts. Kelly and Doyle-Murray, with matching sideburns and moustaches, look more alike than Doyle-Murray and his actual brother do. The shaggy-haired, bespectacled Ramis could pass for a grad student. A beaming Kenney appears to have cut his hair and cleaned up his act. Prager wears a preppy white cotton turtleneck and Beatts is, as usual, in a snappy vintage outfit. A tough Richard Belzer lurks at the back of the photo in sunglasses and a biker hat. It amounts to a *Lampoon* yearbook photo that united most of its print, theater, and radio participants before events whirled them off on trajectories that would have been unimaginable at the time.

As with *Lemmings*, Simmons sent out a cast of then-unknowns, including Belzer and singer Meatloaf, in a touring version with a grueling schedule of eighty-nine consecutive one-night stands. Meanwhile, with the Time-Life run finished, the original cast was at loose ends. Belushi was fretting because he felt his *Lampoon* association hindered his being appreciated as a serious actor. "Nobody considers you legitimate because you're *National Lampoon*. Because you're in a revue they think you can't act. You're not serious," he said in 1975. Belushi's admiration for Marlon Brando and his desire to take on meaty noncomedic roles that would show his full range were well-known to his colleagues. But to get those roles he would have to audition, something he hadn't had to do since he'd come to New York two years earlier, and the prospect unnerved him. Nevertheless, within months he would go through an audition for a television show to be produced by Lorne Michaels, a hip, affable, Hawaiian-shirted writer-producer from Canada who was frequently in the audience at *The National Lampoon Show*. Had Simmons known how Michaels's plans would affect the *Lampoon*'s burgeoning satire empire, he never would have let the Canadian in the theater.

14

CHANNELING

Michaels was planning a comedy-variety show, which he envisioned as a combination of the Muppets, two rock bands, short films by a roster of indie filmmakers, a parody news segment, a different star host each week, "and then this group of supporting players—the cast." Michaels had first presented this somewhat jumbled concept to NBC in 1972 and gotten nowhere, but then two years later had more success with Dick Ebersol, a twenty-seven-year-old executive considered NBC's link to that elusive youth audience. Ebersol's mandate included developing late-night programming, and in February 1975 he persuaded two NBC gatekeepers to meet with the Canadian.

With his elegant manner and fine-boned face framed by dark curls—not to mention his working uniform of jeans, sneakers, and a corduroy jacket—the twenty-nine-year-old Michaels more resembled the girls' favorite sociology professor than a slick network television player. Nevertheless, he was highly professional when it came to delivering the Pitch, the aspiring producer's equivalent of being on the mound at the bottom of the ninth.

Michaels had first persuaded his way onto the airwaves in 1965 with a short radio program for the Canadian Broadcasting Corporation, having made his mark while still an undergraduate by creating the University of Toronto's equivalent of *Beyond the Fringe* the year before. In 1961, he had seen the original *Beyond the Fringe* and been exposed to the whole burgeoning UK satire scene during a summer in London with his future wife Rosie Shuster. This did not, however, make him aspire to be a satirist. "I'm very wary of labels and definitions in these matters because there're a lot of things I like," he declared. "Satire is just one of them." America, he felt, was more into comedy, but not necessarily comedy with a satirical bent. Or, as Shuster said, "American humor is more visceral. I think of Belushi as very American. It's more a cult of personality. You wouldn't see a Canadian showing off, grunting like that."

Shuster was in a position to know as the daughter of Frank Shuster, one of Canada's most popular indigenous comedians. Shuster senior took a parental interest in his daughter's high school sweetheart, advising him to adopt a stage name since Canadians might consider his real one, Lorne Lipowitz, a bit exotic. On returning from England, Michaels developed a stand-up comedy routine with writing partner Hart Pomerantz that resulted in the CBC radio show, and by 1967 the team was commuting to New York to perform at comedy clubs. This led to writing jokes for, among others, Joan Rivers and Woody Allen. By then phasing out of stand-up, Allen never did use the Canadians' material, but he did compliment Michaels on a conceptual gag about tracking down the one person in the world who has exactly the same thoughts as you at exactly the same time only to find that person's line constantly busy.

Providing monologue fodder led to Michaels's signing with a young William Morris agent, the future recording mogul and DreamWorks founder David Geffen, who got the team jobs on an NBC comedy-variety series, *The Beautiful Phyllis Diller Show*. Excited by the opportunity to work on a network show, Michaels managed to overlook the fact that Diller's material (which included a warm-up joke that went, "What's brown and has holes in it? Swiss shit") was not up to his usual standards. The viewing public was more discerning, and the show lasted a mere nine weeks.

In 1969 the team got what appeared to be a bigger break: becoming junior writers on the hot comedy show *Laugh-In*, a collection of unrelated sketches each building to a gag, recurring characters, and catchphrases popular with young audiences at the time. Michaels soon discovered that he was really paying his dues. "Your work was rewritten all the time, and writers weren't encouraged to come to the studio. We weren't part of the show in the same way the cast was," he said. He also found that the head writer, later a Nixon speechwriter, did not appreciate his jokes about the new president. The hugely successful *Laugh-In* was ready to embrace superficial irreverence but studiously avoided any real political or economic critique.

This toothless approach was new to Michaels, but then he had been spoiled at the CBC. "You were allowed to say whatever you wanted to on the CBC. Particularly in political comedy there were no restrictions," he recalled. Just as the *Radio Hour* writers imagined that they were using a commercial medium to subvert the values of commercialism, so he "always used to think we were bringing down the government of Canada every Wednesday. Of course, later we found out no one was listening, or if they were listening they didn't care."

With their *Laugh-In* contract at an end, the two writers returned to Canada, where they were hired to produce TV specials with a format that featured a supporting repertory company, musical guests, and appearances by comedians such as Dan Aykroyd, who by that time had a CBC radio show of his own. Michaels and Shuster bought a large house in Toronto that became the center of a lively scene, a hive of creative (and, by some accounts, procreative) activity. Somehow they found time for another trip to England, where they attended a taping of *Monty Python's Flying Circus*. "It was miraculous to me, a revelation," Michaels later said.

Python revealed to the former gag writer that a sketch did not have to end with a punch line. It also showed that you could carry over elements or characters from one sketch to another—for example, when the three Spanish cardinals introduced in one sketch (threatening heretics with fearsome instruments of torture such as "The Comfy Chair") interrupt subsequent scenes by bursting in and shouting, "No one expects the Spanish Inquisition!"

Besides parodies of specific formats (such as a hard-hitting BBC documentary on men who dress up as mice), *Python* mocked its own processes. For example, in one sketch Eric Idle enters as a policeman and begins to arrest "this entire show" on "offences against the Getting Out of Sketches without Using A Proper Punch Line Act, namely, simply ending every bleeding sketch by just having a policeman come in—" but then John Cleese, also dressed as a policeman, pops up, collaring Idle and saying, "Hold it."

Calling attention to process was just one indication of the Pythons' trust in their viewers' intelligence. Like the Lampooners, they didn't see any reason to limit their escalating circles of absurdity, wide-ranging frame of reference, or highbrow allusions for fear of frightening off viewers. This permitted jokes like the man who's writing anagram versions of Shakespeare ("Two Nentlemeg of Verona, Twelfth Thing, and The Chamrent of Venice"). The Pythons were also allowed to fail, an essential component of taking creative chances, a luxury the big commercial networks felt they could not afford. With millions of dollars at stake, formula ruled the day.

By the time his CBC contract ended in 1972, Michaels had split with Pomerantz and was back in LA, working on everything from comedy specials to a Perry Como Christmas show. To stave off boredom, he thought about what he would do when he was producing his own comedy-variety show. In the fall of 1973, he started having serious discussions with Lily Tomlin, another *Laugh-In* alum who was equally interested in breaking the format's conventions. If *Monty Python* revealed the possibilities of absurdism and format bending, Tomlin, whom he considered "a genius," revealed the potential of realism when he worked with her on a special for CBS, with a commitment to detail so thorough she insisted that the appliances on a kitchen set actually work. She demanded a similar level of believability from the material her writers provided, and Michaels compared writing for her to "being a tailor. You're designing to someone's talent. You tend to write comedy that might be more quirky, more coming out of character. Lily wouldn't string a bunch of jokes together."

For the special, Tomlin wanted to explore a Pythonesque format that would enable her to get out of sketches without building to a gag, and decided to have her best-known *Laugh-In* character, the pinch-mouthed phone operator Ernestine, watching television and switching channels with many acerbic comments and snorts. "Lily used to use the phrase 'cultural feedback'—playing the culture back to itself," recalled Michaels, who, influenced by fashionable Canadian media theorist and Utopia 4 member Marshall McLuhan, had a similar view of the function of mass media comedy.

This commentary was exemplified by "20th Century Blues," a blithe and upbeat Fred Astaire–like musical number, which sees Tomlin romping past overflowing dumps, gun stores, gasless gas stations (a legacy of the 1973 Arab oil export embargo), and other emblems of the grim present while merrily singing of imminent ecological collapse.

The 1975 Tomlin special, which won Emmys for the writers, was not the first time comedy reflecting a contemporary sensibility had made it onto the air. The most notable example was *The Smothers Brothers*, also on CBS. When they first went on the air on Sunday nights in 1967, Tom and Dick Smothers were two nice, well-behaved comedians, more daring than the network's comedy veterans but far milder than boundary-shattering contemporaries like George Carlin. But then Tom Smothers started marching to the proverbial different drum and before long was pushing for guests like Joan Baez and The Committee.

In 1968, the Smothers produced a show that appeared in their time slot during their summer hiatus, packing the writing staff with young dissidents like Steve Martin and Rob Reiner. "*The Smothers Brothers* was a much hipper show than *Laugh-In*," Michaels declared, admitting that he was "very envious" of the people working on it. CBS wasn't as enthusiastic and cancelled the show after a year, despite its Emmy Award.

The Smothers and other attempts to lure the youth market were in prime time, when the price of ads, and sponsors' expectations of audience numbers, ran high. *The Smothers Brothers Show* had met commercial expectations, but their prime-time slot put any controversial material in the spotlight. Late Saturday night, on the other hand, was clearly a throwaway period, fit only for reruns. During his meeting with the NBC executives, Michaels played off this, describing a show with an off-the-cuff look, "as if the network had closed down for the night and these guys had snuck into the studio." The pitch worked and got him a meeting with the president of NBC, the final step to getting the go-ahead.

Ironically, now that he was finally on the verge of realizing his ambition, Michaels had become burnt out on television and was collaborating on a screenplay for Paramount with a writer-producer named Ken Shapiro. Shapiro also had been a writer on the Tomlin special, but unlike Michaels had been unable to subordinate his own way of doing things to Tomlin's approach, and his tenure was brief. "Ken," said his frequent collaborator Lane Sarasohn, "was like W. C. Fields. He didn't compromise."

Shapiro's creative aspirations had started with little radio improvisations while a student at Bard. These sketches were vastly admired by fellow student Chevy Chase, who took to crossing Shapiro's path and performing spontaneous slapstick, like falling out of nearby rosebushes, to attract his attention. After graduating in 1966, Shapiro was among the first people to own a new gadget from Sony: a portable video camera known as a portapack. It weighed a hefty 5.9 lbs and, together with the playback deck, cost almost as much as one of the cheap, fuel-efficient Japanese compacts popularized by the gas shortage.

Shapiro soon began filming sketches, with the portapack acting as the equivalent of the *Lampoon* cocktail napkin. "We taped ourselves doing ideas we had come up with," Chase said, "and if they were funny, we'd use them. We were very open and smoked a lot of pot and tried everything." In 1967, the duo, along with Bard classmate Sarasohn, put together ninety minutes' worth of material under the title *Channel One* and showed it in an East Village theater where Chase's duties included taking the few tickets that were sold. Undeterred, Shapiro decided to produce a second series, largely inspired by the introduction of a huge (and expensive) consumer video recorder that, unlike the portapack, permitted editing.

Although smack-dab in the middle of the East Village in the Summer of Love, when the redolent scents of patchouli and incense issuing from the neighborhood's many Indian clothing boutiques mingled with the more traditional aromas of car exhaust and rotting garbage, the *Channel One* group was not really part of the scene. "Even as we lived down there, we set ourselves apart from it in some way. We felt ourselves above everybody else. We had our own little clique," Chase recalled. This attitude kept them detached from a maelstrom of innovative creative output that included other portapack early adopters like Nam June Paik, widely considered to be the father of video art.

"We were experimental but not experimental like acid TV," Chase said. "We were not anything but just be funny. We weren't pointedly satirical. We were mostly interested in laughs." Their material bore the stamp of television comedy pioneer Ernie Kovacs, like a wordless sketch in which a man goes through his morning bathroom routine as the realization slowly dawns that he has four arms (Chase standing behind Shapiro) or President Johnson's 1967 State of the Union speech with a laugh track substituted for applause.

"It was slick comedy dressed up in dungarees," observed John Lollos, a former NBC producer who started working with Shapiro in 1969. Ultimately, the *Channel One* gang prospered, producing two more shows before releasing a best-of compilation called *Groove Tube*. By this time, however, Chase had become tired of being second banana and left the group, to be replaced once more by his *Lemmings* successor, Richard Belzer.

"We had a bad parting of the ways," Chase said, "because I just didn't get credit for my writing, nor did I get paid for it." Despite their dueling egos, Chase and Shapiro were creatively in sync. Unlike the Second City crowd, their approach to performance was strictly a product of the small screen. "The media babies had very little interest in theater. I remember thinking, 'My God, they let these people come out of school in this condition?' This was a drug culture I stepped into after eight years at NBC and I was in a bit of culture shock myself," the urbane producer recalled.

After runs ranging from days (LA) to a couple of years (Boston), in 1970 *Groove Tube* opened on New York's chic Upper East Side. It wasn't a great financial success, but it did mean that the show could be reviewed (*TV Guide* compared it to "a bop on the head with a sock full of gravel"), which enabled Lollos to send it on a four-year tour, transmitting closed-circuit television broadcasts at some 2,400 colleges. "We did great in Midwestern schools," Sarasohn recalled, "but we couldn't get attention at a place like Harvard." The success of *Groove Tube* led Lollos to form a new company called Video Tape Network, which provided similar closed-circuit tours for other tapes such as the antidrug cult classic *Reefer Madness*, rock concerts, and independent documentaries, all under the rubric "Television that won't rot your mind."

Lollos wanted to make a tape of *Lemmings*, but after Simmons declined to invest, he was reduced to recording a live performance in 1973. The resulting tape suffered from poor audio quality and was not a big draw, although Lollos believed that this had less to do with its technical shortcomings than with the fact that by then Woodstock jokes were already passé. By contrast, at the height of the *Groove Tube* tour in 1971, Sarasohn and Shapiro were each pulling down $20,000 a year (more than $100,000 today) from rentals. Their next goal was a *Groove Tube* for the big screen, but after burning through most of a $125,000 loan from his father, Shapiro shut the production down. He soon started again, this time abandoning video for shooting on more expensive and slicker-looking film after raiding all the money in a trust fund that had already paid for those expensive portapacks.

Much of *Groove Tube* the movie was in the vein of Cheech and

Chong, the less-than-sophisticated dopester comedy team, such as the Vietnam report from villages called "Longh Wang" and "Phoc Hu." A more polished sketch involved a children's program featuring Shapiro as Koko the Clown telling all of the big people to leave the room in a high squeaky voice, then taking requests for the good parts from various dirty books and reading *Fanny Hill* in his normal blasé drawl. This was the source of *Groove Tube*'s appeal to the youth audience: a sense of complicity generated not by political conviction so much as by the feeling that they were initiates into a world of guilt-free pleasures closed to their elders.

Unfortunately for Shapiro, those elders still controlled film distribution, and *Groove Tube*'s R-rated content and funky look meant that he was unable to find a distributor for a year. Eventually ten dentists looking for a tax shelter put up the money to get it into theaters, and *Groove Tube* the movie opened in 1974, three years after it was finished.

It was worth the wait. Produced for $350,000, it grossed over $30 million, and Shapiro was hailed as a boy wonder who had found a way to capture some of the huge youth market's disposable income. After paying back his father and the dentists, Shapiro was left with a tidy $1.4 million. He bought a fanciful house in Beverly Hills, complete with a funicular down to the pool, where he held court as the new prince of Youth Comedy.

In the immediate wake of the film's success, Paramount hired him as a consultant with a mandate to develop youth market films, and he set to work with Michaels on a screenplay (that ultimately remained unproduced). They chose as their subject phone phreaking. This was a phenomenon in which young engineering wizards—whose ranks, legend has it, included Apple founders Steve Jobs and Steve Wozniak—built mysterious "black boxes" that could crack the long-distance codes of the phone company (in those days there was only one), thus enabling their friends to make unbilled nuisance calls to people in Tokyo. Michaels and Shapiro could relate to these daring young prodigies mastering corporate technology and subverting it for their own ends.

Groove Tube also inspired another media parody group: the Kentucky Fried Theater, which was hatched in Wisconsin in 1971. By 1974 the three masterminds—Jim Abrahams and brothers Jerry and David Zucker, who in 1980 became the kings of movie parodies with *Airplane!*—had moved west, joining other comedy writers and producers bouncing around Los Angeles like wandering electrons, occasionally bumping into each other and hoping to latch onto something. Among them was Chase, who, in his own casual just-passing-through way, had managed to land a William Morris agent (the head of the powerful agency's New York office to boot) and acquire some respectable credentials writing for a television special starring the mainstream comedian Alan King.

Armed with the Writers Guild Award he picked up for the special, Chase moved to LA with, he said, "the hope that I would write for Lily Tomlin." Shortly thereafter, all his belongings, including his writing samples, were stolen from his motel room, and soon he was "living on unemployment while trying to find work as an actor. There was nothing," he said. He plugged away while sharing a house with an ascending Guest, who actually *was* hired to write for the 1974 Tomlin special, thanks to the comedienne being impressed by his *Lemmings* performance (but "he never cleaned his room, and I did the dishes all the time," Chase recalled). Eventually a light appeared at the end of Chase's tunnel when he was hired to write for the Smothers Brothers, who had returned in a brief, more bloodless reincarnation on NBC.

Unlike his reticent roommate, Chase was not backward about coming forward. "What I liked about writing for TV," he said, "was that you're always working with other people and going from office to office trying things out." To get the Smothers's attention, he applied the same techniques that had worked with Shapiro years before. "I'd fall into their office without spilling the coffee," he recalled, "or come in with a plate of salt for a cocaine joke."

This combination of writing and falling prepared Chase to exploit a chance meeting with Michaels in March 1975, while they were both waiting in line to see the premiere of *Monty Python and the Holy Grail*. Although they didn't know each other, they had numerous mutual acquaintances and soon struck up a conversation. Once again, Chase literally fell into something and was offered a theoretical job on Michaels's theoretical Saturday-night variety show on the spot. But Chase, having failed to convince Michaels to hire him as an on-camera performer, turned down the offer in favor of appearing in summer stock (he would later reconsider).

The summer of 1974 also found Ramis in LA. He had been invited by a college friend, Michael Shamberg, to write and direct what he termed "a very funky low-budget video trying to look like film" for PBS. Back in 1967, Shamberg and Ramis had shared a group living arrangement with other Washington University students in St. Louis. "It was a big brownstone building and four or five people lived in each apartment and it only cost each person fifteen dollars a month," recalled Allen Rucker, another member of the household.

After graduation, Shamberg worked as a reporter for a Chicago newspaper and ultimately *Time*. This promising trajectory was interrupted when he "did an article on people doing experimental video and that seemed more interesting than *Time*, so I quit," he said, and, moving to New York, started hanging out in the same alternative video circles that *Channel One* distanced themselves from.

Unlike *Channel One*, these videomakers weren't simply out to be funny; their work came complete with a set of theoretical underpinnings influenced heavily by the *Whole Earth* trinity of Marshall McLuhan, Gregory Bateson (an anthropologist who pioneered theories of cybernetics and cognitive science), and Buckminster Fuller. Politics was now "a function of Media America, not vice-versa," Shamberg observed prophetically in his 1971 book, *Guerrilla Television*. Accordingly, "no alternate cultural vision is going to succeed in Media America unless it has its own alternate information structures, not just alternate content pumped across the existing ones . . . and that's what videotape, with cable

TV and videocassettes, is ultimately all about," he proclaimed, though at the time hardly anyone knew what cable television was. Shamberg was forced to note that the publisher was a subsidiary of CBS "whom I have criticized strongly in the text," he wrote preemptively, adding, "Rather than have some reviewer gleefully point out the irony, I do it for you."

Applying Bateson's cybernetic theories, Shamberg declared the "portapack ecology" healthier because it supported "diversity rather than uniformity," was "symbiotic rather than competitive," and tended toward "decentralization and heterogeneity," ideas that neatly encapsulated what was counter about the counterculture in general. When Shamberg applied these evolutionary criteria to the broadcast networks, which he colorfully termed "beast television," he decided the beast was headed for extinction due to being "overly competitive, fabulously over-centralized, and wildly unstable." Not that Shamberg had much use for old-school print, asserting that "print structures are worthless in an electronic culture."

"We didn't divide art and journalism or comedy and journalism or amateur and professional. We didn't cut television between news and entertainment," Rucker said. Instead, "having realized that Abbie Hoffman could put on an American flag shirt and stop the culture in its tracks, we realized we wanted to exploit the media to our own ends." Of course, as Shamberg pointed out, "the Revolution ended when Abbie Hoffman shut up for the first commercial."

As a step toward implementing alternative media structures, Shamberg became a founding partner of a media collective called Raindance. Raindance made low-tech tapes, taught videomaking in schools, and put out a resource guide called *Radical Software*, which proposed that progressive elements had more to gain by infiltrating the media than by going into traditional politics.

One convert was Rucker, who was studying film at Stanford. "There was all this cybernetic and media mumbo jumbo," he said, "but basically it was people playing with technology." The organizational arm of the *Whole Earth Catalog* gave Rucker and some other Stanford students money to set up community video projects. "It was very mild, generous, and civic-minded," Rucker recalled, "but through the *Whole Earth Catalog*, we met the Ant Farm."

The Ant Farm was a group of tyro architects who, influenced by Bateson, Fuller, and similar *Whole Earth* gurus, abandoned traditional architecture in favor of inflatable structures with a small environmental footprint. This led to conceptual art projects like 1974's "Cadillac Ranch," where ten Cadillacs were buried waist-deep in the Texas earth alongside Route 66 to create "a monument to the rise and fall of the tailfin."

After providing the illustrations for *Guerrilla Television*, the Ant Farmers customized a Chevy van with an inflatable shower stall heated by a solar collector and roamed the West, shooting an unsuspecting public (with handheld video cameras). "We'd do things like drive through Scottsdale, Arizona, and see there was a big hotel opening with a ribbon cutting," said Rucker, who became an associate Ant Farmer and was aboard the van for six months in 1971. "We used to wear these long lab coats and sometimes masks and we'd be in and out like, 'Who were those masked men?' That," he said, "was real guerrilla television."

Meanwhile, Videofreex, an East Coast group known for its relatively high technical standards, was also traveling around spontaneously filming. The group had been quickly formed "to take advantage of CBS's money," as Shamberg put it, after the network decided to develop a youth-oriented series to replace the Smothers Brothers. Armed with the network's cash, the Videofreex hit the road in 1969 in *their* media van, documenting alternative viewpoints such as that of Black Panther leader Fred Hampton, who did not stint on either politics or profanity. When the Videofreex invited two CBS executives downtown to view the unadulterated result, the network honchos "were so repelled by what they saw," according to Shamberg, "that they stumbled out early in a nervous fit." The time slot went to the rustic comedy-variety show *Hee Haw* instead.

Nevertheless, three years later, an art/comedy/documentary hybrid would find its way onto the airwaves after Shamberg moved to San Francisco. There, said Rucker, "a liberal documentary mentality which I had, a kind of bigheaded New York media intellectual mentality which Michael and the Raindance people had, and a fuck-you absurdist attitude toward life that the Ant Farm had all came together" in a loose amalgamation they named Top Value Television, or TVTV. In the manner of summoning knights to a tournament, TVTV sent out an invitation to other video tribes to help document the 1972 presidential nominating conventions.

"We said, 'Bring your equipment, we'll supply the tape, we've got plenty of nitrous oxide, we'll give you credentials, go out and shoot what you want,'" all on a production budget of zero, Rucker recalled. But even though they had "no money, no real idea of what we were doing, no experience with the process," nor had anyone made "anything more than maybe a fifteen-minute documentary," they did have what Rucker dubbed "this hot wind that propped us up—a lot of pretentious nonsense about how if you change the way the culture communicates, you change the culture—and we could convince people that what we were doing was heady stuff."

The hot wind managed to blow up $15,000, which covered the hard expenses, although it did not extend to paying anybody. But that was cool. "The point is that in an alternative economic system, you either use straight currency or trust," explained Shamberg in *Guerrilla Television*. Or, as Rucker said, "because there was no money, we laid it out in vibes. So on the TVTV credits where it says 'producer,' there're twenty-five names because of these childish '60s notions of sharing and involvement."

The first TVTV production, a record of the 1972 Republican Convention called *Four More Years*, has a remarkable unity of tone and style despite its numerous filmmakers and exudes zest and lightheartedness. With a focus on process and demystification, there are shots of the

Young Republicans rehearsing their cheers, Nixonettes being briefed on the proper way to distribute buttons and pastries, and Sammy Davis Jr. caught offstage shopping in a drugstore.

While the shaggy videomakers were hardly Republican sympathizers, they avoided editorializing or obvious mockery. Interviews, such as one with some Young Republicans angered by press reports that they were being paid to show up, are evenhanded. Protestors at the convention are similarly allowed to speak for themselves, notably a contingent of Vietnam Veterans Against the War, who parade in their wheelchairs while chanting, "Stop the Bombing."

TVTV did not confuse a dispassionate approach with dull objectivity and employed flashy visual techniques then considered not quite kosher for journalism, such as swinging the camera back and forth between representatives of the Christian Right and demonstrators engaged in an angry confrontation or showing a 1940s publicity photo of Ronald Reagan behind a microphone as a prelude to footage of the real thing giving a speech.

Four More Years was shown on assorted PBS stations before being syndicated together with a sequel covering the Democratic Convention. Not only was it critically acclaimed, it was a big hit with the Republicans, and TVTV was given funding by PBS to document the 1974 gathering of a different faithful—the followers of the pudgy "boy guru" Maharaji assembling at the Astrodome. It became clear to TVTV that they could not approach this subject un-ironically. "Even though we could explain ourselves as having some social purpose," said Rucker, "it turned out we were doing satire."

The resulting documentary, *Lord of the Universe*, won TVTV serious recognition: a prestigious duPont-Columbia Award and commissions for five more documentaries. After completing four of these, including a live-from-the-underground interview with Abbie Hoffman—by then a fugitive after skipping bail following a drug bust—in 1975 TVTV moved away from documentary altogether to do *Supervision*, a multipart fictionalized history of television that concluded nine years into the future (i.e., 1984), for PBS. Although TVTV stuck with portable video to keep costs down, they found that it was far more problematic to use with scripted work. "*Supervision* was a horrendous experience," Rucker recalled. "It wasn't guerrilla television. Guerrilla television is you've got an office, a telephone, a checkbook, some credit cards, and you're off! Suddenly we're doing scripted comedy with sets and wardrobe and so on—that shift is what rent TVTV asunder."

And there, captaining the *Titanic*, was Ramis, brought in by Shamberg to direct. The strain of weaning documentarians away from reality-based productions started to tell. Belushi's Second City colleague Gerrit Graham, who had a leading role, remembered "shooting one afternoon late in the *Supervision* schedule and Harold standing in a hallway sort of looking around, going, 'Uh . . . uh . . .' He was burned out."

In *Supervision*, Graham portrays a video guerrilla named "Gerrit" who is aided and abetted by a "fanatical follower" named "John," portrayed by a post–*National Lampoon Show* Belushi. Gerrit and John's daring idea is to force viewers to live without television for twenty-four hours. Their scheme is to infiltrate the headquarters of the giant network Supervision during the world's first simulcast and shut it down.

But the mission doesn't go quite as planned. Although John makes a suitably aggressive impression on the video security monitors ("I'm John and this is my friend, Mr. Gun"), Gerrit handles the taking of hostages in the Supervision control room somewhat ineptly ("Everybody down! No, this isn't going to work. Everybody up!"). Before this can fully develop into the inevitable Simon Says joke, the simulcast ushering in 1984 goes on the air and Gerrit and John head for the studio to take over the airwaves.

"Peoples of the world—greetings!" says Gerrit. "Supervision can be stopped! Strike at its borders as we have struck at its heart. Off now! Death to the corporate media mongers! Free the videosphere now!" he proclaims with a power salute. As Gerrit prepares to fire a gun at the camera, John, who has been compensating for his lack of lines with much expressive eyebrow arching, whispers into his ear. "But before I do," the ringleader says, "I think we ought to introduce ourselves." Smiling and settling back in his chair, the rapidly cooling firebrand continues: "I think at this point it would be remiss not to thank the many people who've enabled us to get this far, most of all our parents..." And before you can say "teleprompter," the video guerrillas, seduced by celebrity, have become what they wanted to overthrow. It wouldn't take until 1984 for life to imitate art.

15

HEY, LOOKA ME!

I n his pitch to the NBC gatekeepers, Michaels had described his show's style as "raw, disposable" humor, which made it sound a bit like sewage, but he wanted to manage their expectations about its degree of slickness. Surprisingly, even his warning that "we will always be experimenting on the air, responding to our mistakes," didn't faze them.

Securing approval from the then-ruler of NBC's late-night slot, long-time *Tonight Show* host Johnny Carson, was the last hurdle. Michaels agreed that he would avoid overlap with the *Tonight Show* when it came to booking musical acts or well-known comedians to serve as guest hosts, thus practically giving him a mandate to feature the unconventional. Regardless, *Saturday Night*'s initial budget of $134,600 per show made booking mainstream stars an unaffordable luxury.

The miniscule budget also precluded hiring veteran writers, unless they were willing to trade money for creative latitude. Michaels found one such fed-up veteran in Herb Sargent, who, in addition to having been the first head writer for the *Tonight Show*, had been the head writer on the Alan King special that Chase had worked on and Michaels's producer on that first, Emmy-winning Tomlin special.

Michaels also brought in another experienced professional he had worked with on Tomlin's second special. This was Marilyn Miller, who at twenty-three already had writing credits on hits like *The Mary Tyler Moore Show*. Miller suggested to Michaels that Michael O'Donoghue might be another likely recruit. "I didn't know his background," the producer said, maintaining that although he loved the *Radio Hour*, he didn't know any of the writers' names. As for the magazine itself, "what I remember of the *National Lampoon* tended to be covers with pictures of girls with three breasts," he said, "only because I was already in my late twenties and I thought of it as appealing to a younger audience—a hotter version of *Mad*."

Even so, Michaels suggested that O'Donoghue meet him for dinner at the Plaza, a setting designed to remind the cranky writer what vulgar television money could buy. "Yes, the money was an incentive, inasmuch as a drowning man reaches for a rat," O'Donoghue allowed, reluctant to admit just how enthusiastic he was initially.

"Money was definitely a factor," Beatts agreed forthrightly, even though the prospective salary was more or less what O'Donoghue had been making at the *Lampoon*. Still, he hadn't been getting that salary in nearly a year, and since leaving the magazine, the couple had been leading a life of what Beatts described as "grilled cheese sandwiches and putting our pennies into rolls to pay the Con Ed bills." Nevertheless, immersed in editing *Titters*, she too was reluctant to sign up at first. However, she said, "Lorne was very persuasive. I could do the show and finish the book only by giving up eating, sleeping, and sex, but he made it sound easy."

Michaels found himself up against what Beatts called "a certain '*We* are the New Wave of comedy' attitude from the *Lampoon* as well as a certain New York attitude of 'What—is some guy from Hollywood going to come in and tell *us* what's funny?'" But Michaels managed to convince the pair that they could have a regular income *and* creative freedom. "I didn't want to have to tone down ideas and Lorne said I wouldn't have to," O'Donoghue recalled.

Also in Michaels's favor was the fact that he and O'Donoghue hit it off. Both had a sense they belonged in the glamorous life. They saw their rightful place as at the center of a contemporary Algonquin Round Table or any similar coalescing of talent, wit, and self-consciousness. The upshot was that the producer ended up being "charmed by Michael. I always thought he was a brilliant and original thinker," he added, and this may have inclined O'Donoghue to forgive the producer for having the "audacity" to put forward "his kindergarten comedy theories."

However charmed he might have been, Michaels wisely figured that two people with the *Lampoon* sensibility were enough. He rounded out his team of ten with writers from very different backgrounds. One of three apprentice writer slots went to an actor and Off-Broadway playwright named Garrett Morris, who would shortly be shifted over to acting duties. Another went to Alan Zweibel, who was churning out gags for Borscht Belt comedians by night while working in a Queens deli by day when Michaels, impressed by a hand-typed collection of one thousand jokes Zweibel had presented, hired him.

The last apprentice slot went to a stand-up comedy team, Tom Davis and Al Franken (the latter a Harvard alum and unlikely future senator from Minnesota), who were among those young comedians circulating around LA. Their material was designed to appeal to the St. Tunafish crowd and would, Michaels felt, provide a balance to O'Donoghue's more arty, conceptual approach. For once someone took Michaels up on his offer right away. As far as Franken and Davis were concerned, opportunity was pounding on the door, and they were determined to roll out the welcome mat.

There remained the task of selecting the cast, with Michaels checking out the relatively small talent pool performing in New York's few (at the time) comedy clubs. "Comedy was so out of style at that point everybody knew who everybody else was," he said, and his search created quite a stir in that tight scene: the cast of a special performance put together for Michaels's benefit included Billy Crystal, Martin Mull, Andy Kaufman, and Richard Belzer, who, having replaced Chase in both

Channel One and *Lemmings* as well as Ramis in *The National Lampoon Show*, was overdue to be in the original cast of something. Belzer was hired but only to warm up the studio audience before the actual live taping, only appearing on camera sporadically in a few individual episodes.

However, Michaels's primary source for potential members of his television rep company was the improvisational comedy troupes that were sprouting like mushrooms in basement theaters on both coasts. He envisaged the troupe as functioning like the clowns who keep the audience amused between the sword swallower and the high-wire act—crucial as a unit but not as individual stars. He knew by the time he went to see *The National Lampoon Show* in early 1975 that he wanted to hire Radner. He was also fairly decided on Laraine Newman, a member of an LA improv company and alumna of the second Tomlin special. Then, on the recommendation of several mutual acquaintances, he met with Belushi, but the encounter was not auspicious. Perhaps suffering from overexposure to TVTV, an unshaven Belushi marched in and treated Michaels to what the latter called "a batch of rhetoric about guerrilla television and all that stuff, which was not uncommon at the time."

"I had a big chip on my shoulder," Belushi admitted in 1978. "I thought all television was shit and I let Lorne know it. My own set at home was often covered with spit. The only reason I wanted to be on it [*SNL*] was because Michael O'Donoghue was writing for it and it had a chance to be good." While Michaels was prepared to assure O'Donoghue that he would not have to compromise, he saw no reason to extend such assurances to a relatively unknown actor. "John came in and said he didn't want to do television," Michaels recalled. "I'd been working in television for eight years, so I said, 'Fine, thank you very much.' From that point on, we had some pleading on his behalf," primarily from Beatts and O'Donoghue. They also lobbied for Guest, but with less success, possibly because of what Shuster described as "a lack of click between Chris and Lorne."

Besides his reservations about Belushi's attitude, Michaels had not been overly impressed by the actor's *National Lampoon Show* performance and suggested that Belushi try out at the August 1975 auditions. Despite his initial resistance, Belushi came through with a stellar turn as that old Second City standby, the samurai. He may have been soothed by the sight of familiar faces among the approximately two hundred auditionees, who included actors from the second cast of *The National Lampoon Show* such as Meatloaf.

The third slot went to Jane Curtin, another improv veteran, apparently because her New England reserve was thought to balance the more urban, nervy style of Radner and Newman. Plus, since Chase wasn't yet on board as a performer, the show needed a token WASP. Chase, already hired as a writer, attended the auditions, falling off his chair to provide diversion during the slow periods and pushing for his old sparring partner, Belushi. The endorsement of the three writers motivated Michaels to hire Belushi, leaving him with a dilemma: as he only had enough money to hire one more performer, he was forced to decide between the two remaining contenders: Dan Aykroyd and Bill Murray.

Michaels was torn; when he had seen *The National Lampoon Show*, he was "very taken with Bill Murray, who was the only person I *was* taken with," he said, but on the other hand, "there was never a moment's doubt in my mind that Dan Aykroyd would be on the show." If Michaels was sure he wanted Aykroyd, he didn't make his intentions clear. The twenty-two-year-old actor was required to audition like everyone else. Well, not quite like everyone else. He didn't really perform so much as march into the room dressed as a sort of English gentleman complete with bowler, attaché case, and umbrella. By contrast, the previous month he had dropped by Michaels's office wearing motorcycle leathers despite the July heat, a sight that disconcerted even O'Donoghue. "I believe the phrase Michael used was 'rough trade,'" Michaels recalled.

In fact, both costumes reflected aspects of Aykroyd's persona. The son of a Canadian senior bureaucrat and the grandson of a Mountie, he was destined to walk on the mild side. But as with so many at the *Lampoon*, a parochial school education brought any latent sociopathic tendencies to the surface, and he discovered an affinity with motorcycle toughs. This dichotomy became more pronounced in college, where Aykroyd majored in criminology but hung around in such underworlds as Ottawa possessed (perhaps the inspiration for McCall's "The Shame of the North," an April 1973 *Lampoon* depiction of one of "Canada's wide-open way-out border towns," where signs lure tourists to fleshpots advertising "Live Hatless Girls!").

So doubtful was Aykroyd of his place on the show that after the audition, he went off to join Second City's new Pasadena company, Flaherty's new artistic home. However, when the call from Michaels came a few weeks later, "[Second City producer] Bernie Sahlins said, 'Do what your conscience dictates,'" Flaherty recalled. "Dan was gone the next day."

Meanwhile, Murray had already been hired by a rival production on ABC, a prime-time program called *Saturday Night Live with Howard Cosell*, based around the network's football commentator despite his distinctive nasal singsong drone. This meant that Michaels's show could not be called *Saturday Night Live* as originally planned but had to settle for plain *Saturday Night* even though, just to confuse things, it ultimately became officially known as *Saturday Night Live* in its third season.

Simmons, as ever, had an alternative version of events: "When they were putting together *Saturday Night Live with Howard Cosell*, they offered me a lot of money to put on the *National Lampoon* Prime Time Players, and so I said yes. But then they insisted on creative control. I said, 'This group does what *I* say, not what *you* say,' and I said forget it. Belushi, Guest, and Bill Murray were going to do it, but when I walked, Belushi walked. At the same time, Lorne was begging Belushi to do *Saturday Night*," the publisher asserted. At any rate, Weidman recalled "sitting in Matty's office with Matty trying to convince John he was stupid to go on a late-night TV show when Matty was offering him prime-time exposure."

Simmons was not the only one who considered the Cosell show more likely to succeed. However, it turned out to be a three-ring cheesy celeb circus when it premiered three weeks before NBC's *Saturday Night*. As members of the Prime Time Players—the Cosell show's resident repertory company—Murray, Guest, and Doyle-Murray found themselves buried in an onslaught of international acts made possible by the new satellite broadcasts just being adopted by ABC's sports department. This modern technology was incongruously combined with an old-fashioned style characterized by *New Yorker* critic and former 'Poonie Michael Arlen as "the language of kisses blown, of 'God Bless You's', of 'this wonderful human being' . . . in short the language of celebrity 'hype.'" The combination of elaborate production and sentimentality (not to mention Cosell himself) was the opposite of hip, and the show did not last, though it ran long enough to inspire *Saturday Night* to name its rep company the Not Ready for Prime Time Players.

During *Saturday Night Live with Howard Cosell*'s short life, Guest and the Murray brothers got their revenge on sports television by moonlighting in a TVTV documentary on the 1975 Super Bowl. "Some of our people were good at going up to people and drawing them out, so we thought, 'Why not have professionally funny people do that same thing and see what happens?'" Rucker recalled. But comedians are not just bazookas to be pointed in a general direction and fired. Most of the "comedy" ended up being unusable, and the Super Bowl program marked the end of TVTV. Like the *Lampoon*, it had begun as a lark and then become far more viable than anybody had anticipated. But now, Rucker said, "we saw that this little ruse of ours was running its course."

Meanwhile, Michaels was trying to blend his writers' disparate styles into a seamless whole without losing their distinctive voices. "Lorne used to say he wanted a show that was a magazine, and you would be able to tell who wrote it from piece to piece. That was true for the first two years," O'Donoghue recalled. Only magazine writers usually don't have to work around the clock with people they might find unsettling—people like O'Donoghue, for example. "Michael and Anne were the first writers I had ever met who had cultivated these writer personas," said Shuster. "I think Michael had some line like, 'You are who you say you are.' They were inventing their own legends—a Scott and Zelda mythology." Then when the self-invented couple started to speak, she discovered that "O'Donoghue and Beatts were out for blood."

Shuster's own humor tended more toward material like the Bees, a running device in the first few shows that featured bee-costumed members of the Not Ready for Prime Time Players turning up in unrelated sketches, much like Monty Python's Spanish Inquisition, and violating what Beatts called "a sort of rule—no joke costumes, no joke names, no joke props" (a rule that would repeatedly be broken). This taste of Canadian silliness was far too whimsical for those cast members who came out of the hard-edged *Lampoon* tradition. "Maybe here we can become total actors," Belushi said in 1976, "but you can't if the next fucking moment you got to get into a fucking bee costume. I want to *burn* those fucking bee costumes!"

Even worse, in Belushi's view, were the segments featuring the Muppets, who were part of the mix when the show first debuted. If he felt the Bees represented an excess of sweetness and light, the Muppets were enough to induce a diabetic coma, even though Jim Henson had created special puppets that were relatively degenerate—by Muppet standards anyway.

"Belushi *hated* the Muppets. He called them a bunch of blankety-blank green washcloths that should be cut up with a butter knife," said former 'Poonie Michael Frith, who designed them. Although Frith protested that "the Muppets were, at that point, considered adult humor," that wasn't how the show's resident nihilists saw them. "It was when the Muppets were on *Saturday Night Live* that Michael [O'Donoghue] stopped talking to me," Frith recalled. One might wonder how anything so cuddly found its way onto *Saturday Night* in the first place. "Lorne was a Muppet fan," Frith explained. More significantly, Michaels's manager, Bernie Brillstein, had already been Henson's manager for several years.

The dark, vaguely vicious material created by O'Donoghue was more to Belushi's liking. In fact, the first thing ever seen on *Saturday*

Night when the show premiered on October 11, 1975, was a sketch in which O'Donoghue, as a language instructor, teaches his dutiful foreign pupil Belushi such useful English phrases as "I would like to feed your fingertips to the wolverines." At the end, the instructor, struck down by a heart attack, clutches his chest and falls to the floor, an action immediately mimicked by his student. "Michael was as into death as anybody there, but Belushi probably was equally," said Shuster, who once made a list of thirty Belushi *SNL* sketches "where death was the theme over and over again."

O'Donoghue also sensed that the same impulse that led Belushi to test the limits might someday lead the actor over the edge. "The same violent urge that makes John great will also ultimately destroy him," O'Donoghue predicted facetiously in 1978. "He's one of those hysterical personalities that will never be complete. I look for him to end up floating dead after the party."

Not all the *Saturday Night* writers were of this mordant persuasion. Marilyn Miller preferred character-based material where the laughs came from recognition, not shock, like a slumber party sketch in which the company's three actresses play little girls comparing preteen theories of the mechanics of sex. At the same time as it included more material derived from girls' real-life experiences, that source so ignored by the *Lampoon*, the *Saturday Night* mix also downplayed the preppy humor that was so much a part of the magazine's style. "You know, I've always had a problem with the *National Lampoon*'s humor," Michaels told *Rolling Stone* in 1978. "I guess the phrase 'jock' covers it. There was a kind of male-ego sweat sock attitude in it which I have never really been a part of."

"At the *National Lampoon*, we had to do what would please the editors, and their taste was more narrow than Lorne's," said Beatts. "Lorne was an exponent of eclecticism. He genuinely wanted people to go to their strengths and picked people with disparate styles. So there was more room for all sorts of experimental endeavor than there was at the *National Lampoon*, which had a very Harvard WASP attack on humor."

235

Saturday Night was as uninterested in the magazine's commentary on privilege and class distinction as it was in the sweat socks, and the atmosphere around the *Saturday Night* office reflected this approach. According to Beatts, "the *National Lampoon* was a lot, lot tougher. People were meaner, nastier, faster, more cut-and-slash. At the *National Lampoon*, they tended to use the naked blade, but at *Saturday Night Live*, the rapiers had buttons on them. They weren't out for the jugular, or maybe they were less insecure. And the actors could get off on stage. They didn't need to get off in the drawing room." Michaels, she thought, was "a more forceful and benign presence" than the *Lampoon* editors, and his "more maternal and feminine" management style kept things calm and made his team feel secure. At the same time, the producer was not above using guilt to spur productivity.

In O'Donoghue's view, Michaels "ran things like a family. Once you're in, no matter how good or bad you are, he doesn't like to fire you." Rather than reassuring the writer, this acceptance made him feel as though he had found a more subtle version of the manipulative father figure he had just escaped. "Matty tried the same family technique, but it didn't work with micks," O'Donoghue declared. "The only people who Lorne's father thing didn't work with was the Irish Catholics—me, the Murrays, also Belushi. Zweibel would be hooked by the warmth, and Marilyn Miller would stay up all night and feel guilty because she wasn't working."

This pincer movement of warmth and guilt suggests Michaels was less a father figure than a Jewish mother, and in fact, O'Donoghue felt that the producer "brought in traditional Jewish comedy from the West Coast," a development he was not altogether happy about, regarding it as a concession to conventional expectations. "Lorne was not trying to get away from that traditional Hollywood humor. He's a part of it. It's like a fish trying to get away from water—they're not going to get that far away, are they?" the writer inquired. He, for one, missed the good old days of WASPy astringency at the magazine and tried to introduce a little taste of that *Lampoon* competitiveness by terrorizing the apprentices: Morris, Franken, and Zweibel.

Likewise Chase, another *Lampoon* survivor, similarly exploited the junior writers' personal and professional insecurities to establish his primacy, emerging, by the time the show debuted in October 1975, as Michaels's Number One Son. If Michaels was at the apex, Chase and O'Donoghue, now reestablished as Cardinal Richelieu behind a new throne, were his gatekeepers, a troika in Hawaiian shirts. While the other writers sometimes had to wait for hours to catch Michaels at a free moment, O'Donoghue and Chase could walk into his office at any time. "Lorne and I were very close and spent every minute together," Chase recalled, describing himself as "kind of a right-hand man. There were young writers—Zweibel, Franken, and Davis—who would bring material in, and we would have to rewrite it. My recollection is of twenty-four-hour days that were me and Lorne—and Michael a great deal of the time."

To Michaels, Chase may have represented a world of witty sophisticates that Michaels saw as his own natural circle. As *Saturday Night* became the darling of the hip intelligentsia, the producer quickly adapted to a life of limousines, weekends in the Hamptons, deferential maître d's, and Mick Jagger dropping by for a nightcap. However, in the show's first two years, Michaels had very little time to enjoy these perks since, like everyone else, he was either working away in the RCA building (now better known as 30 Rock) or catching up on missed sleep.

Given Chase's affinity with the producer, it is not surprising that he finally managed to get himself in front of the camera. From day one, he had made 30 Rock's elevators, offices, and hallways a stage for his usual brand of impromptu slapstick. Noting how Chase's extroverted style had helped raise his profile, several of the other writers adopted it. "There was a lot of bouncing off each other and a lot of people jumping up and performing in an office, practically jumping on the desk," Shuster recalled. If the name of the game at the *Lampoon* was have-at-you, at *Saturday Night* it was hey-looka-me. As Beatts said, "the volume at *Saturday Night Live* meetings was louder."

"Certain people," added O'Donoghue, "were very brutalized by the system—i.e., Tom Schiller," a director and old friend of Michaels who was enlisted, along with Albert Brooks and Gary Weis, to make short comic films for the new program. Such tender concerns hadn't bothered O'Donoghue at the *Lampoon*, but there, he felt, the competition exposed less-talented writers, while at *Saturday Night* it encouraged what he considered to be the wrong sort of people—those more adept at the battering ram than the poison dart. "It favored someone like Al Franken with the personality of a tank," he said, "and cut down on people who might be more quixotic or fragile." People like McCall, for example, who called the writing job O'Donoghue secured for him during the show's second season "the unhappiest three months of my professional life."

"Bruce was a very quiet person," said Tischler, "and it wasn't a very quiet place at all. You had to do a lot of campaigning to get your stuff on," in contrast to the *Lampoon*, where a word in Beard's ear might be sufficient. This does not mean the reserved never prospered. Jim Downey, another writer on the quiet and conceptual side who joined the staff in the second season, was hired fresh out of the *Harvard Lampoon* on the recommendation of Kenney, his mentor. Despite his lack of bumptiousness, Downey not only survived but became a fixture—enduring, to date, twenty-eight seasons over thirty-three years—and a conduit between future *HL* talent and *SNL*. As for why Kenney didn't turn up on *SNL* himself, "I offered him a job whenever he wanted one," Michaels said, "but he was already committed to writing a screenplay for Matty, and I think that's what he wanted to do." As well, Kenney may not have wanted to enter a whole new pressure cooker.

At least Michaels tried to make sure any pressure at *Saturday Night* was internally generated, not externally applied. "That first year, Lorne fought for artistic freedom, and that year was good," O'Donoghue recalled. Even though Michaels wasn't effusively supportive, his writers believed that he genuinely respected their work and for that alone they would have followed him anywhere, at least in the first years. "There was an unbelievable difference in how writers were treated at *Saturday Night Live*. It so rarely happens on TV for things to come out on the screen how you envisioned them a few days after you wrote them," said Don

Novello, who became an *SNL* writer in 1977. If *Saturday Night* seemed more fresh and spontaneous than other programs, it was largely because Michaels remembered his own frustration as a *Laugh-In* writer and made a point of cutting out the network gatekeepers. On *SNL* the writers were, unusually, encouraged to be directly involved with the production aspects of the show.

Like a good dad, Michaels let his team learn from their mistakes rather than stop them from trying. For example, he wanted some parody commercials featuring the new cast taped before the show went on the air so that they could work together before being hurled in front of a live audience. But Beatts, who wrote many of the parody ads, wanted to use Tischler's approach and employ the voice-over artists who did the real commercials, even though they were an added expense. With the NBC budget managers breathing down his neck on one side and an ornery Beatts on the other, Michaels let the writer have her way. "But later," Beatts said, "I thought, 'You idiot!' Of course Lorne wanted the cast to work together in front of the cameras."

Michaels, who had run improvisation workshops in Toronto, initially sought to knit the company together by doing the same at his SoHo loft, though these fell off once the show started. In any case, Michaels had never intended to create a Second City–type actor-improvised show. This was all to the good as far as Chase, who hadn't grown any fonder of ensemble work since *Lemmings*, was concerned. "I had much less of that Second City experience, and they were all better actors than me," he admitted, "but one thing I could do was look into a camera lens and mug with impunity to a certain degree. Many of the theater people would make a connection with the lens six inches out, but I would look right into the viewers' eyes because I had so much practice from *Channel One*," particularly in his portrayal of a self-important newscaster.

To create a showcase for himself, Chase revived this character in "Weekend Update," an ongoing news parody that was the main outlet for *Saturday Night*'s topical commentary. While Chase's *Channel One* news anchor was literally caught with his pants down, on *Saturday Night* he was caught in the metaphorical sense: the segment often opened with Chase in the middle of a personal call to some offscreen girlfriend, a device that permitted some of the raunchiest but subtle sexual humor ever heard on network TV. After realizing he'd been overheard, an embarrassed Chase would recover his poise with his standard introduction: "Good evening. I'm Chevy Chase, and you're not."

Originally conceived as a way to mock the self-satisfaction of over-paid talking heads, this introduction came to subtly suggest that maybe Chevy Chase was someone the viewer should want to be. Further, it allowed Chase to say his real (although fake-sounding) name on the air. He quickly gained higher public visibility than his fellow troupe members, but he was by no means the only performer who wanted to emerge from the pack. Even a dedicated team player like Radner could say in 1976, "There's no one performer who couldn't carry a whole show by himself. . . . There's so much individual strength here it's driving every-body slightly nuts."

Nor was Chase the only performer coming up with material that showed him to advantage. "It wasn't like saying to the actors, 'Here's this little play I wrote—will you perform it?'" Shuster recalled. "A lot of the spark really came from the performers." As she had on the *Radio Hour*, Radner in particular worked closely with writers on her characters, devoting herself to the show to the point of coming into the office in the middle of the night in her nightgown.

This level of involvement may have contributed to the vividness of Radner's portraits—for example, Emily Litella, a slightly deaf little old lady who offered rambling but passionate "Weekend Update" guest editorials on topics like the "busting" of school children until an exas-perated Curtin, another "Weekend Update" anchor, pointed out the misunderstanding. Curtin's icy rationality served as a foil for another warm but rambling Radner creation introduced in 1977: loudmouthed consumer reporter Roseanne Roseannadanna (so much for the "no joke names" edict), whose reports tended to digress into personal reminiscences and detailed discussions of various bodily functions.

The writers soon discovered that besides being obstreperous in pitch meetings, one way to get their work on air was to create a juicy role for a cast member who would consequently push for it. Belushi was particularly insistent that he was there to act, not just clown around, declaring, "This show's good when we're working together, all of us, in a sketch as comic actors, playing off each other, with each other, not reading cue cards like we have to but memorizing the lines in advance, making eye contact, not dressing like fucking bees!"

Though unconcerned about being typed as a comedienne, Radner felt constrained by Michaels's commitment to realism, recalling that at Second City, all they had to work with was "a revolving doorway, two other doors, and six or seven chairs. And we could make them anything we wanted." For Aykroyd, however, the more prosaic the context, the more it seemed to stoke his inner lunacy. Many of his characters seem like respectable citizens about to snap and go on a rampage. These nuts next door included the hyper salesman pitching the Super Bass-O-Matic '76 blender, "the tool that lets you use the whole bass with no fish waste, without scaling, cutting, or gutting," and small-business owner Irwin Mainway, ready to sell kids useless if not outright dangerous products like the Johnny Human Torch Halloween Costume or the fun-filled Bag o' Glass.

Even real people like Tom Snyder, Richard Nixon, and Howard Hughes seemed like borderline psychopaths when impersonated by Aykroyd. In contrast to Chase, he totally submerged himself in his characters. "Dan," Beatts said, "didn't want his real name used on the air. He always wanted to be the shadow man." Though their approaches to performing were so different, like Chase, Aykroyd immediately proved to be a television natural. But some of the other cast members found the transition more difficult. In O'Donoghue's view, "because you had a live audience at *Saturday Night Live*, people, particularly Second City people, were shouting so the audience in the cheap seats could hear them."

As well, it took actors with a stage or radio background a while to realize that they couldn't throw in action that the camera wasn't expecting to see, since during your ad-lib, the boom mike would probably be moving toward the character with a scripted line, leaving your improvised inspiration unheard and unseen. The exception was "Weekend Update," where the anchor's stationary position permitted a certain amount of improvisation, another factor in Chase's rapid rise. But not much; each segment had to end on schedule, as local affiliates would not delay their commercials just for a punch line.

Another discrepancy arose between the writers' mandate to be as freewheeling as possible and the show's rather staid visual style. Director Dave Wilson was one of the production team's few seasoned television professionals, and he wasn't about to start using handheld cameras, which the short film slot already had covered in any case. Even so, *SNL* incorporated enough innovations to make it appear positively revolutionary. Adapting the Pythons' and TVTV's inclination to call attention to process, it took the camera up to the control booth to show a supposedly drunken, down-and-out Wilson and down to the RCA building's lobby to discover exuberant guest host Ralph Nader striding in, uncharacteristically dressed as a cowboy. Wilson would also periodically shatter the carefully established illusion of reality by having the camera pull back before a commercial break to reveal to the audience at home what the studio audience was seeing: the production crew frantically changing sets, the cast racing back and forth tearing off costumes as they went, and everyone narrowly missing the camera dollies trundling around.

Even though the format discouraged true improvisation, *Saturday Night* still retained the edgy feeling of performers working without a net. This flowed in part from the genuine possibility each week that the show would not come together in time and would instead dissolve into a hopeless mess. The race kicked off late Monday with that noisy writers' meeting. Then, after the NBC office workers with whom the *Saturday*

Night staff shared 30 Rock during the day went home, the nocturnal writers and actors could let loose.

"It was a wonderfully collegiate atmosphere," Beatts agreed. "We had a college student's schedule"—more specifically, a sleepless medical student's schedule. The writers would work straight through from Monday night to Wednesday morning, after which they would squeeze in a nap before the Wednesday afternoon read-through. (Beatts developed "an entire wardrobe of things that looked like pajamas," and she lobbied for three years to get a bed in her office.)

After seeing which ideas worked in the read-through, Michaels—in consultation with director Wilson, the set designer, and perhaps head writer Herb Sargent plus Number One Son and Cardinal Richelieu—would create the show's running order. Meanwhile, the production staff was trying to create sets that met Michaels's demanding standards of realism, all the while praying that they wouldn't have to construct a new sketch's set from scratch on Friday. The last run-through, a dress rehearsal in front of a small invited audience, ended at 10:30 on Saturday evening—only an hour before the actual show. After every run-through, even the final one, sketches would be changed, moved, or discarded altogether. Wandering through the melee would be the guest hosts—getting lost, getting drunk, getting temperamental, and, hopefully, getting their lines down and integrated into the show.

The show was shot in NBC's cavernous Studio 8H on a mainstage with several smaller stages fanning out from it. The mainstage, where the musical guests performed and the guest hosts delivered the opening monologue, looked like the backstage of a theater or nightclub, all ropes and ladders and exposed brick, suggesting the make-believe had been dismantled and the performers were just sitting around jamming for their own amusement. This was as illusory as every other set on the show. Certainly there were no exposed bricks or wood slats to be found in Studio 8H after all of the artifice was removed.

As Michaels had anticipated, the pace and the pressure unified the creative team, at least while they still had enough energy to be exhilarated instead of exhausted by it. Even the jaded O'Donoghue exclaimed, "It was so much fun to be there. It was great!" As at the *Lampoon*, the early days found the writers and performers spending all of their time together in a combination working session–cum–dining club. The team was further united by the widespread expectation that they would fail. Michaels, Shuster remembered, "used to be fond of quoting over and over again that satire was what closed on Saturday night."

16

OVER THEIR HEADS

Nowhere were the low expectations for *SNL* more apparent than among the NBC technical crew assigned to the show, who reacted much like the old-school RCA engineers had to *Radio Dinner*. It was an echo of the late-60s values clash between hardhats and students, only the student radicals had evolved into white wine–and-Brie liberals (and in fact, among the items lurking in *Saturday Night's* prop budget was the producer's supply of white wine). Nor did the creative team embody the kind of professionalism that might have made the crew overlook their subversive brand of humor. The stage-trained designers commissioned sturdy sets built for a six-month theater run, not a television one-night stand; the actors couldn't remember to keep facing the cameras; and the writers, except for the three television veterans, turned in scripts that ignored the practical limitations of production.

As O'Donoghue discovered, *SNL* "had to be much more scripted than the *Radio Hour*. Because of the technical limitations—lighting cues, camera blocking—you couldn't fool around so much." All the while the creatives' salaries stayed the same no matter how long their hours, but the union crew got well-paid overtime.

Not that Michaels minded spending money on giving the main-stage an authentically lived-in look or carrying on the *Lampoon* tradition of verisimilitude in the parody ads. This and similar production expenditures resulted in individual episodes going as much as $75,000 over budget—a sum way out of line with the show's commercial prospects. Initial surveys pegged *Saturday Night*'s average audience to be around seven million people—a drop in the bucket by the gargantuan standards of network television. But research also showed that, while the show may have been a cult, it was at least a cult made up of those elusive eighteen- to twenty-four-year-olds, more of whom were watching *Saturday Night* than anything else on TV. Nevertheless, NBC's head of research continued to predict doom. His December 1975 report concluded that the audience for *Saturday Night* would remain limited because sample viewers felt "much of the humor was simply over their heads."

Michaels was prepared to leapfrog over NBC's middle management, whose job it was to oversee spending, for dispensation right from the top of the network. This propensity led one executive to describe the producer as "a snot-nosed kid, too clever for his own good." But to Michaels's creative team, the fact that he was willing to battle the budget police on their behalf conferred hero status on the producer. "You were comedy shock troops brought together on this mission," Shuster recalled. "There was—especially amongst John and Danny and later Billy—this real gonzo video guerrilla take on it."

"There was a sense of being infiltrators up at NBC. We did feel we were different and pretty cheeky. It was a style, but style," said O'Donoghue, "is content." Like the Radio Ranch, the *Saturday Night* office had its own aesthetic. Practical jokes, defacement of network property, and a standard of neatness more appropriate to a college dorm than a corporate headquarters were the norm. Michaels replaced the standard-issue metal office furniture with funkier wood pieces redolent with '40s atmosphere unearthed from NBC storerooms. The atmosphere in *Saturday Night*'s cluttered, crowded work area was redolent for other reasons as well. When NBC News assistants wanted to get stoned after work, they found that it was usually worth wandering up to the *Saturday Night* offices on the seventeenth floor to see what was happening.

The gonzo video guerrilla attack seems to have been mostly a matter of infiltrating as much borderline material into the show as the NBC censors would permit. Michaels took on this fight as well, developing a number of censor-outwitting strategies. The primary battleground was sex, and the writers amused themselves by including spicy allusions the censors wouldn't pick up on but the young audience would. Sex seems to have aroused the censors' vigilance more than drugs, perhaps because it was a subject that they were more accustomed to policing. In any case, from Chase rolling a square joint as the hapless President Ford to Newman patriotically urging viewers to Buy American in a public service announcement for the American Dope Growers Union, drug jokes slipped through, and Belushi's propensity for conspicuous consumption of controlled substances became a running joke, as Kenney's had in the *Lampoon*.

The third leg of the trinity, rock and roll, proved to be no problem. At that point, having rock bands on television was hardly controversial. Unfortunately, popular music at the time was languishing in the doldrums. The radio oozed with the sounds of Bread, Chicago, and Tony Orlando and Dawn, and by 1975 finding exciting musical talent frequently required looking outside the rock world. As a result, several of *Saturday Night's* most memorable musical guests were niche acts like jazz-blues chanteuses Esther Phillips and Betty Carter, spiky New Waver Elvis Costello, and uncompromising ironist Randy Newman. It also booked (at the insistence of guest host Richard Pryor) Gil Scott-Heron, who had introduced satire into the super-serious Black Power movement with the biting poem/song "The Revolution Will Not Be Televised."

The *SNL* house band was novel in itself. Under Canadian musical director Howard Shore, it was the first on a network show to have the funky sax-dominated sound (an innovation Michaels had envisioned in his jobbing writer days) that subsequently became the new staple of television house bands, not least because house keyboardist Paul Shaffer went on to be the long-term musical director of *The David Letterman Show*.

NBC's censors were far more leery of possibly offensive material about sex and religion than political commentary. "The censors were more out for dirt than politics," said the Credibility Gap's Harry Shearer, "and the game seemed to be to get the dirt in." In any case, politics per se did not particularly engage the *Saturday Night* writers. "It wasn't an area we were interested in," Chase asserted. "We were more into media parody, going after the commercial culture."

Such interest as they had was covered in "Weekend Update" and sketches lampooning politicians' superficial foibles like Carter's folksiness or Ford's clumsiness. Typical was a "Weekend Update" item reporting that President Ford had "pierced his left hand with a salad fork at a luncheon celebrating Tuna Salad day at the White House. Alert Secret Service agents seized the fork and wrestled it to the ground."

To some extent, this focus on personalities instead of policies reflected the influence of Second City, which had always inclined toward character-based humor. But by now, a reaction against the self-righteous and didactic tendencies of dissident ensembles like The Committee had set in, and Michaels was determined to avoid losing mirth in a message. "I think Lorne made a conscious decision to stay away from a certain kind of satire," Ramis said. "He wanted the show to be funny."

The extent to which comedy that promoted political activism was considered passé was made clear to Goodrow when, through Chase, he tried to set up an audition. "Don't you think The Committee's a little dated?" asked Franken, even though he, along with Chase, was considered to be the staff's most politically engaged writer and was already a committed Democrat.

The *Saturday Night* approach encouraged the viewer to see all political figures as either corrupt or buffoons, and implied that politics in general was a sordid, ridiculous business that anyone cool would not waste their time on. "*Saturday Night* was far more into iconoclasm than they were into satire," observed Carl Gottlieb, another Committee veteran and former writer for 1969's *The Music Scene*, ABC's short-lived precursor to *SNL* that showcased musical acts along with Tomlin and The Committee. "Iconoclasts aim to shatter images, ideally in the rudest way possible. Satirists achieve the same effect by making intellectual connections between real events and the comic extension of those events. Mr. Mike's poking the sharp sticks in the eyes [a recurring bit featuring O'Donoghue's on-camera alter ego] was a great shocking joke but not at the expense of any institution. After you get over the shock of it, you hadn't learned anything."

Moreover, the *Saturday Night* team would have agreed with this assessment. "It might have made people look at political figureheads a little differently," Shuster suggested, "but they were pretty much on our side to begin with, so it was preaching to the converted." As well, after several years of being preached to, even the converted were ready for a welcome respite. Ford and Carter seemed relatively harmless, the Vietnam War was over, the Senate Intelligence Committee was reining in the CIA, the Justice Department had temporarily suspended its attack on the First, Fourth, and Nineteenth Amendments, and it seemed safe to lighten up a little. Although Dick Ebersol was inclined to refer to *Saturday Night* as "the post-Watergate victory party for the Woodstock generation," that party had actually been going on for quite a while. By 1976 it was more like the morning after. Watergate, however, did play a big part in *Saturday Night*'s getting on air at all, as Nixon's impeachment suggested to NBC that the balance of power was shifting toward the iconoclasts. Also, the economy had plunged in 1974, and hard times do a lot to widen satire's fan base. The upshot was that at that particular and unique moment in history, *Saturday Night* was an acceptable risk.

Distracted by monitoring prurient interest, the NBC censors were caught off guard when it came to scrutinizing the one area where the program really was on dangerous ground. Like the *Lampoon*, *SNL*'s main breakthrough in troublemaking was to undermine its own context—

commercial television—described by Chase in 1975 as "a medium that exists to sell products, not to supply hard-hitting entertainment." Such subversion was accomplished directly by the parody ads, or more subtly by the juxtaposition of a sketch next to an apparently related ad, like putting Belushi's updated version of the *Official Pogrom*'s groovy army recruitment pitch immediately before an actual army recruiting ad. (NBC eventually thwarted such irreverence by putting *SNL* commercials on separate cassettes instead of one continuous reel, allowing their order to be shuffled.)

Besides attacking the nature of advertising in particular, the show also sniped at corporate power in general. One reason *Saturday Night* may not have devoted much energy to skewering the government was that by this time the White House and Congress were perceived as mostly puppets of corporate interests (a phenomenon the *Lampoon* had explored in a July 1973 piece by Cerf, "America's changing its name to Nixxon"), and it was seen as more productive to go after the true Masters of the Universe, multinational corporations. Michaels was surely aware that merely by giving consumer movement guru Ralph Nader a public forum on network television in the second season, *SNL* was provoking some of its advertisers. Nader made the most of his appearance by portraying the chairman of the energy conglomerate Texxon, explaining that as part of its plan for developing solar energy, Texxon would need to own the sun and so should have a solar depletion allowance because the sun was a natural resource that would decay over time.

O'Donoghue in particular gravitated toward similar attacks, producing material like "The following program is brought to you by Exxaco. Exxaco—yesterday's technology at tomorrow's prices. Where life is second only to money. Stay out of our way or we'll kill you."

NBC was not entirely insensitive to these jabs at its corporate hide and, O'Donoghue claimed, ultimately prevented him from doing fake institutional ads because its parent company, RCA, objected to a joke he had written about them. "Lorne said, 'This is pure censorship. I'll take this to the press if you block this,' and they had a big, big fight," the writer recalled. On the other hand, NBC gamely went along with Nader's opening monologue, which reported on his investigation into RCA until it was apparently cut short by sudden technical difficulties.

More often censorship efforts directed against O'Donoghue involved jokes that did not threaten to undermine anything except standards of taste, like several dead baby jokes. Michaels himself removed an O'Donoghue ad for "Tarbrush, the toothpaste for Negroes," that would have been delivered by the cast's lone black performer, Garrett Morris. Unfortunately, the censors did not discriminate between jokes that were simply in pointless bad taste and jokes where the bad taste showed up the even tackier reality, as in one censored "Weekend Update" item that reported, "FBI Director Clarence Kelley denied rumors that the Bureau's entire investigation into Dr. Martin Luther King's death consisted of asking a Ouija board, 'Who shot the monkey?'"

Although *Saturday Night* was widely perceived as a new departure simply because it didn't underestimate its audience, the *Lampoon* circle did not consider the show all that daring. O'Donoghue thought that, far from breaking new ground, the show "was so overdue that all we were doing was a mainstream show twenty years too late. I never felt we were doing an avant-garde show. I just felt, 'Thank God this show which should have been on the air in 1960 was getting on the air in 1975.'"

Likewise, Ramis felt that *SNL* was "a show whose time had come, a way to bring Second City and the *Lampoon* to TV with rock music," while Harry Shearer, who ended up spending an unhappy year on *SNL* in its fifth season, felt that *Saturday Night* "seemed to bear the mark of the *National Lampoon* in its taste for attacking the underdog and its lack of energy for going after the powerful."

This kind of statement tended to irritate Michaels. *SNL*, he felt, was more than the sum of its parts—it was an entirely fresh and superior entity. "It wasn't that I said, 'Well, let's get the *Lampoon* people,'" he protested. "If it was that simple, then other people would have just gotten a few *Lampoon* people and that's what they did and it didn't work. *Saturday Night Live* on any given week didn't come out of Second City or out of the *Lampoon*—it evolved the way it evolved. The point people can't see is that it actually was its own thing."

SNL was not the only television show that season climbing on the irreverence bandwagon. Its rival for favorite cult comedy of 1976 was the quasi-satirical soap opera, *Mary Hartman, Mary Hartman*, which was shown weekday late nights in syndication. Populated with characters at once more believable and more absurdist than those on the regular soaps, *Mary Hartman* walked a tightrope between condescension and affection in its depiction of small-town America. Several members of the *Mary Hartman* cast served as guest hosts on *Saturday Night Live*, including its nominal star, Louise Lasser, who, suffering from a well-publicized drug problem at the time, turned in such a rambling and disorganized performance that O'Donoghue "wanted to force her to eat her goddamn pigtails at gunpoint."

Mary Hartman also propelled Martin Mull out of the underground, displaying his unctuous yet smug stage persona in all its slimy glory as the glib self-satisfied host of local television program *Fernwood Tonight*, which broadened Fernwoodians' horizons by offering segments like "Talk to a Jew."

Mull was invited to be an *SNL* guest host but declined. He wasn't the only one. Woody Allen turned the offer down, as did Richard Nixon, Muhammad Ali, Andy Warhol, and Jack Nicholson. Some hosts, such as Buck Henry, Candice Bergen, and Steve Martin, became cast favorites. Others, like Lasser and, surprisingly, Frank Zappa, were less welcome. And a few, such as Michaels's idols Tomlin and Richard Pryor, who hosted early in the first season, were respected enough to put the cast on good behavior (even O'Donoghue minded his p's and q's around Pryor).

By the end of that first season, it was becoming increasingly clear that it didn't really matter who the guest host was because the rep players had become a sufficient draw on their own. As their star ascended, the other elements in Michaels's original variety concept became correspondingly lower profile. The first half of the second season saw, to the cast's great joy, the departure of the Muppets. As the Muppets were being phased out, the rep players' individual names and hand-tinted head shots were added to the show's opening credits, which till then had been lumping them together as the Not Ready for Prime Time Players. Their position on the show and Michaels's leverage within NBC was further enhanced when *Saturday Night* was nominated for five Emmys, winning best director, comedy-variety program, and writing for its first season.

"When we got the Emmy, there was very much this sense of bringing this trophy back to New York from the showbiz capital," Beatts said. The award resulted in the writers receiving more than something shiny to put on their bookshelves: they also got substantial raises. Meanwhile, the actors' per-show salaries more than doubled. With the mantle of boy genius fitting a little more comfortably, Michaels was able to renegotiate a second-season salary of $300,000—a 100 percent increase. Even better, he got the show's per-show budget beefed up, so now he was regularly only $25,000 in the red.

Ordinarily an Emmy unsupported by lots of viewers would not result in a higher budget, but in a season that had seen the network sink to third place overall, NBC was willing to consider a critical success better than no success at all. Also, *Saturday Night* had from the first generated more press attention than its audience numbers might warrant. Although more than a few reviewers called the show uneven and sophomoric (which O'Donoghue defined as "the liberal code for funny"), the most influential critics praised its originality and daring.

However, a network's star-making machinery does not make stars out of ensembles. The media required an individual personality to celebrate, and it found one in the *Saturday Night* player who told them his name. As early as December 1975, when the show had been on air for three months, an article in *New York* magazine dubbed Chase "TV's hot new comedy star"—heady stuff for someone who had been on unemployment only a year before. Then, when the Emmy for best supporting actor in a music or variety program was announced, Chase bumbled his way onto the stage all by himself to accept his award while his fellow Not Ready for Prime Time Players had to stay in their seats. This did not go over well, nor did *Rolling Stone*'s suggestion that Chase "could be, besides the smartest of *Saturday Night*'s staff, its most thoughtful, most complex member."

"Once we bend to a fucking star system here, everything changes," Belushi told the same publication at the end of the first season. Or, if there was going to be a star, Belushi had a better idea of who that should be. "John was sure he would be the first person to become a star. It just killed him when Chevy was the first," Tischler recalled. This led Belushi to offer some advice to Flaherty in 1976, when the latter had started appearing in a Canadian television show called *SCTV* featuring the Toronto Second City troupe. "John would call up," Flaherty recalled, "and say, 'Use your real name. The audience isn't going to remember you. You'll never get anywhere if you don't use your real name.'"

Chase, meanwhile, seemed ambivalent. "I sure as hell never discouraged it, this 'star' number that's happened," he told *Rolling Stone* after winning the Emmy. "I have spent the last ten years commenting on that cliché, shitting on it, satirizing it. So how long can you poke fun at it after you've become it?" Probably not very long, as even he realized. "I had a lot of trouble taking it seriously, but I always knew I wouldn't have any perspective on it until about ten years in retrospect. Apparently I was a very big deal, and looking back, I felt like a big deal, but not even as big as I was. As much as I wanted to say—and I always did in interviews—'I'm one person who won't fall prey to anything,' I always knew in the back of my mind I probably would because I was so important to everybody," he said, even though he considered what he was doing "not particularly deep—basically parody and falling down."

Unfortunately for intercast relations, Chase did not display such modesty in the first flush of his stardom. For one thing, under pressure to be sharp and amusing on three hours of sleep, he had increasingly started to substitute energizing cocaine for nap-inducing marijuana, which exaggerated any media-induced tendency toward grandiosity. Chase soon gave his colleagues the impression that he thought he was bigger than the show, and his actions confirmed this perception; even before the Emmy results were announced, he had already made plans to leave.

Chase claimed this decision was motivated at least in part by creative frustration, saying, "I thought we'd pretty much parodied the medium and we'd have to wait a year before the medium did something new that we could parody." As well, he was exhausted and conducting a long-distance relationship with his future wife who lived in LA. Then there was money. When Michaels originally negotiated the rep company's contracts, the terms were that all the Players would be paid the same. If one got a raise, all the others had to get similar raises. Chase realized that NBC would never agree to give the whole troupe the kind of salary he could now command. As well, he now had movie offers.

It became clear that Chase no longer considered himself a player on Michaels's team when the nascent star replaced the producer's long-term maven Bernie Brillstein with new management who promptly arranged for him to leave *SNL* and produce two NBC specials of his own. He could have done this and still stayed at *SNL* but, although he would later claim that he hadn't really wanted to leave, he arranged to phase himself out over the first five shows of season 2 in the fall of 1976.

Michaels put a good face on it, telling the press, "This show was conceived as a *starting* place for people, like off-Broadway, from which, inevitably, people want to move uptown. As soon as anybody starts staying because of loyalty, or some similar fucked reason . . ." But loyalty was exactly what Michaels expected, and the break with Chase became more than professional. However, the star-making machine took Michaels at his word and eagerly waited to see which *Saturday Night* cast member would be the next to leave the others in the dust.

17
THE CEILING OPENS

By the fall of 1976, the feeling of being left behind was becoming all too familiar to some Lampooners. Two years before, NatLamp had been ubiquitous: the magazine, with circulation and ad sales approaching their zenith; *The National Lampoon Show* on the road; the *Radio Hour* on the air; and anthologies in bookstores. The same year, 1974, also saw the publication of what turned out to be the most special of the *Lampoon*'s special editions: the *1964 High School Yearbook Parody*, a huge success that ended up selling over 1.5 million copies.

The *Yearbook* began as a way for Kenney to redeem himself after his return from Martha's Vineyard. "Doug was in Dutch for walking out and staying away for a year, and I was junior man on the block, so Matty more or less ordered me to undertake this project," said O'Rourke. "This project" was an expanded version of a 1956 high school yearbook written by O'Donoghue and Kenney for the November 1970 issue. "Everyone said it couldn't be padded out to be a whole special edition," O'Rourke recalled, "and basically Doug and I had this thing dumped on us, because we didn't think it could be done either."

What everyone, or at least the art department, had actually said was that it couldn't be done by swiping old photos from real high school yearbooks as O'Donoghue's original article had but would require shooting new photographs with models. Kenney and O'Rourke started looking at hundreds of yearbooks, a survey that convinced them that high schools, wherever they might be, had more similarities than differences. They found that life imitated Archie comics: students inevitably conformed to one of a limited number of cultural archetypes. "It was chilling to see how much they were all the same—bully, clown, intelligent introvert, politician, proto-homosexual," Kenney said in 1978. "It was Nazi social engineering. By weight of social pressure people became these things."

"Doug and I were sitting around smoking dope, and somebody brought up that Kurt Vonnegut once wrote that if you want to understand anybody, think about what they were like in high school," O'Rourke agreed. "So we started to talk about the types, and pretty soon we had a cast of characters." To embody these quintessential high schoolers, the *Lampoon* enlisted students from a private school in New York, even though the *Yearbook* supposedly emerges from the C. Estes Kefauver Memorial High School in Dacron, Ohio, named after a prominent Democratic senator and majority leader. Those students who volunteered to model soon found that they had to give up more than their Saturdays. "One of the big surprises was when we had to cut all the students' hair," O'Rourke recalled. "It got a tremendous amount of coverage even though their hair wasn't all that long in the first place."

The editors had decided to set the *Yearbook* in 1964 for a number of reasons. "Part of it was because it was simply ten years ago, and part of it was that Doug and I figured that 1964 was the last year before the sort of hipness explosion," O'Rourke explained. Once again, Kenney was invoking an idealized age, in this case the days when Harvard students still wore ties to dinner, when authority figures still had credibility, when traditional values could be believed in without irony, and when everyone knew who was on the right track and who was deviant.

In the first category are students like Robert Baxter, "well-rounded, well-groomed, well-liked... terrific gun collection... saving him-self for marriage... pet peeve: people who are trying to be 'differ-ent'"; student council president Charles "Chuck" U. Farley, a member of "Young Americans for Freedom, Kanga-Young-Republicans, and Future Real Estate Speculators"; and cheerleaders "Winky" Dempster, "Pinky" Albright, and "Twinky" Croup, all "neat, cute, and pert" and busy with such school-spirited activities as the Christmas Poverty Poor Folk Perk Up, the Kangarettes, the Kangarooterettes, and the Kangaran-garettes. The outsiders include "French" Lambretta ("Grecian nose and roamin' hands"), Madison Avenue Jones ("sure can sing, dance and play baseball... a credit to his homeroom"), and, a love tribute of sorts, glum Emily May "Preggers" Praeger.

Just how high the standards of conformity were is revealed in the sample Confidential Permanent Records. Under "religion," the record offers five choices: Methodist, Presbyterian, Lutheran, Episcopalian, and Other ("specify and explain"). Fathers have a choice of three occu-pational categories: white collar, civil service / military, and laborer. Mothers are scrutinized for such lapses as "cigarettes," "fidelity prob-lems," "excessive dress or makeup," "previous marriages," and "work-ing mother." To make sure standards of behavior are maintained in the school itself, there are the hall monitors, headed by acne-plagued Carl Lepper ("Junior Police, Lavatory Patrol, Student Court Prosecutor, Bay of Pigs Club"), whose duties include "guiding lost freshmen and helping them obtain respect for proper authority."

"There could not be a less democratic institution than high school. High school is the single most fascist thing you have to put up with unless you go on welfare," O'Rourke told *Newsweek* in 1974. Though some reviewers like *Newsweek* lumped the *Yearbook* in with cheerfully nostalgic movies and TV shows like *American Graffiti*, *Grease*, and *Happy Days*, there is little to suggest the editors had a rosy view of the repression and intolerance that was the other face of the security pro-vided by those stable norms. If Kenney was nostalgic for anything, it was for the defiant reaction these narrow conventions stimulated, a defiance that was already waning. As O'Rourke said, "by 1974, things had almost changed again. We were already deep into the disco era, and the world as we know it now was well under way."

Even so, there were a few Kefauver students who resisted conforming, most notably Faun Laurel "Weirdo" Rosenberg ("free spirit . . . artsy-craftsy-spooky-kooky . . . future Freedom-Rider . . . Peace Corps after college") and Forrest "Swish" Swisher, who edited the largely unread school literary magazine and contributed "authentic bohemian song readings of 'Greenleaves'" to the student talent night.

The *Yearbook* is lifted beyond mere parody by the scribbled farewell messages to and doodles by student Larry Kroger, owner of this particular copy, which create a fictional universe. Kroger is the *Lampoon* Everyreader, neither an obvious geek nor an obvious go-getter. Instead, he blends into the woodwork, a "nice guy . . . mows lawns in the summer," a not-very-good but game athlete, neither a rich boy like classmate Woolworth "Lunch Money" Van Husen III nor a blue-collar hunk like Dominic Xavier Brocolli ("Manual Arts Club"). Kroger's father works at Van Husen Mobile Homes, the local economic powerhouse owned by Woolworth's father, and, according to Kroger's permanent record, has debts and income running neck-and-neck.

As it had on the *Encyclopedia*, O'Rourke's capacity for organization and attention to detail complemented his collaborator's scatter-shot conceptual brilliance. The detail work extended to coming up with approximately four hundred names to put under the sixteen (swiped) photographs of junior and senior homerooms, names such as T. V. Dinners, Mandy Lifeboats, Hugh G. Rection, Bertha D. Blues, and old favorite Lawrence Nightinjail. "There was unbelievable detail, very complicated work," said Gikow, who herself remained at the office every night until midnight rendering all of the kids' handwritten notes. Nevertheless, she remembers the experience as "just joy."

The two editors apparently felt the same way. As always, Kenney was happiest dissecting a social microcosm, and he threw himself into the work. "Doug and P. J. just relished it," Michael Simmons declared, especially since both were "obsessed with childhood and adolescence." They also shared a Midwestern perspective. Kenney, as Latimer said, "looked at everything from the point of view of a real smart kid from Middle America who is exploring the absurdities and incongruities of contemporary hip culture." Just as "*Mad* was Kurtzman's point of view, a second generation Jewish kid from the Lower East Side, the *Lampoon* was a bright Middle Western nerd looking at the same scene."

However, the *Yearbook* by no means reflected the two Ohioans alone. "It was a pretty collective enterprise," O'Rourke recalled. "When something like this was under way, there was not a lot of personal fame or individual career at stake. It was how much interest did it rouse in you personally."

Several of the *Lampoon* staff were recruited to serve as models. Hirsch, who had contracted polio as a child and walked with crutches, was cast as crippled student Ursula "Wobbles" Watersky. "P. J. came up to me," she recalled, "and said, 'This is a delicate question, but if we had to rent crutches, it would be so expensive, so will you be the handicapped girl?'" Always game, Hirsch soon found herself posing with corsages on her crutches, wistfully watching the rest of the class bunny hop at the prom.

O'Rourke himself appeared in a dual role as a nerdish social studies teacher and as pinch-mouthed Miss Marilyn Armbruster, girls' phys ed coach and advisor to the Junior Police. A clear-eyed, crew-cut Kenney turns up in a photo from his own actual yearbook used, at his suggestion, for the "In Memorium" tribute to a deceased classmate.

With all of this group enthusiasm, the *Yearbook* was completed in five months. By the end of 1975, it had sold eight hundred thousand copies and been acclaimed as "the finest example of group writing since the King James Bible" by *Harper's*. One would think that this critical *and* commercial triumph would make Simmons a happy man. But there was a worm in the apple. As 21st Century's earnings continued to soar, so did the amount of money he would have to pay to Beard, Kenney, and Hoffman, who, according to their original contract, could force a buyout at any time after October 1, 1974. One reason Simmons had brought Reitman in to produce *The National Lampoon Show* was so he could focus on renegotiating the original deal, as 21st Century couldn't afford the existing buyout terms either in cash or in stock.

Though the rest of the staff assumed that Hoffman had vanished from the picture in 1970 except as a friend, in fact he had been meeting with Simmons throughout 1973 and 1974. "Matty and Len never expected to pay us in cash," he hypothesized. "They thought the stock might hit thirty-one times earnings so they could buy us out with paper, and whoever thought that by 1974 we'd be making millions of dollars?" Who'd also have thought that by 1974 the stock market would be at a historic low? Not only that, but potential investors were in no hurry to buy stock in a company known to be facing a massive payout. In any case, as the deadline loomed, *National Lampoon* stock was down to three times earnings.

Simmons and Mogel faced a dilemma. If they used stock, the three Harvard founders would end up owning 80 percent of the company. But based on the soaring 1974 revenues, the cash amount was just under a hefty $9 million (over $42 million in 2012 dollars). With the magazine's circulation soaring, 21st Century had an incentive to renegotiate before the cash price went up even further, but no alternative agreement was reached, and in July 1974, Hoffman, Beard, and Kenney each received $100,000 as a down payment.

This was a tiny amount of the total owed; a balance of $4 million was due in the spring of 1975, with another $3.5 million to be paid out over a period of five years (the Harvardians had agreed to reduce their price to $7.5 million in order to close the deal). In the interim, the *1964 High School Yearbook* appeared, pushing earnings up even further. "Here I was, an experienced negotiator. I was the chief negotiator for Diners Club," Simmons mused, "and I used to go to bed every night thinking 'how could I let this kid out-negotiate me?'"

The busy editorial staff was only dimly aware of these financial machinations. But those close to Beard felt that change was coming.

Weidman recalled that "by the spring of 1974—when I joined the staff—it was already in that slightly uncomfortable stage where Henry was getting ready to take a hike and Doug was still sort of there, hanging out with the *Radio Hour* and *The National Lampoon Show*, and the next regime was about to bubble to the top. For a period, Henry, Tony, Sean, and Brian ran the magazine, with Henry starting to phase himself out." A true milestone was reached at the end of 1974 when Gross left, to be replaced by his deputy, Peter Kleinman. Even though Kleinman was trusted and liked, Gross's departure left the staff with what Weidman termed "inchoate feelings of entering a new era."

Weidman may have been more aware than most that this new era was imminent because, like O'Rourke, he had a foot on the business side. Having realized almost as soon as he entered Yale Law School that he didn't want to be a lawyer, he had phoned Simmons toward the end of his first year to ask if he could work for the *Lampoon*. Simmons suggested that Weidman finish and *then* come to work at the magazine. "The idea of hiring an editor who was also a member of the Bar appealed to Matty enormously," Weidman said, and as a result, he joined the magazine as an editor/lawyer.

If most of the staff had only a vague sense that changes were afoot, even one of the principals was not entirely sure what was happening. "Hardly anybody reads contracts. I certainly don't. We lucked into something I don't even totally understand," Kenney said in 1978. Rumors swirled, but there was no direct impact until March 1975, when Beard, Hoffman, and Kenney got the balance of their initial $4 million payment. "It was an incredible meeting," Hoffman recalled. "We sat around this conference table in the lawyers' office, and all they did is pick up the phone and say, 'Wire them the money.' Then they all walked out of the room five minutes later and theoretically we had the money." By the end of the day, Beard and Kenney were richer by approximately $3 million between them and Hoffman by half that amount.

This sudden influx of wealth did not turn Kenney into a conspicuous consumer overnight. "After Doug was paid off, he still wore these same dungarees with his balls hanging out that he always wore," said Peter Kaminsky, who worked in the *Lampoon* publicity department at the time. But Kenney had always been known for his simple tastes. "We once had dinner with Doug and someone asked him, 'What's your favorite food?' and he said, 'Potatoes and water.' That was perfect for Doug," Beatts recalled, adding, "Michael used to say, 'Doug has beer taste on a champagne budget'" (a line Kenney would adopt as a self-description).

Nor did Kenney have any big dreams beyond that he wanted to escape to a carefree land. "When Doug got his $3 million, I asked him what he was going to do, and he said he was going to go to Disney World," said Kelly, who, while admitting that he never really got to know Kenney, nonetheless thought that this modest whim "seemed like Doug all over—the all-American boy. In some senses, his horizons were demarcated by TV and pulp novels."

Kenney may have been reluctant to spend money on himself because, given that even in small matters he "didn't know what he thought about anything for two minutes running," as Beatts said, such a major increase in options put his normal ambivalence into overdrive. "He was saying things like, 'Oh God, now I'm getting all this money. What does it mean? What am I going to do with it?' Other times he'd be very proud he got it," Prager recalled. "He always thought he deserved it. It was more like, 'What now?'" He did, however, quickly decide on one new toy: a red Porsche (Hoffman's first luxury purchase, by contrast, was a painting by artist Helen Frankenthaler).

If Kenney had doubts about buying things for himself, he had no reservations about sharing his wealth. He bought his parents a house in Greenwich, Connecticut; he sent his sister to Madeira, a prestigious girls' boarding school in Virginia; and he gave ex-wife Garcia-Mata several thousand dollars, with Prager getting a trip to Europe. Kenney also remembered some old friends, giving O'Donoghue $30,000 in his post-*Lampoon*, pre-*SNL* days when the writer was strapped for cash. Trow, who had stopped contributing to the magazine at the end of 1974, was another beneficiary. "When Doug came into dough, he came by and gave me a check and shook my hand and said, 'You never needed us.' I didn't say anything, but he was wrong," the writer recalled, describing his usually buoyant friend as "a tub toy under sedation" in the wrenching weeks following the buyout.

More than ever, Kenney picked up the check at restaurants and paid for drug supplies. He was also always good for a loan. When some years later Miller repaid a few thousand dollars Kenney had lent him, "Doug looked at me in amazement and said, 'You are the first person to ever pay me back.' He was extremely generous, almost compulsively so," Miller said, suggesting that Kenney "had some guilt feelings about the buyout." Beard was another matter. "Henry felt like he had earned it," Hoffman declared. "He had really worked hard and stood up for the writers. He's a person of strong loyalties and strong feelings, and I just think he was tired of dealing with Matty. He didn't feel any guilt at all."

"Henry was patient, he was there, he was the only one talking to everyone when none of them were talking to each other," Cerf said in 1978. "But he paid a terrible price. Underneath he was furious, and when he let go, boy did he let go," Meyerowitz agreed, noting that "for five years, Henry was at the *National Lampoon* office for fourteen hours every day. Everyone took him for granted" until one day when, like the long-suffering wife who suddenly packs her bags and leaves, Beard dramatically served notice that he had had enough. The day the check cleared he cleaned out his desk, told the stunned staff that working at the *Lampoon* was worse than his time in boot camp, and left, never to return.

In the months following his departure, not even his intimates knew what had become of him, and in the absence of hard information, rumors abounded: Beard had become a Sufi; he had become a follower of the Russian mystic Gurdjieff; according to Simmons, he had joined some sort of cult that required building furniture; according to Hoffman, he was driving a cab. But there was no mystery about the effect that his departure had on the magazine. Since the spring of 1974, Beard had been carefully delegating more of his editorial responsibilities, so it wasn't as if the magazine's process suddenly fell apart. But even if the transition was smooth on an organizational level, there was emotional fallout. "The '75 buyout was devastating," Kelly declared. "It was as if the Rolling Stones lost Mick *and* Keith and also they took all the money."

Those *Lampoon* veterans who did not receive sizeable tokens of appreciation from Kenney were resentful of the three founders. "Suddenly the ceiling opened and a staggering amount of money fell through the roof, and Doug and Henry and Rob picked it up and left. When there's that much money around, people get bitter," Weidman said. What made it worse was that some core writers had stock options and were supposed to have been given more, but this fell through and the promised windfall failed to materialize.

What they did inherit was a magazine with no operating capital and a missing linchpin. Subsequent to Beard's departure, his position was filled by a committee, though just who was on it is open to debate. "When Henry left, the magazine was basically left leaderless, and an informal committee was put together to run the magazine. Basically it was Tony, Sean, Brian, Doug, myself, and someone else," O'Rourke said. Sussman disagreed, saying, "Sean, Tony, P. J., and myself picked up the reins." Not so, said Kelly, asserting that "Tony, Brian, and I became the editors, and we went hunting for new talent." One thing at least was clear: "This was a group of people in a state of flux," said Danny Abelson, some of that new talent. "One felt those people were not going to be there forever, and one went on feeling that year after year."

Abelson, from South Africa via the University of Pennsylvania, had first come into contact with the *Lampoon* via Ellis Weiner, a fellow U of P grad and fellow employee at New York's Strand Bookstore. Weiner had sent the *Lampoon* a sample parody even though he'd never actually read the magazine. "I addressed it to the submissions editor," he said, "and of course there was no submissions editor." Later he submitted a collaborative article with Abelson that was accepted by Kenney, who promptly disappeared.

Eventually Kenney called the two writers to apologize for letting their story languish and invited them to come in. They met in an office Abelson remembered as being empty save for "a little bottle of Jack Daniel's," and subsequently the pair found themselves "being welcomed into the fold. We only realized later," he said, "that very few survived the gauntlet," a gauntlet he characterized as "a bunch of extremely opinionated, cynical, snotty people who were fairly unhappy at the time because it was their position to be unhappy—and also because three people had just walked out of the room with enormous amounts of money and another group of former colleagues were becoming very famous very quickly."

Weiner penetrated the inner circle in the fall of 1975 when he collaborated with Kelly on a parody of the fine arts trade journal *ARTnews*, a piece very much in the Kelly vein that required knowledge of subjects like contemporary avant-garde video artists or the 1920s Italian futurist movement to fully appreciate its focused skewering. Unsurprisingly, this led to Weiner and Abelson being labeled "the eggheads of the group," the latter recalled, "even though we weren't really. There was a certain amount of redneck posing there, but we weren't that different from anybody else."

The difference was that Abelson and Weiner were unapologetic about their high-culture orientation. Their new colleagues, by contrast, "were very erudite and witty and well read, but people did cultivate a kind of anti-intellectual style," Abelson observed, a style he felt was the result of Kenney's influence. "Doug had set the tone," he said, "and was ironic about anything to do with intellectual attainment."

Like Frith before him, Weiner was not at all sure that Kenney's influence was a beneficial one. He saw a clear dichotomy that the magazine's original editorial cohort might not have considered quite so black and white. "The *Lampoon* was always Dr. Jekyll and Mr. Hyde, half Kierkegaard jokes and half big-tit jokes. Dr. Jekyll was Henry Beard, and Mr. Hyde was Doug," he declared, adding, "I didn't think Doug was a genius the way some people did." To Weiner, there was something almost decadent about the Mr. Hyde approach. "Why should any of us, including Doug, write about big tits and masturbation, in that way especially?" he wondered, although Kenney was hardly alone in addressing these subjects, and the push for the breast factor came from Simmons.

Kelly and Hendra had never been Kenney's biggest fans and were now in a position to do something about it. "They beat Doug up—not all the time but a time or two," said Kaminsky, who had moved over from the PR department to become another new contributor, swept from the edges toward the center of the vortex—not without meeting resistance, however. According to Kelly, "Matty in particular hated Peter and always wanted to fire him."

McConnachie, on the other hand, was marginalized and decided to leave. For his swan song, he supervised a March 1975 *New Yorker* parody as dense and detailed as any O'Donoghue effort. Even the magazine's standard publishing boilerplate is covered, stating, "*The New Yorker* is published at the sort of intervals a magazine such as *The New Yorker* ought to be published at, by the sort of corporation which ought to publish it," while Nightlife listings offer information on venues such as the Stork Club ("a good address, just off the avenue. Used to have tea-dances back when people had money and neckties. Not like now, though").

In Kelly's estimation, McConnachie was altogether too taken with the days when people had money and neckties. "Brian wanted to turn the magazine into *The New Yorker* because Brian wants to turn his life into *The New Yorker*," he said, and the new regime did not consider *The New Yorker* a publication that should have any influence on the *Lampoon*. They determined that the *Lampoon* would no longer be as effete (no more Deco Desperados dishing the décor) or elite as the original version, and the hovering spirit of the insouciant 'Poonie was exorcised forever. "They could be forgiven for thinking they were to the '70s what *The New Yorker* was to the '30s. I don't blame them for making the parallel and having their little fantasy," Weiner said forgivingly, "but politically I don't like it. When I was there, there was less of this pseudo–*New Yorker* style, the source of which was O'Donoghue and Trow, these sort of guys with style. It got more populist and more concerned with who has power than with who has wonderful style" (though Trow would have argued that in '70s America, style had become indistinguishable from power).

Power and its permutations were the lifeblood of another new regular contributor, Jeff Greenfield, who arrived as a sort of emissary from the world of realpolitik. Unlike the other *Lampoon* writers who, except for those with prior experience in advertising, knew no other craft besides humor writing, Greenfield had written speeches for Robert Kennedy and by 1975 was working for a high-powered political media consultant. He also freelanced for respectable publications like the *New York Times Magazine* and *New York*. Unlike some of the other new recruits, Greenfield readily admitted to having read the magazine before he wrote for it, "because it was such a departure from what humor was expected to be. What struck you," he said, "is that those guys were out for blood. A lot of people in journalism or politics might make jokes like that in the bar, but you wouldn't see it in a mainstream publication."

Greenfield did not completely convert to this brand of carnivorous comedy. "I tended to write more gentle stuff," he acknowledged, like the Kenneyesque "What Every Young Girl Should Know," a July 1977 guide to the facts of life and love. This useful pamphlet defines impotence as "what happens when a girl fails to stimulate her man properly. This can happen when her figure is not perfect, or when she tries to talk to him for too long before getting into bed with him," and, after assuring girls that "the average man's penis is 2½ to 3 inches long," responds to the question "What is a multiple orgasm?" with the answer "There is no such thing." In September 1977 he also contributed a similarly helpful "Guide to Grown-ups" that offers teens hints on how to communicate in Adultspeak. For example, "We should do this more often" translates into "Fuck off," while "Let's have lunch after the first of the year" means "Fuck off."

Once the highly focused Greenfield became a contributing editor and gained access to the monthly editorial meetings, he made an interesting discovery. "It was completely outside of anything I'd worked in before—law school, Bobby Kennedy, political consulting. This was all mainstream stuff, and that's where you sort of think the smart people are," he said. "Then you go over to the *Lampoon*, and here are these people from a totally different world who can blow you away with how good they are at what they do."

The Lampooners, for their part, found Greenfield as much of a novelty as he found them. "I was much too straight for them," he admitted. "I had a wife, kids, wrote for mainstream magazines." However, there was common ground—notably, a suspicion of the New Left and the emerging ecofeminist perspective, which fingered technology, militarism, and patriarchal values in general as prime culprits in the destruction of the environment.

Greenfield's dim view of this outlook fueled the *Earth Mother News*. Printed on what appears to be skins and illustrated with cave painting–style drawings of animals, it features articles by correspondents such as Hairy Fart Woman and Shaman Hungry Rock Taster. One correspondent warns of a world where "the temperature is 70 degrees, so hot no life could survive. Imagine walking through clouds of inky black poison, breathing through wet moss, stinging eyes closed against the pain, easy prey for tooth tigers. This is what shamans tell us may happen if atmospheric testing of fire continues."

This jab at the doomsday predictions of environmentalists (a switch from the 1970 Blight issue, which took jabs at those who dismissed environmentalists' predictions) was coauthored with Ted Mann, another newcomer. When he came on staff as an associate editor, Mann made a strong bid to fill the House Wild Man slot vacated by O'Donoghue—for example, by arranging for canisters of nitrous oxide to be delivered from drug hobbyist magazine *High Times*. Mann also shared O'Donoghue's penchant for finding humor in things like savaging kittens, but instead of using such jokes to explore the gap between cruelty and the sentimentality used to mask it, Mann's target often seemed to be compassion itself.

After the buyout, Sussman, too, gained a higher profile in the magazine, receiving a regular salary and starting a slow rise up the masthead—a climb he must have found especially gratifying after being considered a second-class citizen by the likes of O'Donoghue.

"The *Lampoon* was snob heaven. There was the A group, which was George, Henry, Doug, and myself," said the departed arbiter of taste. "The B group was Anne, Michel Choquette, McCall, Miller, and McConnachie. Then with the C group, we're starting to get people like Gerry Sussman. There's the people who found it, then there's the second wave who are the people initially attracted by the first people, then we're beginning to get down to the carbons of the carbons." But now the A group was history, and instead of a sneering O'Donoghue, Sussman was working with someone like Greenfield who thought, "If there is one guy who deserved to become a world-famous humorist out of that magazine, it was Gerry Sussman."

Indeed, Sussman could now afford to declare, "There weren't that many funny guys [let alone gals] who could write our kind of stuff." One reason the editors may have had trouble finding compatible new blood, Kaminsky suggested, is because by the mid-70s, "we were so much defined by our common experience, there was nobody else we could accept. We definitely had a stamp of deep '60s on us, and there were no new '60s acidheads to come in because they were all old like us." At the same time as new recruits weren't coming aboard, more old hands were jumping ship. McCall started drifting off after the departure of Beard and McConnachie, his main links to the magazine. "The spring of 1975 was when it all fell apart," he said, plaintively adding, "I'm always the last to know."

"After the buyout, there was instantly a diaspora. All that talent which had been contained in the magazine exploded in every direction," Miller recalled, comparing the postbuyout *Lampoon* to "a college football team where the whole first team graduates except for maybe two guys, and the next year becomes a building year and then there's another building year and it never builds because the sensibility that had existed when the original group of people came together was not there anymore. After '75, the fun was gone. The more time that passed after Doug and Henry left, the more the afterglow faded and it became really just a job."

Weidman, on the other hand, was more actively involved than before, once he finished collaborating with Stephen Sondheim (an old family friend) on the thoughtful musical *Pacific Overtures*, which opened on Broadway to general acclaim. However, he said, talking about the show in *Lampoon* circles made him a little uncomfortable because "it was a serious work. It wasn't being a wise guy."

In spite of his old school ties to the former regime, Weidman was socially comfortable with the new crowd. The same could not be said of O'Rourke, who took O'Donoghue's place as Hendra's pet peeve. As Kaminsky said, "P. J. really didn't fit in with that group, so he sort of became his own guy and worked pretty much by himself," although apparently this didn't stop him from collaborating promiscuously. For example, he worked with Kelly on more highbrow humor, the gossipy *Myth & Legend Mirror*, a first-century forerunner of *Poonbeat* with articles such as "Icarus: On His Way to the Top, but Has It Been Too Much Too Soon?," "Isis: 'I Want to Be More than Just a Cult Figure!,'" and a special report, "Who's Going to Be the Next Big God? Don't Look Now, but He Just Might Be Jewish!"

O'Rourke and Kelly also collaborated on a considerably more accessible article, a Trowish game that penalized players for bad taste in consumer items. The offending articles include beanbag chairs, shag rugs, paper lampshades, gerbils, water beds, the *Whole Earth Catalog*, Frye boots, safari jackets, white suits, and any *National Lampoon* product. The list sounds, in fact, like the items that might be found in a *National Lampoon* editor's fall 1976 garage sale.

Your score tells you what the editors think of you, the reader— "Patronizing indulgence? Simple contempt? Actual dislike?" At the pinnacle of the editors' estimation is a person who is "a quiet dresser with inherited wealth and no political or religious beliefs. . . . There's always plenty of whisky and ice at your house. . . . You never raise your voice, have public arguments or discuss money or your sexual partners. And you have a large, quiet, shabby house in the country to which we are frequently invited." You are, in short, very much like Henry Beard.

O'Rourke even collaborated with his adversary Hendra on what seems to be largely an exercise in sour grapes: the "Tail of Monty Snake," subtitled "A Faerie Story." It appears the authors' main problem with Monty Python is that the troupe is insufficiently rugged. "How did all this come about? By the wave of a wand of some fairy godfather? Not on your nelly," the tale begins, and goes on to assert that the heart of the British humorists' approach is to "dress up like women and shriek." As might be expected, this effeminate group is short on hard-hitting substance, avoiding subjects like Vietnam, the United Kingdom's "collapsing economy," or "class privilege" in favor of jokes about "Absolutely Sweet Bugger-All"—unlike the *Lampoon*, which was busy taking on shag rugs, beanbag chairs, and Frye boots.

O'Rourke's being excluded from the in crowd went beyond personalities. He was still seen as an agent of the front office, "the guy who consolidated the magazine in Matty's interest. I was close to him until '76," Latimer said. "Then he went executive in a big way. When Doug and Henry took off, he became managing editor or something and was too busy to hang out and get drunk." Having further proved his organizational skills on the *Yearbook*, O'Rourke took over the production management aspects of Beard's job, becoming managing editor in 1976, but Hendra and Kelly seemed to find it hard to see him as an equal instead of a callow hanger-on. As Abelson said, "they had been around when P. J. was really a pal and assistant, so they weren't used to the idea of him being a writer and then an editor."

Furthermore, O'Rourke's wagon had been hitched to Kenney's star, and that didn't burn as brightly as it used to. For example, Kaminsky, like his mentor Kelly, regarded the founding editor as a sort of Amadeus figure, "just a nice hippie who happened to have God's ear that let him say great things. That's how we regarded him—as this acid-guzzling bozo who just happened, when he wrote, to do the best stuff we ever did. But," he said, "one didn't hang out with Doug a lot."

This acid-casualty image might well have been only another of Kenney's protective colorations, very different from what those who knew him better saw. For instance, while Prager often found herself with the Kenney who dressed like a fifteen-year-old in torn jeans and sneakers, she also sometimes went out on the town with the reincarnation of the Harvard social butterfly, a suave figure who, she said, "would take me dancing at the Pierre anytime," the Pierre being a hotel that, even as New York's municipal finances teetered on the edge of default, remained an emblem of the city at its swankiest.

Nor did Abelson view Kenney as some sort of idiot savant, instead finding him "very on the ball and professional. I didn't know the Doug of the Great Eye in the Sky, the ultimate space cadet." However, he *was* struck by Kenney's characteristic ambivalence. "Obviously he was extremely ironic and cynical," Abelson recalled, "but I was always a little surprised that Doug didn't seem more centered."

Lacking any clear alternative plan, Kenney haunted the magazine's offices like a senior partner who is past retirement age but has nowhere else to go. To the extent that he was still around, he made a convenient target for any free-floating buyout resentment and anxieties about proving equal to editors past. As well, even though the new team might have thought they were a refreshing change from either trivial-minded fops, drug-addled flakes, or apolitical would-be *New Yorker* editors, they were fighting a public perception that the golden age was over. When Susan Devins started as Gikow's assistant in early 1976, it seemed to her that "that very exciting time from 1970 to 1975 had already ended and they were conscious of it." Nevertheless, the building-year crew was determined to make its mark, though keeping the magazine flying would prove far harder than launching it in the first place.

273

18

THE FOREST
IS LEVELED

I f internally all was not well at the *Lampoon*, it wasn't apparent from
the outside. Product poured forth: Cerf's *Official National Lampoon
Bicentennial Calendar*, which found a dark moment in the nation's
history for each day; *Gold Turkey*, the *Radio Hour* greatest hits collection; an art poster book, launched with a publication party that offered
guests the chance to tag a replica subway car; and *The 199th Birthday
Book*, another salute to the upcoming bicentennial.

The *Lampoon*'s attitude toward this impending celebration of
national values may be gauged by Weidman's guide to the American
System and its constituent parts: "labor, industry, government, the press,
the church, and a small group of wealthy Jewish businessmen." Recycling the device that worked so well in the "Defeat" section, he adopts
the voice of a right-wing curmudgeon and supposes, as an example of
the System in operation, that it has "organized itself to fight a friendly
little war in some silly country on the other side of the world." At that
point, the wheels start to turn: "A President's elected, appropriations
bills are passed by Congress, newsmen write patriotic editorials, negroes
get drafted, the economy gears up, tanks and planes roll off the assem-

bly line, unemployment drops as more get drafted, the Red Sox win the pennant . . . and everything hums along in harmony and happy union."

All this output did not indicate an abundance of energy but rather a feverish enervation. "We put out three times the product," Kelly said. "The magazine was operating on a shoestring, and we were desperate." Kelly himself was especially busy, in charge of not only the art poster book but also *The Very Large Book of Comical Funnies*, an extremely ambitious pseudohistory of comics told entirely through parody comic strips of assorted periods and faithfully re-created styles, like a *Justice League*–type comic called *The Legion of Elements* in which the entire Periodic Table of Elements bursts into President Eisenhower's office with explosive results when Oxygen and Hydrogen make up a fight by shaking hands.

Kelly was also the issue editor for the fourth *Lampoon* album, *Goodbye Pop*, which was recorded in the summer before *Saturday Night* went on the air. The record was created in response to the recognition that, as Tischler said, "the music business was now pretty much like everything else. *Lemmings* was about how the counterculture was played out; *Goodbye Pop* was that now the music itself was played out." The driving force behind the album was Guest, back from LA to portray legend-in-his-own-mind Sid Gormless, lead singer of the British prog-rock group Dog's Breakfast and a forerunner of Guest's best-known creation, *Spinal Tap*'s Nigel Tufnel. The listener is treated to an excerpt from Gormless's latest work, a bombastic pseudoclassical hodgepodge in the style of then-ascendant prog-rock bands Emerson, Lake & Palmer and Yes.

Murray and Radner were two other creative forces behind the album. Radner is showcased in another parody of "I Am Woman," this one written by Kelly. "I'm a Woman, I'm a Human, I'm a Sister," Radner belts out staunchly in a recording session until a voice from the control room informs her, "You're not singing it right." Radner's singer listens calmly, then gives it another shot, but this, too, is interrupted. "You're using your whine voice," her manager (Murray) says, to which Radner responds by whining, "I wasn't using my whine voice!" Alternately

berated and condescended to by a bitchy engineer, a snotty British producer, and the patronizing manager, she starts another take but breaks
down crying in the middle. "I thought she could hack it but it looks like
she's having a tantrum," the manager apologizes. "I am *not* having a tantrum," the New Woman shrieks.

The voice of the petulant engineer was provided by future *SNL*
house keyboardist, Paul Shaffer. Although there is no record of the
blues coming up the Mississippi from New Orleans and then blowing
across Lake Superior to his hometown in North Ontario, somehow the
mild-mannered Shaffer developed a Stax-inspired funky style that could
have come right out of Memphis. As well, that language of celebrity
hype identified by Michael Arlen somehow became his mother tongue,
though the extent to which it reflected his genuine persona remained
a mystery even to his friends. "I always wondered if you woke Paul up
in the middle of the night if he'd go, 'Hey, that's beautiful!' But he was
always like that," said Shuster.

Shaffer had met Radner when they were both in a Toronto production of *Godspell*, where he also met future Second Citizen Martin Short,
who introduced him to the delights of putting on a tux and parodying
Vegas lounge acts. Soon Shaffer was passing the tradition along to the
Murray brothers when they all gathered to watch Sammy Davis Jr.'s syndicated TV show.

After that Toronto version of *Godspell*, Shaffer's next project was
to compose the music for Reitman's *The Magic Show*. When the show
moved to Broadway in 1974, Shaffer moved with it. Once in New York,
he looked up his old friends Radner and Flaherty and started hanging
around the *Radio Hour* studio, where it was soon clear that his ability
to parody R & B music complemented Guest's expertise in the folk and
rock areas.

Absorbed in their own internal conflicts, the magazine editors
stayed away from the recording studio, aside from Kelly and, as always,
Kenney. There he encountered Harry Shearer, who also was hanging around although not actively involved. "There was a sort of lingua

franca in that scene, which consisted of, upon first meeting someone, making as many rude personal comments as possible. That," Shearer recalled, "was my first impression of Doug—'Oh, more of this.' Later he seemed like an OK guy."

Meanwhile, in the *Lampoon* offices, this battle plan was still in effect. Abelson noticed that "enthusiasm was a dangerous commodity there. It was a hell of a lot easier to say, 'Stanley Kubrick—give me a break' than to say, 'I kind of liked *Dr. Strangelove.*'" It also remained true that while scorn was the only appropriate reaction to worthy efforts by outsiders, within the group a mutual admiration society prevailed. Like its predecessor, this self-selected elite had celebrated dinners, or at least celebrated lunches and after-work cocktails, and it was still at these social gatherings that the real work of the magazine got done, or so the participants told themselves.

However, there wasn't the same seamless merging of work and social lives that had characterized the *Lampoon*'s early days. For one thing, the staff's average age had inexorably crept upward. "Part of it was that they were getting older. That kind of living in the office wasn't going to last forever," O'Rourke observed and, as Greenfield said, "it's a lot easier to be a twenty-five-year-old guerrilla satirist than a thirty-five-year-old one."

Still, the group brainstorming session remained at the heart of the magazine's process. "We would sit down and have ideas together, and we were all equal in that respect, although Sean and Tony were ultimately deferred to for yea or nay," Kaminsky recalled. The two veterans assumed the mantles of the founders, with Hendra, according to the loyal Kaminsky, occupying "the role Henry had had in a certain leadership sense" and Kelly taking over Kenney's role as "the free-floating genius. Sean, just by his smartness and fastness, set the tone of every conversation. If he was in a room, the conversation went his way. It was natural," in a way it hadn't been before the departure of the initial A group.

Hendra presided, in his own fashion, over a process that hadn't altered much from Beard's day, with an ever-changing roster of issue editors. If there was a difference in the process, a rickety contraption at the best of times, it was in the efficiency with which it functioned. "Tony drove a lot of people nuts with his work habits. Supposedly he had a habit of not being where he was supposed to be, of being not exactly organized," said Greenfield, while noting that this was not his own experience of the editor, recalling, "When I worked with Tony, things got done." Weiner, too, held Hendra's editorial skills in high regard, saying, "I came to realize when I got out into the world and dealt with other editors what a great editor Tony is." That said, with strengths more in the areas of inspiring, conceptualizing, and prose improving than in scheduling and time/money relationships, Hendra was the kind of editor more likely to be admired by writers than by publishers. Michael Simmons, for example, felt that while Beard was a "very meticulous and hardworking editor, Tony and Sean were perhaps less so."

This was definitely O'Rourke's view, and he made no effort to conceal it. "Initially it was a collective enterprise with Henry at the head—collective in the sense of everybody having fun and working together, constantly bouncing off of each other about what they were working on. But by the end of 1977," he asserted, "it had become a progressive disaster. The process became yelling and screaming. What little order there had been about deadlines and budgets began to fall apart. That was one reason I was made managing editor [in 1976]—to keep budgets and deadlines in order. And it was, I may say, a thankless job."

Still, at least there were less smashing of walls and breaking of doors than before. "There was a lot of cut and thrust, but it wasn't uniform. It existed on certain axes," Abelson said, these axes of confrontation being between those holdovers from the first generation, whose hostilities had apparently not mellowed but only simmered with time.

Some other old habits remained as well. "When I looked at the *Lampoon* masthead before I got there," Weiner recalled, "I thought, 'Jesus Christ, this is supposed to be a humor magazine and most of the staff isn't Jewish. Most of the staff is Irish Catholic!' It was the first place that

I'd been in where Jewishness was the butt of humor as everything else was." After "sort of shivering a bit when it first started happening," he decided that because "it was stylistic anti-Semitism in the form of satire, it didn't strike me as anti-Semitic." Although, he admitted, "occasionally certain things would be said that I did take exception to."

This was Kaminsky's position as well. Like Sussman before him, he felt that "there was definitely good-spirited, bad, large-spirited, and petty anti-Semitism," he said, "but we hated everybody. I gave it to the goys every chance I could," finally resulting in a brief fistfight with O'Rourke. This incident may have been behind a February 1977 Letter to the Editor that asked, "Does P.J. sometimes use this column to set-tle little personal grievances around the office, or was that letter telling Peter Kaminsky to jam a cantaloupe up his cunt a joke?"

In any case, according to Kelly, any feathers ruffled in the give-and-take of the magazine's rough camaraderie could be soothed later in the bar, where "the same guy who called you a nickel-nosed Jew five minutes ago was buying you a drink and saying, 'Hey, we have more in common than those stupid Protestants.'" This approach to socialization mystified even those who weren't targets of abuse, like Flenniken. "I never could understand the anti-Semitic thing there," she said. "It became a tradi-tion, but it wasn't there at the start."

Ironically, if on a rhetorical level ethnic tensions were escalating, this was mitigated by Hendra and Kelly's bringing Jews into the inner circle. These "real Jewish editors" appear on the masthead of the Jan-uary 1976 *New York Review of Us*, a parody of the distinguished lit-erary monthly *The New York Review of Books*, along with Editor Anthony Hendraov, Advisory Editor Sean Kellybaum, Assistant Edi-tor Ted Mannstein, and contributors such as Elie Weisel ("The Basic Anti-Semitism of Almost Everything"). The *Review*, at the Beard-like Dr. Jekyll end of the spectrum, carries ads for books such as influen-tial literary critic Harold Bloom's "'An Enormous History of the Jews', a vast, lavishly un-illustrated work in ten volumes proving yet again why everyone in the whole world should pay so much attention to a small, obscure, intractable, historically powerless and culturally eccentric tribe of Hamitic Semites, and in particular, Harold Bloom."

However, there were still no representatives of another often-mocked group to add the spice of inside knowledge to the jokes. This was because, according to Kaminsky, the *Lampoon* was simply "a real guy clique—women got battered. The humor was guy stuff, and it was a male sensibility, editorially." At the same time, he felt that whatever the magazine's hiring and editorial practices, the editors did not hold particularly reactionary views on the personal level. "I think in the main the guys there—and most of us had had rotten marriages—insofar as we were aware of the women's movement we were for it, but subconsciously you acted like your swine uncle. I don't think we were ahead or behind the culture," he said. "We just expressed anxiety as humor does." Furthermore, women artists and illustrators continued to be welcome; the *Lampoon* under Hendra was one of the first places to print the dark, savagely political work of graphic artist Sue Coe.

Fortunately for Simmons, Hendra, and Kelly, the support staff still tended to view the absence of women's voices in the magazine or in decision-making positions as a function of their own lack of interest. Devins felt that she "would have been welcome to do things, but I never pretended to be a comedy writer, so I never had that as a goal." Also, in the tradition of women at the *Lampoon*, she was "very intimidated," although "even on a bad day it was better than most places." As for those women on the outside who did aspire to write, their submissions still couldn't make the grade. And even if some intrepid woman had met the magazine's standards, she would still be in trouble because, as Abelson said, "the women who were funny there seemed to be disliked for it."

Even if they weren't around anymore. The Letters column of the February 1977 issue contained a submission from "Anne and Deanne Titters, Remainder Rack, Val-U-Mart Book-O-Rama," which asked, "What has two legs and a fly and has oppressed women for centuries? Give up? *You*! And who says women don't have a sense of humor?" The previous month's issue had featured a (fake) ad for "Wisecracks—a slightly lower collection of humor by women," which garnered such critical praise as "yeasty, infectious," and "no pussy-footing or beating around the bush!" The publishers promise "future minority kneeslappers" such as "*Sniggers*, a collection of Negro humor."

Always a close call, it became increasingly difficult to tell whether the Lampooners were making fun of their own prejudices or if they were simply reinforcing stereotypes. Even as early as June 1974, the editors' confusion was visible in articles like "Cloo," a parody of the English country-house murder mystery board game. Instead of the library and billiard room, possible scenes of the crime are the trash-strewn Afro Cola Pool Room, the Pink Pussy Lounge, and the Hotel Geraldo Rivera. Instead of Colonel Mustard and Miss Scarlet, the suspects include the likes of Ms. Blowjangles (a huge hooker in large platform shoes) and the nattily dressed pimp Black Jack. The point of the game is to find out "1. Wha's happenin'? 2. Where at? 3. Wif wha? 4. Who cares?"

The editors may have felt that these stereotypes were deployed to rouse the ire of liberals, that favorite *Lampoon* pastime, as the concluding sentence of the game's directions—"The crime of the guilty party is our crime, the crime of society, the crime of humanity"—might indicate. However, with the success of boundary-pushing sitcom *All in the Family*, the *Lampoon* device of satirizing bigotry by exaggerating it did not seem quite so daring. "What happened partly is that they said all that they had to say. It had been a vessel into which the gifts and rage and experience of all those people was poured. It was molten at the beginning," McCall observed "and now it was finally played out."

"There was a time when the attitude of the *Lampoon* cut a little loose from the content and the pieces weren't as special," said Weidman, who coauthored "Cloo" with Hendra, acknowledging that "one did get into cranking it out." The process, the social habits, and the style of the *Lampoon* may have stayed the same, though the tone now reflected Hendra's forcefulness as opposed to Beard's essential circumspection, but the zest had gone out of it. As Beatts put it, "it was like trying to keep a relationship going with your college roommate after five years."

Not only were they burned out, they were burned, or so they thought. If anyone had a right to feel resentful, it would have been the newcomers, whose paychecks bore the brunt of the new austerity. It wasn't that *Lampoon* starting salaries became unusually terrible, but that by 1975 they were merely average as opposed to two years earlier, when they had been on the high side. "The guys who came after the buyout never made much money at all," Kaminsky contended. "The pay rate didn't improve—it got worse."

For those who remembered the glory days, the uneasy feeling that the good times were over was compounded by the feeling that they were now happening somewhere else. Even during *The National Lampoon Show*'s run, the magazine was still the place to be. But now the action had moved on. As McCall said, "it seemed that the energy just went from Madison Avenue to Rockefeller Center in six weeks." Not that the Lampooners would admit this was troubling. "We were above it all," Kaminsky declared. "We didn't think it was quite up to our standards. It was just people we knew doing what they'd always done. *Saturday Night Live* was just like the *National Lampoon* except it was on TV." Despite these professions of indifference, Weiner noticed that "there was some jealousy and edginess in the office and some sneering, so I was never able to watch the show without feeling a little guilty if I liked it."

"They all wanted to write for *Saturday Night Live*, but they wouldn't say so," said Devins, who remembered that when she came on board in February 1976, "there were little mumblings all around that *Saturday Night* was stealing a lot of their jokes." These little mumblings soon developed into a distinct burble. Evidently still feeling more sinned against than sinning, Hendra "had a real anger towards *Saturday Night Live*," Kelly said. His ire may have been fueled by the fact that in 1969, he had been hired to write for *The Music Scene*, ABC's earlier attempt to create a comedy-variety show for the youth audience. But it was cancelled after ten weeks, and now Hendra could only watch as his old rival O'Donoghue found the television success that had eluded him.

Hendra vented his feelings by, Kelly recalled, "copying down stuff he thought they'd stolen from the *Lampoon*," suspicions that were shared by Sussman. "When it first came out, we all agreed that there was definitely a rip-off of our ideas," he asserted, and having amassed a list of some thirty *Saturday Night Live* sketches that they felt were of *Lampoon* origin, they planned to use it in an ad in *Variety*. Fortunately, cooler heads prevailed, and what Weidman called "a stupid, misguided, sour-grapes ad pissing on *Saturday Night Live*, claiming they had stolen all the *National Lampoon*'s jokes," appeared only in the pages of the magazine itself.

The Lampooners' charges were not completely without foundation, but it was common knowledge that with ninety minutes to fill on a weekly basis, the *SNL* writers were desperate characters; a chance remark, a joke recounted in casual conversation, or a cocktail party anecdote, let alone a piece submitted to an *SNL* writer in the days when he or she was a *Lampoon* editor—anything was fair game. Also, given the *Lampoon*'s, and especially one particular editor's, reputation for "borrowing" work, these outraged protestations rang a little hollow; there was no shortage of freelancers ready to complain that the *Lampoon* had stolen their ideas.

The prevailing feelings of envy, according to Abelson, were diluted by doubts that success in television meant very much. "People were likely to say on a Monday morning, 'Yeah, I saw the parody they did of game shows. I guess they really see through game shows.' There was a certain sense in which it was considered safe humor and a certain sense in which it was painful," he said, "like half the class stays home and half the class gets picked to go on a school trip to the South Seas for six months. The trouble is the *National Lampoon* editors saw through stardom and fame and money along with everything else. So," he speculated, "it was very difficult for them to have a straightforward envy for people who had become either rich or famous or both"—people like Kenney, for example, whose very presence made it clear that money couldn't buy happiness.

If the Lampooners weren't sure they wanted to deal with the anguish and misery of fame and fortune, there were plenty of comedy writers who did. *SNL* replaced the *Lampoon* as the brass ring for emerging humorists, and the magazine was losing potential talent, not to mention cachet. In addition to the beer-and-babes young male readership, initially the magazine's audience had included "a lot of people in the less-literary literary community. It was what was In—something you felt you had to read," Greenfield recalled. But this relatively sophisticated reader was leaving, and now the talk of the less-literary literary community would probably be Radner as Patti Smith spewing booze all over the recording studio on *SNL*.

The rocket had fallen out of Simmons's horse. "The *Lampoon*," Abelson observed, "was based on an obsession with sex and drugs and on seeing through conventional success," but while sex and drugs retained their appeal, a critique of conventional success was no longer so interesting and neither was profound alienation. It could be argued that the magazine was in trouble from the moment President Nixon resigned in 1974. "You can't wheel out a tactical nuke against Gerald Ford the way you could against Nixon and Agnew, whose sins were so outsized and hilarious," Greenfield pointed out, and now the Lampooners were left wondering, "When you go in with flamethrowers blazing, what do you do when you've leveled the forest?"

This, among other questions related to the magazine's loss of creative energy, might have been raised at those conference room meetings, but introspection was not on the agenda, although Kelly maintained that he and Hendra had always encouraged discussions about the magazine's direction. "Doug would throw up his hands and walk away from these '60s-esque self-criticism sessions which Tony and I were very keen on holding. We'd say, 'We're going to do an issue on injustice—who are we attacking?' We ended up giving people their heads" in the sense of incorporating more lowbrow material, Kelly sighed, "but Tony and I didn't want to."

The editors could be forgiven for not devoting time to considering how they might boost the magazine's popular appeal because there was no sudden falloff in business to dramatize the point. Even though 1975 saw a contraction in the magazine business in general, the *Lampoon*'s ad sales were up 30 percent by the end of the year—higher than ever—and while average circulation did decline, it did so slowly, as if wasting away from TB (or in this case, TV).

However, the editors were not entirely oblivious to the magazine's sinking fortunes. "There was a certain amount of anxiety about the magazine's sales figures, and we vaguely knew, even though we were too hip to care, that this was a business and the business wasn't doing well or well enough," Abelson recalled. If they weren't thinking about it, it was mostly because reflection was not in the nature of the beast, and that fatal ambivalence made it hard to get exercised, even about one's career prospects.

To the extent that the editors noticed circulation declining, they were inclined to take a philosophical attitude. As Abelson said, "a humor magazine has a natural life span in the same way that very few rock groups sustain themselves. There was a collective perception on the part of the people there that the *Lampoon* had reached the end of its natural life span. Maybe it could be protracted or even given new life, but nobody was betting on it."

19

THE ROCKET
FALLS OUT

One person who was not prepared to accept that humor magazines had a natural life span and that the *Lampoon*'s was at an end was Simmons. It might be necessary for his editors to make a greater effort to be accessible to the widest possible audience instead of writing what they damn well pleased and expecting a self-selecting audience to come to them, but an indulgent attitude was a luxury Simmons could no longer afford—not with a $3.5 million debt to pay off.

This was by no means a new dynamic. From the start, Beard and Kenney had held Simmons's editorial suggestions at bay. "They were always fighting, wondering, 'How do we keep our editorial integrity and at the same time make it financially successful?'" Hoffman recalled. In his view as a major stockholder, "the magazine was Henry and Doug and we should stay with what they wanted to do and it would be successful anyway." The responsibility for maintaining this editorial integrity fell mainly to Beard, and for his successors, it was truly a case of not missing their water until their well ran dry. "The first five years, Henry dealt with Matty and we didn't appreciate it," Kelly said. "Matty was a joke figure to us. He'd walk through the office and say, 'Mention matzoh balls' and walk out. We had no idea how much Matty wanted to meddle. We found out the day Henry left," and Kelly came to realize that "Henry earned every nickel he took from the *Lampoon*."

As a major stockholder who could exercise a buyout option at any time, Beard had enjoyed a certain amount of leverage unavailable to the ordinary staffer. "Matty had tremendous respect for Henry," Meyerowitz said, "but after Henry left, the editors were just employees and they were made to know it."

The new senior editors lacked not only Beard's economic clout but also his editorial authority. "Matty was not only embittered about the two of them having left but also there was no longer a leadership that had a sense of what the magazine was," Abelson declared. "People would fight with him, but that's not the same thing." Nor did Simmons provide a vision of his own to fill the vacuum beyond keeping sales figures buoyant. "He was very panicked about money. He was willing to make any compromises he thought necessary, and I don't think," said Abelson, "that Matty had any great respect for any of us, though I do think he had an affection for P. J. and respect for P. J.'s ability to run a tight ship."

The feeling was mutual. Of all the original Lampooners, Hendra and Kelly were the most likely to strike sparks with the publisher. If Simmons and Beard were like fire and ice, Simmons and Hendra—the former mercurial, the latter volatile—were like fire and gasoline. Also, whatever differences of taste Beard may have had with Simmons, he was unlikely to hold the publisher's being a capitalist against him. "Henry wasn't that angry at society. His articles were about the use of words. But with Hendra and Kelly," Meyerowitz recalled, "the magazine took on a little nastier tone because Tony and Sean were angrier at the world."

A capitalist Simmons might have been, but things could have been a lot worse. At least Simmons was the old-fashioned kind of capitalist who saw his company as an extension of himself; otherwise, he might have sold the magazine to a media conglomerate and instead of a publisher who, however irritating, was at least a recognizable human being,

Hendra might have found himself answering to an army of faceless accountants.

Though less confrontational than his coeditor, Kelly was similarly inclined to dismiss Simmons's right to influence editorial decisions. "Sean and Tony didn't like taking orders from anyone. They didn't like having to buckle under when Doug or Henry told them to do anything or not do anything, and they certainly didn't like it from Matty," Latimer said. If Hendra had it in for Simmons on political grounds, Kelly's objections were aesthetic: his natural inclination was to give the people what was good for them, while Simmons's was to give the people what they wanted. Even if he had totally agreed with Simmons's priorities, Kelly was perhaps the staffer least likely to be able to implement them. Then, too, there were simmering resentments. Kelly maintained that when he was offered a writing job on one of the Tomlin specials, Simmons told him that if he spent his vacation writing for Tomlin in California not to bother coming back.

The bad feeling was not a one-way street. Meyerowitz remembered Simmons telling him, "'I gave Sean ninety-seven chances and Sean screwed up ninety-eight times.' That's simply not true," the artist said, "but Matty blamed Sean for everything that went wrong." The end result was that communication between the editorial and business spheres plummeted just when it was most needed. Hendra and Kelly's primary gripe against Simmons was that he did not trust them to reshape the magazine in their image, to make it their own instead of a pale shadow of the Beard-Kenney product.

Abelson believed that the magazine's decline might have been arrested or even reversed if only Simmons had not been "insisting we keep on doing everything that had worked yesterday and just allowed a new group to evolve a new magazine. . . . Matty's inability to relinquish his control squelched whatever genuine rebirth there might have been."

"My argument with Matty was, 'You hired a group of people who are specifically not hacks who give the people what they want and now you're asking them to be that. If unleashing these lunatics on the world means everyone gets to take home a nice paycheck, why screw with that formula?'" Kelly asked. But Simmons might have felt that, postbuyout, he could not afford a leap into the unknown.

In any case, a magazine had appeared in 1976 to tempt those readers in search of a more mature approach to humor. Intelligent, sophisticated, and obviously richer in good intentions than working capital, the *Real World* did not exploit naked ladies, but its contributors included numerous younger *New Yorker* writers, Chris Cerf, and a resurfaced Henry Beard. Even though the *Real World* resisted pandering to adolescents, Hendra and Kelly probably would not have felt at home there either. Aside from the fact that it was riddled with Harvard grads, the magazine avoided the *Lampoon*'s bare-knuckled body blows in favor of a more genteel approach. For example, its parody of the much-discussed 1976 sexology tome *The Hite Report*, *The Spite Report* (coauthored by Beard), explodes "the myth of the penile orgasm" by revealing such believable male responses as "nothing turns me on more than to get a six-pack and a pizza, and slowly apply thick gobs of creamy paste wax to the trunk and firm sides of my '73 Plymouth Barracuda." However, whether because of its unslick art direction, its limited distribution, its miniature ad base, or its relatively sophisticated humor, the *Real World* was not long for same and its fate can only have strengthened Simmons's resolve.

The *Lampoon* editors may have been blaming Simmons for what was essentially the readers' fault. If *NatLamp*'s original college-age audience had stayed with the magazine into their late twenties, Simmons might well have followed Kelly's game plan. However, said Mogel, "the theory was that people would grow up into the *Lampoon* from *Mad*," which suggests the publishers wanted to target high-school seniors and college freshmen, not ancients in their late twenties.

Hendra and Kelly, on the other hand, wanted the magazine to mature. "We said, 'We're growing up and so are the readers,'" the latter recalled. "Our argument was 'We can't make jokes for the kids in college in 1978 because one, there're fewer and fewer of them; two, they're watching *Saturday Night Live* for free; and three, they've changed and we don't know how they've changed.'"

The choice was between going for an older audience or hiring new editors more in sync with the younger readership. Hendra and Kelly knew which alternative they preferred. "Tony and Sean tried to maintain and even build on a sense of political consciousness," Abelson said, "but on the other hand, the *Lampoon* wasn't for people who were really aware of what went on this week. It was a magazine read by a very young audience, like Doug and Henry and those people were when they started it." It had never bothered the editors that the audience might not get many of the jokes. "We both assumed a wide range of knowledge and didn't care whether readers had it or not," as Kelly said, but this was an assumption that would apply to less and less of the readership, and Simmons *did* care.

Needless to say, the perceived gap between the magazine and its audience provided humor fodder. "Well, it's been lovely," began an early 1977 Letter to the Editor. "We've been together what, six years? Remember the time we made love in your bedroom and your mother almost walked in . . . when you came all over my Foto Funnies? I absorbed every drop. I loved you. But people change, don't they? I guess what I'm trying to say is that I'm leaving you . . . no hard feelings. (signed) *National Lampoon*."

"I know certain judgments were made—e.g., we have to do the sex issue twice a year. It became more and more like that, although," Kelly maintained, "Tony and I tried to hold the line." Yet without a buyout option, they couldn't argue with figures that showed sales jumping by 15 percent whenever a busty lady graced the cover. In fact, they didn't really mind busty ladies, but Simmons was also pressuring them to soft-pedal the more serious aspects of their critique. This was not an ideological stance but a business decision. Simmons might have been able to live with RCA's withdrawing its ads in response to December 1974's Judeo-Christian Tradition issue, but distributors in the Midwest had refused to carry the offending issue and newsstand distribution was the magazine's lifeblood.

Consequently, after that issue, Simmons declared that religious jokes were off-limits. To Kelly, this was the equivalent of telling Chris Miller that he couldn't write about sex. "I was the one who did the religious shit," he said. Ultimately, the subsequent years of pent-up heresy meant that Kelly's first project after finally leaving the *Lampoon* in 1978 was a parody of the Bible that contained "every antireligious joke I'd thought of for four years and couldn't use."

The original editors had always known that without its blithe indifference to the good opinion of advertisers, the *Lampoon* would quickly become just another magazine. Awareness of this had informed an October 1971 parody of *Mad* by Kelly, Beard, and John Boni, who created a cautionary tale in the form of "Citizen Gaines" in the style of one of *Mad*'s movie parodies. The story begins when *Mad* publisher William Gaines expires murmuring the word *satire*. In search of the meaning of this mysterious term, a reporter interviews the current *Mad* editor, who recalls Gaines urging him to "go easy on the kind of humor we've been printing up to now. You know, what Kurtzman used to call . . . to call . . . sorry can't remember. It's been so long." Current *Mad* writers offer guesses like "Satire? It's a Jewish holiday." Finally Kurtzman confronts Gaines, asking, "What about adult satire?" Gaines replies, "Huh? What does satire have to do with anything?" When the *Lampoon* started following a similar course, Kelly may have felt he was bowing to the inevitable.

However, Simmons himself disputed that he ever tried to censor the editors. "I cannot run the magazine at the whim of advertisers. We publish what we think is funny and meaningful. My attitude has always been we can do anything if it's redeemably funny. Of course someone had to decide if was redeemably funny, and that," he said, "was me."

This view was not without support. "Matty never interfered as far as I could tell," said Greenfield, and it seemed to Weiner that "Matty may have wanted a cover occasionally, but other than that I don't remember any editorial interference." Even his detractors admitted that Simmons gave the editors their heads, along with a large budget, to produce the issue that is universally viewed as the best of the Hendra-Kelly years, a February 1977 chronicle of the five JFK administrations that never were. This long-overdue correction to the Kennedy hagiography gave Hendra an opportunity to simultaneously smash two of his favorite but rarely overlapping targets, saints and politicians. "Tony was of the basic view that the Right was a lunatic fringe and these people would blow us all up," Greenfield recalled, "but he was much more interested in listening to the sound of bad faith, political mush, phony sentimentality."

A foldout time chart gives an overview of the many highlights of the Kennedy years: the 1963 assassination attempt in Dallas, in which the president was merely wounded but his wife Jacqueline tragically mown down by the press bus; the Summers of Love, 1965–1968; the institution of a minimum wage for housework; an inflation rate of 25 percent; the establishment of local CIA precincts; Kennedy's remarriage to Christina Onassis; Che Guevara running for governor of Cuba, the new fifty-first state; and the repeal of the Twenty-Second Amendment banning more than two presidential terms. On the cultural front, "Robert F. Dylan" records songs like "The Times They Are Terrific" and "Highway 61 Repaved," Ian Fleming wins the Nobel Prize for literature, NBC's *Saturday Night* is cancelled after its first show, and in 1970, the "first and last issue" of the *National Lampoon* is published.

So proud were the editors of their baby that they urged Simmons to publicize the issue and serve notice that the *Lampoon* was more than zits and tits. Kaminsky remembered "telling Matty he should spend $25,000 to take out an ad and Matty's going along with it," until Ted Mann, yet another Canadian, walked in and deposited himself on Simmons's desk. Convinced that money was being deducted from his paycheck to pay for green card–related legal expenses, Mann called the police and reported Simmons for theft. Despite this performance, Simmons went ahead and bought full-page ads in the New York and Los Angeles *Times*. Sadly, the outlay did not bring in that new audience. The issue sold no more than averagely. He also, said Kaminsky, "fired Ted at that point, although he reinstated him sometime later."

This revolving-door phenomenon was apparently standard. "A lot of people were fired and rehired," said Devins, who also recalled "all these fabulous rows between Matty and Sean and Ted." Because Simmons was perceived as being generationally, intellectually, and temperamentally out of sync, decisions that might have been considered prudent were not given serious attention, and because the editors found it hard to respect Simmons himself, they also found it hard to respect his very real financial problems.

If they were going to have to pander to the lowest common denominator and be considerate of advertisers' feelings, there seemed to be no reason for *Lampoon* writers not to go after television-level money, particularly since it was clear that their counterparts on *Saturday Night* weren't being asked to pull many punches. As well, although Simmons "to some extent persuaded people that they were so weird and unprofessional they would never survive in the real world," as Abelson said, further proof was coming in every day that *Lampoon* experience was a marketable commodity. Not only had O'Donoghue and Beatts won Emmy Awards, but even the otherworldly McConnachie had landed a job writing an NBC pilot in collaboration with the Murray brothers and cartoonist M. K. Brown, a project produced by TVTV's Michael Shamberg.

Consequently, said Latimer, Kelly and Hendra "were absolutely impatient to go, impatient and disgruntled," while Devins added, "It was the start of screenplayitis." They may also have been tired of coping with the job's emotional fallout. When the steam generated by "internecine squabbles, and feeling ripped off by Doug and Henry, and Matty coming in and telling you you can't do this joke because it's too political" blew at home, Kelly said, it was made more scalding by the fact that "the *National Lampoon* editor feels as if he's doing everyone a big favor when he vents. We thought the most outrageous, negative, vulgar, scurrilous thing we said wasn't only permitted, it was cute, so it was hard not to stop at home."

As the chief editors' attention started to wander, the leadership vacuum that began with Beard's departure grew. At the beginning of 1978, with Kaminsky off skiing in Vermont and Hendra in England, the issue missed its publication date. Simmons had had enough. As Abelson recalled, "Matty wanted things to be less collective and more hierarchical, to run more like a magazine where people got their assignments, knew what they were doing, and didn't sit around in five-hour meetings."

After being frozen out by Hendra and Kelly, Simmons probably also wanted someone who not only could make the trains run on time but to whom he felt personally close. There was only one possible choice: "Sure wish you would let that P.J. fellow edit more issues, as we know he hates Communists as much as we do, and we aren't so certain about some of the rest of you," a "Billy Bob and Lee Willy Bucket" wrote in to the Kennedy issue. They were about to get their wish.

20

VISITING THE HAREM WITH SILKS

While Kelly and Hendra were struggling to create their own version of the *Lampoon*, Murray also was trying to measure up to former colleagues' achievements. April 1976 found him still in Los Angeles, working with Ramis, Rucker, and Shamberg on a TVTV look at the Oscars that offered glimpses of the stars in unguarded moments, such as nominee Lee Grant asking Goldie Hawn to say, "And the winner is . . . Lily Tomlin!" as they ride over to the ceremony so Grant can practice being a good loser on camera, or Steven Spielberg watching the announcement of best director nominees and groaning, "I didn't get it" as his associates rush to comfort him.

Murray, meanwhile, stands among the throngs along the red carpet, shouting comments through a megaphone at the arriving stars. They ignore him completely as do his fellow fans; in early 1976, no one in a crowd of starstruck movie enthusiasts had the slightest interest in Bill Murray. But Murray was not in pursuit of movie stardom. He just wanted a context to be funny in and by the end of the year was back in New York working on the fifth *Lampoon* album, *That's Not Funny, That's Sick*. Although Hendra, Ramis, Belzer, McCall, and Kenney are credited as writers, the driving creative forces were Guest and the two Murray brothers, whose improvisational talents came to the fore on a record that was largely unscripted.

Unfortunately, reflecting the *Lampoon*'s new financial realities, the recording gang were expected to come up with a crowd pleaser, and the resulting album might be more aptly titled *That's Not Funny, That's Dumb*. With much gratuitous grossness, the material illustrates the growing schism between the *Lampoon*'s Dr. Jekyll and Mr. Hyde components. "We didn't try to be as smart as on the other albums," Tischler admitted. "We were under so much pressure from Matty to make a shocking record that we decided to do a parody of a bad taste album. Still, sometimes it's hard to tell it's a parody."

However, the album does have its inspired moments, notably a Mel Brooks tribute by Richard Belzer in which terrorists hijack a plane to Miami only to be kvetched to death by a planeload of passengers moaning, "Haven't we suffered enough? In Egypt, in Germany . . . and now no meal or movie!" Another highlight is the big production number the "Height Report Disco," arranged by Shaffer. By the mid-70s, the idealistic movement that had wanted to free sexuality from the shackles of repression and guilt was being reinterpreted as the encouragement of sex without attachment. With penicillin to control VD and the specter of botched illegal abortions banished by 1973's *Roe v. Wade* decision, the ancient linkage of sex and death seemed to be truly broken, at least until AIDS appeared some ten years later. The "zipless fuck" one-night stand and "swingers' clubs" flourished, and where only a few years before radio play of the Rolling Stones' relatively demure "Let's Spend the Night Together" had caused outrage, being stuck in traffic could now be enlivened by the pseudo-orgasmic moans of singers groaning with all the genuine passion of a hustler.

This manufactured, mass-produced libertinism provided the basis for the "Height Report," which featured a chorus crooning, "Give it to me lover, slip it to me lover, ram it to me lover," and so forth as singer Donna Detroit and Murray have an audio orgasm over a thumping bass. Or at least he does. Detroit is left grumbling, "What about me, Mr. Rocketship?" but her complaints fall on deaf ears. "I'm going to fix myself a double-decker sandwich, finish an entire bag of potato chips and maybe a couple of beers," Murray rambles on cheerily, like a sort of Disco Dagwood.

Unlike the magazine editors, the eleventh-floor team didn't agonize over whether they were being more juvenile than they would like. However, with the success of *Saturday Night*, "it became clear that this was not just for fun, that it was turning into a little industry," as Tischler said. As if to underscore the point, Belushi, who only two years before had been working alongside them for $300 a week, would come over in his limousine to visit the album's midnight recording sessions.

Chase, too, dropped by "and quoted Lorne as saying, 'No one gets laid because they work at the *National Lampoon* anymore,'" Weidman recalled, adding hastily, "That wasn't meant to be taken literally." But despite having already been tapped to replace Chase, Murray did not appear distracted by visions of celebrity and, Weidman said, "seemed quite happy in what he was doing." The actor would not feel that way again for quite some time.

Although he was hardly an unknown quantity, Murray found he still had to pay some dues when he joined *SNL* in September 1976. "I spent six months as a second banana," he recalled, and especially coming off the *Lampoon* records and TVTV where he had been given as much scope as he wanted, he found it frustrating. To make matters worse, his frustration affected his performances. "I blew a joke in one of Anne Beatts' sketches and she still hasn't forgiven me," he told *Rolling Stone*'s resident 'Poonie Tim Crouse in 1984.

Then, too, just because Murray took over Chase's slot in the cast did not mean that he inherited the position of Number One Son. On the contrary, the down-to-earth actor and the upwardly mobile producer mixed like beer and white wine. Nor was Murray's life made any easier by the letters pouring in from irate Chevy Chase fans making disparaging comparisons. It was a lot of pressure for a twenty-five-year-old to handle, especially one who had only been in the business for four years.

Ironically, it was Murray's portrayal of a man rising above difficult circumstances that provided his breakthrough. Inspired by some soap-on-a-rope in the shape of a microphone, he created a character who not only sings but also creates a whole Vegas persona in the shower. "Thank you, thank you, thank you very much," he says to no one in particular before launching into the Beatles' "Something." When his wife, played by cowriter Radner, ventures into the bathroom, he pulls her under the showerhead, introducing her with "Ladies and gentlemen, a very special guest." Then he introduces "the man she's been seeing behind my back for the last two years" and pulls him into the shower as well. "Well, honey, are you going to break it off with him for the good of our marriage or are you just going to stick the knife in and twist it?" Murray asks amiably.

Where Chase's characters usually appeared to have everything under control until he shattered this impression with a pratfall, Murray's usual persona had nothing under control but was able to blithely ignore this reality by taking refuge in that "everything's beautiful, baby" language of celebrity hype. He hit his stride with characters like the fanzine-minded Entertainment Reporter from "Weekend Update" and Nick, a mediocre but always-game lounge singer, two legends in their own minds blissfully unaware of their own limitations.

When people began ending ordinary conversations with the Entertainment Reporter's sign-off "Now get *outta* here! I mean it" (delivered after giving some totally unasked-for advice to a celebrity he doesn't know), it was clear that Murray had prevailed. As the show entered its third season in the fall of 1977, creating regular characters that captured the audience's imagination became the key to success on *SNL*. The surest indication of this was a character's signature catchphrase being picked up by the public. Thus, Emily Litella's meek "Never mind" on learning she had once again made much ado about nothing and the would-be trendy Czech Brothers' (Aykroyd and Steve Martin) confident if mistaken self-description "Two wild and crazy guys" were heard in bars and on campuses across the nation, the verbal equivalent of hand signs to denote being a member of the hip gang.

The extent to which they were penetrating public consciousness left the perpetrators somewhat dazed. Shuster remembered going to restaurants with Beatts on Monday nights to write while they ate and hearing "people on either side talking about stuff we'd written, or talking like experts about the personal lives of Belushi or Gilda—outrageous weird things that were often not true. I think we were swept away in the excitement that it was actually happening," she said.

For a new writer, coming up with a good recurring bit was essential. "It's hard for anyone joining anything like that, especially when it's been going for a while," said Novello, who established himself immediately thanks to writing a Greek restaurant sketch that introduced Belushi as a diner owner taking cheeseburger orders. Novello further strengthened his position when his urbane Vatican gossip columnist Father Guido Sarducci became an audience favorite.

This growing affection for recurring material was a departure from Michaels's original goal of raw disposability, and not everybody was happy about it—especially O'Donoghue. Discouraging risky innovation was, he felt, smothering creative fire in a security blanket because "danger was the most important thing in *SNL*. Acrobats are never more exciting than when they're falling—it's never going to get better than that. But gradually there began to be cheeseburger sketches and you knew what the end would be."

Even those actors who benefitted from the familiarity grew tired of the characters that endeared them to the audience. By the end of the first season, Belushi was declaring, "Get rid of *all* the old standard characters, the stale stuff, catchphrases! Lorne's pressured, the network, like always, wants to go with a winner, but fuck 'em, we've got to build on what we've learned this year, see how far we can *reach*."

"Belushi was always angry about selling out," said Gottlieb, who felt that the entire *SNL* cast "was always muttering about selling out and were always trying to see how much more they could get away with." However, the situation was not quite the same as the *Lampoon*'s, with finance-minded management determined to stick to established formats and writers chafing to explore new artistic directions. O'Donoghue did not turn down many opportunities to appear on camera as Mr. Mike, portraying, for example, the entire Mormon Tabernacle Choir having their eyes put out with needles, nor did Belushi suddenly refuse to say, "But *noooo*."

Michaels himself was of two minds. "Uniformity of product is an enormously important thing when you're a businessman. For an artist, it's anathema," he declared, identifying himself as a hybrid, an "artist-businessman." This was, after all, a man who had refined his concept for the show not by studying audience demographics but by meditating in the desert, or at least spending several introspective weeks at the Joshua Tree resort taking magic mushrooms and talking over ideas with Tom Schiller. Clearly, this was a project that grew out of a vision, not a formula. "I wanted it to be devoid of definition much the way I wanted my life to be. . . . The mandate was to be experimental. Whenever it was getting to the point where smugness was about to creep in I tried to kick it around a little," he declared in 1979.

But Michaels's businessman side could only be cheered by the steady increase in viewers. With the third season, *SNL*'s audience had grown by ten million viewers to a thirty share, making it a genuine, as opposed to cult, hit. Ad prices went up and the show went into the black, and NBC was happy to provide the cast with rock star perks.

There was a trade-off, however; as more of the public grew accustomed to their faces, it became harder for the cast to anonymously observe human behavior, thus cutting them off from a rich source of inspiration. At the end of the first season, Belushi and Aykroyd could go on a cross-country road trip without being recognized. By 1977, those days were gone. "The main change that I noticed in them was when people started to recognize them," Hirsch recalled. "Gilda got very nervous because a single woman in the city doesn't need strangers patting her on the ass. John got nervous. When a character actor suddenly gets some fame, it throws them."

It was all happening very fast; in the summer hiatus between the first and second seasons, Belushi had performed his Joe Cocker imitation at a garden party in honor of Paul McCartney's birthday, for which he was paid $6,000. He was mingling with the superstars, but as the paid entertainment. Between the second and third seasons, the *SNL* cast had a superstar-studded garden party of their own at which *they* were the guests of honor. The party was a leisurely affair that migrated from a Hamptons beach house where O'Donoghue and Chase were holed up writing a movie script (the never-produced *Saturday Afternoon at the Movies*) to a beach house Michaels was sharing with musician Paul Simon. It was the realization of the dream Michaels had dangled in front of O'Donoghue at that first Plaza meeting, the epitome of that eclectic, appreciative, amused, fickle, and perverse style.

Accustomed to wearing clothes they could sleep in if necessary, the *SNL* team found they could adapt to silk and linen. Initially, *Saturday Night Live* struck Prager as "similar to the *Lampoon* in the sense that everybody was completely dedicated to what they were doing and spent day and night doing it." But, she felt, as the glare of the spotlight grew hotter, this changed. "When *SNL* started, people's attitude was that they weren't that excited about television. They soon realized how powerful they could be," she said, "and it became something else, a major power and fame trip, a lot more high-powered than the *Lampoon*."

"They were absolutely torn between the commitment to ensemble comedy and a certain purity of purpose—'We're going to do funny stuff that's *about* something'—and the pressure of being pop stars," Gottlieb agreed. "They were caught up in the rush—especially Belushi and Aykroyd. They had the best of everything, the cachet of being the hottest ticket in New York."

"We were lifted on a current of chic," Beatts admitted. Like the Lampooners before them, the *SNL* team took everything as their due and soon grew blasé. "We'd go to parties where there'd be the Rolling Stones, the mayor, Baryshnikov, Nicholson, you name it, and *we* were the stars. I mean, impress me after that," she challenged. At the same time, she maintained, the relentless grind of getting the show on the air kept them grounded. "During the show, it was still a lot of eating with plastic utensils out of Styrofoam dishes and ordering a lot of food from Pastrami & Things. The good news was that you're invited to the party. The bad news," she said, "was that you can't go because you have to work." And as for hobnobbing with the stars, "hobnobbing wears off real fast. All you do is find out your idols have feet of clay."

Likewise, the cast was finally making decent money but had no time to shop. Consequently, vendors would come to the office—"like visiting the harem with silks," Beatts recalled—leading a visiting Canadian to inquire, "How come everybody dresses the same?"

"Some people went crazy behind the money. Lots of people went hog wild. I know I did," said O'Donoghue, and the first vacation the stylish couple took after they started writing for the show was a cruise to Europe on the fabulously art deco *Queen Elizabeth 2.* Even so, when a *Rolling Stone* reporter went to visit Murray's apartment in 1978, he found it decorated in Early Doug Kenney—bare except for a mattress on the floor and assorted books, papers, and clothes scattered around (Meyerowitz described Kenney's Greenwich Village apartment as "three empty rooms with a bed on the floor, virtually no furniture, piles of papers and books, and different kinds of garbage. It didn't look like anybody lived there. It looked like a crash pad for terrorists").

"They expect you to be around a lot, even if you're not doing that much. It's sort of like a family. You sort of feel you should stay around to share the agony," Murray explained in 1978. This total immersion in the *SNL* world led to the writers' becoming increasingly isolated from real life, and so, like the cast, from sources of inspiration. "There's a factor of not experiencing enough life to be able to satirize it," Beatts observed. "Lorne used to joke he got his news from 'Weekend Update.' There's a lot of things I'm not sure if they really happened or if we made them up."

As at the *Lampoon*, being buried alive together led to a certain amount of turmoil. O'Donoghue hadn't given up his old telephone-throwing ways, and his temper wasn't improved any by an acrimonious breakup with Beatts during the third season. On top of having to see each other at work nearly every day, they were engaged in a true New York custody battle over the lease to their apartment (although Beatts might have been secretly glad to unload it, telling Flenniken, "We've got this beautiful apartment and it's got these floor-to-ceiling mirrors and this chandelier, but nobody told me I'd have to *clean* them!").

Aykroyd, too, became prone to eruptions, which, while not as predictable or frequent as O'Donoghue's and Belushi's, were equally ferocious. Unlike his two testy colleagues, Aykroyd's fuse was not naturally short, but it had been increasingly frayed by stress and overwork. Incensed more by moral outrage than wounded ego, Aykroyd tended to take his anger out on hapless property, smashing glass display cases or ripping out the ceiling tiles from his dressing room. "Hell, I'd rather be psychotic than quietly neurotic if my psychosis comes out on breakable objects. Considering the pressure we're under, what people expect of us, what's a few mail chutes here and there?" he asked.

One notable outburst in 1977 was triggered by his discovery of a major discrepancy between the amount budgeted for the writers' salaries and what they were actually paid. Aykroyd made a rousing speech urging his fellow writers to join him in confronting the producer, then punctuated his argument by kicking a hole through the wall into Michaels's office. It was a clear turning point: the team's trust in Michaels as fearless guerrilla leader was undermined. Hurt by this questioning of his motives, Michaels retreated from hands-on production, preferring to stay in his office and work the phones, although he tried to relieve the exhausted writing team by sending in reinforcements Novello and Doyle-Murray.

The writers' ranks shrank once again when Miller and O'Donoghue, *SNL*'s most and least naturalistic voices, respectively, quit at the end of the third season. As the show aimed for a bigger audience, O'Donoghue's quirky influence was diminishing while that of Franken and Davis, the *SNL* writers most after Matty Simmons's heart, was on the rise. According to Shuster, O'Donoghue saw this ascension as "the potato eaters, the *lumpenproletariat* rising up and taking over. And here was Baudelaire, shoved to one side."

Nevertheless, Baudelaire denied that he wanted to create television too precious and obscure for the audience. "You can have subtlety and complexity of ideas as long as you don't make an entire piece depend on it," he asserted. "If you give them nurses with big tits running around for four minutes, give them medicine for five. Art can be commercial. But try convincing commercial entities of that," he said. "The commercial people always win in the short run and lose in the long run." Unfortunately for O'Donoghue, *SNL* sponsors and NBC executives were interested in the short run—that week's ratings.

As he had at the *Lampoon*, O'Donoghue believed that humor without edge wasn't worth bothering with. "I know about edge, but most of these people don't even think about it," he declared, and by the third season, he felt that *SNL*'s edge had dulled to the point where "comedy had become a limitation, not a springboard."

Partially this was because, as at the *Lampoon*, life itself was providing less to react to. Some of President Carter's appointees displayed an affinity for the party lifestyle, and it was possible that some of Them had turned into Us, and vice versa. Also, as at the *Lampoon*, the lack of a clearly defined enemy contributed to the troops' turning their fire on each other, a situation aggravated by *SNL*'s coed staff being distracted by hormones. Aykroyd's flare-up with Michaels, though triggered by a perfectly rational labor grievance, may have been especially intense because the actor had started seeing Shuster, by then the ex–Mrs. Michaels. On top of this situation, Murray, following in the footsteps of his brother once again, began a relationship with Radner in the third season, with Doyle-Murray joining the writing staff just in time to witness it. Besides these liaisons between officers (the creative staff), a certain amount of fraternization with the enlisted ranks (the production team) raised the general level of tension as well as the general level of romantic intrigue and excitement.

The volatility quotient of interoffice relationships was especially high in the second half of the '70s because relations between the sexes were even more incendiary than usual. "When the feminist movement came along, I remember thinking, 'They're right, but what it's doing to relationships is weird,'" Chase recalled. "Relationships that were budding and breaking up all had to do with this great shift." In the aftermath of this upheaval, he saw "men much more frightened, not sure of what their identity was. They didn't know how to behave with girls anymore. There were these extremes, and it was driving people nuts."

The *Lampoon* had had a simple solution to the Woman Problem: ignore it. But with a core group that included an almost equal number of women, this was not an option for *SNL*. "The *National Lampoon* was beyond tokenism," said Beatts. "By *SNL* at least there was tokenism, like, 'We better get some girl writers, even if they still won't be as funny as we are.'" It also rankled that the women working in this high-pressure situation had to give up domestic comforts that were available to the men because the latter, as Beatts pointed out, "had wives. Franni Franken used to bring Al changes of underwear at *SNL*. Nobody did that for me."

Still, at least there was that different attitude at the top, with Dad Michaels taking a more supportive attitude than Dad Simmons or Older Brother Beard. But, inexorably, the working atmosphere of the show took on a more macho cast. "In the early '70s, men were getting their wrists slapped for infringements. Then there was a kind of resurgence of the bravado male, and what better place for that 'move over—I'm here' kind of person than live TV," as Shuster said. As well, the more hairy-chested backstage climate at *SNL* reflected Chase being replaced as leader of the pack by Belushi and Aykroyd. "This was just after the white heat of the women's movement. The women on the show were very strong and it seemed that it was the men on who were in disarray at the time," Michaels recalled. "And along came Danny and John, who were both very much guys' guys," delighting in boyish pranks like throwing frozen pizzas onto Rockefeller Center's skating rink seventeen floors below.

Guys' guys they may have been, but like Beard and Kenney, they formed a partnership of opposites: Aykroyd was a careful and meticulous writer, while Belushi was scattershot but occasionally inspired; Aykroyd learned his lines immediately and perfectly, while Belushi read them from cue cards; Aykroyd preferred the company of honest working men with the kind of jobs he had had before becoming an actor—warehouseman, railroad brakeman—while Belushi enjoyed the company of other showbiz types; Aykroyd wanted to stay in the shadows, while Belushi enjoyed calling attention to himself; Aykroyd's wallet was chained to his belt, while Belushi, like Kenney, would take off into the night without money or ID; or, as Belushi put it, "He's Mister Careful and I'm Mister Fuck It."

However, despite his fondness for things mechanical and tough guys like the Hells Angels, Aykroyd's masculinity was not expressed by a loud antipathy to strong women or by dominating more submissive ones. Not so his pal: Belushi didn't hesitate to express harsh judgments about some of *SNL*'s female writers and cast, making no secret of his hostility toward Curtin, who had little patience for macho blowhards and people who didn't learn their lines.

As well as uppity women, Belushi also dismissed men he considered overly domesticated—men like his producer, for instance. By the third season, the Michaels-Belushi relationship had not improved much from its inauspicious beginnings and, if anything, had deteriorated. Taking a leaf from O'Donoghue's book, Belushi quit often and was occasionally fired. The situation was compounded by his increasingly starlike behavior, which included skipping rehearsals. Sometimes, even if he did show up, after a night spent cruising clubs in the limo, it was hardly worth it.

On the other hand, a bad attitude and hearty partying were not entirely responsible for the actor's poor attendance record: during the course of the third season, he made three movies in quick succession—a grueling schedule that might require him to leave New York on Sunday and return to do the show on Thursday with no time off. Nor, as Belushi's admirers pointed out, was he the only cast member becoming more inclined toward displays of artistic temperament.

Those who loved Belushi forgave the undisciplined, self-indulgent bully for the sake of the generous and exuberant friend underneath. But that was a side they were seeing less and less often, thanks to a combination of drugs and media attention. Belushi himself said as much to a journalist in 1979. "What'd you expect to find, some nice, gracious guy?" he inquired truculently. "You've heard of wild and crazy guys? Well, I'm a wild and *really* crazy guy. Sex, drugs and violence—that's what it's all about."

"Suddenly Chevy was gone and the burden of leadership fell to John. He just collapsed under it, just went away," was Michaels's assessment of the situation, with the result that "there was the problem of having to pull him through a very difficult period, an incredibly self-destructive period." Or as Hirsch said, "all the attention made Belushi uncomfortable, even while he craved it." In the summer of 1978, the actor observed that with success, "everything becomes more heightened, takes on more urgency, and the tendency to self-destruct heightens too. I get nervous," he admitted, "and I am capable of doing something to blow it on purpose." The widening of Belushi's self-destructive streak was especially apparent to old friends. "Bill Murray has not changed from day one in my relationship with him," Tischler said, "but Belushi became impossible to talk to because he was so caught up. He always wanted to make it and he did and it wasn't enough."

Belushi had always had a complicated relationship with the image of the gifted hipster whose talent is blighted by too many late nights and the grip of an addictive drug. This self-exiled outsider, described by sperm conservationist Norman Mailer as the "white negro," had already surfaced in his work. "John and I often discussed the roots of hip com-

307

edy in the Bohemian American Beat scene," Dan Aykroyd said in 1982. "John did a character called Shelly Bayliss: a guy in a black suit, white shirt and black tie . . . a suit to fool the cops . . . shades to hide the eyes. It was the touch of the hippie, the beatnik, the hipster that helped us to impart a weird novel approach to our work."

After appearing in *The National Lampoon Show*, Bayliss was introduced to *SNL* in a sketch called "Beatnik Coffee House." Shuster described the character as "a kind of down-and-out Lenny Bruce, mumbling to the band, kind of paranoid. He may even have been based on [Second City director] Del Close, who was sort of an underground folk hero to some of them. That was part of John's fantasy."

The hipster turned up in yet another incarnation as Joliet Jake, a small-time hood who favored cheap black suits, white shirts, black fedoras, and shades. Aykroyd, portraying Jake's brother Elwood, wore the same costume down to the crosses on his hands. The crosses, Aykroyd explained, were "the junkie's cross. Ask any con, when a white man wears that cross he is the low one on the inside scale. We were playing guys who had nothing, who always had to start at the bottom and work up. . . . John knew the full implications of the hipster's addiction and," Aykroyd contended, "it's not the way he wanted to go out." Nevertheless, as *SNL* took off, it started to look as if this figure was becoming less Belushi's alter ego and more the main event.

Joliet Jake also provided the means for Belushi to realize another, more conscious fantasy. "John wanted to be a rock and roll star more than anything in the world," his manager Bernie Brillstein said in 1986, and he took to sitting in for a couple of numbers with surprised bands at New York clubs. Belushi was hardly alone in this fantasy, but he and Aykroyd went further: they didn't just showcase their musical talents to entertain their guests, they created an entire performance piece in which they portrayed two down-and-out Chicago bluesmen, a context that prevented the pair's renditions of R & B classics from becoming only an exercise in nostalgia.

Christened the Blues Brothers, Elwood and Jake's first public appearance was as the warm-up act Michaels used to put the studio audience in a receptive mood before the show started. The audience became so warmed up that in April 1978, Michaels put the Blues Brothers on the actual broadcast, backed up by the *SNL* band. A contract with Atlantic Records, the label of several of the artists the Brothers emulated, materialized in short order. Like Beard and Kenney before them, only on an even larger scale, Belushi and Aykroyd found themselves in a dreamlike state where the slightest creative whim could be realized as a viable commercial product (indeed, it was as "a viable commercial product" that Shaffer, in showbiz mode, introduced the Blues Brothers' first *SNL* appearance).

Displaying impeccable musical taste, Belushi and Shaffer, the act's musical director, assembled an all-star lineup of R & B heavy hitters that included members of the legendary Stax/Volt studio band who had accompanied Otis Redding himself. For Belushi and Aykroyd, it was yet another instance of fantasy merging with reality—the musicians whom they had listened to so often were now backing them up.

The whole thing was all the more remarkable because Belushi had only recently been turned on to this kind of music between the second and third seasons, when he was in Oregon filming *Animal House*, the first *Lampoon* movie. "The music just blew me away," he recalled. "I thought to myself 'Man, where have you been all these years, listening to the Bee Gees and that disco shit?'" Filled with the missionary zeal of the recently converted, he told Aykroyd that the Blues Brothers "was our chance to bring back some of the greatest stuff that's ever been recorded. We'd make people *listen*," although according to Tischler the act did not inspire their younger, overwhelmingly white audience to track down the Brothers' sources of inspiration.

Belushi and Aykroyd's enthusiasm for the music led them to open a downtown hangout called the Blues Bar, essentially a cleaner re-creation of the seedy after-hours club Aykroyd had run in Toronto. The new club's main attraction was a jukebox stocked with the soul favorites so popular among late-60s 'Poonies, as well as with more esoteric blues and R & B singles. Open by invitation only, the ersatz but funky juke joint drew an unlikely combination of blues musicians, Hells Angels, and movie/rock stars.

As for whether enthusiasm could substitute for dues, "I realized you didn't have to be black to sing the blues, you just had to have the emotion," Belushi opined in 1979, and he wasn't going to let either his race or his status as a highly paid television star get in the way of feeling sufficiently oppressed. Unfortunately, one problem remained.

"The only weakness was the frontmen," the clear-sighted Aykroyd admitted. "We got by, we did a pretty decent job, but we knew our limitations," he said with a humility his partner may not have shared. At any rate, Aykroyd usually refrained from singing except for growling out the bass harmony and stuck to playing harmonica. In the end, it may have been irrelevant whether Belushi could sing or not. Having grown up in a world that—unlike the sheltered '50s—was perhaps a little *too* exciting, the band's young fans did not mind authenticity at one remove, and the Brothers' cover versions might have been more appealing than the originals, resonant with echoes of injustice and suffering.

If the Blues Brothers' success had little to do with their musical ability and still less to do with a renewed public interest in the blues, it had everything to do with *Saturday Night Live*'s high profile and the fact that it was great party music interpreted by America's premier party animal. When on the eve of *SNL*'s fourth season the band recorded nine concerts in LA, "the response was incredible," Tischler recalled. "People showed up in Blues Brothers costumes. The album sounded like a party"—a party partially financed by Belushi, who sunk $100,000 of his own money into the live recording. It proved to be a wise investment. The result, *Briefcase Full of Blues*, sold a million copies within a month.

As the Blues Brothers became a more-than-viable commercial product, the line between fantasy and reality blurred even more. "Everyone was knocked out by how the album took off," said Tischler, who produced it. "John and Danny *became* the Blues Brothers. They became more important than *SNL*," and Belushi's coworkers were made to know it. In January 1979, Belushi, who had just turned thirty, had "the Number One record, the Number One movie, and the Number One TV show, all at the same time. And I was a madman, okay? I was *mad!*" he said three years later, explaining, "It's just so much pressure, so many things going on, so many parties, so many people paying attention to you." The TV show—not actually number one, but close enough—was *Saturday Night Live*, the record was *Briefcase Full of Blues*, and the movie was *National Lampoon's Animal House*.

21

CHARLIE MANSON GOES TO HIGH SCHOOL

Low-budget and unheralded, *Animal House* was one of those fairy-tale movies that scattered box-office gold over everyone connected with it. Success, as the saying goes, has a thousand fathers, and *Animal House* was no exception. First to claim paternity was Simmons, who had a succinct account of the movie's genesis: "In 1975 Doug came to me and said, 'I can't write magazine stories anymore. I have to leave.' I said, 'You can't leave.' He said, 'Why?' I looked at him and finally I said, 'Because we're doing a movie! You're writing a movie with somebody else.' " He then, he said, told Kenney that the movie would be based on the *1964 High School Yearbook* and put him together with Ramis in an office where "they'd start working and then talk to me and kick around ideas every day."

If only it had been that easy. According to Reitman, during *The National Lampoon Show*'s run, he approached Simmons with the idea of turning the production into a film. "By using that as a lever, I got Matty to agree to make a film with me as opposed to the various other people who were getting the smell," he said. However, "the studios still didn't get it, so there was no real great interest." In light of this indifference,

312

Reitman financed an initial treatment with his own money and in the summer of 1975 enlisted Ramis, who was in LA working on *Supervision*, to write it.

In the meantime, among those getting the smell was a junior executive at Universal, who, said Simmons, "called me out of the blue and said, 'Isn't there anything we can do together?'" to which the publisher replied that he would meet "with the head of the studio *only*." At this meeting, said Simmons, Universal chief Ned Tanen agreed to consider making the *Lampoon* project if the budget stayed under $2.5 million, despite finding Ramis's treatment "too rough and too crazy."

Reitman had a somewhat different version of events, declaring that the suggestion for making the *High School Yearbook* the basis of the film came from him. Then, he said, "we made the most basic kind of development deal you can make at a studio: they have all the control, all of the power, and most of the profits, and you keep writing and someday they either make your film or you can turn it around." Following this meeting, Ramis decided that after six months in California with TVTV, he had lost that *Lampoon*-ish edge and requested a collaborator from the magazine—specifically Doug Kenney. "They wanted a shot at writing it by themselves without any interference," Reitman recalled, "so I left them alone for six weeks."

This was not the first time the *Lampoon* had been approached about turning the *Yearbook* into a movie. For example, Thom Mount, who ended up shepherding *Animal House* through Universal's production process, asserted that he had called Kenney a week after the *Yearbook* came out in 1974 "and said, 'I think there's a movie in this. I'd like to figure out how to make that movie.'" Kenney's response, Mount recalled, was to "immediately say all the stuff he would say many times during his life—stuff like 'Maybe there's not a movie in this' and 'Who knows?' and 'Matty's driving me crazy. This place is insane. I gotta get out of here' and 'I think there's some kind of TV show in the works.'"

Mount's advances were spurned by 21st Century because at the time he was working with some "small-time independent producers" and, he said, "it's hard to get anybody to take you seriously when you're not powered by a lot of cash." By the time Ramis and Kenney delivered their outline to Universal, Mount had become Tanen's assistant and so was able to see "two pen-and-ink drawings of scenes from a proposed movie and a sort of treatment written by Doug and Harold. It had Doug's stamp all over it."

"What came in," said Reitman, "was 'Charlie Manson Goes to High School.'" Even with Kenney trying to convey a full sense of the drama by picking up one of those children's toys that spin a swirl of concentric circles while giving off sparks and explaining, "For example, Charlie Manson will go up to girls and hypnotize them with one of these things to make them go out in the country with him," Reitman remained unimpressed by what he termed "this extraordinary story. I sat there quietly for half an hour while they made this presentation, and then I said, 'You can't do that.'" As for the Universal executives, Reitman described their reaction to the Kenney-Ramis treatment as "Holy shit! Let us out of here!"

Similarly, Simmons's reaction was, "Everything was dope smoking, sex—everything like that. I thought, 'Jesus, we'll get lynched.'" At this point, he recalled, two ideas suddenly occurred to him: "I said, 'Let's do it in college,' and everybody agreed that would be a good idea. Then I just came up with a name—'Animal House.'"

Whatever Simmons's inspiration might have been, another factor contributed to bumping the story up to college. George Lucas's *American Graffiti*, which looked at a graduating class of the early '60s, had just been released to great success, "and that really handled high school," Reitman said. Once the project's focus shifted to college life, the subject of fraternities inevitably popped up, and once the word "frat" started popping up, so did the name Chris Miller. "Doug called me into his office in December 1975," Miller recalled, "and said, 'We'd like to do your frat stories as a movie. How do you feel about that?' He didn't say, 'You're invited.'" In response to this rather tactless approach, Miller, with steam coming out of his ears, told Kenney, "I would feel terrible about that because I was planning to do it," whereupon Kenney asked him to come aboard.

The three screenwriters spent the next three months thrashing out a script in Kenney's Village apartment, working eight hours a day. The project attracted what Miller described as "mild curiosity on the part of some of the other *National Lampoon* writers, but no jealousy that I felt." For one thing, the magazine's writers had their own internal rivalries to keep them busy, and for another, their attitude toward Simmons led them to discredit any of his enthusiasms. "We just didn't take it seriously because it was Matty's project, because it was Hollywood," Kaminsky recalled. The actual screenwriters, on the other hand, were fired up. Although none of them had ever written a screenplay before, "from the minute Harold, Doug, and I sat down, there was an excitement about this movie," Miller recalled. "We really felt it was going to be great, even though writing it was exhausting and horrible sometimes."

"We thought we were onto something new. We used to sit around and talk about how *Animal House* was going to be the most successful comedy ever," Ramis agreed, "and we actually believed it." The novelty they thought they were introducing was "the humor of cruelty—anything for a laugh," the cheap laugh at the expense of others less in the know that has since become a staple of teen comedy. But Ramis maintained that they only incorporated such humor to illuminate "the morality of the early '60s. It was very specific to a time and place"—namely, that age of perceived innocence after McCarthy but before the Kennedy assassination, when 'Poonies still wore jackets and ties to dinner but loosened them up to dance to "Louie Louie" afterward. To Ramis, it seemed like "1962, 1963 were the peak years of that old-style frat life," not like after the assassination and the civil rights movement when "there was a major shift in consciousness and all institutions were suspect."

The finished movie has a few hints of what is to come (the civil rights movement is mentioned, but only as a good conversational gambit—along with modern art and folk music—for picking up girls at

Dickinson, a nearby liberal arts women's college where the *Yearbook*'s protohippie Faun Rosenberg is a student).

But the main focus of the script is not outward on changes getting under way in the larger world, but inward on the microcosm of frats, exploring the dynamics of male bonding with its peculiar combination of aggression and affection, undermining and support, and use of humor as a weapon of group defense and internal offense. "It was used as a crucible," Ramis explained, "to keep attacking someone until you found out what they were made of, if they could take it and then give it back." In the presuspicious days of 1962, before there were Us and Them, the enemy was those who deviated from the norm, not those who upheld traditional values. Ramis, Kenney, and Miller were concerned with how the nature of the enemy came to be reconsidered, how Them-in-training turned into Us.

In pursuit of this high purpose, they were unflinching in their depiction of frat man's inhumanity to frat man. "There was a meaner and truer quality to that first draft than was in the final movie. Along with the hijinks, there was some cruelty to unfortunates, but that's part of frat life," declared Miller, the expert. His original idea was to make "the upper-middle-class *Mean Streets*, to frighten people as well as make them laugh." By the time the script had gone through several revisions, he felt the end result had become "not very dangerous. It acts like a rebellious movie, but it's really a St. Bernard that comes up and licks your face." This was a positive shift as far as Reitman was concerned. "The first draft had all the basic elements that made *Animal House* a great film," he maintained, "but it was so strong and strange that it was unmakeable as a film. It was just mean-spirited."

"A lot of the writing revolved around throwing up on things," Mount recalled. "It was very keyed to Dartmouth," Miller's alma mater and the Animal House of the Ivy League, with a winter carnival so notorious students at neighboring women's colleges were routinely warned to stay away unless they were in the market for not remembering who they were waking up next to and how they got there.

However, Miller cautioned against judging all of Dartmouth's twenty-four frats by a notorious few. "Most of them were preppy, upscale, snobbish, conservative, and so on," he said, "but there were four or five that were messy, wild Animal Houses. Their raison d'etre was parties, outrageousness, and rebellion against social norms, to the point where throwing up became something that was engaged in voluntarily and with zest. There was definitely a boorish cast to all this," Miller admitted, but on the other hand, he'd "never had so much fun in my life. Drinking, parties, rock and roll. Even then I knew I would write about it."

When the script finally appeared, said Mount, Universal "thought there was a wonderful movie there, potentially. The basic dean versus the wayward fraternity was in, the neo-Nazi attitude about straight fraternities was in. Anyway, we said yes to further development," pending the excision of episodes like a victory bonfire being extinguished by the brothers throwing up on it and other less tasteful scenes, such as the moment during a grand homecoming parade where a beer keg goes through the forehead of a giant papier-mâché JFK on a New Frontier float and exits out the back in an approximation of the fatal bullet's trajectory.

It took a further nine months for the deal to be concluded, with Simmons making sure the writers only communicated with the studio through him. This may have been intended to avoid a repeat of the January 1975 incident when Kenney and Miller had appeared on Tom Snyder's talk show to promote the magazine. Unfortunately, Kenney had developed an antipathy, as strong as it was irrational, toward Snyder, whom he had never met. The situation was not helped by the host's obvious unfamiliarity with the *Lampoon*. When Snyder asked whether Kenney considered himself a satirist, a writer, a comedian, or what, his guest replied genially, "Actually, Tom, I think of myself as a cheap hustler, just like you," though that may have been just the preshow hashish talking. This prompted Snyder to note that the magazine was doing very well and to suggest, "Maybe we can do something about that."

Without any direct contact with Universal, the writers passed an anxiety-filled nine months. They kept occupied by writing new drafts and found that the vagueness of their situation did not extend to their working habits. Indeed, Ramis felt that "in a way, we attacked *Animal House* with even greater efficiency than we would later projects. We told each other every anecdote we could remember, both true and apocryphal. We threw in every great character we'd ever met. We totally exhausted ourselves talking about college—every tradition, every small bit of frat lore—and that gave us a well of material."

He could participate with authority, having been an officer of his fraternity at Washington University, even if he was ultimately impeached. Kenney, one would think, might have been at a disadvantage, having been deprived of the true fraternity experience by going to Harvard. However, he had been able to attend what Miller deemed "notoriously great Phi Gamma Delta Fiji Island parties" as a teen visiting his older brother at Kent State, and so had experienced an Animal House in its pure form.

Once the raw material had been pooled, the trio brainstormed until they had an outline, then divided up the scenes, with each writing a third and rewriting the other two's scenes. This meant that the entire script got the benefit of each writer's strengths: Miller's feeling for what Ramis called "the philosophy, the edge, the taste level" of the frat spirit and Kenney's ability to create sympathetic characters and depict clearly defined social hierarchies.

As for Ramis, "Doug and I really didn't know how to write a script," Miller acknowledged, "but luckily Harold did, so basically Doug and I were coming up with funny ideas and good lines and Harold was writing the body of the script." Also, as he had on *The National Lampoon Show*, Ramis functioned as a sort of grounding wire for his more zapped colleagues. His steadiness lent him a reassuring, almost guru-like quality, so much so that Miller suggested, "There should be a little book, *The Wise Sayings of Harold*. I once asked Harold, 'How do you deal with anxiety?' and he said, 'Try to think of it as excitement.'"

This ability to deal with stress was being tested to its limit during the development process. Not only was *Animal House* constantly on and off again, Ramis was awaiting the birth of his first child. As well, he had been tapped by the Toronto Second City troupe to be the head writer on their new television show, which he commuted to Canada to write between bouts of writing *Animal House*—a double life that required moving every three or four months. "It was distracting," he recalled with typical understatement.

How Ramis managed to get so many key writing positions dropped in his lap might seem puzzling; apparently he didn't even have to ask, let alone hustle. On the contrary, like Chase, he failed to formulate career goals, moseying along doing whatever seemed interesting at the time, and just happened to stumble into the perfect showcase for his talents. "After I joined Second City, I never once looked for a job again in my life," he said. "I always took the Chinese approach to my career—whatever my destiny was would reveal itself without my doing anything."

Delivering a commencement address, Ramis urged the graduates "not to do anything about their careers and to have fun while they're young because everything good that happened to me happened by my choosing the path of least resistance, always committing myself to having as much fun as possible," and while there are several underemployed creatives who might question whether this is one of Harold's wiser sayings, the approach worked for Ramis, who, like Belushi and Aykroyd, found viable commercial contexts for his creative urges arising with dreamlike ease.

"Harold," Miller recalled, "once said he felt fortunate because he'd been able to run his life so as to get people to pay him to learn the next thing he wanted to learn." With the television version of *SCTV*, he got paid to learn how to create a TV show on a shoestring. *SNL* was managing on a per-show budget of $200,000, but *SCTV* had to get by on $5,000, though admittedly each episode was only one-third as long. The lowliness of the show's budget was matched only by its near-invisible profile. "It was a half-hour show once a month. Imagine trying to find *that* on your dial," said Flaherty, who was an associate producer along with Ramis. *SCTV* could not afford a separate writing staff, so the performers—among them Flaherty, Ramis, John Candy, Eugene Levy, Catherine O'Hara, and Rick Moranis (later replaced by Shaffer pal Martin Short)—did double duty, at least until the third season when a separate writing staff that included Peter Aykroyd and Doyle-Murray was brought on board.

The one advantage *SCTV* had that the NBC show did not was time. The Canadian shows were taped, which meant sketches could be polished. However, this meant sacrificing the working-without-a-net immediacy of live TV. "We couldn't be topical so that put us in a limbo world where there was no news. Our show," Ramis said, "always seemed otherworldly to me, in a goofy world of its own." This was a world of loopy Canadian silliness, in contrast to *SNL*'s knowing New York edge.

Another difference, Ramis pointed out, was that *SCTV* had "no supervision, no censors, no sponsors to appease and no network to please." Possibly because there were no censors to outwit, the Canadian show had far fewer double entendres and sly references to sex and drugs. Instead, there was an almost naive quality to *SCTV*, in part because they couldn't afford glossy production values. "[SNL] had all this money to spend, and they were able to get the look of a network show in a parody form when they wanted to," Ramis recalled. "In a sense, we felt we had to counter what *SNL* was doing."

SCTV decided on a visual style that, as Ramis said, "would make the show look like it was coming from a small independent station somewhere," specifically the mythical town of Melonville, and much of its humor derived from low-budget substitutions for dazzling special effects. In one classic sketch, invading aliens commandeer the bodies of unwitting station personnel, the only sign of the transformation being a single cabbage leaf sprouting menacingly from the back of each victim's collar. Also, without the celebrity guest hosts and musical groups, *SCTV* remained free of a hipper-than-thou tone that had begun to characterize *SNL*. And without NBC's star-making mechanism in operation, the audience stayed far less conscious of the actors behind the roles.

They *were* aware that the Melonville actor (Flaherty) who played Count Floyd, the host of the station's scary movie program, knew that the movies he was introducing weren't all that scary and occasionally had doubts about his own power to terrify, but would gamely rally with a rousing wolf howl or two. Some recurring characters, like Candy's Johnny LaRue, the resident star whose complacency remained undisturbed by his complete lack of talent, were also observed behind the scenes, interacting with other station personalities like Levy's Woody Tobias Jr., a hunchbacked actor doomed to be cast in character roles, his aspiration to play a romantic lead constantly ignored. To further complicate things, there were characters like Flaherty's sleazy station owner Guy Caballero who appeared only in the behind-the-scenes scenes. This dense layering of actors portraying fictional characters who are themselves actors portraying yet other fictional characters gave *SCTV*'s material a postmodern complexity that was in contrast to the simplicity of its production values.

The show's sense of media parody was equally sophisticated. In response to the Canadian government's decree that indigenous programs had to devote 10 percent of their content to specifically Canadian-oriented material (in order to counteract the presumed cultural domination of the United States), *SCTV* came up with *The Great White North*, a talk show hosted by locals Bob and Doug McKenzie. *The Great White North* would invariably start out with the flannel shirt–wearing, somewhat inarticulate McKenzies discussing some important Canadian issue of the day, but almost immediately, the conversation would veer off into a fraternal squabble, usually involving beer, before concluding with the phrase "You hoser," soon adopted as a popular catchphrase in the United States.

While *SCTV* gained a small but devoted following south of the border, it never reached the mass audience of *SNL* even after it was picked up by NBC in 1981 for its fourth season. Cast salaries in the first four years were far below what the *SNL* cast was getting, but the routine was just as punishing. For Ramis, it was "a great effort physically—the hours, the pace, working around the budget restrictions," on top of the new baby and the movie script.

As *SCTV* was gearing up, changes were under way in the movie industry that would work in *Animal House*'s favor. "There was still a real clear sense of Them and Us in the country, and the studio in those days was divided between young executives who thought they could make fresh, exciting movies that would make a difference and the people who felt these kids didn't know what they were doing. When I arrived in 1975, Universal was still making John Wayne vehicles, but within thirty-six months, all the executives in the movie division, with the exception of Tanen, had changed. That was true all around town," Mount asserted. "It was a changing of the guard."

Certainly there was little in Mount's own background to suggest studio executive potential—no law school, no MBA, not even a stint at a talent agency. Another Bard grad, he had spent time painting in SoHo, then got an MA in film and worked as a reporter for the Liberation News Service, a leftist newswire. When he was able to hire an assistant of his own, Mount brought in Sean Daniel, who became *Animal House*'s most enthusiastic in-house champion. Daniel had attended Bennington College, the model for *Animal House*'s Dickinson, and knew he wanted to work on the *Lampoon* movie as soon as he read the purported Dickinson newspaper headline "Sophomore Dies in Kiln Explosion." "That *was* Bennington," Daniel said delightedly. His enthusiasm was further fueled by the fact that he was a regular reader of the magazine.

Unfortunately, Reitman said, he "was about the lowest guy on the totem pole, so his advocacy was not powerful." But like Rob Hoffman, Daniel concealed a keen business sense behind an open, boyish manner and within two years he was supervising the production of *Animal House* as well as other films. Familiarity with the *Lampoon* was another of those things that made Mount and Daniel anomalies around Universal. "No one at the studio had any real sense of what this was," Daniel observed. "When the *Animal House* script went out into the bureaucracy, there were howls of 'What the hell is *this*?' It was this weird fringe screenplay that some people thought was funny and others thought was disgusting. It was a project from the lower depths."

These judgments were being made toward the end of 1976, when the big film was *Rocky*, a modest but upbeat story of a blue-collar underdog determined to better himself through hard work. The heroes of *Animal House*, by contrast, are middle-class layabouts who have no goals beyond having a good time and avoiding undue effort. "The prevailing wisdom among our fellow executives, particularly the older ones, was that fraternity life was a privileged experience," Mount said, and since most people didn't go to college, let alone belong to fraternities, the studio view was that the story would only appeal to a niche audience.

Not everyone on the other side of the generation gap was opposed to the project. "Tanen certainly saw the humor in it," Daniel said. Reitman's recollection, however, was that "every time Tanen read the script, he hated it more," and the script lingered in development hell throughout much of 1977. The writers' sense of the situation was that "one or two guys at Universal who were cool championed it, or it would never have gotten made," as Miller put it.

Around the same time, Mount was also championing a Richard Pryor vehicle coscripted by Gottlieb called *Which Way Is Up?* Unfortunately, like so many Pryor movies, it didn't do well at the box office. He had better luck with the low-budget *Car Wash*, one of the few nonexploitation films aimed primarily at African-American audiences, about one day in the life of the eponymous business. Aided by great music, it ended up turning a respectable profit.

Still, the modest success of Mount's low-budget projects didn't increase his clout around Universal. But then his *Smokey and the Bandit*, a Burt Reynolds vehicle linked to the fad for CB radios, "just went crazy," Mount recalled, "and helped us to have the power inside the studio to make the things we wanted"—things like *Animal House*.

Mount, who shared the Yippie/Ailes/Shamberg view that "the politics of the future is the politics of media," thought he detected the same sense of infiltrating the System when he went to New York to meet with the screenwriters, who were, he found, "going through their own various conniptions and personal battles. . . . And all of us were suddenly getting real incomes for the first time in our lives. It was like somehow the gypsies had snuck into the Vatican dinner. We couldn't believe the Establishment machinery was giving us money to do things we would all be doing anyway." Miller was similarly astonished, feeling, "I got to make money being myself and doing what came naturally. I couldn't believe it. It was like a dream come true."

Like Greenfield before him, Mount was struck by the Lampooners' dismissive attitude toward their boss. At the end of each draft, there were, he said, "always two meetings—one to allow Simmons to pass judgment on the script's shortcomings, and a real one. 'This isn't funny,' Matty would say and point out something and we'd all nod, and then he would get bored and leave. Then we'd all go to that back room and get some deli sandwiches sent up" and write what they wanted. "I think that's how the magazine was run," Mount suggested, "to keep Matty positioned." The idea that Simmons accepted that his interventions would not be seriously considered strains credulity, but Mount believed that "Matty understood that he provided a source of creative tension for them, and as a result got better work out of them."

Relations between Simmons and his movie boys such as Chase and Ramis remained relatively untainted by the condescension and acrimony that characterized his dealings with the magazine's editors. For example, Gerrit Graham, who starred in a subsequent *Lampoon* movie, thought Simmons "very nice in an avuncular way" and felt that much of the mockery the Lampooners directed toward the publisher arose out of a conflicted sense of gratitude. "They knew damned well they owed him a great deal," Graham said, "and, as boys will, they made a certain amount of sport at his expense."

Simmons was not the only one feeding this group whose hand got bitten. "They were ruthless about anybody they wanted to poke fun at. They weren't thrilled to be working for Universal either," Mount recalled, "and whatever the current Universal release of the day was—and there were usually some lousy ones—they'd be all over me about it." Even Reitman came in for a little nibbling, being dubbed "the Roger Corman of Canada."

All three—Simmons, Universal as represented by Mount, and Reitman—were targets since all three were offering the writers advice on the screenplay. Simmons, as usual, was in no doubt about his contribution. "The script was written by Doug, Harold, and Chris, with input from me and Ivan. I worked with them every day. There were actual lines and scenes that I put in," he stoutly maintained. Reitman basically agreed with this account, aside from the minor detail of reversing the producers' roles. "It was me working with the writers on a regular, almost daily basis," he said, "with Matty making notes at the end of each draft."

"It was mainly Ivan Reitman's two cents that were put in on those eight drafts," Miller agreed. As with *The National Lampoon Show*, Reitman acted as trusted sounding board and representative audience member, trying to keep the characters more engaging and the tone less astringent. His efforts were not altogether welcome, especially by Kenney and Miller, with the latter getting "angry with him again and again because I thought he was getting between us and the true story," but the years have mellowed this view. "Now I think Ivan's suggestions were very canny," he said. "He had a very strong sense of what the public would go for and would reel us in from some of our excesses."

Very much unlike the writers, Reitman valued making the audience happy. "The first question for Ivan is: 'Will it work for an audience?' It's not like Fellini sitting down and saying 'Express,'" as Ramis said in 1986. Reitman brought something else to the team: unlike everybody else on the *Lampoon*, he had actually made a film. This, as far as Simmons is concerned, was why the Canadian had been brought on board. "Ivan was hired because he knew the technical end of it," he declared, while inaccurately assessing Daniel's contribution as being limited to telling him, "'My girlfriend is a script supervisor on a picture. You want to go to a screening with me?' I went to the screening. The picture was *Kentucky Fried Movie*. I didn't like the picture but I thought the director was very good." The director of the film, which was written by Kentucky Fried Theater veterans David Zucker, Jim Abrahams, and Jerry Zucker, was a twenty-five-year-old newcomer named John Landis, who had made his directorial debut with a movie called *Schlock*.

22

TIE A YELLOW RIBBON ROUND THE DILDO, PLEASE

I n the spring of 1977, after several drafts of the screenplay had come and gone, the search for a director began. Simmons had sent a letter suggesting candidates to Universal, but Daniel felt that if his superiors ever saw this list, filled with pricey Academy Award–winning directors like Billy Wilder and Robert Altman, "it would make them incredibly nervous. So," he recalled, "I went up to Tanen's secretary before he'd seen it and said, 'Maybe you could just give me the letter.'"

Daniel, by now the executive in charge of *Animal House*'s production, vetted potential directors along with producers Simmons and Reitman. The latter could not put forward the man he really wanted. "Having only directed *Cannibal Girls*," he admitted, "I knew there was no way Matty or the studio would let me direct it." Meanwhile, both Daniel and Mount were impressed with *Kentucky Fried Movie*, despite it being primarily an uneven collection of broad *Groove Tube*–ish media parodies, like the energy company ad touting new sources of oil such as Italians' discarded combs, carryout food, and teenagers' faces.

However, at least some sketches show the Abrahams-Zucker talent that would flower in *Airplane!* and *The Naked Gun*, like the beer ad featuring Hare Krishnas bellying up to the bar ("You've just sold your last case of incense and pestered over sixty pedestrians. You're only reincarnated six or seven times in life, so you've got to reach for all the gusto you can").

Landis's special talent for depicting a gradual slide into anarchy was evident in a chop-socky movie parody in which the hero single-handedly dispatches the villain's bodyguards to the accompaniment of loud squishing and crunching sounds. This penchant for punching up visceral noises reflected one aspect of the *Lampoon* sensibility; affinity with another was demonstrated in scenes like the trailer for *Catholic High School Girls in Trouble*, which shows a pair of large breasts squashed up against a steamy shower door as their owner is obviously being entered from behind ("Never has the beauty of the sexual act been so crassly exploited" booms the soundtrack, borrowing the old *Lampoon* trick of simultaneously satirizing and making the most of such exploitation).

A feeling for anarchy, a cartoonish yet juicy approach to sex, and an inclination toward broad, not to say gross, humor clearly marked out Landis as *Lampoon* material. Indeed, *Time* described *Kentucky Fried Movie* as "a sort of *National Lampoon* that talks and moves." What's more, Landis had made the movie on a budget of $1 million, and it had ended up being a hit. "John was the guy. It was a natural fit," Mount said, and a groundswell of support grew. "*Kentucky Fried Movie* was a little broader in its sensibilities than *Animal House*," Reitman said, "but we liked John and I told Sean to hire the guy."

According to Simmons, Landis was overwhelmed by the honor. "He was a big *Lampoon* fan," the publisher-producer recalled, "and the first thing he said to me when I met him was, 'Mr. Simmons, this is the proudest day of my life.' That—and I've said this to John—was the last humble thing John has said." Landis appeared similarly bowled over by the prospect of working with a major studio. When invited to lunch at the Universal canteen, the young director was so nervous that he spilled three glasses of Coke in a row.

Humility and uncertainty were not usually the first words that people connected with Landis. What he *was* known for was the kind of zest that carries all before it. "He had enough energy for five people," said Miller, while Simmons described the director as being "like he's sitting on the electric chair—volatile, wired, totally on edge. He screams, he yells, he jumps, he hops, he skips," and a *Rolling Stone* reporter noted that Landis was enthusiastic about everything and rarely expressed this enthusiasm below ten decibels.

This energy and enthusiasm was very much in evidence as Landis tackled his new project, and he started supervising the last rewrite of the *Animal House* script during a long weekend in Toronto, with a harried Ramis racing between the *SCTV* studio and Landis's hotel, writing for both at once. Landis's contribution to the mix, said Mount, was to introduce "a level of emotional compassion for the characters that substantially lowered the level of meanness." No longer were the Deltas, the *Animal House* brothers, to be presented merely as a bunch of irresponsible goof-offs with a penchant for nasty pranks. "I don't think *Animal House* worked because it was—as people have said—outrageous, wild, zany, gross," Daniel asserted. "None of those words apply. This was a movie about heartwarming heroic people who were wonderful friends to each other," a far cry from the unvarnished picture of frat life the writers originally hoped to depict.

One can imagine how Kenney must have liked yet another infusion of warmth. Hearing this kind of talk from Mount and Daniel was one thing—he could at least relate to their combination of laid-back aspiration and residual bohemianism. But it is easy to see how Kenney, Ivy League golden boy and preppy sympathizer, would chafe at the intrusion of Landis, a native Angeleno who had left school in tenth grade and whose education was rooted in movies and television rather than the literary canon.

As well, ambivalence, not to mention nuance, was an alien concept to Landis, and Kenney may have felt daunted by someone who had known exactly what he wanted to do since his midteens. Though he may have sported a beard and shaggy longish hair, Landis had escaped any '60s-ish tendency toward introspection and questioning of values and so had never veered from the path of ambition, not even to flirt with drugs, a flirtation that, for Kenney, was now a full-blown affair.

Although there was much common ground between Kenney and Landis—notably a reluctance to leave behind their youthful fondness for science fiction, fantasy, and cartoons—Kenney was more inclined to focus on their differences. "Doug could be very nice to people he liked and very snooty and defensive to people he didn't like," Prager said, and Landis's undisguised desire to get ahead and lack of a gentlemanly sense of irony would have roused both Kenney's snootiness and defensiveness. But Miller felt it was nothing personal. "John did run into hostility from Doug," he admitted, "but Doug was hostile toward a lot of people if he thought they were going to fuck around with his work. It was the same attitude that the *SNL* people had toward commercial TV; he was concerned that the movie would become Hollywoodized."

Such feelings, Miller maintained, were not shared by the entire writing team. "Landis likes to say that when he came onto the project, he ran into tremendous hostility from the writers, but it is simply not true," he said. He himself, for example, "liked John from the minute I met him. He impressed me with his weirdness and his kind of cocky wise-guy streak, and he made me laugh." Ramis's relationship with Landis was characterized less by enmity than by a lack of connection. It was simply a matter of temperament. "Harold is the most laid-back character in the world, and John's totally the opposite," Simmons said. "Landis never sleeps where Harold never moves."

Any hostile atmosphere did not prevent the director from offering Kenney what the writer most wanted: a chance to act, prompting him to drive across the country in his new Porsche. This was not Kenney's film debut. During 1976, while waiting for *Animal House* to get the green light, he had appeared in a film called *Between the Lines*, the story of how the staff of an underground newspaper deals with the disappearance of its original audience after new management insists on a more commercial approach. In a small role as a philosophical hippie barfly, Kenney was long haired and pudgy. But by *Animal House*, he had shape-shifted again, sporting a spiky punk do and sharp cheekbones in the role of a silent, withdrawn science whiz. Miller found his collaborator's choice of supporting character significant. "Doug could have made himself anyone. And who does he choose?" he asked rhetorically. "Stork, the weirdo."

Weird Stork may have been, but in his short-sleeved chartreuse shirt (with several pens protruding from the breast pocket), pegged pants, and heavy black-framed glasses, he was the embodiment of geek chic. And even though *Animal House* was made before anyone knew that today's disparaged nerds would become tomorrow's idolized IT millionaires, Stork's fate, according to Miller's *Animal House* novelization, was to become an independently wealthy holder of several patents.

Not all casting questions were settled so easily. Tanen wanted the suave Brother Otter to be played by Chase, who was at that point trying to decide on the appropriate vehicle for his film debut. "Chevy," said Mount, "was the item that was going to make this picture a go-ahead." Unfortunately for *Animal House*, while the fast-rising star thought the movie's script was "very funny," he also thought it was too much like what he was already known for. His other option was *Foul Play*, a lightweight romantic comedy-thriller that proved to be a hit and made Chase a romantic lead. "I didn't particularly think the script was very good," the actor said candidly, "but it gave me the opportunity to do something different."

Two other factors influenced Chase's decision. One was that he shared Kenney's view of Landis. "I thought he was loud and offensive," Chase said equally candidly. Worse, "I didn't think he was funny." The other was he felt the role was too good a fit—not surprising considering that Ramis and Kenney wrote it with him in mind. "That's the way I *was* in college, except that we didn't have fraternities, and I didn't behave that broadly. But," he said, "there wasn't much about the script that I hadn't already seen or done. I thought that I had lived it." This is saying a good deal considering that Brother Otter—good looking, well off, unflappable—is possessed of an uncanny ability to inveigle his way into women's hearts and pants with a combination of charm, chutzpah, and fast talking, rather like a human Bugs Bunny.

Instead, the part went to Tim Matheson, another handsome actor, who, according to Mount, "was the hot guy in the cast at the time as far as the industry was concerned." Chase's decision was all to the good in Miller's view, and he was similarly relieved when Aykroyd declined to play biker Brother D-Day, a part written for him. Miller didn't doubt the actors' abilities, but he "didn't want it to become an *SNL* movie. I felt that would skew the impact." Despite these reservations, he agreed with his collaborators that the role of Brother Bluto, an elemental mass of raw id and pure appetite, could only be played by Belushi.

Just as Otter incorporated much of Chase's inherent nonchalance, so Bluto incorporated Belushi's force of nature-ness, nowhere more so than in a scene in the university cafeteria where he moves down the food line grabbing plates off the shelves with both hands and swiftly gobbling leftovers off abandoned trays (Belushi was renowned for the speed with which he could make a meal disappear), a display of voraciousness the director pointed up by adding gurgling digestive noises on the audio track. He may have been inspired by the memory of his first meeting with Belushi at which the actor ordered ten shrimp cocktails, twenty beers, and ten Perriers.

Further, Bluto instigates *Animal House*'s two most notable episodes of anarchy and ecstasy: a food fight in the cafeteria and a Roman-themed "toga" party at Delta House. He is a creature of instinct, natural man unhampered by the rules of civilization, as is evident from the first moment he appears on the screen, standing on the Delta House lawn clutching a beer as he woozily greets two potential pledges. Hearing a loud drizzling noise, they notice the bottom of their pants have been moistened, and not by the dew. "Sorry," says Bluto sincerely, mimicking Belushi's tendency to do beastly things and then, in a more conscious moment, apologize profoundly, a tendency that led Landis to describe him as "basically a sweet person who is very sorry for much of what he does, a combination of Harpo Marx and the Cookie Monster."

Also like Belushi, Bluto is a combination of apparent slobdom ("That boy is a p-i-g pig," as a cheerleader girlfriend of one of the Omegas, the upright and uptight fraternity, says) and unexpected physical deftness. Physicality is in fact far more central to Belushi's characterization than speech. For example, when Bluto is discovered perched on a ladder in order to get a better look through a bedroom window at disrobing sorority girls, one raised eyebrow conveys his thoughts far more effectively than words.

Although he got on well with Landis, who recognized the future star's potential appeal to the extent of designing the film around Bluto's entrances and exits, Belushi, too, almost turned the role down, accepting it only after being lobbied heavily. "Doug was a very good friend of John's, and Harold was among the few people John trusted in those days," Reitman recalled, "and we all put tremendous pressure on him to make sure he did it. We all felt he was the critical one."

If the creative team thought Belushi's participation was essential, it was considered immaterial on the business end. As Mount said, they "squeaked Belushi by because we had Tim Matheson, which made the studio feel secure," and because the studio was not really concerned about who would play a character perceived to be unattractive and unsympathetic. The hip studio executives may have been *SNL* fans, but in 1977 the upper echelons still didn't have the show on their radar ("This was a conservative, moribund, culturally bereft community, and by the time news got here, I promise you it was over elsewhere," said Mount of his industry) and, far from wooing Belushi as a star of tomorrow, Universal paid him a mere $35,000 to do the picture.

The relatively small fee would increasingly rankle the actor, to the point where shortly before the film's premiere, he was throwing darts at an *Animal House* poster and muttering to the press about "bullshit money, no points, but I'm going to be a star anyhow, those cheap bastards" (Belushi must have been even more apoplectic when, after the movie opened, Landis publicly boasted about how his percentage of the film's profits would make him a millionaire). On the other hand, when Playten visited Belushi backstage at *SNL* in 1978, she thought the actor would be thrilled about his role in *The Missouri Breaks*, another of the films he made during the third season, because it had given him a chance to work with his idols Jack Nicholson and Marlon Brando. Belushi surprised her by replying, "It was OK, but Alice, I've done this other movie, and it's the greatest thing since *Lemmings*!"

Even with a cast and director in place, the greatest thing since *Lemmings* could still not start shooting until a location was found to serve as Faber College. As soon as officials from a prospective campus read the script, they would back off, but at long last the University of Oregon agreed. Shooting started in Eugene in October 1977, but then the rains came, on top of which the director got sick. However, it would take more than the flu to decommission Landis who, despite running a fever, soldiered on wrapped in a blanket. "John did a wonderful job directing the movie," Mount said, "given that they were having to move the location constantly because of the rain and they had no money and were in general an undernourished group."

With a few exceptions, notably Donald Sutherland—the film's lone star name, portraying an English professor so cool he admits to his class that Milton is indeed boring and, displaying the Dr. Jekyll side of the *Lampoon*, cogently explains why—the actors, even Belushi, were happy to be there during the monthlong shoot despite the rain. The cast of unknowns included a youthful Tom Hulce playing an appealing version of the *Yearbook*'s Larry Kroger (which was, in fact, his character's name); Peter Riegert, who portrayed Brother Otter's savvy golfing buddy Brother Boon; and in his first, very small film role as a snot-nosed preppy Omega pledge, Kevin Bacon.

No one was as yet in a position to insist on star treatment, and camaraderie prevailed. "We all stayed at a Rodeway Inn," Miller recalled, "and after work, music would be played, drugs would be done [the woods around Eugene are known for their fine crop of psychedelic mushrooms], and we had some good parties"—parties that were no doubt further enlivened when Riegert's then-girlfriend Bette Midler came to visit. The cast, however, was more excited by another visitor: author and alternative lifestyle icon Ken Kesey, who came over from a nearby commune with some of the remaining Merry Pranksters.

Simmons, too, found time to drop by and, as always, had advice to offer. For instance, the producer happened to observe a scene that depicts Otter advising Boon on how to resolve his relationship troubles. The suggestion, which Otter pulls out of the doctor's bag he brings along on dates, is an exceptionally tall rubber dildo. "She'll take *this* seriously. Try it," he urges. "Matty was grossed out at the sight of this giant cock and said, 'Can't we do something to make this less offensive?' He then found a piece of ribbon," Miller recalled, "and tied it around the dildo saying, 'Use it *this* way!'"

Meanwhile, Daniel and Mount were in LA watching dailies, the results of the previous day's shooting that, in predigital days, were processed overnight to provide a sort of progress report for studio executives. Screenings of dailies for a relatively obscure movie like *Animal House* were usually not that well attended, but as the word began to spread, "the movie went from a backwater, disreputable little enterprise to where we began to have quite a crowd," Daniel said. "It didn't matter if you were me—an ex-Yippie who saw some of my own story in this— or a class of '35 ex-football player."

The ex-Yippies could relate to the portrayal of Faber's dean as a Nixonian figure who maintains that there is a "little-known clause" in the college constitution that gives him "unlimited power to preserve order in times of campus emergency" and the general celebration of the quirky, cranky individual who resists indoctrination or regimentation. In fact, some of Delta House's brothers bear a distinct resemblance to those other scruffy rule benders, the MASH unit depicted in Altman's 1970 film, with Otter as fast-talking lady-killer Hawkeye, Boon as down-to-earth-but-irreverent Trapper, and vague but decent nominal Delta leader Hoover as vague but decent nominal MASH leader Col. Henry Blake.

At the same time, older viewers could yearn nostalgically for the happy days of irresponsibility. Like *Time's* review of *Lemmings*, they might also have been heartened by the sight of young people destroying property for no good reason instead of as some sort of political statement. This prompted a reviewer in the Canadian magazine *Maclean's* to observe, "The people who bring you *National Lampoon's Animal House* are obviously relieved the 60s are finally over. Who needs to worry about little things like war and civil rights when everyone knows that the really important things in life are being able to squash a beer can against your face, losing your virginity, and pledging the fraternity?"

Not that *Animal House* completely endorsed a return to traditional values. In its total cynicism toward authority figures, distrust of arbitrary paramilitary rituals as embodied in the campus ROTC, and disdain for normal rules of polite behavior, it still had one foot in the land of incense and peppermint. "*Animal House,*" Mount pronounced, "said the following things: education does not take place only in the classroom; by their nature, bureaucracies are evil; and it's not cool to be John Wayne and we're never going back to finding that to be cool again," though the election of Ronald Reagan in 1980 would prove this prediction wrong.

Like the *Lampoon*, *Animal House* wanted to have it both ways, mocking that John Wayne model of manhood but still playing off his traditional fears of the Other, although the film's three writers were among the least swaggering and macho of the *Lampoon* crew. "This was a generation of guys who grew up understanding how to cure yeast infections with yogurt," Mount said. "We tried to have good politics and attitudes about women, and yet we were all very conscious that you couldn't take any of this shit too seriously."

The creators of *Animal House* go back and forth on whether to depict women (Vagino-Americans, as the *Lampoon* put it) as actual characters or simply as joke opportunities. Almost every cute girl in the film has her naked breasts showcased at some point, but on the other hand, the Deltas' female party guests look like normal girls as opposed to super babes. Several jokes can be forgiven their political incorrectness because they are just too good, such as when during the homecoming parade debacle a Bunny goes flying off a Playboy-themed "GEKE" float (adorned with the slogan "When Better Women Are Made, Faber Men Will Make Them") only to land in the bedroom of a twelve-year-old boy absorbed in reading *Playboy*, eliciting from him a fervent "Thank you, God."

The main problem was that, as Ramis observed, "none of us understood women, it's safe to say," and so even a well-intentioned attempt to include a three-dimensional female character misses the mark. Though depicted as warm and intelligent, The Girl, Katy, constantly bugs her boyfriend Boon about when he's going to start acting more responsibly and stop getting drunk with the guys every night. She has a point, but she inevitably sounds like Wendy urging Peter Pan to grow up and get a job.

"I was kind of sure we would get some hostility from women," Mount recalled, "and on some level we did," umbrage being taken mostly at a scene where four Deltas flee a potentially threatening situation, leaving their dates to trudge back to Dickinson at night. The studio, however, was more concerned that the same scene might trigger umbrage from a different quarter, since the threatening situation is a funky roadhouse on the wrong side of the tracks where large African-American men apparently have their eyes on the Deltas' Dickinson dates. Tanen, Mount recalled, "thought it would incite hostility in the black community and argued vehemently to remove it."

One can understand why Tanen was concerned: shot from the Deltas' point of view, the black men appear exaggeratedly massive and looming. They are romanticized as bigger, badder, and impossibly cool, so removed from protected middle-class experience as to make communication impossible, leading one of the Deltas to ask a glowering roadhouse patron, "What school do you go to?"

But at least communication is being attempted. The attitude of the Deltas bumbling into this unwelcoming atmosphere is not so much hostility as what Miller called "a cultural wistfulness" based on unfamiliarity. This may have illustrated less a racial than a class divide. When an

African-American *Animal House* appeared ten years later in the form of Spike Lee's *School Daze*, it revealed that black fraternity brothers could be every bit as devoted to drinking, dumb pranks, and peculiar bonding rituals as the Deltas, and might themselves have felt somewhat uncomfortable and callow in a bar full of lowlifes, even of the same race.

The bridge over this social and racial gulf is music, and the *Animal House* soundtrack suggests the Deltas have more in common with the roadhouse patrons than with other white boys in more restrained fraternities. In contrast to the Omegas' excruciatingly proper, snotty rush party, where the music is provided by a cocktail pianist, the accompaniment to the Deltas' rush bash is the Motown classic "Money," belted out by an offscreen Belushi.

This spirit of genuine festivity saves *Animal House* from being overwhelmed, like several of its lesser imitations, by its sophomoric elements, and nowhere is this more in evidence than in the Delta toga party, which, exuding good fellowship and good cheer, is clearly a Dionysian revel, and not just because everyone is wearing vaguely Grecian costumes.

In 1964, this kind of abandon had been in itself a political statement. The secret weapon of the "counterculture" was that it was able to make politics sexy. "One of the nice things about the Left movement," as Mount said, "was that it was hard to separate the question of mass demonstrations from the tradition of Fort Lauderdale. Everybody showed up at rallies to meet girls and see what Washington looked like in the springtime." A decade later, the link between pleasure and activism had been broken. Far better, given the perceived futility of struggle, to channel that angry and rebellious energy into actions that would prompt the approving cry "Outrageous!"—something like Bluto's propelling a cheekful of mashed potato from his mouth in his celebrated zit impersonation.

"It's behavioral humor of outrage," Landis said when the film was released. "It's definitely offensive. It's antagonistic." But no need to worry because "it's all in good fun." Under such circumstances, it is hardly surprising that, as the *Lampoon* had anticipated, "Party on" replaced "Revolution now!" as the favorite cry of defiance. Given the increasingly grim nature of reality, a little unedifying fun was refreshing. It certainly was for O'Rourke. "A lot of this is a backlash against the enormous serious-ness of the 1960s," he said in 1978 as the film opened. "All the good vibes and piousness . . . look what happened; after all the folk songs and can-dlelit marches it didn't change a thing. You could argue that the world's a worse place now." As well, many young people were tired of being sen-sitive and concerned, and cheered when Bluto impulsively seized the guitar of a sensitive and concerned folksinger and smashed it to bits right in the middle of "I Gave My Love a Cherry," returning the pieces with an apologetic "Sorry."

Despite doubts among Universal's marketing gurus as to whether anyone would respond to this brand of humor, it was apparent from the first public screening that *Animal House* was going to confound expec-tations. A sneak preview in Denver that summer was not particularly promoted, yet the line to get in started forming before noon. When the Universal contingent arrived, they found hundreds of kids milling around outside the theater in the hope of obtaining no-shows' tickets.

The movie benefitted from what Mount called "a jungle drum sys-tem, a kinetic cultural thing that happens and has nothing to do with marketing or anything that's quantifiable." To prolong this ripple of excitement, the studio spent almost double the film's production budget on advertising. After opening in New York in July, *Animal House* went into four hundred theaters nationwide and within a month had demon-strated that, as Mount said, "this picture was going to make a phenome-nal amount of money for a very small investment."

The movie had cost $2.7 million to make; by the end of October, it had taken in $60 million, and a toga-clad Belushi, crowned with a laurel wreath, was gazing out from the cover of *Newsweek* under the headline "College Humor Comes Back." The movie was more than a hit; it was a phenomenon, far outdistancing the movie that had been expected to be the big youth smash that summer, *Sgt. Pepper's Lonely Hearts Club Band*, starring the Bee Gees.

Animal House's success was even more unexpected because for years, comedy films, with the exception of Mel Brooks's movies, had been box-office duds. Now, suddenly, a comedy was hotter than hot with that elusive youth audience. The Lampooners celebrated the opening with their own memorable toga party at *Lemmings* Central, the Village Gate, where Belushi was in his element, with a white limousine and a suite at the exclusive Sherry-Netherland at his disposal.

With *Animal House* rapidly heading toward a spell on the list of the top ten box-office successes, critical reaction was somewhat irrelevant, but a range of opinion similar to the reviewers' could be found among those with a closer relation to the creators. Former jock Conn Nugent gave it a "three out of five," finding it reminiscent of "my roommates and the piano and rock and roll singing and rowdy behavior." Frith, an incurable Dr. Jekyll, found it "a wonderfully strung-together collection of single-panel cartoons without any substance except 'Let's be outrageous one more time.' I came close to walking out."

And while one might expect that editors from the intellectually serious, politically committed Hendra-Kelly regime would all agree with Weiner that "it was the Doug side of the *Lampoon*; it was OK," Kaminsky was far more enthusiastic. "It was a fucking great movie," he declared, although he didn't see it until years after it opened because, he said, "we distanced ourselves from *Animal House* the way *Saturday Night Live* was never very important to us, and so I missed it." From this lofty vantage point, the movie's success was somewhat bewildering, but, said Weiner philosophically, "after you write satire for a while, the taste of the public, whether they vote for Nixon or like *Animal House*, doesn't surprise you except for extreme exceptions."

The screenwriters themselves had mixed reactions. Miller had not been present for the final rewrites because he was in New York working on the *Animal House* tie-in book. When the movie opened, he found that "it had got softened a bit. I couldn't tell if I liked it or not." Kenney, as usual, was of two minds. "While he was very delighted with *Animal House*'s success, underneath I think he knew that it was junk," Chase suggested, "because here you're talking about somebody who founded a magazine based on really good parody writing at Harvard and knew what was intellectually sound and viable."

When Latimer ran into Kenney in the Bells of Hell, he thought his former editor, who was about to move to California on the heels of the movie's success, "seemed dazed and dazzled. He was real ambivalent about Hollywood—whether he wanted to be successful, whether he could be, whether he didn't really want to. He was a lovely, lovely guy," Latimer said, "but he had wheels within wheels in his head, like a Swiss clock." The pressure of being a hot property in Hollywood would make the wheels spin even faster. As Mount put it, "this second cash infusion into Doug's life was really fatal."

23
REMODELING

Saturday Night Live was one of the main beneficiaries of *Animal House*'s golden fallout. The fourth season, which began shortly after the movie was released, saw the audience grow by some eight million viewers, numbers that made advertisers pay attention. Consequently, the ad price went up and the per-show budget almost doubled. So many of the new viewers were perceived to have come to the show through allegiance to Bluto (*SNL* was the most popular show on television among men eighteen to thirty-four years old) that Michaels described them as "the undeserved audience."

As at the *Lampoon*, a gap began to emerge between the blasé, sophisticated (i.e., aging) creators and their young mass-market audience. As Shuster said, "it was embarrassing. We were the TV literati, very hip, the darlings of some intellectual culture. Then it sort of degenerated into people who thought the more shrill the better." For his part, Belushi dismissed his new fans as "the angel dust crowd." There were compensations, however. Everybody's salary went up, and the writers were in a position to demand more perks. Beatts was finally able to get a bed in her office (a hospital bed at that) while Michaels got a private bathroom.

As for the cast, more perks were the least of what some of them could expect. If the studio heads hadn't been staying up to watch the show before, they were now. "After the success of *Animal House*, the whole country was *Saturday Night Live*–conscious," said Bernie Brillstein, who was by then managing Belushi, Aykroyd, Michaels, and Radner. Just how conscious was brought home to him one morning in 1978 when a group of Warner executives showed up at his door bearing bagels and lox, not to mention offers of "more money than I'd ever heard of for all my clients. The week before *Animal House* came out they didn't know who I was. Suddenly the savior of the movie business was young comedy, dangerous comedy," and what Warner got for their bagels was a multipicture deal with Michaels.

First in line among the eager suitors was, naturally, Universal. This meant that the whole matter of a Blues Brothers movie could be settled with one phone call from Brillstein to Daniel (who had been rewarded with a vice presidency for his services in the *Animal House* campaign), with Landis on board to direct. No two years of rewriting for this project—it was set to go as soon as the two stars could fit it into their busy schedules, with Belushi adding another zero to his *Animal House* fee. But first he had to finish *1941*, Steven Spielberg's tribute to his friend Landis's loose anarchic style, a frenetic comedy with a big cast—Aykroyd and Matheson also featured—and $30 million of sound, fury, and elaborate stunts that ended up signifying not much.

Although *1941* was a box-office bomb, Landis similarly laid on the sound, fury, and elaborate stunts for *his* frenetic comedy. The plot of the Blues Brothers movie involves the quest of good Catholic boys Elwood and Jake to raise money for the orphanage that nurtured them. Unsurprisingly, not all of their methods are strictly legal. Landis saw the Brothers as nothing less than "a metaphor for America—with everything that's good and bad about it. They're essentially good and innocent, but at the same time totally destructive." With the accent on the latter, most of the movie consists of Jake and Elwood eluding the Chicago police in the Bluesmobile, a merry chase that required no less than three hundred on-screen collisions, the totaling of sixty cars, and the destruction of an entire shopping mall.

All this activity overwhelmed the lively but essentially slight initial concept. Brillstein was distressed by this grandiosity even as his bank balance swelled accordingly. "*The Blues Brothers* should have been a small movie about two guys who loved each other. Comedy is faces and nuances and looks," he observed. "Instead Landis set off World War III." Tischler, another staunch fan, was similarly disappointed, so much so that he "walked out during the movie, incredibly angry."

Enormous but without substance, the movie is prevented from totally floating off like a runaway Macy's Thanksgiving Day Parade balloon by anchoring performances from soul legends like James Brown, Ray Charles, and Aretha Franklin, and such charm as it possesses comes from Belushi and Aykroyd's obvious desire to swing some of their spotlight toward the artists who had inspired them. Critics, certainly, were reserved, except toward these artists, but audiences responded to the Brothers and Belushi's star rose still further. Released in 1980, by 1983 the movie had made some $115 million worldwide.

Even before *The Blues Brothers* started shooting, the *SNL* staff was seeing more and more of Belushi's Cookie Monster side, as his substance abuse and physical exhaustion increased. Also, like Chase, Belushi was not shy about letting his coworkers know he had become bigger than *SNL*, and his casual attitude toward preparing for the week's show grew even more cavalier. At the same time, his irritation with Michaels grew because the producer refused to treat him like a Star with a capital *S*.

The rift was formalized when the actor decided to quit the show after the fourth season, leaving Aykroyd in the Ramis-like position of having to write two demanding projects at once, unable to throw himself into either one with his usual single-minded intensity. The situation was finally resolved when he quit the show at the same time as Belushi did during the filming of *The Blues Brothers*.

Aykroyd wasn't the only one having to choose sides. Inspired by the success of *Briefcase Full of Blues*, Michaels and Radner had decided to record a live performance album during the 1978 Christmas break that would feature some of Radner's characters singing original material. Shaffer and Tischler were all set to produce it when Belushi declared that they could either work on the Radner record or do the Blues Brothers movie and tie-in tour, but not both. Put off by Belushi's failing to introduce Shaffer during the live shows recorded for the first album, they stuck with Radner.

Although Radner's ego stayed considerably closer to life-size, her project, like the Blues Brothers, soon expanded from being an intimate expression of personal enthusiasm to a big production number. The original concept was to record the show in front of a small audience of friends but then grew to encompass a film version of a theatrical run to be directed by Michaels's buddy Mike Nichols. And so, in August 1979, as *SNL* was reeling from news of Aykroyd's departure, *Gilda Live* opened on Broadway.

Radner was no more able to divide her focus than was Aykroyd, and, having spent her 1979 summer break from *SNL* working feverishly on *Gilda Live* instead of recharging, she became physically run-down, a condition aggravated by her constant dieting and the deterioration of her relationship with Murray. Nor was Michaels, distracted by more side projects like *Meet the Rutles*, a Beatles parody album and follow-up TV special spearheaded by Monty Python's Eric Idle, able to give *SNL* his full attention. Those remaining cast members who were not starring in movies felt even more neglected. The result was that even as audience numbers were rising, group morale was plummeting.

Despite this, the start of the fifth season in 1979 found Murray's personal morale in good shape. For one thing, with Aykroyd and Belushi gone, he was in nobody's shadow. For another, he had a movie of his own opening. During the 1978 summer hiatus, Murray had visited Canada to star in a low-budget comedy directed by Reitman, who had been feeling like the *Animal House* parade was passing him by. Even the fact that he was "probably going to make more money than anyone connected with *Animal House*" couldn't console the producer because, he said, "none of the creative acknowledgment was going to come my way. So I decided to make a film as fast as I could."

When Reitman says fast, he means fast: *Animal House* opened on August 3; on August 6, he started filming *Meatballs*, a story set in a summer camp. It was essential to get going before September because, determined to shoot fast, tight, and cheap, he needed to use an actual camp while there was still a supply of actual kids (unpaid extras) available.

When Reitman initially approached Murray about starring as a head counselor who coaxes a lonely, depressed young boy out of his shell, the actor was reluctant, despite not being swamped with film offers. He had a dim view of the script, an assessment Reitman shared. "The first draft was terrible," he admitted. After enlisting Ramis as script doctor, he finally brought Murray around with the argument "If it's terrible, it was made in Canada and no one will know about it. You're not doing anything this summer anyway."

Like *Animal House*, *Meatballs* takes place in a closed society, a pricey camp so plush a camper can "stalk and kill his own bear in our private wildlife preserve." Its main distinction is Murray's inspired comic riffing, and audiences found his screen persona of the smart-ass with a heart of gold so appealing that the hastily conceived and executed movie ended up bringing in close to $70 million. Reitman found this unexpected success especially sweet because, he said, when he was looking for a studio to distribute the film, he had been snubbed by Universal, a claim Daniel disputes.

Even if Universal was not eager to pick up the movie itself, they *were* eager to get their hands on the fourth bankable star to emerge from *SNL* and signed Murray to play "Dr." Hunter S. Thompson himself in another Mount project. Released as *Where the Buffalo Roam*, it turned out to be a better idea on paper, but it did give Murray the chance to spend a lot of time with the Doctor, a man who shared his penchant for stiff drinking and hard living.

This acquaintanceship would add to *SNL*'s woes: Hurricane Belushi had moved on but then Murray, up till now a fairly regular guy—or as regular as someone who is a star on a hot television show can be—returned for the fifth season having adopted some of the more temperamental aspects of the Thompson persona, behaving like a less epicene but equally volatile O'Donoghue. Fortunately, his original more easygoing personality returned after the movie's release in the spring of 1980, around the same time the film version of *Gilda Live* opened.

Having these two ex-lovers' projects in direct competition did nothing to improve the backstage atmosphere, which already had problems enough. The staff was now three times as large and the lowly new assistants to assistants were given to understand they were not to deal with the writers and cast members as equals. This was very different from the original spirit of one big happy family pitching in together, a change embodied in renovations on the seventeenth floor. As well as doubling the show's office space, NBC spent almost a million dollars accommodating the stars' individual demands. Now instead of gathering around the communal refrigerator, they holed up in their private retreats, there to bug their agents about getting them more movie work.

Meanwhile, thanks to *Animal House* revenues, a similar phenomenon was taking place at the *Lampoon*. "It was like How Architecture Reveals Psychological Truths 101," Weiner said. "When we were on the fourth floor, everyone hung out on the couch and threw Frisbees and ate lunch in the little central lounge area. Then when we moved up to the eighth and ninth floors, there was no communal space at all, so when we had meetings, we had to commandeer Matty's office. It meant appealing to the authorities to do a group thing."

Like the wider society, the *Lampoon* compensated for spending less on public areas with increased private opulence. The editors' individual cubicles became luxurious reflections of the occupants' personal tastes, which tended toward the exotic. A new staffer, Tod Carroll, decorated his office in what Weiner described as "the style of a British colonial administrator's office in Borneo, with dark green walls, an antique wooden desk, and a turning ceiling fan. It was very nice, and subsequently Ted Mann made his office into this sort of mosquito-netting jungle with camouflage gauze everywhere. It had a certain military, sinister quality."

Also like *SNL*, the Lampooners moved from a casual attitude toward establishing personal power bases to the traditional system of competing ambitions held in check by a strong centralized authority. The magazine's strong man at the top was a delighted O'Rourke, who had been made editor in chief in early 1978. Meyerowitz remembered the new chief editor telling a resurfaced Beard, "'You should have seen Tony and Sean's faces when they found out I had their job.' P. J. was gloating. He said it with oil sliding down his face. Henry was wincing."

To those more sympathetic, like Flenniken, who was brought back from California and made a staff editor, O'Rourke was perceived as bringing order to chaos and instituting much-needed reforms. "P. J. loved the magazine," she declared. "He was actively seeking to build it up again and approached it with a real plan and incredible energy." Because the *Lampoon* had been getting on newsstands late, resulting in large financial losses, O'Rourke felt that his mandate was to run it "more like a regular magazine, with planning two, three, four issues in advance." His efforts were largely successful, but there was a non-economic price to pay. "It was very efficiently run, and he was great to me personally," Devins recalled, "but I think some of the early magic was gone. A lot of the zaniness in the office got diluted, and a lot of the energy was dissipated."

The new seriousness was impressed on Miller when he returned in early 1978 shortly after O'Rourke's installation to write the *Animal House* novelization. "I would be sitting in an office and lighting up a joint and people would stick their heads in the door and look at me in amazement," he said, noting that in the early days "the place was just roiling with pot smoke. Now there were carpets in the hall instead of people scrawling graffiti on the wall." The new businesslike attitude extended to personal style as well. O'Rourke traded in his army surplus jackets for suits and rep ties. Even Flenniken, emerging from the Birkenstock stronghold of the Pacific Northwest, tried to fit in with what she described as "a real conservative feeling" by dressing for success.

"People would always think the *Lampoon* was a wild and crazy place, people shooting up at work and a laugh riot and so on when in fact," Devins pointed out, "there was an element of 'Oh, another day at the humor factory,'" and under O'Rourke, this disciplined attitude was encouraged. There was a corresponding change in the nature of the brainstorming sessions. As Mogel put it, the new editor "had a totally different management style. He was becoming a dictator," and Meyerowitz was shocked to find O'Rourke "acting like a boss, not a compatriot. It was like, 'You say something. OK, now you say something.' I went to one editorial meeting under P. J.," the illustrator said, "and decided I'd never go back."

The introduction of an established hierarchy may have streamlined the meeting process, but it did nothing for the free flow of ideas. "I can remember meetings where everyone would sit around and there would be dead silence in the room. P. J. made everyone nervous," said Weiner, another Hendra-Kelly loyalist. "Not that he browbeat people like some cartoon corporate executive, but we would all sit in this fucking room trying to come up with funny stuff, and everyone was waiting for somebody else to say something."

As well, O'Rourke was able to run the magazine with what an envious Kelly called "less interference than any editor had ever had before or since" because Simmons was spending most of his time in Beverly Hills. The publisher had never been happier than after being hailed by *Time* in August 1978 as deserving "particular credit" for the growth of the *Lampoon*'s "comedy empire." *Time* even identified Simmons as the perspicacious scout "who raided Chicago's satirical Second City troupe to bring Belushi to New York" for *Lemmings*, a statement that probably came as a surprise to Hendra.

His hand firmly on the tiller, O'Rourke still had to decide which way to steer a ship that, before *Animal House* sent stock prices and circulation soaring, had given every indication of being about to sink. He knew he had to keep the new readers coming back after the movie's glow had faded and believed that determining the magazine's direction rationally, as opposed to the former instinctual approach, was key. The days of the writers doing what they damn well pleased and letting the readers self-select were over. As Weidman put it, "P. J. was the only person who ever theorized about what the *Lampoon* was doing."

This conscious search for a new identity led to what Weiner called "a big corporate retreat, and at one point, everyone was supposed to say what they thought was wrong with the magazine." But the pervasive nervousness that had paralyzed the editorial meetings kicked in, and nothing substantive emerged.

The silence may have been related to a feeling that the magazine may have outlived its usefulness. "When the *Lampoon* started to get into financial trouble and it seemed no longer hip, there started to be a lot of self-criticism sessions about what was wrong," said Weidman, who considered the very fact that they had to identify the readership "an indication that Altamont had happened." When Weiner's turn came around, "I felt like Jack Lemmon at the climactic scene of *The China Syndrome*," he said. "I had my forum and I couldn't talk." However, he eventually managed to nail the problem on the head, blurting out, "Who do we think we're writing for? We're doing all these masturbation jokes and articles on how to get your wing-wang pulled. If we're writing for fifteen-year-olds, let's admit it, and if we're not, let's not do it."

Weiner would be gone within a few weeks, but the question would linger. Demographic studies offered little help. "If you believed the advertising indexes, the readers were twenty-four-year-olds with a $25,000 disposable income," Devins recalled, "when we *knew* they were fourteen-year-old boys. And if you ever asked people who were twenty-five if they read the *Lampoon*, they said, 'No, but I used to.'" After *Animal House*, Gikow said, "the audience P. J. and everyone else had in mind was the very young male smashing beer cans against his head."

Inevitably, a kind of schizophrenia set in. O'Rourke commissioned more stories about relationships and families, with writers encouraged to go on at length, while simultaneously "there were actually memos coming down saying, 'More tits and ass,' and there was this real rampage to have Foto Funnies with tits,'" Devins recalled. But O'Rourke maintained that he gave the raunchy material a higher profile purely for commercial reasons while his actual goal was "to open the magazine up to a broader range of writing and to aim at an older, more sophisticated readership. I was struggling to make the *Lampoon* a little more than adolescent, and my hard work was going unappreciated. Of course," he observed philosophically, "you'll never find a humorist who doesn't feel his hard work is going unappreciated. It is the curse of the humorist to be laughed at."

"P. J. always knew who his audience was, but he personally wanted the *Lampoon* to be a more highbrow and literary humor magazine," Devins agreed, "something on a par with *The New Yorker*, something people talked about at cocktail parties," and a wistful "For Adults" was tacked onto the magazine's long-standing subtitle, "The Humor Magazine" (a misguided impulse in Simmons's view. "The early O'Rourke was one of the magazine's best writers. But then," the publisher said sadly, "he started getting a little too literate").

Occasionally O'Rourke's frustration emerged in articles like August 1978's "Great Works of Literature Translated for Today's Teens," which he cowrote with Greenfield. This translates several well-known classics into "an entertaining and highly accessible format" of tweet-like concision. Thus *A Tale of Two Cities* becomes a teen in a frock coat explaining, "Me and this other guy looked exactly alike. Everybody wanted to kill me but they killed him instead and he let them."

Another O'Rourke innovation was to discourage the magazine's traditional distrust of corporate intentions and the free market. "Consumerism and corporations definitely became less suspicious than in the early *Lampoon*. There's no place in an adult magazine for that sort of nonsense," he declared. This new respect for the interests of capital coincided with a tilt in the magazine's political outlook. "There's a strong right-wing bent to most of the people here," O'Rourke confided to the *New Republic* in 1978, adding nonironically that if there were anyone he wouldn't be inclined to make fun of, it would be "a guy my age making $500,000"—a guy like, for example, Doug Kenney.

This conservative drift may have been inevitable with Jimmy Carter in the White House. If only to be contrary, it behooved the *Lampoon* to shift to the other side of the political spectrum. Moreover, O'Rourke had come up with a new political animal he dubbed the Pants-Down Republican—"Republicans who took drugs and wanted to screw Deborah Harry"—later renamed the Republican Party Reptile. "We look like Republicans and think like conservatives, but we drive a lot faster and keep vibrators and baby oil and a video camera behind the stack of sweaters in the bedroom closet shelf," he wrote. Things Reptiles oppose include "government spending, Kennedy kids, seat-belt laws, being a pussy about nuclear power and busing our children anywhere other than Yale." In other words, they were in favor of keeping the personal morality of the '60s in terms of its hedonism and latitude but wanted it unencumbered by that period's feelings of social responsibility.

O'Rourke's main gripe with liberals was that they were now the boring Straights who would want him to be *careful*. "Some people are worried about the difference between right and wrong," he wrote. "I'm worried about the difference between wrong and fun"—that and the kind of people "who worry themselves sick over sexism in language and think the government sneaks into their house at night and puts atomic waste in the kitchen disposal."

And yet basically, O'Rourke may have been less Reptile and more just plain Republican. Writing somewhat later in the genteel pages of *House & Garden*, he characterized Hollywood as filled with "ordinary men and women freed by money and social mobility to do anything unencumbered by family pressure, community mores, social responsibility, civic duty, or good sense. There's a little streak of it in us all," especially if we're gonzo *Lampoon* editors.

Whether the *Lampoon*'s practice of ridiculing conventional prejudices by exaggerating them reinforced stereotypes more than it undermined them had long been open to debate, but its primary object had always been to make fun of the editors' ambivalence about their own privilege. Now what was once a refreshing refusal to pretend to be more politically correct than they actually were was transformed into using political incorrectness as a provocation. "We take the stance of the white, educated, upper-middle class," O'Rourke told *Newsweek* proudly in 1978, shortly after being quoted in *Time* as saying, "We are ruling class [though any actual blue bloods were long gone] . . . our comic pose is superior. It says 'I'm better than you and I'm going to destroy you. It's an offensive, very aggressive form of humor,'" a form that would be given a blue-collar twist in the '80s by comedians such as Sam Kinison and Andrew "Dice" Clay.

The tone was nothing new, but whereas the Lampooners once took on targets their own size or bigger, now they were mostly kicking those who were already down—a reflection of the Reptiles' inclination to identify with rich winners instead of dispossessed losers. As Greenfield said, "when the exclusive focus is on minorities, then you probably have abandoned what a magazine like that should do—it's got to be an equal-opportunity offender." However, Taylor felt that this new approach was in tune with the new readership. "There's more materialism today," he said in 1981. "These young people want to make money and spend it now. The emulation of the poor is over." Meanwhile, advertisers were no doubt happy to see that impressing peers by status brand purchases was once again an effective carrot for the young.

There were those prepared to argue that despite his authoritarian management style and ideological sympathies, O'Rourke was still an anarchist at heart. "His basic sense of humor and his attitude were still subversive even if his politics and dress were not," Michael Simmons asserted. And indeed, in the true *Lampoon* tradition, O'Rourke's writing was sharpest when he was going after his own. "Like Democrats, we've allied ourselves to an embittered racial group with whom we have nothing in common and for whom we intend to do zilch," he cautioned in a 1988 issue of the conservative journal *National Review*. "Personally," O'Rourke confided, "I didn't become a Republican to hang around with extra Y-chromosome types who pester God on cable TV and have cars up on blocks in their front yards. But, hey, whatever works."

But if O'Rourke had retained his original bad attitude, it escaped other of his colleagues. "P. J. was into all that Midwestern 'Grab your gal, nuke the Reds, and take a six-pack along' stuff with no irony at all," Abelson said, displaying a little prejudice of his own. Of course, Kenney, too, was known for his allegiance to Midwestern values, but he "was being cool and ironic when he talked about a bottle of beer and a dame on your arm. I didn't think P. J. was in on the joke." On the other hand, O'Rourke's *Lampoon* map of Minnebraska, a heartland region boasting such towns as Alimony Park, Awfulsex, Bumpkin, and Usedford, suggests he may have been just another New York smarty-pants.

If O'Rourke was in fact dedicated to returning the *Lampoon* to solid Middle American (as opposed to snotty Ivy League) values, he found a strong ally in John Hughes, a *Lampoon* writer so rooted in Middle America he never actually left his base in the Chicago suburbs even after he was put on the *Lampoon* staff, instead flying in for meetings at the magazine's expense.

Like Zweibel and Michaels, Hughes had slogged as a gag writer in his youth, selling jokes to the likes of Rodney Dangerfield, Joan Rivers, and Phyllis Diller. Like Miller, he had been a copywriter and became an agency vice president by the time he was twenty-five while freelancing for *Playboy*. In fact, it was Miller's work that had inspired Hughes to contact the *Lampoon*. "I read all of Chris Miller's stuff and a couple of things by Doug Kenney and the stuff drove me insane," he recalled, and in late 1977, he called and ended up talking to Flenniken, who told him to get in touch with Hendra, at that point incubating his own satire magazine. But the socialist-leaning, literary Hendra and the basically apolitical-though-Republican-if-anything Hughes (who would make his name in 1985 as writer and director of *The Breakfast Club*, a movie in which five high school kids are confined to a library and generally avoid reading, bored stiff though they are) were not a good fit.

O'Rourke and Hughes, however, were another story. "He became real tight with P. J. They were both proud Americans, for a strong defense, that kind of thing," as Flenniken said, and soon Hughes was installed as trusted lieutenant and heir apparent. Weiner recalled that at the big brainstorming retreat, "at one point P. J. said, 'We're not going to do parody ads because people get confused and they don't know what's real and what isn't,' and John Hughes said, 'Yeah, I agree with that. Let's stop fooling people.' It's one thing to be at the *New York Times* or *Time* and say ass-kissing things to ingratiate yourself to power," Weiner declared, "but the *Lampoon* should be—and used to be—the place where its whole existence was to see through that shit." In fact, the *Lampoon* did keep doing parody ads but shifted the target from the ostensible corporate sponsors. Ted Mann's 1978 "Senior Vittles" ad, for instance, mocked hard-up senior citizens' apparently amusing inclination to eat pet food.

Hughes did not turn out to be unquestioningly supportive. He took a dim view of his editor's aspirations to join the gentry, providing satirical reenactments of the fashionable Hamptons dinner parties O'Rourke dragged him along to. As well, Hughes may have been a Republican but he was hardly a Reptile. Instead, he was a self-described "really heavy homebody" who got married at twenty and had "not been on a date as an adult, not even close." Moreover, he thought it was "real dangerous to be hip and try to write funny stuff, for me anyway. I don't want to be too cool," he said in 1985.

Hughes was clearly the ideal person to collaborate with O'Rourke on the *Lampoon*'s next special project, a follow-up to the *High School Yearbook*. This was the February 1978 *Dacron (Ohio) Republican-Democrat*, a parody of a small-town Sunday newspaper, the town being the home of the *Yearbook*'s Kefauver High. As the *Lampoon* proved so often, familiarity breeds the best satire, and the two Midwesterners were able to mock Middle American values without condescending to them, a trick another group of Midwesterners would later pull off even more spectacularly with the ongoing small-town newspaper parody *The Onion*.

The big headline of the *Republican-Democrat* refers to yet another attack by a notorious local criminal, the Powder Room Prowler, a menace still at large after several months despite his trademark high heels and bag over his head. This local story is given far more attention than such minor (and faraway) events like "30,000 Feared Dead in India" and "Japan Destroyed" (which receives a bit more play because the tragedy "has marred the vacation plans of Miss Frances Bundle and her mother, Olive").

The true flavor of Dacronian life is conveyed in the ads for eateries like the White Curtain Inn, known for its "Time-Saver One Dish Breakfast," a ham, cheese, and coffee omelet. Meanwhile, an advertising supplement created by non-Midwesterner McCall for Swillmart, "where Quality is A Slogan," promotes goods like perpetual lunch meat, Snak Paste ("liver, peanut butter, mayo, lard, cheese—all in one E-Z squeeze tube"), and a digital grandfather clock.

Like the *Yearbook*, the *Sunday Newspaper Parody* succeeds in creating its own universe through an accumulation of interrelated detail. The society page brings us up to date on what has become some of the *Yearbook*'s Kefauverites. Rich kid Woolworth Van Husen III is, unsurprisingly, in the family trailer business, while artistic Forrest Swisher is director of the "Dinner Theater in the Dell." Elsewhere we learn that lone African-American student Madison Avenue Jones is a city councilman, class clown Herb Weisenheimer is now proprietor of "Hollerin' Herb's Psychopathic Chevrolet and Lunatic Used Cars," and former beatnik and Dickinson grad Faun Rosenberg heads up a conservation group that is trying to stop hunters from shooting the wildlife that flocks to the warm (160 degrees centigrade) waters of the Lake Muskingum nuclear cooling pond. Meanwhile, Everystudent Larry Kroger, now a Kefauver High guidance counselor, has attempted suicide by jumping from the second story of his parents' home.

However, when Dacron's Malcolm X Lounge offers "Free Coke and V.O. to every white girl," the Black Slant on the News column reports on a "Minority Math Course," which accents "relevant arithmetical concepts" like odds and numbers, and every classified ad for questionable legal services ("Sue the @$'& Jerk! Let's Go to Court!") is placed by either Meyer "The Rabbi" Saperstein or David Goldstein or Krepstein, Shepstein, Weinstein, Feinstein, and Smith (not forgetting real-estate ads from local slumlord Swinestein), it's not clear whether the writers are mocking small-mindedness or embodying it.

The *Sunday Newspaper Parody* was equal to the *Yearbook* and the *Encyclopedia of Humor* in its maniacal attention to detail. From the classifieds to the obituaries to the movie ads (all for fake movies except *Animal House*, which is acclaimed as being "much like *American Graffiti*," "really a lot like *American Graffiti*," and "so much like *American Graffiti* I understand there are a bunch of lawsuits being brought"), no opportunity for a joke or an appropriate typeface has been overlooked. "P. J. is a perfectionist," Mogel said, "and every one-inch classified had to be funny." *Now* he admires such zeal, but at the time, he "was screaming, 'Why are we spending so much money?'" Fortunately, the newspaper parody became the *Lampoon*'s second biggest-selling special issue and served notice that O'Rourke was in charge.

It also smoothed Hughes's path considerably, sparing him the worst of the still-harrowing initiation rites, which O'Rourke found himself "perpetuating in spite of myself." This was attested to by a former *Harvard Lampoon* editor hired in 1979, the first 'Poonie to join the *National Lampoon* staff since the original group. "Here I was, the new kid; they're supposed to teach me and take me under their wing but instead," he recalled, "it was like having a Gila monster as an arterial clamp during open-heart surgery."

At first, Hughes tried to come up with Milleresque pieces such as his April 1979 "My Vagina," his own version of the transformed-into-a-woman story. With a keen sense that biology is destiny, the hero moans, "Next thing I knew I would be down in the basement doing a load of laundry with Mom!" In contrast to Kenney's essential sympathy for his date-raped heroine, when Hughes's protagonist is gang-raped, her main concern is that she will have to "use up most of my money I was saving for new skis . . . having to get an abortion."

This kind of raunch was not really Hughes's forte. In September 1979, he found his true subject with an article called "Vacation '58," a memoir of a family trip as seen through the eyes of a twelve-year-old boy. Four years later, this story would provide the basis for *Vacation*, written by Hughes, directed by Ramis, and the second hit movie from the *Lampoon* stable. While the magazine story is set in the '50s, the film takes place in the '80s, and the only way it can convincingly establish this very retro family structure of Chief Dad, Vice Chair Mom, and the Kids—all on a cross-country road trip—is by depicting it with a knowing irony. Just as the Reptiles could not embrace the Colonel Teddy Jingo attitudes of the past without a certain defensive self-consciousness, so these traditional gender roles could not be presented straightforwardly.

Casting Chase as would-be patriarch Clark Griswold ensured that any paternal authority was undercut by borderline buffoonery. In the original story, Dad's authority is never questioned, even though all of his decisions turn out to be disastrous. In fact, the more he becomes a Bluto-like instigator of destruction and anarchy, the more his son respects him. For example, when Dad orders his son to throw an ice chest onto the road to slow down an approaching cop car, the boy exclaims, "This is *so* cool!"

In the film version, Dad is merely a bumbling incompetent. Any moral authority is vested in the kids, who appear to be the only calm and intelligent people present, humoring their parents' simple enthusiasms. So while Clark is happily singing the theme song of Walley World, the Disneyland equivalent that is their ultimate destination, his son is rocking out to the Ramones on his Walkman. Even Clark's role as sole breadwinner is undermined by the fact that he works in a totally superfluous and possibly harmful industry, food additives.

It's as if Mom and Dad Griswold have come through the '60s with their squareness untouched. "Clark Griswold is not a real person by a long shot," Chase observed. "It's a burlesque, and it's very broad, so I could clown and mug more. I loved it." One reason the role may have showcased Chase's talents was because he had a large hand in writing it. "At first, I was supervising John Hughes's rewrites," Ramis recalled, "then Chevy and I took over when we thought he'd gone as far as he was going to go." As for how Hughes felt about having his baby taken away from him, "I think John was happy to get the movie made and that it was successful," Ramis hypothesized, saying it was only later that Hughes "learned to resent it."

In presenting the middle-aged Clark as already on the verge of senility and vastly less able to cope than his composed son, Hughes was starting as he meant to go on. Much of his work for the magazine, not to mention his subsequent screenplays, is pervaded with the feeling that once you're over eighteen, you're past it, a notion that was naturally flattering to a teenage audience. For example, his August 1978 *Real teen Magazine*, another parody of the kind of publication that inspired *Poonbeat*, gives ample evidence of his ability to view life from the teen perspective. A special report that asks, "Is it okay to kill your parents?" attracts responses such as "The best," "Except for detention it was a good idea," and "I should have done it a long time ago before they used up all the money sending my brothers and my sister to college."

Other articles offer hints on "Breaking Up Your Parents' Marriage," "Household Drugs," and, for girls, "Pretend Rape—Using It to Get What You Want from Older Men" (this accompanied by a photo of a guilty-looking Simmons passing money to a young girl). "Whenever I have a man teacher in school," our correspondent reports, ". . . I just tell him on the first day that if he doesn't do what I want, I'll tell my parents he fucked me"—certainly one explanation for why teenage girls were starting to outperform boys academically.

Although O'Rourke made it clear that he viewed Hughes as his successor, his *Republican-Democrat* collaborator had other plans. Even when, with a family to support, Hughes finally gave up his advertising job in 1979 for the more chancy life of a *Lampoon* editor, it was only as a means to an end. "Turning 29 was *really* tough for me," he said. "I thought 'if I don't move now then I'm too old.' I didn't want to be on my deathbed thinking I should have written a movie." Having achieved this goal, he was already aiming higher. During the making of *Vacation*, Ramis recalled, "John was already telling me the idea for *The Breakfast Club*, so he was definitely planning to direct even then, and I'm sure the offers were already out there."

Five years later, thanks to *The Breakfast Club*'s huge success, Hughes would not only be directing but would have total creative control of his films, which ultimately became generational touchstones for '80s teens. But first, he had to languish in what Mount called "some kind of indentured servitude" to Simmons.

24

SPINNING OFF

Even before *Animal House* went into production, Simmons was meeting with studio executives, "trotting out the full panoply of *Lampoon* people at all times," Mount said, "but he hadn't had a hit yet, so there was some resistance." After *Animal House*, Simmons was in a position to realize his dream of making the *Lampoon* a farm team for Hollywood, with himself as owner-cum-manager. He saw Hughes as his hottest prospect and used his new clout to circulate what Mount called "compromised screenplays. It was clear that there was talent there, but Matty's footprints were all over them, and that tended to diminish their value."

Hughes had originally impressed Simmons with his scripts for *Delta House*, an ABC television spin-off of *Animal House* rushed into production so swiftly that it was ready to go a brief six months after the movie opened, albeit minus Belushi, Sutherland, Riegert, Matheson, drinking, drugs, and sex. What's more, it was on at 8:00 p.m., when standards were stricter than in *SNL*'s late-night slot. "Trying to do a slob comedy on mainstream network television without fart jokes and vomit jokes and bare breasts—it wasn't going to be that easy," said Gottlieb, who directed some episodes.

When the show was cancelled after thirteen weeks (despite featuring Michelle Pfeiffer in one of her first roles), Simmons partnered Hughes with Tod Carroll on the *Lampoon*'s next film project, which was based on a story by Simmons himself. Entitled *Jaws 3, People 0* (and later retitled *Jaws 3-D*), it was to be the second spin-off of the enormous Spielberg hit *Jaws*. The script reprises some familiar *Lampoon* themes, such as anarchy (the destruction of a swanky Beverly Hills restaurant) and biting the hand that's feeding them (cartoonish movie moguls are shown taking meetings at a funeral), but they are presented with a ham-handedness that makes *Animal House* look like Chekhov. In the spirit of O'Rourke's Social Darwinist approach to satire, fun is poked at targets that include the disabled (a blind and deaf man tries to push into a phone booth as someone else is making a call), the mentally handicapped (a man asks for an autograph explaining, "This means a lot to us—we're retarded"), and the old. The magazine had gone for these targets before, but the *Jaws 3, People 0* script uses cruelty casually, with little sense of its power, and the resulting attempts at humor are dim rather than dark.

The script was well into preproduction when Universal saw sense and dropped the project, leading Simmons to withdraw from his deal with them. Despite this setback, the studio was sufficiently impressed by Hughes's work on *Jaws 3* as well as on a screenplay version of the *Sunday Newspaper Parody* to hire him for rewrite work. The break with Universal did not mean that Simmons withdrew from the movie business. As Devins recalled, "Matty was golden in Hollywood." This bolstered his position within the *Lampoon* itself because, as Greenfield said, "after *Animal House*, everybody was thinking they could become screenwriters and go to Hollywood where the dough was one hundred times as much," and Simmons controlled the pipeline to that Hollywood money.

In 1980, everybody got into the act with a portmanteau script written by Sussman, Carroll, Weiner, and Flenniken under the leadership of O'Rourke, who hated the movie industry. *Movie Madness* (as the script was retitled) parodied four different genres of popular fiction: a tough urban cop story, a drama of personal growth among the upper middle class, a terrorism-related action adventure, and a glossy fantasy called "The Success Wanters," the saga of a beautiful woman who not only becomes a margarine magnate but also wins the Nobel Prize by discovering a margarine-based cure for cancer.

The project was further complicated by the decision to use two directors with diametrically opposed styles. One, Bob Giraldi, had directed slick, fast-moving commercials (a style that would flower in his Michael Jackson videos, including "Beat It"). The other, Henry Jaglom, made slow, talky, quirky, intensely personal low-budget features. It was not a happy combination. "My wife and I were at a screening in LA," Weiner recalled, "and it was one of the worst experiences of my life."

Undaunted, Simmons had Hughes churn out two more scripts until they finally hit it big with *Vacation* in 1983, followed by Hughes's successful sequel, *European Vacation*, two years later in 1985, which also saw the less-heralded release of the *Lampoon*'s *O.C. and Stiggs*. Stories featuring the eponymous alienated teens, avatars of Beavis and Butt-Head, had been reader favorites since they first appeared in the magazine in 1980, and within weeks, writers Ted Mann and Tod Carroll had a movie contract with MGM. The resulting film, something of a curiosity, sat on the shelf for five years despite the participation of its unlikely director, Robert Altman.

These film efforts "pulled some of the spirit out of the *Lampoon*," Gikow observed. "It's hard to generate enthusiasm for a product you know is going down the tubes because the audience isn't there when you also know there's another medium where the audience is." Beard and Hoffman could have predicted this day would come. "Henry and I had the donut and the hole theory," Hoffman explained. "There was a tendency on the staff's part to get involved with snazzy new stuff— the *Radio Hour*, *Lemmings*—on the periphery, and the people were forgetting about the magazine in the middle, which was becoming a hole. Henry held it together when he was there, but when Tony and Sean got in, it started to drift apart." In his view, the donut activities "were an enormous drain on staff and creativity, but Matty [not to mention Ken-ney] loved them."

It wasn't only the lure of showbiz that drew Simmons to the periph-eral projects; his business sense had grasped the potential of synergy, spinning off one idea into several different media. Unfortunately, the best *Lampoon* side projects were created before suitable delivery systems were really in place; had personal VCRs—let alone streaming video—been widely available in 1972, producing a stage show and later selling the video of it along with a tie-in podcast would not necessarily have been a money-losing proposition.

Ahead of the curve again, Simmons was one of the first produc-ers to develop a comedy special for the fledgling Home Box Office—although in November 1978 few households had the cable to receive it—and, overlooking their past battles, put Hendra in charge. With the publisher busy with *Delta House*, Hendra had a freer hand than he had ever had as an editor at the magazine. "Matty and Tony had been sort of warring at that point, but it was Tony's show—he was the boss," said Joshua White, who Simmons hired to direct the HBO show, christened *Disco Beaver from Outer Space*. The sunny-dispositioned White—the Joshua behind the legendary Joshua Light Show that had accompa-nied concerts at '60s rock temple the Fillmore East—was already in the *Lampoon* circle as a *Delta House* director and long-standing husband of *Lemmings'* Alice Playten.

Unusually, *Disco Beaver* was one *Lampoon* project that Simmons did not take credit for, instead asserting that he "had almost nothing to do with it." Hendra took the same organizational approach to producing television as he had to editing the magazine, and with things still in dis-array as the shoot's starting date drew closer, White began to get worried. He took it on himself to organize a headquarters at the *Lampoon* offices, unaware that the remodeling had been designed to thwart this possibil-ity. "Downstairs there were just cubbyholes. There wasn't any room big-ger than a postage stamp where six or seven people could talk, except," he said, "for Matty's office." Unfortunately, this space was off-limits even when Simmons was away because the writers were "famous for being absolute pigs—cigarette burns everywhere—so Matty's secretary would lock his office when he was out of town." Finally, White found one large room on the eleventh floor, which he had painted and cleaned because "it was disgusting." The former Radio Ranch had come to this.

Much of the script was still being written up to the last minute, with several sketches still mere concepts, but somehow Hendra managed to put it into production without showing HBO an actual shooting script. Inevitably, the resulting program has an off-the-cuff feel. A flimsy over-arching device, the picaresque adventures of a giant alien beaver who has landed on Earth, is stretched to contain sketches ranging from a rousing anti–substance abuse speech on the dangers of excessive Perrier consumption to a game show where contestants stand at podiums in the shape of giant breasts with lights in the nipples. The true organiz-ing principle of the script was that, as White said, "Tony was anxious to develop themes that were funny to Tony and Peter [Elbling, his for-mer partner in the two-man act who had been brought in to collaborate on the script]." These included flatulence (a redoing of *Radio Dinner*'s public service announcement on behalf of the terminally flatulent) and homosexuality (addressed in, among other sketches, an adaptation of the *Dragula* comic).

The small cable production *Disco Beaver from Outer Space* labored under the shadow of the big network hit *Saturday Night Live*, which White viewed as being made "in a big old-fashioned facility, and they had to work in a funny old-fashioned way." He, on the other hand, was looking forward to creating a lean, mean comedy machine, "liberated from the crushing problem of the studio," not to mention large $400,000 budgets. His solution was to shoot *Disco Beaver* quick and dirty in a mere ten days using a mobile video unit in a van, a process that meant that a small team "could just roll up, shoot it, and be gone" in true Ant Farm / TVTV guerrilla video style.

At the same time, the other *Radio Dinner* mastermind was creating a one-off NBC special called *Mr. Mike's Mondo Video*, a pilot for a proposed series that had been set up through Michaels. The linking concept behind *his* collection of unrelated bits was a parody of *Mondo Cane*, an early '60s Italian "documentary"—a hodgepodge along the lines of a filmic *National Enquirer*—which turned out to be a surprise cult hit and a landmark in preironic kitsch/sleaze. O'Donoghue compared his "soufflé of trash" to "MTV comedy rather than live television, which," he said, "I thought had run its course." Some of the oddities exposed include Dan Aykroyd displaying his webbed toes, soon-to-be-deceased Sex Pistol Sid Vicious howling "My Way," and a tour of an academy for feline fitness, which teaches cats to swim by throwing them in a pool (O'Donoghue's own cats portrayed the academy's star pupils).

Mondo Video turned out to be stronger in theory than in actuality, and Mr. Mike's frequent appearances to point out how sick and bizarre it all is, parodying the original *Mondo Cane*'s moralistic narration, seem more self-congratulatory than funny. Tischler, who was the video editor, tried to tell him. "I ended up just screaming at Michael and not talking to him for a few months, although we got to be friends again after time went by," he recalled. "It was a great fiasco."

The competing video projects stirred the embers of the old feud, leading to the terminal flatulence appeal's principal sufferer being called O'Donoghue, changed from the original O'Rourke after, White said, "Matty called up and said, '*Please* don't do O'Rourke jokes!'" Even as Hendra and O'Donoghue hoped this final duel would prove once and for all who was the real genius behind *Radio Dinner* (a question that had long ceased to be of any interest to anyone else), the end results were more likely to make one wonder if there hadn't been a third party responsible for the album's good moments.

In any case, NBC demanded that Mr. Mike make some major changes and, when O'Donoghue refused, dropped the show. *Mondo Video* was distributed to movie theaters by New Line, a company that had handled John Waters's films and was used to cult material, and, if not a commercial success, at least ended up contributing to what Kelly called "the legend of Michael O'Donoghue as 'the man who makes audi-

ences crazy," as opposed to the tape's just being bad and vanishing without a trace."

Disco Beaver fared no better at HBO. "[HBO president] Michael
Fuchs freaked out," White recalled. "It was full of beaver jokes and
porn, and it wasn't *Animal House*." It was also, as Simmons said, "a
mess. It was poorly put together, and they overdid things, like the gay
stuff." Fuchs decided to reedit the show into a *Groove Tube*-ish parody
of television, so that instead of a wandering alien beaver the framing
device is an unseen viewer's channel surfing, with the original sketches
greatly (and wisely) shortened. Hendra, said White, "washed his hands
of the whole affair."

Any ego damage this might have inflicted on Hendra was greatly
soothed by the fact that, in print, he was on a roll. In October 1978, he
had spearheaded a project that became the talk not only of less-literary literary circles but even of more-literary literary circles, along with
political and media circles. This was a parody of the *New York Times* that
was given added impact by appearing when the real *New York Times* had
disappeared from newsstands due to a strike by the city's press unions.

Like so many of the *Lampoon* team's best ideas, the project was generated in a restaurant. Cerf and Hendra happened to have drinks scheduled at the time the strike started, and in the course of this get-together,
the former 'Poonie mentioned that ever since the fuss generated by the
Harvard Lampoon's mock front page, he had always wanted to do a parody of the entire *Times*. Hendra's response, Cerf recalled, was to say that
"it so happened he had a friend who could probably find us a printer
and money, and he asked me if I was game." Even the normally gung-ho
Cerf doubted they could pull it off before the strike was settled but was
swayed when he started calling potential contributors and "everyone
wanted to do it," even though this meant writing pieces overnight.

Out of the woodwork contributors came: "Carl Bernstein was always
the person to write the lead story," said Rusty Unger, a book editor and
friend of Cerf's who became the project's third prime mover. Bernstein
and then-wife Nora Ephron immediately got to work on the lead story

announcing the tragic and sudden death of Pope John Paul John Paul I, who had served for a total of fifteen minutes. "The first idea was to make him Polish," Unger recalled, "but everyone said that's too much. No one would believe a Polish pope," shortly before John Paul II became just that. The accompanying photo of the late Pontiff reveals an amazing resemblance to a beatifically smiling Hendra.

Bernstein and Ephron were not the only high-profile writers recruited. Others included Terry Southern, Jerzy Kosinski, and George Plimpton (who handled the sports pages), prompting one critic to remark, "Sounds as if they emptied the back room of Elaine's for this one." There was also a large contingent of what Unger called "younger *New Yorker* people" who had been part of the *Real World*, plus, of course, Hendra-era *Lampoon* alumni including Sussman, Weiner, Kelly, and Greenfield. With the participation of so many leading journalists, the project, under the legally acceptable name *Not the New York Times*, became the New York media world's version of a prairie fire. "People started calling us," Unger recalled, "and after it got going, people would just show up," which required moving the editorial headquarters from Unger's small apartment to Plimpton's town house.

The atmosphere remained more early *Harvard Lampoon* than late *National Lampoon*, what Unger described as "like Mickey Rooney and Judy Garland—'Let's start a newspaper right here in the apartment!' It was really done for the pleasure of it. It couldn't be about egos because no one was going to get billing. In fact, they had to hide their names in case we got sued." This last may account for the editorial masthead listing "Who Me?" as publisher, "You've Got to Be Kidding" as managing editor, and "I Work for Them" as assistant managing editor. But, as Unger pointed out, "because there was no time for egos and there was no thought of making money, it was a community effort in the most ideal, unreal . . . you get that once in a lifetime. It was clear that it was everybody's best experience up to that time in their life."

Not everyone approached the project with such blithe altruism. "It was a lark for some," Kelly said. "Everyone involved—Plimpton, Cerf, et cetera—was dabbling in this amusing little thing, except for Tony, who was saying, 'I've got kids to feed!' Tony was the only one thinking professionally. He was determined to wrest something ongoing out of it." Nor was Hendra the only participant for whom there were serious implications; the parody was certainly no laughing matter for the striking *Times* staffers who worked on it. "It could have cost them their jobs, and some of them had children," Unger recalled. "They were nervous—nervous and in heaven."

Not the New York Times was able to achieve *Lampoon*-like verisimilitude after discovering that an Ohio paper, the *Toledo Blade*, used the same typefaces and was willing to print the parody (another account had two of the actual *Times*' real designers smuggling out the newspaper's font book and then matching it). Nothing fuels good satire like employees getting back at the boss, and *Not the New York Times* has the edge that only comes with inside knowledge. For example, an account of Studio 54 being burned to the ground because the firemen couldn't make it past the doorman captures the newspaper's occasional fusty pedantry by informing readers that "'disco' is a term that refers to both the music characterized by an insistent repetitive rock and roll beat, and as an abbreviation of the French word 'discotheque', an establishment where patrons dance to recorded music rather than to a live band or orchestra."

Displaying a similar grasp of contemporary trends, "a six-month investigation by a team of 35 *Not The New York Times* reporters, buttressed by lawyers, editors, corporate officials and mapmakers" comes up with the scoop that "an exotic drug, 'Cocaine', appears popular." Also, since Cerf was by then heavily involved with the Children's Television Workshop, the TV listings had to mention that on *Sesame Street*, "Big Bird will show Rita Moreno why he's *really* called Big Bird."

Nothing could have been more appealing to Hendra than a high-powered assault on the voice of the Establishment. Also, the speed of the operation (from concept to newsstand in one week) lent itself to his managerial style, which was more suited to a swift guerrilla strike than a long siege. And, of course, it offered Hendra the chance to orchestrate a newspaper parody that would compare favorably to the one supervised by his other adversary—imagine if he could do in one week what it took O'Rourke months to complete and do it better! He threw himself into the project with total dedication. "I don't think it could have been done without the three of us," Unger said, "but there's no question that Tony did the most and was the editor in chief. His sensibility and whatever he learned at the *Lampoon* was absolutely crucial."

Hendra's politicized approach is evident in the "Having" section, which replicates media aimed at the newly identified demographic of upwardly mobile young professionals, or yuppies. Its articles include guides to converting one's "boring old townhouse" into "pure raw space" as an "exciting alternative to moving way downtown"—another example of today's satire becoming tomorrow's reality.

Not the New York Times was both fun and, it turned out, profitable. Not that this meant any money for the three editors. According to Unger, they eventually spent four years in court after the printer Hendra's friend had found made off with the parody's profits. But this was still in the future. For the time being, *Not the New York Times* seemed to portend nothing but good. Buoyed by the public's warm response, Hendra, Cerf, and Unger decided to start that elusive satire magazine for adults. "It had always been a dream of Tony's, and now with the success of *Not the Times*, he saw it happening," Unger recalled. "He badly wanted that magazine, and he had a definite concept for it." What he didn't have was financing. At one point, Unger said, she procured a definite commitment from record and film producer (and former Michaels agent) David Geffen, but ultimately nothing came of it, and the grown-up satire magazine remained a dream.

However, the *Times* parody did result in a lavishly illustrated history of the '80s, published in 1979. The idea for this piece of futuristic nostalgia originated with Hendra's *Disco Beaver* cowriter, Peter Elbling, "and we got all excited about it," Unger said. But almost immediately, it became apparent that *The 80s: A Look Back at the Tumultuous Decade*

1980–1989 was not going to be another happy one-for-all-and-all-for-one collaboration: two weeks into the meetings, when Unger had already brought in her heavyweight connections, she was informed that the editors of *The 80s* would be Hendra, Cerf, and Elbling. "It was the only time in my life I was ever mad at Chris," she said, "and I didn't talk to Tony for a few years," thus joining the rather sizeable club of people who have stopped speaking to Hendra at some point or other.

It seemed as if everyone (except P. J. O'Rourke) was called up. Senior writers included Plimpton, Harry Shearer, Gottlieb, Janis Hirsch, and the usual suspects (Beard, McCall, Meyerowitz, Greenfield, Weiner, and Kelly), along with Abbie Hoffman, a real coup considering the fugitive Yippie was still living underground. Hoffman contributed an account of the sinking of the Pentagon, reportage prefaced by an editor's note explaining that "Ms. Abbie Hoffman, having undergone a sex-change, came out of hiding in 1982. In a triumphant gesture she sent her penis to the FBI, prompting the famous response from a bureau spokesman, 'We'll need a much bigger file on him than we thought.'"

Other contributors included Abelson, Goodrow, Krassner, former rock journalist and Springsteen manager Jon Landau, the founders of *Monocle* (who had moved on to editing the *Nation*), and possibly anyone else who'd ever bought Hendra or Cerf a drink. The acknowledgments for special thanks are beyond eclectic, running the gamut from Roy Cohn and Watergate burglar G. Gordon Liddy to Lou Reed, stopping along the way to pick up Gerrit Graham, Ephron, Bernstein, and Steve Martin, to name just a few.

How accurate were the satirical soothsayers' retrospective predictions? Their crystal ball was pretty clear with the forecast of a late-80s stock market crash followed by an economic rebound (it was off by a couple of years and happened on a Black Friday instead of a Black Monday, but close enough). Another major '80s economic trend was foreseen in an account of a merger that saw General Motors acquire General Tire and Rubber, General Mills, and General Foods to become General General, which then merged with the remaining seven conglomerates to form the "First National United Texas American General International Corporation, otherwise known as the Seven Brothers." In blocking this entity's attempt to merge with the combined oil companies, or Seven Sisters, the Justice Department scored "its lone anti-trust victory of the decade," which turned out to be fairly close to the Justice Department's actual 1980s record.

Beard, too, proved prophetic with some proposed changes to a revised Bill of Rights—for example, Article 15, which suggested that "no pregnancy may be terminated without the written consent of the fetus." An even more glaring example of today's satire becoming tomorrow's news was Shearer's account of a suit (an "*amicus feti*" brief) brought on behalf of Cher's unborn child after witnesses saw the pregnant actress light a cigarette. Sure enough, Cher is convicted of endangering the fetus; before the end of the '80s, the concept of the *amicus feti* brief would be considered far from risible and a woman would be convicted of endangering her unborn child by exposing it to crack.

Some '80s trends were easy to predict since they were really '70s trends that had grown and flourished. "The redefinition of 'journalism' as 'gossip' apparently boded well for the medium . . . but no, no, 'the people' would rather 'read' the *fotonovella* of *Captain Kirk Meets Bluto in Animal Planet* than the *Quixote*," wrote Weiner under the prophetic heading "Adieu, Print," with a little sideswipe at absent friends. *The 80s* also accurately predicted that America would get a national daily newspaper, only instead of *USA Today*, it came up with the *New York Variety Times*, a combination of those two publications that produced the apparently timeless headline "Afghan War Is Held Over for 6th Big Week." In other respects, their powers of prediction failed. "Where Are They Now '89" informed us that "voters repaid Mr. Reagan's patriotic fervor by ignoring him during the 1980 elections."

Conservatives in general were still so obscure a target that they escaped pretty much unscathed, with much more of the book dedicated to beating the almost-dead horse of the counterculture and traditional liberalism. The exception was a piece by Greenfield, loyal mainstream

Democrat that he was, which described a neoconservative utopia. Founded on the principles of the free market unhindered by the "dead, stifling hand of bureaucrats who went to fancy colleges and got big fat foundation grants ... and wanted to tell everybody else what to do, including being sexually perverted," a town lifts all zoning requirements (except for restrictions on the sale of pornography), all auto safety requirements, all "restrictive regulations" governing factories and utilities, and all traffic regulations including stop signs and traffic lights. Soon the water system breaks down, the "Adam Smith nuclear power plant" releases a vapor that may or may not be related to the subsequent rash of babies born with three nostrils, five Supreme Court justices are killed in one of the town's frequent car crashes, and the community becomes another failed utopian experiment.

If Greenfield did not anticipate that the entire country would come to resemble a failed neoconservative utopian experiment during the 2000s, at least he grasped where the Supreme Court was heading. His "A Court for Our Time" offers some key opinions, such as *ITT v. United States*, which, uncannily anticipating 2010's *Citizens United* decision, states that "in the 1970s, we held ... that corporations may spend any amount of money to influence the outcome of public referenda, and that individuals may spend any amount of money to elect themselves to office. We take judicial notice of the fact that 'money talks.'"

In some ways, *The 80s* was undermined by its own ambitions, trying to report on all aspects of the next decade's life and relate them to each other. There was also an editorial diffusion that accompanied a horde of contributors and, as with *Disco Beaver*, a complicated conceptual framework. Such pressure might fray the temper of any editor. As it was, "a lot of people didn't want to work with Tony again after the *80s* book," said Unger. The book also resembles *Disco Beaver* in its tendency to go on at great length about some relatively flimsy concept just because it happened to be an obsession of the project's guiding force. One of the big events of the '80s, it turns out, was the prohibition of meat, leading to a subculture of "meatheads" springing up around its illegal consumption.

But not everyone found meat as hilarious as Hendra and, in any case, by 1979 satires on potheads were already a little stale, George Carlin and Cheech and Chong having been around for quite a while.

Hendra's determination to ride the parody wave would keep him busy throughout the first half of the '80s. In 1982 he supervised a follow-up talk-of-the-town sensation, the *Off the Wall Street Journal*, which gave him the chance to puncture another self-important publication while going after capitalism in general, and supply-side economics in particular. This was followed by a second *Journal* parody and, with considerably less originality but considerably more sales-boosting naked ladies, yet another *Playboy* parody with Jerry Taylor on board as publisher.

By 1984, the *Not the Times* spirit of happy camaraderie was wearing thin, to the point where Hendra's partner in the *Off the Wall Street Journal* venture, Rob Vare, put out his own *Playboy* parody at the same time as Hendra's, using several of the people who had worked on the *Times* and *Wall Street Journal* parodies. The duel was on: Vare fired off a parody of the *New York Post* (headlined "Kaboom!" to indicate the explosive start of WWIII); Hendra retaliated with the *Irrational Inquirer*, a parody of another well-known tabloid. As if all of this were not enough, Sussman got into the act in 1984 with *Not Quite TV Guide*. And somewhere in there, Hendra produced the parody that landed him on the cover of *Newsweek*: *Not the Bible*.

All of this was more than enough product to satisfy the public's never avid desire for parodies. But it was fun while it lasted. "In the creative sense, the parodies were very enjoyable," said Kelly, "so people were willing to work very cheap," which was good because, without advertising, none of the post-*WSJ* parodies turned much of a profit. Kelly's sentiments were echoed by Kurt Andersen, *Time* staffer, former 'Poonie ('76), and one of those working cheap. "In all these parodies, people were essentially writing for themselves," he said. "This was what this group of people liked to do and liked to do together, so I think that demographic notions were far from how those projects were conceived."

Bearing in mind the parodies' lack of economic viability, Andersen took demographics more seriously when, in 1986, he started planning *Spy*, another stab at that elusive adult satire magazine, observing, "*Spy* was much more MBA-ish than the magazine parodies because it wasn't conceived as a one-shot deal." As well, Andersen and his *Spy* cofounder, Graydon Carter, later editor of *Vanity Fair* (who, legend has it, hitchhiked around his native Canada at nineteen with a copy of the *National Lampoon* in his back pocket), were products of a much more business-like era and realized that "you need to do some demographic research and some test mailings, and so we did some. Then you need to round up a significant amount of money to start it up and sell ads to sustain it. We thought through the business and editorial product of the magazine very carefully," as opposed to just plunging in, like a satire magazine started in 1970.

Spy, according to Andersen, was always aimed "more at twenty-seven- to forty-year-olds than the original *Lampoon* audience of eighteen-to twenty-five-year-olds"—in other words, "the people who had read the *National Lampoon* at twenty-two and loved it but who at thirty-four didn't. The magazine parodies tried to appeal to them later and *Spy* still later." Perhaps because of this more mature orientation, it seemed to Andersen that the atmosphere at Hendra's parodies was "less self-consciously post–frat house" than at the *Lampoon*, a difference he attributes mostly to "the average age of contributors being twenty-eight as opposed to twenty-three." Of course, by the '80s much of the *Lampoon* staff was hardly twenty-three either.

In pursuit of that more sophisticated audience, the *Spy* editors recognized that plutocrats and celebrity culture were to the early '80s what rock stars and the counterculture had been to the early '70s. Instead of the *Lampoon*'s tendency toward surreal or gonzo rambling, sharpness and succinct epithets were the order of the day (such as, for example, constantly referring to Donald Trump as "the short-fingered vulgarian," a characterization that reportedly infuriated him). *Spy*'s particular strength was that it was the *Gawker* or *Deadline Hollywood* of its day in terms of being able to acquire embarrassing insider information. It soon became a must-read, generating more excitement in humor circles than any publication (except for the one-off *Not the New York Times*) since the early *Lampoon*.

Further competition for the satire dollar came from numerous humor books that resembled extended *National Lampoon* articles. If Simmons capitalized on the *Lampoon* sensibility in the film industry, Workman, publisher of *The 80s*, seized the momentum when it came to print. Its most visible success was 1980's *The Official Preppy Handbook*, a book that had greater appeal for those who weren't preppies than for the genuine article. As Groton alum Gerrit Graham said, "The mania for Top-Siders and alligator shirts was ludicrous. If they could only see those guys smearing dog shit on each other on a football field."

Drawing on the legion of contributors who had worked on *The 80s*, Workman brought out books such as Beard and Cerf's *The Pentagon Catalog*, composed of items actually purchased or ordered by the Pentagon with prices based on documented research. Fully justifying the claim "We will not be oversold," it offers such bargains as a $12,000 Lockheed Lunch Pack Refrigerator ("Senses dulled by an insufficiently chilled sandwich, a radar operator's attention wanders—and a Red missile sub escapes detection").

The *Catalog* was an anomaly. Most of Workman's books were along the apolitical lines of Sussman's *Official Sex Manual* or Rich Hall's linguistically imaginative *Sniglets*. Hall was one of the standout performers on HBO's *Not Necessarily the News*, an ensemble topical comedy show that went on the air in 1983 and whose writing staff, during its seven-year run, included Shearer, Krassner, and *Channel One*'s Lane Sarasohn. According to Kelly, *Not Necessarily the News* was yet another outgrowth of *The 80s*, with its roots in a television pilot of the book commissioned by ABC to be called *Not the Network News*. After this came to naught, the idea, said Kelly, was picked up by HBO "without anyone [such as Hendra or himself] who had developed it." But then

"Tony had ripped it off from the BBC's [topical comedy show] *Not the Nine O'Clock News.*"

In fact, HBO had bought the format rights to the BBC show, which had started before *The 80s* (its British producers never denied that the show's title was inspired by *Not the New York Times*). Despite this set-back, Hendra remained undaunted. "Tony goes from one horrible experience to another horrible experience to another horrible experience, and it always ends up with him being fired or fucked over or he's suing somebody," said White, "but I've never seen him look backward. That's part of his charm."

So, as the '80s dawned, Hendra, like several of his fellow *Lampoon* alums, found himself stuck in print with his nose pressed up against the glass of the more lucrative film and television world. A few had gained a foothold, but were their lives as golden as they seemed to their envious former colleagues? Or were they flying too close to the sun, soon to crash and burn?

25

A MEMO FROM GOD

I n the summer of 1978, Ramis had moved to LA to work on *Meatballs* and *SCTV*'s second season simultaneously. Like Reitman, he realized that if he really wanted people to return his calls, he needed to get into directing and in 1979 started writing a script with the understanding that he would direct it. His collaborators were Kenney and Brian Doyle-Murray and the theme was golf, that most suburban of pastimes to which all three had remained loyal underneath all the countercultural enthusiasms.

The resulting script is another exploration of social dynamics in a closed society—in this case, a snooty country club. When a caddy from a large Catholic family (not unlike the Murrays) who is hoping to win a scholarship offered by the club expresses his fears that he won't be able to afford college, a stuffy member of the old guard responds cheerily, "Well, the world needs ditch diggers too." Into this hotbed of pompous petty snobbery breezes unapologetically vulgar Rodney Dangerfield, spreading lots of new money around, driving a bright red Rolls-Royce, and sporting orange golf balls and tees in the shape of naked ladies. While this was not someone Kenney might have been drawn to in real life, the story is weighted in Dangerfield's favor: How can we resist a guy who throws money at the bloodless club orchestra to play "Boogie Wonderland" while telling an equally stiff matron, "You're a lot of woman . . . Wanna make fourteen dollars the hard way?"

The stars were Chase and Murray, performing together for the first time. Chase, not cast against type, plays a rich smoothie who becomes remarkably successful at the game despite having no clear goal in sight, to the point where he puts on a blindfold before teeing off only to hit a perfect shot. He also shares Chase's apparent nonchalance, airily saying, "Keep it" when a date finds an uncashed check for $70,000 in his apartment (this may have been inspired by an incident when Peter Ivers, Kenney's Harvard buddy, found an uncashed check for $186,000 in one of the writer's books).

Murray, meanwhile, portrays the club's eccentric groundskeeper, a driven man whose goals are to eradicate the course's gopher population and to become head groundskeeper. Murray perfectly captures his character's sad bravado, foreshadowing the mature talent that would later make him an Oscar contender. As usual, his dialogue was largely improvised, with the script reduced to a jumping-off point.

While Chase found that the off-the-cuff aspect of the production "made it so much fun to do," even he had to concede that it was difficult to structure the improvisation into a story the audience could follow. This was the problem Ramis came up against when he tried to edit "the inspired nonsense you get from Chevy or Bill. We had a good script," he maintained, "but it was unfortunately 150 pages long [which would make the finished film run to over two hours], so we were tearing out pages on the set, which, when you come into the editing room, leaves you with terrible continuity flaws." This may have been one of the hard-won lessons that led him to describe the making of *Caddyshack* as "a $6 million scholarship to film school."

As it had in the early days of *SNL* and the *Lampoon*, the line between work and life blurred during the two-month shoot. "We all lived at this motel for golfers," Chase recalled, "and the evenings were spent rabble-rousing, partying, and chasing golf carts around," an atmosphere more old-school performers like Dangerfield found disconcerting. Even more disconcerting was the fact that "there was plenty of coke on *Caddyshack*," Chase admitted, "because there's plenty of coke in Florida. None of us brought it to the movie. It seemed to just arrive," he declared, conjuring up images of people finding little foil packets left on their pillows instead of chocolates. The prevailing attitude toward the drug threat is indicated in the scene where Chase's Zen golfer asks the caddy, "Do you take drugs, Danny?" and, on receiving the answer "Every day," replies "Good."

Even without recreational chemicals, "no one," said Chase, "had any perspective on their lives then." He himself was facing dilemmas such as whether his marriage could be saved and whether he really wanted to be packaged as the next Cary Grant, able to glide from slapstick to suave. *Foul Play*, he thought, was "me doing what I was told. I felt so awkward because anybody who knows me knows me to be broad and physical. It was just an experiment; 'I'll play this type—let's see what happens,'" so of course he was hailed as a new romantic screen lead and just as inevitably undermined this new image in *Caddyshack*.

The chaotic atmosphere may have derived from the producer being Kenney, never known for his outstanding organizational ability. "It was the first thing Doug had produced, and I'm not sure he felt totally on top of all the details," Ramis said. Apparently exhausted by his responsibilities, Kenney took to napping in the bedroom of a house being used as a location, a practice that led to a Three Bears–like situation when the house's owner discovered him and asked, "'Excuse me, who's that sleeping on my bed?'"

A better question is why the studio (Orion) would entrust a $6 million project to the same Doug Kenney last seen wandering the halls of the *Lampoon* being dismissed by the Hendra-Kelly recruits as a leftover hippie, aimless and erratic. But that is not the Doug Kenney that appeared to the studio. Instead, they saw a young man with neatly trimmed hair and given to casual but expensive sportswear (Prager observed that after he moved to California, Kenney "finally got some nice clothes") who drove up in a red Porsche he had bought with money earned from starting the publishing sensation of the first half of the decade and writing the most successful screen comedy to date. "Doug," Mount said, "moved to California, and the adulation here was intense."

Nor, contrary to the view around the new *Lampoon* office, was Kenney stuck in adolescence to the point where he couldn't be taken seriously. Those who knew the former editor better thought his intellect a thing of subtlety and sophistication. And if Kenney hadn't yet achieved full emotional maturity—although he was making strides in even this direction, maintaining an ongoing if tumultuous relationship with actress Kathryn Walker, another well-bred, high-style girlfriend—he would hardly be the first to prosper in Hollywood despite this.

Even more mysterious is why Kenney had wanted the job in the first place. Certainly he had been delighted to leave the managerial aspects of the *Lampoon* to Beard. Trow had one possible explanation: "The movie business retains a vague authority," he wrote, "partly because the idea of stardom adheres to it (and stardom . . . is not really an adult state but is, rather, the ultimate adolescent fantasy of adulthood)." Or as Graham put it, Kenney "loved the joke of being a twerp from Harvard who all of a sudden could schmooze the big shots in Hollywood. The very incongruity of it appealed to him."

Becoming a producer offered more than yet another identity to try on. "Doug loved the Hollywood schmooze and he liked money, for Christ's sake. All of a sudden, every morning's mail had a check for $200,000 in it. Who wouldn't go nuts? The wheeler-dealer was a veneer, but he very much wanted to be rich, rich, rich," Graham declared. "Doug was very ambitious and wanted to make a lot of money. He came out here wealthy and wanted more," Chase agreed. The chameleon had changed again, but Kenney had not completely abandoned his former casual attitude toward wealth. "It was more the idea of money than the fact of it that he liked," Graham explained, noting that Kenney mostly spent those big checks on his family.

Just before *Caddyshack* went into production, Kenney had established a production company in partnership with TVTV's Michael Shamberg and Shamberg's production partner Alan Greisman, an arrangement instigated by an agent who realized that Kenney needed what Shamberg called "some down-to-earth people to manage his ideas." The company, called Three Wheel Productions, combed Kenney's extensive network for projects and began developing an idea from Miller, a comedy set in one of the informal, youth-oriented resorts operated by the then-trendy Club Med. It was dubbed, inevitably, *Club Sandwich*.

In the aftermath of *Animal House*, Miller hadn't found the same success as his cowriters. Shortly after the movie opened, Universal had approached him about writing a sequel in collaboration with Weidman. Miller had wanted to work with his original collaborators, "but they had other plans. They went straight to Hollywood to do their own things. I hadn't been invited and," he said, "I wasn't going to ask." *Animal House II* never happened and instead Miller went where he knew he was welcome, going on the college speaking circuit and, as Mount said, "wandering from campus to campus, being a hero."

Miller's first attempt at *Club Sandwich*, created in collaboration with a former colleague of Ramis's from *Playboy*, was "surrealistic, stoned out—like the Marx Brothers on LSD. It was on Doug's advice we had done such a far-out script," Miller recalled. "'Follow your instincts', Doug said." The more pragmatic Shamberg felt that druggy surrealism had had its day, and Miller was taken off the case, replaced first by Harry Shearer and his writing partner Tom Leopold, then by Ramis and Doyle-Murray.

The finished product, retitled *Club Paradise* and released in 1986, is a jumble that can't decide whether to be a satire on singles' mating habits, a semiserious exploration of Third World tourism, or a romantic farce. "It was educational to see it not be a hit," said Ramis, the lesson he drew being that "people aren't comfortable with the mix of real political values and broad comedy."

For Ramis, who also directed it, *Club Paradise* marked the end of a hot streak of collaborations with Reitman and Murray that began with *Caddyshack*, continued with 1981's *Stripes*, and culminated, with help from Dan Aykroyd, in 1984's all-conquering *Ghostbusters*, perhaps the most successful blend, both commercially and creatively, of the *Lampoon-SNL* smart-ass sensibility and Reitman's more crowd-pleasing approach. It also marked Murray's arrival as a leading man and viable star.

Another former fixture of the *Lampoon's* recording studio made a splash in Hollywood in 1984, although in a cult hit rather than a box-office behemoth, when Guest, along with Shearer and former Credibility Gapper Michael McKean, starred in the enduringly hilarious *This Is Spinal Tap*, which also featured Hendra as an irascible British band manager. Even more than *Animal House*, this brilliantly observed improvised "mockumentary" (a term and genre it introduced) about a hapless legends-in-their-own-minds heavy metal band was the film most likely to appeal to readers of the early *National Lampoon*. Guest's stock continued to rise when that same year he took over Chase's old slot as the anchorman of "Weekend Update" during his one season on *SNL* before that lack of a click kicked in.

But back in 1980, Three Wheel decided to make its third production a follow-up to *Groove Tube*, starring Chase. However, its director, Shapiro, had trouble accepting that his former sidekick was now the main attraction and kept trying to turn Chase into his doppelganger. As a result, the film's title, *Modern Problems*, was all too appropriate. "I love Ken, but it really was a hideous chore," Chase recalled.

Clearly, while not as broad as the movies that were to appear under the banner of the *Lampoon* itself, the post–*Animal House* output of its creators was not designed to be stinging satire. "My films are similar in intent—the intent is to be as funny as possible as much as possible," said Ramis in 1988. "You'd like to think your audience is the top 10 percent on the college boards, but it's everybody"—everybody, but some more than others. "You can safely say young males liked the movies better than anyone else. There's a lot of thirteen-year-old male fantasy operating in this work, but juvenile is not a criticism; it's a description," he protested, comparing condemning his films for this reason to "going to the opera and saying, 'It's a good play, but why do they have to sing so much?'"

During the gestation of *Caddyshack*, the first film where the *Lampoon* veterans were given a free hand, it never occurred to them to choose between being good and being popular. Until now, they had done exactly what they wanted and received both acclaim and money. "Some people would take success over quality. Other people would always take quality over success," Ramis said. "At this point, everyone wanted both. Everyone probably had hopes of finding new kinds of success." Shamberg certainly didn't think that his partners were lowering their standards or blunting their edge in return for monster ticket sales. "People weren't co-opted by Hollywood or NBC," he asserted. "It was what they always wanted. It was never highbrow or experimental, and I don't think people got into it thinking there was going to be a revolution."

But of course when they were doing the *Radio Hour* or the first years of *Saturday Night* or writing books advocating the abolition of network television, that *was* what they thought. "We used to sit around putting down everything and everyone on television," said Ramis of those more alienated days. "And even now," he declared, "the people I know tend to resent people who got successful by doing substandard work or by selling out their artistic, as opposed to political, values." Such edge as remained in Three Wheel's movies came from the energy of the individual performers. The main excitement in *Caddyshack*, for example, lies in watching Murray and Chase (and Dangerfield) do their respective shticks. Who would have predicted that several of the people who emerged out of such a hip, innovative scene would increasingly become associated with predictable star vehicles? Only, perhaps, the kind of cynic who used to write for the *Lampoon*.

"More and more these old Lampooners have gone into the comedy factory," said O'Donoghue. But Chase, for one, became a little tired of having his mainstream work belittled by old colleagues. "People like Michael O'Donoghue get on my case about selling out. I love Michael, incidentally," he said in 1987, "but the day that Michael has a big popular success will be the day that I'll come back at him and say, 'Oh, Michael, what have you *done*?'" Chase may have gotten his chance a year later in 1988, when O'Donoghue cowrote *Scrooged*, an updated version of *A Christmas Carol* starring Murray as a powerful but friendless network programming chief that proved to be a holiday hit. Murray's gleefully mean Scrooge phase gives O'Donoghue the chance to express his dim view of network television, Christmas, and human nature. But then Murray's character follows tradition by repenting and ending up a generous, all-around nice guy.

Chase maintained that there was no way he could be a sellout because his rise was not the result of any calculated career moves. "I was a crammer in college, and ever since I've done things impetuously or impulsively or whatever it doesn't seem like a person who is supposed to succeed in life should do," he admitted. So when he was asked (frequently) "'What happened to you? You were such a counterculturist and cult item and now you're rich,'" his response was a simple "I got lucky." Moreover, he said, "I don't know anyone out here being honest who wouldn't say, 'I bullshitted my way into this.'"

It may have been this very lack of introspection that helped propel Chase. "Chevy doesn't doubt his own motives—why he does what he does or if he deserves what he gets," Ramis said. "Chevy and John always acted like they were successful, and no one ever doubted that they would be. Other people are consumed by self-doubt or philosophical speculation," a tendency Ramis himself was somewhat more afflicted by. "It was hard for me to reconcile being commercially successful," he said. "People who had strong leftist values had a lot to overcome. A lot of us espoused egalitarian political beliefs that would seem to work against the star system, and I think I was perceived as one."

It may have been inevitable that some of the former Lampooners' work would become less biting as life's rough edges were smoothed out for them. "When you're on the outside, you develop a certain resentment for people at the top of the show-business heap, so when you get to the top, can you keep that cynicism?" Ramis wondered. Furthermore, several former snipers found themselves transformed, like Chase, into targets. "There was a lot of pride in those who had been successful," Ramis recalled, "but at the same time, as certain people got wildly successful, the envy might have grown."

While those who weren't quite as famous were still able to distinguish between quality and success, the judgment of the few in the winner's circle became clouded. "You can be successful and not good," Ramis observed, "but because it was successful, you can allow yourself to think it was good. It's a comfortable illusion." Some people, however, were unable to take refuge in comfortable illusions. "In order to make sense out of life, it's necessary to be oblivious to a lot of things or twist them around so they fit with everything else. Doug was unable to do this.... This made his life uncomfortable at best and sometimes an agony," as O'Rourke wrote in a June 1985 *Lampoon* editorial. Although Kenney gave the appearance of relishing his climb to the top of the pile, he had serious reservations as to what it might be a pile *of*, and he wasn't quite cynical enough for this question not to matter.

Up till now, Kenney's starting point had been an irony-pervaded consideration of the gap between how we would like the world to be and how it really is. But irony, except in the most shallow sense, seems not to have come with him to Three Wheel, perhaps because Kenney wasn't prepared to give up those big audiences. "It wasn't a question of Doug coming out here to sell out," Chase said, "but he was willing to sell out if he could hold onto a modicum of credibility with his friends and still make the big bucks, because in the end, he laughed at all of it. He had a lot of hate in him for the bullshit out here, for the hustle, for the very thing he pretended to be a part of."

Other friends also noticed that Kenney felt superior to the game he was trying to master. Although he enjoyed LA's nightlife, "Doug definitely felt he was much smarter than everyone else and that LA was nonintellectual. He hated the kind of people he was meeting in the industry, who were crass by his standards. Given his old Harvard East Coast WASP prejudices, this was a very strange world," said

Ramis, apparently under the impression that Kenney had never been employed by the *National Lampoon* and so had never worked closely with Matty Simmons. Perhaps Ramis was simply projecting how he might have felt if he had come from a New York that seemed to him "dominated by the old-boy WASP network" to "a place like this—it's like an antiuniverse in a way."

Possessed of a strong sense of self and an equable temperament, along with the added ballast of family life, Ramis was better able to stay grounded in the headier atmosphere of this new antiuniverse. "Harold handled it better than most," Mount recalled. "He did his homework and started working on projects that he cared about and kept his nose down and just dealt with it." Not so Kenney, who swooped and dipped and got tangled up like a kite given too much string. "This is a bad town to be in if you want to keep your head screwed on," the producer observed, "and Doug was conflicted about it all the time. He was in some sense the conscience for all of us."

Being the designated conscience for a group of people who are beginning to think that they should forget about changing the way the whole bakery operates and just concentrate on getting a bigger slice of the pie does not make for an untroubled life. In the Fitzgerald tradition of the talented Ivy League writer who arrives in Hollywood only to disappear into a bottle, Kenney disappeared into a more contemporary cloud of white powder. When Meyerowitz went to Kenney's suite at the Chateau Marmont, his host asked the cartoonist if he wanted to see $20,000 of cocaine, then showed him "a bag with about sixteen ounces of coke in it."

After buying (half in cash) an expensive house in the Hollywood Hills, Kenney moved out of his hotel and started to furnish it with his usual minimalism. "Doug had always had real style problems, but he finally stumbled onto one out in Hollywood," said the interiors-conscious O'Donoghue, describing Kenney's residence as "the ultimate Hollywood house—almost no furnishings and a giant bowl of cocaine. Well, it was *a* style. I think he sort of backed into it."

Unfortunately, these large amounts of cocaine were not for display. "I knew Doug did a lot of coke," said Miller, "but I didn't realize he was out of control," until the day in June 1980 when Miller and his *Club Sandwich* collaborator met with Kenney at the Three Wheel office. "Doug was busy and very scattered, and it had been hard to get hold of him," Miller recalled. "Finally, the day our plane was leaving, he deigned to have a meeting with us early in the morning. His mind was like a broken mirror. It was," Miller said, "very upsetting to see him that way." When a Three Wheel secretary interrupted the meeting to announce the arrival of a visitor, Kenney left the room briefly, then came back and told the two screenwriters to "'just go ahead. Keep talking,' while he laid a rail from his elbow to his thumb and snorted the whole thing—at 9:15 in the morning."

On the other hand, Shamberg, who saw Kenney almost every day, declared, "I never saw Doug do drugs in my life." Even more-observant friends were not especially alarmed. For one thing, many of them were able to function normally despite doing quite a bit of cocaine themselves. For another, they had all been doing copious amounts of other drugs for several years yet had prospered. This was, after all, the same Doug Kenney who had consumed large quantities of LSD, pot, hash, and even booze without passing the point of no return. "We all did coke," Miller said, "but some people can do it and put it away. He couldn't, but we were so into letting everyone do their own thing we thought, 'Doug knows what he's doing; he can take care of himself.'"

There are several possible reasons why cocaine proved to be the drug that Kenney couldn't put away. Perhaps its ability to generate short-term but intense focus gave him a welcome single-mindedness. Or perhaps the drug enabled him to adopt a kind of blunderbuss overbearing quality that could be useful in dealing with studio executives. Graham, however, asserted that Kenney's cocaine use had less to do with developing a type A personality to fit in with the power breakfast crowd and more to do with his propensity for, when not depressed, revelry. "It was fun to get high, be a movie mogul, screw girls. And it *was* fun, my God. It was even fun for me and I was never on the big gravy train," he said. "For Doug, that first elevator ride to the top floor must have been incredibly exhilarating. Drugs were not a way of pumping up to get into gear with industry schmucks. They were about getting high, partying, and becoming paranoid."

This last tendency became more evident in July 1980 as the opening of *Caddyshack* approached and Kenney became convinced that those who had lionized him as the new young genius of comedy were about to turn on him. "He became convinced *Caddyshack* was going to fail," Hoffman recalled. "*Animal House* set him up to have a lot of insecurities. How do you top it?" When Kelly saw Kenney after the first screening, he found the novice producer to be "one depressed guy. Most of us, our rule is everything in life pays half as much and takes twice as long as you think it will. You do a load of compromising, and if it comes out anything like what you were hoping—hey! Doug had never caught a whiff of that until *Caddyshack*."

Kenney's anxieties may have been exacerbated by what Ramis called "the big splashy Times Square opening" Orion had set up for the movie's official premiere in New York. If even the relatively unflappable director felt that "given the film's level of sophistication, they shouldn't have had all the spotlights and the limos and the critics dragged in," one can imagine how the hoopla played into Kenney's fears that he was being set up to fail. Just in case others hadn't set him up properly, he decided to do it himself. The postopening party at Dangerfield's eponymous nightclub provided the perfect opportunity. Kenney, Chase remembered, "was dead drunk, falling over and yelling at people," including reporters, before passing out.

The incident roused the concern of his old friends on the East Coast. "It was really terrible because everybody saw Doug being depressed and couldn't do anything," said Tischler, who thought that Kenney "felt he couldn't top himself and that a lot of the attention paid to him wasn't deserved." It was no secret to any of Kenney's intimates that he, like Belushi, had always been casual when it came to personal safety. "Doug had a death wish you could cut with a knife, which is probably why he was so good, or why John was so good," O'Donoghue speculated. "They were out there, and anyone who's out there has a good chance of getting snuffed."

Kenney had sometimes seemed depressed before, but now these down moods were balanced less often by periods of good cheer and optimism. He appeared to be wandering ever closer to the edge, living with what Weidman called an "incredible recklessness." This was brought home to Meyerowitz when he went for a ride with Kenney in the writer's Porsche along twisting Mulholland Drive in the hills above Los Angeles. "I thought, 'I could die on this ride,'" the illustrator recalled. "He drove like a loon."

Kenney's New York friends implicated the Hollywood lifestyle itself as a factor in his decline, in the sense that it discouraged the kind of discipline that might have held in check his self-destructive tendencies. "He was doing what everyone else in Hollywood was doing," Weidman said, "and it was not very good for him." Prager was less diplomatic. "LA is a particularly pernicious town for people with money. It encourages decadence. I always felt the thing with Doug and John was too much money and not enough to do. Also, Doug didn't have a lot of willpower to begin with," she said, remembering that Kenney's preferred dieting regime was to "not keep food in the house, because if it was there, he would eat it." However, she was not so naive as to think that success was in itself the problem. "Drugs change people more than success, of course," she observed. Or as Meyerowitz put it, "Doug was still the same guy, but a little lost."

At least Hollywood's pernicious effects on him did not include becoming infected, like Belushi, with the Star virus. When Kenney had one of his frequent parties, his old friends remained on the guest list whether or not they were professionally useful, proving that even though he "presented to the world a man who was concerned about profit participation, deals, grosses, and so on, underneath he wasn't really like that at all," as Chase said. Graham agreed, saying that, despite

Kenney's attempt to appear worldly and hardheaded, "there was always a positively naive streak in him. If there's ever been a human being to whom the word *ineffable* applied, it was Doug."

As well, Kenney's impersonation of a grasping executive kept being undermined by his innate generosity and his willingness to help his friends. Loyal, generous, driven but not ruthless—try as he might, Kenney couldn't quite transform himself into a Hollywood shark. If any further proof were needed that he remained at heart a spaced-out creative type as opposed to a pragmatic dealmaker, it was his continuing close friendship with Ivers. After serving a Kenney-like role during their college years as designated group conscience and barometer of integrity, Ivers had pursued his own path, which included writing the score for David Lynch's debut feature *Eraserhead* and putting out four records that received more critical praise than popular acceptance.

However, Ivers did not share his friend's desire to be rich, rich, rich. On the contrary, he enthusiastically embraced a bohemian attitude. Art, for Ivers, was a vehicle for transformation and even a means of redemption. "Real art always has some stack of the unknown woven into its spine. Yes, there's nothing like the unknown to make people stop, to fulfill art's purpose as change-maker," he asserted, clad in a pink-spangled jacket as the host of cable program *New Wave Theatre*.

Before gaining national exposure on the USA Network, *New Wave Theatre* began as a local cable show designed to highlight the furiously loud, furiously fast, and just plain furious bands of the early LA punk and thrasher scene, the kind of bands Belushi had become partial to and started hanging around with (in fact, he made a guest appearance, as did Chase and Ramis). *New Wave Theatre* seemed a step toward realizing the goal Ivers had set forth in a 1978 manifesto—namely, "to market high-energy, raw-talent artists in new video forms." With his whimsical boy-man persona, Ivers seemed an odd choice to host this showcase for the noisy and nihilistic, but he approached the task like an ambassador of residual hopefulness from the '60s seeking to instill purpose in the prematurely burned-out youth of the '80s, assuring them, "We know it looks hopeless, but it's up to us together and you alone to effect the changes we need."

Perhaps it was this sense of responsibility that kept Ivers from being beset by the same demons as Kenney. Or perhaps it was just that he kept his distance from Kenney's principal demon, the thin white line (a Warner executive remembered visiting the *Caddyshack* set and finding Ivers practicing yoga on the lawn instead of indulging like everyone else).

Though possibly a harbinger of the '90s, Ivers was clearly not an '80s kind of guy. But Kenney was, or at any rate was trying to be, and if Ivers represented where he had been, by August 1980 the writer had a new best friend who represented where he wanted to go. "There were some things where he emulated me. He really did admire me, although he knew underneath it all I was just a buffoon," said Chase. It seemed to others as well that Kenney was patterning himself after his lucky friend, and it was certainly true that, by coincidence or not, when he first moved to Los Angeles he rented one of Chase's former residences.

The source of this attraction, Chase hypothesized, was Kenney's impression that "I had it in hand, that I knew how to be on top of this world out here, and indeed I did to a certain degree. Doug felt perhaps that I'd been able to wile and guile and somehow finagle myself into this big position." It is easy to see why the more Kenney's insecurities were exacerbated by the strain of living up to a reputation he wasn't sure he deserved in the first place, the more he'd be drawn to Chase, self-assured but not self-important, lionized but not troubled about whether he deserved such acclaim. Chase had known Kenney peripherally for years, of course, but the friendship really took root during the *Caddyshack* shoot and blossomed after Kenney's premiere party meltdown, when Chase was struck by Kenney's unhappiness and "started to befriend Doug." He wasn't in much better shape himself and, feeling that he needed to get away and dry out, suggested to Kenney that they repair to a tennis camp for a few health-filled weeks of chasing nothing more dangerous than tennis balls.

In pursuit of yet more clean living, Chase proposed that their next stop should be Hawaii for what he called "three weeks of recovery." They were both in a mood to get out of town, with Kenney upset over *Caddyshack*'s lukewarm reception and Chase depressed over his separation from his then-wife. Both adrift despite their apparent good fortune, they were able to sympathize with each other's situation in a way others might have found difficult to do wholeheartedly. This, plus their complementary temperaments, led to their becoming what Chase described as "lovers. Not literally," he clarified, "but we just had the same outlook on life and got along great." It was as if Kenney thought some of Chase's star power would rub off on him and he would be transformed from a reasonably good-looking but bespectacled, slightly balding, unmistakably writer-type person into someone with that mysterious chemistry that appeals to thousands of people on the other side of a camera lens.

"Doug used to consistently think he was the most handsome man in comedy. It was a joke with us in Hawaii," Chase recalled. "He'd get in front of the mirror, flex, and say, 'There he is—the most handsome man in comedy.' Then I'd walk up behind him and I'd be half a head taller and I'd go, 'No, *here's* the most handsome man in comedy,' and then we'd both laugh, but underneath it," Chase said, "I think Doug's yearning to be a star was real."

Not everyone welcomed this new bond: in Chase's company, they feared, Kenney would fall deeper into those aspects of Hollywood life that were not good for him, and while the confident Chase could handle life in the fast lane, Kenney would have a harder time. Among those who had their doubts about the relationship was Kenney's girlfriend, Kathryn Walker. Despite these reservations, she joined comedy's two most handsome men on Kauai, where it became clear that Kenney hadn't disbanded the party so much as changed its location, telephoning friends in California and urging them to come out and join the fun. "Doug was in the midst of making a choice. He was deciding whether he wanted to be an adult," said Lucy Fisher, a Warner studio executive and Ivers's girlfriend since Harvard.

Off on Kauai, Kenney seemed in a generally positive frame of mind, the shadows in retreat. Opinions differ on whether he and Walker were closer together or further apart by the time she left at the end of August, but in any case she flew back to Los Angeles to ensure that Kenney would for once in his life live with some real furniture in that big new house they would now share. Chase had returned some four days before Walker's departure, and Kenney was scheduled to fly back on the thirtieth. But on August 31, the news came from Hawaii: Doug Kenney's body had been discovered in a gorge at the bottom of a cliff, his Jeep abandoned by the side of the road. His best girl and his best friend, along with Alan Greisman and a lawyer, went out to bring him home.

* * *

When a dear friend dies an untimely death, especially if that person is bright and talented and lovable, the bereaved look around for someone to blame. Some blamed those who saw him last. "There was something about Doug that if you loved him, you knew you always had to take care of him a little bit," one friend said. "It's about drugs and making sure he didn't get too crazy," she elucidated. "There was a feeling with Doug that there was this innocence and you had to keep him from getting into too much trouble."

Another blamed the criminal element, suggesting that Kenney encountered muggers who robbed him and then pushed his body over the cliff. Still others blamed Kenney himself, angry at him for either actively throwing himself off of the bluff or for passively getting stoned enough to ignore warning notices and stroll to the edge of a scenic but crumbling lookout point. The hardest thing to accept is that there is no one to blame; tragedies happen every day, and most of them are senseless. For example, three years later, Peter Ivers would be found in his bed beaten to death by an unknown assailant.

"Three years in a row at the beginning of the decade, people started dropping like flies—Doug, Belushi [who died in 1982 in classic rockstar fashion from a much-publicized drug overdose], and Ivers. This group of people," said Graham, "found itself jerked to its feet and forced to face the music in a really harsh way," and they were left blinking in the bright light of day. "It was one of the first times real life had intruded on this little dreamworld we'd created for ourselves," Ramis recalled. "Even though people were very worried about Doug for many months before he died, the actual fact of it was quite shocking, and people came together in a very strong emotional way around his death."

In Los Angeles, they gathered at what became known as the "Sushi Wake" because of the large piles of same heaped behind the podium from which eulogies were delivered. Kenney would no doubt have loved the absurdist touch of having his wake in a Hollywood Hills Japanese restaurant designed to resemble a samurai's palace, adjacent to a small pseudocastle that was a magicians' club, a setting that epitomized the blend of fancifulness and pretension Kenney found so amusing about his adopted city.

Standing in front of the sushi, Chase delivered what Krassner called "a beautiful eulogy." It seemed to the *Realist* editor that Chase had obviously fallen "in love with Doug, not," he said, "romantically, but in the same way I fell in love with my daughter when she came to live with me." He also carried away impressions of "smiling Japanese waiters carrying flowers, people from *Saturday Night*, *Animal House*, the *Lampoon*—all these people from the comedy world all trying to look sad but all joking with each other." Even at this solemn moment, Krassner could not repress his anarchic urges. Inspired by the piles of sushi, "I said, 'I'm going to start a food fight. Doug would have wanted it this way.' I was torn," he recalled. "It would have been so appropriate, but I was afraid I would become known forever as the asshole who did that."

The difficulty a group of professionally irreverent people had in observing the social niceties out of respect for the deceased, even though the deceased would have probably made the most inappropriate comments of all, later became a talking point at the funeral, which was held on the other side of the country in Connecticut. "Humor is all about unpleasantness," O'Rourke observed. "We always used to talk about who would be the first to go and what the others would do. We couldn't imagine a group of professional humorists would stop for somebody's funeral," and so they didn't. A young cartoonist remembered it as being "awful. All these people were incredibly miserable, and they were trying to be funny on top of it. It was painful." Similarly, Tischler found the event "very strange. It was a gathering of all these comedy people, and when we went back to the wake, people could not stop. It would have been ridiculous that they could not be funny." One suggestion going around was that the staid Motor Lodge where the East Coast wake was held might be improved by the addition of a sign proclaiming "Kenney funeral—mourners welcome."

A number of other jokes circulated: one of the better was that Kenney had slipped and fallen while looking for a place to commit suicide. Another true word said in jest, which Prager attributed to Ramis, was that "Doug jumped off a cliff, and as he was falling, he saw a better place to jump from." A more slashing, truly *Lampoon*-ish remark came from the magazine staffer who joked that when Kenney died, he probably had a review of *Caddyshack* in his hand (in fact, the reviews were mixed but far from dismal, and the film has accrued devoted fans).

But even in this group some things resisted becoming jokes, like the extemporaneous eulogy given by Tim Mayer, one of Kenney's closest Harvard friends, which Graham called "one of the most extraordinary few minutes of public speaking I've ever heard in my life. It was incredibly moving." Another thing that wasn't funny at all was the number of people who still weren't speaking to each other, even at a time like this, which resulted in a big file of limos because no one wanted to travel together. O'Donoghue, for example, "was hardly talking to anybody," Tischler recalled, and the same went for Beard. Still, when one of the designated pallbearers didn't show up and a substitute had to be improvised, someone pointed to a tall figure who happened to be standing nearby and said, "Henry—you," and Beard took up the casket.

Krassner theorized that some of the tears shed at the memorials sprang from self-interest as much as grief. "I don't think anybody would admit it because you can only carry bad taste so far, but it was not only him personally but also the opportunities he represented that people were sorry to lose," the erstwhile gadfly said. But that people mourned Kenney as a professional as well as a personal loss wasn't as dark a secret as Krassner imagined. Flenniken, for one, readily admitted that "Doug was responsible in a lot of ways for so many people working: he founded the magazine and wrote the movie that saved the magazine and started a new career direction for everyone." Consequently, she said, around the *Lampoon* office it felt like "the ship losing its captain," even though Kenney's connection to the magazine had for years been tenuous at best.

Kenney's death was seen as having significance beyond the personal loss in another way. It came, as O'Rourke put it, "like an urgent memo from God about life's brevity," and people were moved to make changes in their lives, to get off that elevator ride. "For me," said Graham, "the issue was 'I'm not happy in this life anymore. I want something better,'" and before too long if you visited his house, you would, as at Chase's, be more likely to stumble over baby toys than empty champagne bottles. Flenniken quit the magazine immediately after the funeral "because," she explained, "Doug's death was like realizing things were serious— you couldn't just fry yourself and keep going." This was O'Rourke's reaction as well. He turned the editor-in-chief job he had gone through so much to get over to Sussman and left the *Lampoon*. "After Doug died," he said, "the fun went out of it. I guess the fun had been going out of it for a while."

Several other mourners soon found themselves at a personal cross-roads. The September of the funeral marked the first fall that Michaels would not be back hands-on producing *SNL*, nor would any of the original cast members be in the show. *Disco Beaver, Mr. Mike's Mondo Video, Gilda Live, Where the Buffalo Roam*, and *The Blues Brothers* had all opened in the previous months and, along with *Caddyshack*, indicated that not everything this group did would be greeted with rapturous acclaim—an unexpected reminder that the elevator could also go down.

Things were changing in the larger world as well. The immediate future held the long-awaited release of fifty-two Americans taken hostage by Iranian militants, an event that would trigger an orgy of flag waving and gluey sentimentality of the kind that used to rouse the *Lampoon* to its most scathing heights. But even if they had been able to rise to the occasion, the overall public was in no mood to listen. It was Morning in America, and anyone who still wanted to point out how the country was failing to live up to its promise was pushed to the margins. The iconoclasm gravy train had pulled out of the station, or so it seemed.

For all its snotty, puerile, exclusionary, and cruel aspects, the humor of the early *Lampoon* and *SNL* at least discouraged susceptibility to slick PR campaigns and mindless acceptance of dogma. If it encouraged a cynicism that promoted apathy and disengagement by suggesting that no ideal was worth believing in or taking action on behalf of, it also encouraged questioning authority, resistance to regimentation, and an ability to distinguish between patriotism and jingoism, religion and religiosity, and morality and moralizing. Just because *Lampoon* readers had stopped taking to the streets didn't mean that they were swallowing the official line. They would not be programmed into following predictable demographic patterns to make life easier for marketing teams; they would not be manipulated by appeals to emotion into swallowing half-truths; and if they believed very little was worth dying for, they also thought carefully about what was worth killing for.

That spirit would be missed in the coming years, but it was not dead. When the video guerrillas' dream was realized twenty-five years later and the means to make and distribute low-cost media became available to almost everyone, it turned out that there were hundreds of satirists out there as able to puncture hypocrisy, parody fatuousness, deflate the powerful, and come up with great gags as the *Lampoon/SNL* at its best. Then again, all this irreverence failed to divert the course of events from heading in the direction deplored by the '70s satirists: corporations and plutocrats tightened their grip on the political apparatus; the media grew ever more reluctant to challenge either the status quo or the mighty as it drifted increasingly toward the shallows; and the public was increasingly offered what Trow called "the exercise of preference in trivial matters" in place of actual democratic clout, all perhaps demonstrating that satire is indeed the revenge of the powerless.

Starting in the '80s, it seemed the Lampooners themselves couldn't do it anymore, at least not with the same brio, even had they wanted to. The specter of mortality had fatally tempered the arrogance required to bring it off with style, and Kenney's death had demonstrated that joking about terrible things would not stop them from happening. No matter how fast and slashing your repartee, Fate, God, Chaos—call it what you will—would have the last laugh. Suddenly, having realized this, everyone was run over by a truck.

EPILOGUE

DANNY ABELSON After writing the obscure 1984 television show *National Lampoon's Hot Flashes*, Abelson wrote narration for several more highbrow public television programs on opera and classical music, culminating in a long-term stint on *Live from Lincoln Center*. He also wrote two Muppet-related books and operates his own communications firm.

KURT ANDERSEN After leaving *Spy* in 1993, Andersen went on to edit *New York* magazine and write three well-received novels, two nonfiction books, columns for *Time* and *The New Yorker*, and a satirical stage revue called *Loose Lips* with casts including Harry Shearer and Martin Mull. He is the host of NPR's cultural magazine program *Studio 360*.

DAVID AXELROD After consulting on *Lemmings*, Axelrod went on to direct the Video Tape Network recording of the show for Lollos, episodes of *Saturday Night Live with Howard Cosell*, and the TVTV comedy/documentary on the Academy Awards. He subsequently wrote and directed episodes of the *Mary Tyler Moore Hour* and documentaries for the highly regarded PBS programs *Nova* and *The American Experience*, among several other projects.

DAN AYKROYD Aykroyd has continued to promote the Blues as a cofounder of the House of Blues clubs and hosting (as Elwood) the *House of Blues Radio Hour.* He has also kept the Blues Brothers going, both in concerts and the film *Blues Brothers 2000* (1998). He has appeared in other films ranging from interesting indies to major studio films like *Driving Miss Daisy*—for which he received an Oscar nomination—and Landis's *Trading Places*, in addition to frequently appearing on television. In 2012 he started cowriting a new screenplay with Chevy Chase.

HENRY BEARD Beard has written, to date, some thirty-nine short books of largely linguistically oriented humor, several involving golf or cats (including the very O'Donoghue-sounding *French for Cats*), three guides to politically correct language written with Cerf, and three handbooks of Latin adapted to contemporary usage. Some have sold more than a million copies. In the early '80s he was often Miss Piggy's ghostwriter and in the mid-80s collaborated with former *Harvard Lampoon* president Andy Borowitz on *Young Bucks*, a screenplay about preppies based on a draft script (*Little Gentlemen*) Kenney was working on when he died.

ANNE BEATTS After leaving *SNL*, Beatts created and produced the successful semiautobiographical sitcom *Square Pegs*, executive produced the *Cosby* spinoff hit *A Different World*, and wrote the book for the 1985 jukebox musical *Leader of the Pack*. She currently teaches sketch comedy writing at the University of Southern California and is developing a *Blues Brothers* TV series with Aykroyd and Judy Belushi.

RICHARD BELZER Finally originating a role, Belzer has played Detective John Munch—an unlikely combination of policeman and conspiracy-minded '70s radical (the latter quality modeled on Belzer himself)—first in *Homicide: Life on the Street* (1993–1999) and then in *Law & Order: Special Victims Unit* (1999 and counting). Munch has also turned up in *The Wire, Jimmy Kimmel Live, Arrested Development,* and *30 Rock*, while Belzer has provided voices for *South Park* and *Sesame Street*, as well as appearing in movies directed by Oliver Stone, Spike Lee, and Chris Guest.

PETER BRAMLEY Bramley continued to provide illustrations for magazines and covers for leading book publishers. In later years, he turned to painting and died in 2005 at the age of sixty.

M. K. BROWN Brown's work has appeared in publications including *Playboy*, *The New Yorker*, and the *Atlantic Monthly*. Her animations alternated with *The Simpsons* on *The Tracey Ullman Show*, and she is the author of several children's books.

TERRY CATCHPOLE Catchpole went on to be editor of *Boston Magazine* and then two publications aimed at the IT industry. He now runs a communications company whose clients include Microsoft and AOL.

CHRIS CERF Cerf has for the past forty years written songs for the Muppets and *Sesame Street*, winning Grammys and Emmys. He also cocreated and produced two award-winning educational children's series for PBS—*Between the Lions* and *Lomax, the Hound of Music*. Prior to this, he collaborated with Marlo Thomas on the best-selling *Free to Be . . . a Family* book and Emmy-winning TV special. Writing for an older audience, he collaborated with Beard and Kelly on *The Book of Sequels* (1990) and with *Monocle* founder Victor Navasky on *The Experts Speak*, a collection of "authoritative misinformation" (1984 and 1998, plus a special 2008 edition devoted to the Iraq War). He has coauthored numerous humor books with Beard, most recently *Encyclopedia Paranoiaca* (2012).

CHEVY CHASE After *National Lampoon's Vacation*, Chase starred in two *Fletch* films, the Michaels-produced *¡Three Amigos!*, and two further *Vacation* sequels, as well as hosting the Oscars in 1987 and 1988. His film career languished in the '90s, but he nevertheless received a Lifetime Achievement Award from the *Harvard Lampoon* in 1996. The new century has seen him making a renewed foray into television, most notably in the well-received sitcom *Community*.

MICHEL CHOQUETTE Choquette currently teaches screenwriting and comedy writing at Canadian universities McGill and Concordia. He is the editor of *The Someday Funnies*, a graphic anthology-history of the '60s told through the work of a wide assortment of writers and artists. Originally started in 1971, it was finally published forty years later.

SEAN DANIEL Daniel spent twelve years at Universal, including five as president of production, before going on to be an independent producer. He has produced more than twenty-five films including Richard Linklater's *Dazed and Confused* (1993) and the Coen brothers' *Intolerable Cruelty* (2003).

SUSAN DEVINS Devins ended up as managing editor of the *Lampoon* before going on to work as an entertainment reporter for publications including *Variety* and Australian *Vogue*. She is also the author of three books for children on cooking and baking.

BRIAN DOYLE-MURRAY In addition to serving three seasons on *SNL* (1979–1982), Doyle-Murray has worked steadily in film and television, appearing in *Lampoon* alumni movies including *National Lampoon's Christmas Vacation*, Ramis's *Groundhog Day* and *Club Paradise*, Reitman's *Ghostbusters* and its sequel, Guest's *Waiting for Guffman*, and Hughes's *Sixteen Candles*, as well as Mike Myers's sublime *SNL* spin-off, *Wayne's World*. His TV work includes roles in comedy classics such as *Seinfeld*, *King of the Hill*, and *SpongeBob SquarePants*.

PETER ELBLING Elbling has made frequent appearances on television in series ranging from *L.A. Law* and *Murphy Brown* to *Barney Miller* and *Cheers*. He is the author of a novel called *The Food Taster* and coauthor, with Tony Hendra, of the sequel *The 90s: A Look Back*.

JOE FLAHERTY After appearances in *1941*, *Heavy Metal*, Reitman's *Stripes*, and Ramis's *Club Paradise*, Flaherty had character roles in films such as *Back to the Future II* (1989) and *Happy Gilmore* (1996) and television programs including *Freaks and Geeks* (1999) and *Family Guy*. He currently teaches comedy writing at a Canadian university.

SHARY FLENNIKEN Flenniken lives in Seattle where she continues to freelance as a cartoonist and develops animated productions and avatars for Microsoft.

AL FRANKEN Franken contributed intermittently to *SNL* until 2008, as well as working on several *SNL* spin-off documentaries, specials, and "best ofs." He also scripted *One More Saturday Night* (1986) and the 1994 movie *When a Man Loves a Woman*, provided material for the 1988 Emmy and 1995 Oscar ceremonies, and wrote for Bill Maher's *Politically Incorrect* in 1996–1997. He has written five books, hosted an Air America radio show for three years, and in 2008 was elected as a Democratic senator from Minnesota. His writing partner Tom Davis died in 2012.

MICHAEL FRITH As the long-time creative director for Jim Henson Productions, Frith was deeply involved with the design of Muppet projects in television, film, and print, codeveloping *Fraggle Rock*. He left in 1995 to set up Sirius Thinking Ltd., a multimedia children's educational entertainment company, with Cerf and two others. He is also a cocreator of *Between the Lions*.

PETER GABEL Gabel taught law for over thirty years and was president of the progressive New College of California School of Law in San Francisco. He is currently an associate editor of *Tikkun*, a journal of culture, politics, and society from a liberal Jewish perspective.

LOUISE GIKOW Gikow is a writer and producer for *Between the Lions* and codeveloped *Lomax, the Hound of Music*. She is also an executive at Sirius Thinking Ltd., the programs' production company. Part of the Muppet Mafia, she was editorial director of Jim Henson Productions' publishing arm and subsequently created a publishing division for Nickelodeon.

GARRY GOODROW Goodrow has continued to work steadily as a character actor, appearing in films and numerous television shows including *Laverne & Shirley* and *Remington Steele*.

CARL GOTTLIEB Gottlieb cowrote the screenplay for *Jaws* (1975), the Richard Pryor vehicle *Which Way Is Up?* (1977), and the Steve Martin vehicle *The Jerk* (1979). He also cowrote musician David Crosby's memoirs.

GERRIT GRAHAM Graham appeared in films including *Demon Seed* and *Pretty Baby* (and the less-celebrated *National Lampoon's Class Reunion*) throughout the '70s and '80s and subsequently on television programs ranging from *Star Trek: Voyager* to *The Larry Sanders Show*.

JEFF GREENFIELD Greenfield was a commentator on media for CBS until 1983 and then became a political analyst for ABC until 1997, often appearing on *Nightline*. He then returned to CBS as senior political correspondent, where he remained until 2011. Besides winning three Emmy Awards, Greenfield has found time to write several books on television and politics, most recently *Then Everything Changed: Stunning Alternate Histories of American Politics* (2011).

MICHAEL GROSS Gross started a design consultancy after leaving the *Lampoon* in partnership with David Kaestle, working for clients including John Lennon and the ubiquitous Muppets. Moving to LA in 1980, Gross served as an associate producer on *Ghostbusters* (for which he designed the *No Ghosts* logo) and the film version of 21st Century's *Heavy Metal*, and subsequently was a producer or executive producer of Reitman projects including *Kindergarten Cop*, *Twins*, *Dave*, and *Ghostbusters II*. More recently he has returned to painting.

CHRISTOPHER GUEST Guest is best known for directing wry, sharply observed comedies about distinctive subcultures like dog shows (*Best in Show*, 2000), amateur dramatics (*Waiting for Guffman*, 1996), and folk music (*A Mighty Wind*, 2003) using scripts developed through structured improvisation by an informal repertory company that includes *SCTV* alums Eugene Levy and Catherine O'Hara, *Glee*'s Jane Lynch, and *Spinal Tap* bandmates Michael McKean and Harry Shearer. In 1985 he spent a year as a writer/performer with *SNL* and has appeared in several other film and TV roles. He continues to play music (sometimes at *Tap* reunion concerts) and was briefly a member of the British House of Lords, having acceded to his father's title shortly before reforms eliminated most of the hereditary peers.

TONY HENDRA Hendra has been prolific on many fronts, writing humor books including *The 90s: A Look Back* (1989, of course) and an unauthorized biography of George H. W. Bush (1992), plus making guest appearances on television programs such as *Miami Vice*. He also wrote two memoirs—*Going Too Far* (1987), an account of his life in satire and baby boomer humor in general, and the best-selling *Father Joe* (2004)—as well as a novel, *The Messiah of Morris Avenue* (2006), and a collaboration with George Carlin, the comic's posthumous autobiography (2009). Hendra also worked on the first episodes of landmark British television satire show *Spitting Image* in 1984 and from 1993 to 1994 served as editor in chief of a reconstituted version of *Spy* started after the original folded following the departure of Carter and Andersen. He recently returned to old stomping grounds by launching *The Final Edition*, a news parody site that began as a parody of the online *New York Times*.

JANIS HIRSCH Starting with Beatts's *Square Pegs*, Hirsch has been a writer and/or producer for leading television comedy programs including *Murphy Brown*, *Will & Grace*, and *Frasier*.

ROB HOFFMAN Post-*Lampoon* buyout, Hoffman joined his father in the family soft-drink business, growing it into the country's fifth largest bottler of Coca-Cola. He became active in Dallas civic life, ultimately donating a 224-piece collection of notable modern art to the Dallas Museum of Art. He died in August 2006 at the age of fifty-nine.

JOHN HUGHES As the writer-director of films such as *Sixteen Candles* (1984), *The Breakfast Club* (1985), and *Ferris Bueller's Day Off* (1986) and writer of *Pretty in Pink* (1986), Hughes became a cultural icon to a generation of '80s teens. He subsequently wrote and directed the comedies *Planes, Trains & Automobiles* (1987) and *Uncle Buck* (1989), both starring SCTV alum John Candy, in addition to writing *Home Alone* (1990) and its two sequels, along with numerous other projects including NatLamp's *European Vacation* (1985) and *National Lampoon's Christmas Vacation* (1989). Between 1983 and 2002, Hughes stacked up a remarkable record of having one and sometimes two screenplays produced per year (excluding 1999). He died in 2009, age fifty-nine.

PAUL JACOBS After playing with Meatloaf's band for five years in the early '80s, Jacobs, along with wife Sarah Durkee, began writing songs for *Sesame Street* and now does the same for *Between the Lions*.

DAVID KAESTLE Kaestle went on to be a partner in a design company with Michael Gross. He died in January 2004.

PETER KAMINSKY Kaminsky specializes in writing about food and fishing (a pastime he took up while at the *Lampoon* to help him relax), acting as *New York* magazine's "Underground Gourmet" for several years and producing books on both enthusiasms. He created and produces the Kennedy Center's Mark Twain Prize ceremony, whose honorees have included Michaels, Tomlin, George Carlin, Steve Martin, and Tina Fey.

SEAN KELLY Kelly has written more than fifteen books, including three about saints, two relating to Irishness, and several for children. He has also written for several PBS children's television programs and spent one season writing for *SNL*. Returning to his roots in academia, he teaches at the Pratt Institute in Brooklyn.

PAUL KRASSNER Krassner revived the *Realist* as a newsletter in the mid-80s, with the final edition appearing in 2001. He published his memoir,

Confessions of a Raving, Unconfined Nut, in 2004 and has collected his work into four anthologies, one with a foreword by Harry Shearer. He continues to work as a stand-up comedian, lecturer, and columnist.

JOHN LANDIS Landis has directed more than a dozen feature films, mostly comedies, horror, or horror-comedies, including *Coming to America* (1988) and *Trading Places* (1983), both starring Eddie Murphy, and *¡Three Amigos!* (1986) and *Spies like Us* (1985), both starring Chase, as well as *An American Werewolf in London* (1981) and *Blues Brothers 2000* (1998). However, he is now probably best known for the landmark video of Michael Jackson's *Thriller*, which perfectly fuses his love of pop music and horror movies.

DEAN LATIMER Latimer wrote regularly for drug hobbyist magazine *High Times* throughout the late '70s and into the '80s. *Flowers in the Blood*, his book on the history of opium, was published in 1981.

JOHN LOLLOS Lollos produced TV specials with broadcasting personalities Dr. Ruth and Howard Stern in the early '90s and coauthored the 2002 Off-Broadway show *Mr. Goldwyn*.

TED MANN Mann has gone on to write for several television series, notably *Miami Vice, NYPD Blue,* and *Deadwood*. He also wrote the screenplay for sci-fi satire *Space Truckers* (1996).

BRUCE McCALL After his ill-fated season on *SNL*, McCall became a frequent contributor to *The New Yorker*, creating more than forty covers. In addition to contributing illustrations and articles to other magazines including *Vanity Fair* and *Esquire* and Op-Ed pieces to the *New York Times* (the real one), McCall has produced two collections, *Zany Afternoons* (1982) and *All Meat Looks like South America* (2003), as well as a memoir, *Thin Ice* (1997). In 2011, the $70,000 production budget for an animation based on one of his *New Yorker* covers was raised entirely by crowd sourcing.

BRIAN McCONNACHIE McConnachie wrote for *SNL* during the 1979 season and then for *SCTV* in 1982 during its short-lived incarnation on NBC. He has had a late-blooming career as an actor, appearing in some four Woody Allen movies as well as *Sleepless in Seattle*, in addition to his earlier appearances in *Mondo Video*, *Caddyshack*, and *Strange Brew*, an *SCTV* spin-off featuring the McKenzie Brothers.

RICK MEYEROWITZ Meyerowitz is the writer and artist behind several illustrated humor books for both adult and young readers, as well as a *New Yorker* cover artist. He is also the author of *Drunk Stoned Brilliant Dead* (2010), a large-format illustrated book showcasing the work of the *Lampoon*'s artists.

LORNE MICHAELS Michaels has become his generation's preeminent producer of television comedy and one of the most influential figures in comedy in general. As executive producer of *Saturday Night Live* for more than thirty years (only missing seasons six through ten, when Dick Ebersol took over), he has launched the careers of countless prominent comedians. He has also executive produced two other tentpoles of late-night television: *Late Night with* [former 'Poonie] *Conan O'Brien* (1993–2009) and, starting in 2009, *Late Night with Jimmy Fallon*. Beginning in 2006, he was the executive producer of the multiple-award-winning *30 Rock*, created by *SNL*'s first female head writer, Tina Fey. He has produced movies including *Mean Girls* (2004), based on Fey's screenplay; *¡Three Amigos!* (1986), which he also coscripted; and the sublime *Wayne's World* (1992), along with numerous other films, TV series, and specials.

CHRIS MILLER After writing for television programs including *Delta House* and Beatts's *Square Pegs*, Miller wrote the screenplay for *Multiplicity* (1996), directed by Ramis. *The Real Animal House*, a memoir about his Dartmouth frat days, was published in 2006, and he is currently at work on a follow-up volume covering his pre-*Lampoon* copywriting and freelancing years.

410

LEN MOGEL Mogel has written ten educational books on forging a career in the communications industry, most recently *This Business of Broadcasting* (2004).

THOM MOUNT Mount spent eight years as president of production at Universal, where he oversaw the so-called Youth Unit responsible for such films as *Fast Times at Ridgemont High* (1982) and Hughes's *The Breakfast Club* (1985). In 1983 he went independent, producing films including *Bull Durham* (1988), *Tequila Sunrise* (1988), *Natural Born Killers* (1994), *Chéki* (2009), and *Death and the Maiden* (1994), one of three Mount projects directed by his friend Roman Polanski.

BILL MURRAY Murray has become one of the most respected actors of his generation and, moreover, a living national treasure with a fan website devoted to recording his impromptu interactions with the public. He has taken roles in big crowd-pleasers such as *Garfield* (2004) and *Charlie's Angels* (2000), but his heart really lies with offbeat independent films such as Tim Burton's *Ed Wood* (1994) and five Wes Anderson films—*The Royal Tenenbaums* (2001), *Rushmore* (1998), *The Life Aquatic with Steve Zissou* (2004), *Fantastic Mr. Fox* (2009), and *Moonrise Kingdom* (2012)—among many others, with his most acclaimed performances in Ramis's *Groundhog Day* (1993) and Sofia Coppola's *Lost in Translation* (2003). He has even portrayed FDR, in Roger Michell's *Hyde Park on Hudson* (2012). After writing and starring in an adaptation of Somerset Maugham's *The Razor's Edge* (1984), he moved to Paris for a couple of years to study philosophy and history at the Sorbonne, then later made an excursion into directing with *Quick Change* (1990). He retains his enthusiasm for baseball—he co-owns two minor league teams—and golf, even producing a sporting memoir called *Cinderella Story: My Life in Golf* (1999).

DON NOVELLO As his alter ego Father Guido Sarducci, Novello has appeared not only on *Saturday Night Live* but also on programs including *It's Garry Shandling's Show*, *Married . . . with Children*, and *The Col-*

bert Report. A writer on *SNL*'s third season, he is also the author of three collections of letters allegedly written by one Lazlo Toth (a sort of print Borat) to public figures and corporations. He produced *SCTV* episodes in the early '80s and collaborated with Belushi on *Noble Rot*, an unproduced screenplay.

CONN NUGENT Nugent is currently president of the Heinz Center for Science, Economics, and the Environment, after managing similar philanthropic or nonprofit organizations including the J. M. Kaplan Fund, which supports international environmental, immigration, and historical preservation programs, and the Nobel Prize–winning International Physicians for the Prevention of Nuclear War. Despite all this high-mindedness, he stayed in touch with his *HL* side enough to create the comedy website WeLoveTheIraqiInformationMinister.com in 2003, which went viral in the run-up to the Iraq War.

MICHAEL O'DONOGHUE After leaving *SNL*, O'Donoghue wrote a number of unproduced screenplays (including one called *Planet of the Cheap Special Effects*) before making it to the screen with *Scrooged*. In the early '90s, he contributed a regular free-ranging column called Not My Fault!, a protoblog, to *Spin* magazine until 1994, when he suffered a fatal cerebral hemorrhage at the age of fifty-two. His wake, like Kenney's, was full of the cream of American comedy all trying to be funny despite their grief. The room was adorned with the deceased's CAT scans—a touch he would surely have appreciated.

P. J. O'ROURKE Certainly the most prolific and highest-profile (and arguably the most accomplished) prose writer of the former Lampooners, O'Rourke is the author of more than sixteen books, including three *New York Times* best sellers, on subjects ranging from foreign policy to domestic politics, economics, travel, driving, manners, and more. They include *Holidays in Hell*, *Parliament of Whores*, and *Eat the Rich*. For fifteen years he was *Rolling Stone*'s chief foreign affairs correspondent and currently writes regularly for the *Atlantic Monthly* and for the conservative journals *Weekly Standard* and *American Spectator*. A fellow at the libertarian Cato Institute, he has filled William F. Buckley's slot as the face of witty, literate conservatism, appearing regularly on NPR, *Real Time with Bill Maher*, and C-Span, and has been profiled on *60 Minutes*. He has also carved out an unlikely lucrative sideline as the voice of commercials for British Airways and Honda.

ALICE PLAYTEN Playten continued to do highly regarded stage work, appearing in shows including *Caroline, or Change*; *Spoils of War*; and *First Lady Suite*, for which she won an Obie. She also provided character voices for several animated features and appeared in numerous television roles. She died in June 2011 at the age of sixty-three.

EMILY PRAGER Prager is the author of three novels, a memoir, a short-story collection, and a compendium of humor writing largely drawn from her satirical columns for the *New York Observer*, the *Village Voice*, and the *New York Times*. She did a stint as an *SNL* writer in 1981 and currently teaches fiction writing at New York University.

GILDA RADNER After leaving *SNL* in 1980, Radner started forging a career in movies, appearing in Buck Henry's *First Family* (1980), Sidney Poitier's *Hanky Panky* (1982), and *The Woman in Red* (1984), directed by co-star Gene Wilder, whom she married that year. Shortly after filming Wilder's *Haunted Honeymoon* (1986), Radner was diagnosed with ovarian cancer. Her autobiography, *It's Always Something*, came out the week before she died in May 1989 at forty-two. Wilder subsequently established Gilda's Club, a network of support facilities for cancer patients and their families.

HAROLD RAMIS After the acclaimed *Groundhog Day* (1993), Ramis went on to direct, among others, *Analyze This* (1999) and its sequel *Analyze That* (2002), the remake of the Peter Cook/Dudley Moore vehicle *Bedazzled* (2000), and, for producer Judd Apatow, *Year One* (2009), also acting as screenwriter for the last three. As an actor he's appeared in films including *As Good as It Gets* (1997), *Knocked Up* (2007), and

Walk Hard (2007). In 1996 he directed *Multiplicity* from a script by Miller. The main character was called Doug Kinney.

IVAN REITMAN Reitman has continued to direct and produce audience-pleasing comedies such as *Twins* (1988), *Kindergarten Cop* (1990), *Dave* (1993), and *My Super Ex-Girlfriend* (2006) and is set to direct a football comedy, *Draft Day*. He has been involved with developing a mooted *Ghostbusters III* for several years, but its realization has been frustrated by Murray's nonparticipation. In 2009 he produced two films by new-generation filmmakers—*I Love You, Man* and the Oscar-nominated *Up in the Air*, the latter directed by his son, Jason, whose first film, the mordant comedy *Thank You for Smoking* (2005), suggested a distinct affinity with the caustic side of the *Lampoon* sensibility.

JIM RIVALDO Rivaldo became one of California's leading political consultants, working largely for minority candidates. He got his start as campaign manager for San Francisco supervisor Harvey Milk, one of the country's first openly gay politicians. He died in 2007 at the age of sixty and a year later was portrayed on screen as a character in Gus Van Sant's *Milk*.

ALLEN RUCKER Rucker collaborated with Martin Mull on the HBO series *The History of White People in America* directed by Harry Shearer (1985) and has scripted several television documentaries. He is the author of eleven books of humor and nonfiction, including one on becoming paralyzed after contracting transverse myelitis at the age of fifty-one.

LANE SARASOHN Sarasohn went on to write for HBO's *Not Necessarily the News* from 1983 to 1990 and is currently managing editor of weekly online satirical newspaper *Ironic Times*.

PAUL SHAFFER Shaffer has served as musical director for *The David Letterman Show* since its start in 1982, as well as for the Rock and Roll

Hall of Fame induction ceremonies, the 1996 Olympic Games, and 2001's Concert for New York City. He has recorded with artists ranging from Yoko Ono to Robert Plant, released two solo albums, and authored a 2009 memoir called *We'll Be Here for the Rest of Our Lives*, in addition to cowriting the disco classic "It's Raining Men."

MICHAEL SHAMBERG Shamberg has produced, along with business partner Stacey Sher and former partner Danny DeVito, some of the most notable films of recent decades including *A Fish Called Wanda*, *Get Shorty*, *The Big Chill*, *Pulp Fiction*, *Out of Sight*, *Ghost World*, and *Erin Brockovich*. His most recent projects are Quentin Tarantino's *Django Unchained* (2012) and Steven Soderbergh's *Contagion* (2011), with several more in the works.

ROSIE SHUSTER Shuster continued to write for *Saturday Night Live* until 1998, after which she wrote for *The Larry Sanders Show* in 1992 and subsequently other television comedy shows.

MATTY SIMMONS Simmons continued as publisher of the *National Lampoon*, retaining an ever-firmer grip on the magazine's content, particularly after his son Andy became the editor, until 1989 when he sold his interest in the company. He continued to be involved in films produced under the *Lampoon* banner including *National Lampoon's Christmas Vacation* (1989) written by Hughes, its sequel *National Lampoon's Christmas Vacation 2* (2003), *Vegas Vacation* (1997), and *National Lampoon's Pucked* (2006). He has also written two memoirs of his time at the *Lampoon*—*If You Don't Buy This Book, We'll Kill This Dog* (1994) and *Fat, Drunk, & Stupid: The Inside Story behind the Making of Animal House* (2012)—as well as a novel called, going back to his roots, *The Credit Card Catastrophe* (1995). In 2002 he rejoined National Lampoon Inc., formerly J2 Communications, as director of classics with a mandate to reconnect with former *Lampoon* contributors.

MICHAEL SIMMONS After serving as an editor of the *National Lampoon* in the mid-80s, Michael Simmons contributed to publications including *MOJO, LA Weekly, Rolling Stone, Penthouse, High Times,* the *Los Angeles Times,* and the *Progressive* and blogged for the *Huffington Post.* He was a producer on *National Lampoon's Class of '86* (1986) and is currently making a solo album.

GERRY SUSSMAN After leaving the *Lampoon* in 1984, Sussman returned to advertising, becoming an associate creative director in the sales promotion department of Saatchi & Saatchi. He died in 1989 at the age of fifty-six, having authored seven humor books.

JERRY TAYLOR Taylor went on to be publisher of *Spy* and is currently general manager of Lippe Taylor, a brand communications company specializing in marketing to women.

BOB TISCHLER Tischler was brought in by O'Donoghue to write for *SNL* after Dick Ebersol took over producing it in 1981. He became Ebersol's right-hand man and stayed until the producer left the show in 1985. During the '90s, he worked on several sitcoms as a writer/producer, most notably *Empty Nest.*

GEORGE TROW Trow's best-known book, *Within the Context of No Context,* a long essay originally written for *The New Yorker* on what he saw as the leaching of significance from public discourse and the increasing vulgarization of culture, was published in 1981 and reissued in 1997. It was followed by a short-story collection, a novel, a collection of criticism, and another long essay. He also wrote several plays and the screenplay for Ismail Merchant's *The Proprietor* (1996). He resigned from *The New Yorker* after a nearly twenty-year association when Roseanne Barr was commissioned to guest edit the magazine. With the beginning of the new century, his depression worsened and he led a vagabond existence until, after a spell in a psychiatric hospital, he settled in Naples, Italy. He died in 2006 at the age of sixty-three.

RUSTY UNGER Unger has continued to write for magazines and was a blogger for the *Huffington Post* in its early days.

KATHRYN WALKER Walker appeared in films including *Neighbors* (1981), with Belushi and Aykroyd, and *D.A.R.Y.L.* (1985). Since 2000, she has directed several productions of classical Greek drama for New York's 92nd Street Y and is the author of a novel, *A Stopover in Venice* (2008), inspired by her ten-year marriage to James Taylor, with whom she lived on Martha's Vineyard.

JOHN WEIDMAN Weidman has written the libretto for several musicals, including three collaborations with Stephen Sondheim and the revised book of *Anything Goes* in collaboration with Tim Crouse (whose father, Russel, cowrote the book for the original production), receiving three Tony Award nominations (for *Pacific Overtures*, *Big—the Musical*, and *Contact*). He has won several Emmy Awards for his work on *Sesame Street*, for which he wrote from 1998 to 2007.

ELLIS WEINER Following a stint as a columnist at *Spy*, Weiner has continued to freelance widely with a specialism in humor, writing articles for, among others, *The New Yorker*, the *New York Times Magazine*, and the *Paris Review* as well as producing nearly a dozen books, most recently *Atlas Slugged AGAIN* (2011), a parody of the novel by Ayn Rand.

JOSH WHITE White continued to direct comedy for television, including a Cinemax talk show featuring cult character Max Headroom in the '80s and a *Seinfeld* episode in the '90s. For the last several years, he has been collaborating on art/comedy videos and installations with artists Michael Smith and Gary Panter.

SATURDAY NIGHT LIVE *Saturday Night Live* has become an oxymoron—an institution based on iconoclasm. Over its thirty-seven years (as of this writing), the show has unsurprisingly varied in quality and drifted in and out of relevance, with its demise often predicted during creatively fallow periods. Nevertheless, it continues to bounce back (during the 2008 election campaign, it again became a must-see thanks to Tina Fey's dead-on impersonation of Sarah Palin), and its preeminence as the major launching pad for American comedy talent is beyond doubt. Among those it introduced after the original cast left are Eddie Murphy, Robert Downey Jr., Mike Myers, Dana Carvey, Nora Dunn, David Spade, Will Ferrell, Phil Hartman, Conan O'Brien (a writer), John Cusack, Joan Cusack, Chris Farley, Chris Rock, Maya Rudolph, Tracy Morgan, Jay Mohr, Jimmy Fallon, Kristen Wiig, Stephen Colbert (a writer), Sarah Silverman, Seth Meyers, Amy Poehler, and, er, Adam Sandler, to name just a few. As of 2011, it had received 126 Emmy nominations (winning 28)—the most for any one show in television history—and won two Peabody Awards. Moving with the times, it now creates popular Internet-friendly content in the form of *SNL* Digital Shorts.

THE NATIONAL LAMPOON Like some of its early contributors, the *Lampoon* has had a rather tragic trajectory from gilded youth to becoming a shell of its former self. Searching for that vanished circulation, during the '80s female nudity and sophomoric humor featured ever more prominently, even with 'Poonies Al Jean and Mike Reiss, later long-serving executive producers of *The Simpsons*, on the staff—but to no avail. By 1988 NatLamp Inc. was losing half a million a year, while circulation was down to 250,000. In 1989, actor Tim Matheson (a.k.a. Otter and later President Bartlet's VP on *The West Wing*) and a business partner acquired control of the company, becoming cochairmen when Simmons resigned.

Plans to take the magazine more upscale and bring in writers like Bruce Jay Friedman, Richard Belzer, and Will Durst came to naught, and in 1990 the company was sold to J2 Communications, who also pledged to revive the magazine but ultimately put out only one issue a year before finally pulling the plug in 1998. J2's major success was *Van Wilder: Party Liaison* (2002), a gross-out comedy that makes *Animal House* look like Chekhov.

That same year, the company's largest shareholder, a venture capitalist called Daniel Laikin, bought NatLamp Inc. and became the new CEO. Like J2, the new team's main interest was in licensing the *Lampoon* name, producing lackluster films like *National Lampoon's Barely*

Legal (2003), *Pucked* (2006), *Pledge This* starring Paris Hilton (2006), and *National Lampoon's The Stoned Age* (2007). Other ventures included *National Lampoon's Strip Poker* (with attractive lady players) for pay-per-view, events like *National Lampoon's Greek Games* (spring-break hijinks), and aggregating comedy websites under the umbrella National Lampoon Network. Even so, the company lost $5.1 million in 2004.

In 2008 Laikin was charged with conspiracy and securities fraud, with the SEC alleging that he tried to artificially inflate the value of NatLamp stock. Following Laikin's arrest, Indiana businessman Tim Durham took over as CEO, after which the company produced nothing new but simply exploited existing assets. Laikin pleaded guilty and was sentenced to nearly four years in prison in September 2010, by which time NatLamp shares were trading at seventeen cents. In March 2011, Durham was arrested on charges of running a Ponzi scheme (not related to NatLamp) and defrauding investors of more than $200 million. He was convicted in June 2012 and is currently appealing the judgment. In 2010, the *Harvard Lampoon* sued NatLamp Inc. over nonpayment of licensing fees.

ACKNOWLEDGMENTS

The good thing about writing a book as opposed to winning an Oscar is that you can express your thanks to all the people on your list without worrying about the band striking up and the microphone sinking into the floor before you've finished.

So—first of all, I'd like to thank everyone who agreed to be interviewed and share their memories and experiences with me. This means you, Danny Abelson, Kurt Andersen, David Axelrod, Anne Beatts, Ed Bluestone, M. K. Brown, Terry Catchpole, Chris Cerf, Chevy Chase, Sean Daniel, Susan Devins, Peter Elbling, Amy Ephron, Joe Flaherty, Shary Flenniken, Michael Frith, Peter Gabel, Louise Gikow, Garry Goodrow, Carl Gottlieb, Gerrit Graham, Jeff Greenfield, Janis Hirsch, Paul Jacobs, Peter Kaminsky, Sean Kelly, Paul Krassner, Dean Latimer, Richard Lingeman, John Lollos, Brian McConnachie, Rick Meyerowitz, Lorne Michaels, Chris Miller, Len Mogel, Thom Mount, Don Novello, Conn Nugent, P. J. O'Rourke, Emily Prager, Harold Ramis, Ivan Reitman, Allen Rucker, Lane Sarasohn, Michael Shamberg, Harry Shearer, Rosie Shuster, Matty Simmons, Michael Simmons, Deanne Stillman, Jerry Taylor, Bob Tischler, Rusty Unger,

ACKNOWLEDGMENTS

John Weidman, Ellis Weiner, and Joshua White. I hope you feel your input has been used to illuminate rather than distort.

As well, although they are unlikely to care, I nevertheless feel I need to thank those interviewees who are no longer with us: Rob Hoffman, David Kaestle, Michael O'Donoghue, Alice Playten, Jim Rivaldo, and Gerry Sussman. I hope these previously unheard words will evoke their memories for those who knew them. Similarly, I must mention the late Ned Chase for his encouragement and his persuading his son to talk to me, and Doug Kenney, who allowed a very young person to interview him when the magazine first started.

My thanks to all at Norton, especially my editor, Brendan Curry, for his perspicacity and patience and his faith in this project, Nancy Palmquist, Francine Kass, the meticulous Kristin Roth, Will Glovinsky, and Melanie Tortoroli for her astute feedback.

As well, I have to thank the great Bruce McCall for his brilliant cover illustration (as well as agreeing to be interviewed). The only downside was that this left me with the difficult challenge of making the actual content as witty, pithy, and elegant as his artwork, so please do judge this book by its cover.

The book would never have become a reality without the sterling efforts of my agents, Jon Elek at AP Watt and Chris Parris-Lamb at the Gernert Company. I hope eventually they get something more tangible than my sincere appreciation out of it. I also have to thank Jon for additionally serving as humor sounding board, proposal guru, and occasional knight in shining armor. And I cannot fail to thank Carol Mann, who got the ball rolling and was so instrumental in getting the project off the ground in the first place, along with Charles M. Young, who lent me his extensive collection of *National Lampoons*.

Like anyone who is interested in the history of the *Lampoon*, I have to tip my hat to Mark Simonson and his Mark's Very Large National Lampoon Site, an invaluable aid for clarifying who was doing what when. I also have to express my appreciation to ace microfilm wrangler

Jianai Jenny Chen and to Ellen Tumposky for trawling the *New York Daily News* database.

It may take a village to raise a child, but apparently it takes a small metropolis to help a writer finish a book, and I owe more friends for their positive reinforcement and putting up with my moaning than I can possibly list without the microphone disappearing, so this is just a representative sample. For the many I haven't mentioned, please don't think that you're unappreciated. I know who you are and what I owe you.

The early drafts of the book were greatly improved by editorial input from ace reporters Nina Biddle and Alice Ritchie, whose keen journalists' eyes cut out filler, cut down editorializing, and got me off most of my soapboxes. I also have to thank fellow writers Cynthia Brown and Susan Zakin, along with men of letters Wade Carey and Ted Coltman, for their ongoing faith in the ultimate outcome, and Paul Rider for giving me the Mirren treatment. I am grateful to Robin Rue not only for her belief in me but also for generously sharing her professional insights into the mysteries of the book business.

Finally, as the band lifts their instruments, I offer profound thanks to Esta and Lewis Ress for their affection, moral support, and generally being in my corner. My love and gratitude for the same, in spades, to my husband, Chris Fagg—soul mate, in-house publishing expert, and supreme arbiter of funny.

NOTES

All quotations in the text are from author interviews unless cited in what follows. Specific *National Lampoon* issues are cited in the text itself.

CHAPTER 1

3 "The Supreme Court of the United States": *Boston Post*, May 8, 1936.

6 "The bacon must be crisp": Christopher Cerf and Michael Frith, *Alligator* (Cambridge: Vanitas Press, 1962).

7 "None of us approached the world": Roger Wilmut, *From Fringe to Flying Circus* (London: Methuen, 1980).

7 "anti-reactionary without being progressive": Kenneth Tynan, "English Satire Advances into the 60s," *Observer* (London), May 14, 1961.

11 "You would get down to what you thought": Robert Sam Anson, "The Life and Death of a Comic Genius," *Esquire*, October 1981.

12 "We do get problems": David Handelman, "Candy Goes to Harvard," *Vanity Fair*, February 1986.

14 "It was not uncommon among members of my generation": George W. S. Trow, *Within the Context of No Context* (New York: Little, Brown, 1981).

CHAPTER 2

30 "an unattractive but annoying people": Henry Beard and Doug Kenney, *Bored of the Rings* (New York: Signet Books, 1969).

36 "probably the only used car salesman": Tony Hiss and Jeff Lewis, "The 'Mad' Generation," *New York Times Magazine*, July 31, 1977.

CHAPTER 3

38 "it's better to commit rape than to masturbate": Paul Krassner, "An Impolite Interview with Norman Mailer," *Realist*, December 1962.

39 "to be somebody": Richard Pryor, "Uncle Sam Wants You Dead, Nigger," *Realist*, May/June 1971.

39 "Two governments have": Mae Brussell, "Why Was Martha Mitchell Kidnapped?," *Realist*, August 1972.

40 "Media is free": Abbie Hoffman, "The Yippies Are Going to Chicago," in *Best of the Realist* (Philadelphia: Running Press, 1984).

41 "Homecoming Day at the Pentagon": Abbie Hoffman (writing as "Free"), *Revolution for the Hell of It* (New York: Dial Press, 1968).

43 "Boom-a-lark-a! Chick-a-lark-a!": Chris Cerf and Michael Frith, eds., *Official Pogrom* (New York: Domesday Books, 1969).

44 "Comedy collectives": Charles M. Young, "Michael O'Donoghue Pokes Fun till It Bleeds," *Mother Jones*, December 21, 1983.

48 "The culture, for reasons": Trow, *Within the Context of No Context*.

50 "When I was growing up": Thomas Carney, "They Only Laughed When It Hurt," *New Times*, August 21, 1978.

CHAPTER 4

58 "Blotting her cherry-frost lipstick": Doug Kenney, *First Blowjob*, in *The National Lampoon's Encyclopedia of Humor* (New York: National Lampoon Inc., 1974).

60 a poll in the May 18 issue: "A Newsweek Poll: Mr. Nixon Holds Up," *Newsweek*, May 18, 1970.

60 "what the men in power were thinking": Trow, *Within the Context of No Context*.

65 "putting out a monthly": "Postgraduate Humor," *Newsweek*, March 23, 1970.

66 "When the commercial reality": Rose DeNeve, "National Lampoon: The Art of Bad Taste," *Print*, July/August 1974.

CHAPTER 5

73 "the master safecracker": Anson, "The Life and Death of a Comic Genius."

77 "bubblegum cards to the Edict of Nantes": Mopsy Strange Kennedy, "Juve-

nile, Funny, Puerile, Sophomoric, Jejune, Nutty—and Funny; Lampoon," *New York Times Magazine*, December 10, 1972.

83 "summered at the shore and went on dates": ibid.

85 "who wrote out of": ibid.

87 "The magazine had an almost": Joey Green, "Last Laughs: Why the National Lampoon Isn't Funny Any More," *Rolling Stone*, September 29, 1983.

88 "To much of the public": Trow, *Within the Context of No Context.*

88 "Comedy requires peer support": Carney, "They Only Laughed When It Hurt."

CHAPTER 6

90 "The first year it was fun": Carney, "They Only Laughed When It Hurt."

92 "A lot of people were looking at the time": Tony Schwartz, "Forever Young," *New York* magazine, September 15, 1983.

93 "unmentionable places, unspeakable hosts": Carney, "They Only Laughed When It Hurt."

98 "Light your faith and you can": Michael O'Donoghue and Tony Hendra, "Public Service Announcement," *Radio Dinner* (Blue Thumb Records, 1972).

98 "Yoko is a supreme artist": Michael O'Donoghue and Tony Hendra, "Magical Misery Tour," *Radio Dinner.*

98 "Speak your truth quietly": Max Ehrmann, "Desiderata," in *The Poems of Max Ehrmann* (New York: Dodge Publishing Company, 1910).

98 "Know what to kiss": Christopher Guest and Tony Hendra, "Deteriorata," *Radio Dinner.*

99 "I'm the world's Madonna": Tony Hendra, "Pull the Tregros," *Radio Dinner.*

99 "Like, bombing North Vietnam": Christopher Guest, "Teenyrap," *Radio Dinner.*

105 "went across the board, like": Anson, "The Life and Death of a Comic Genius."

CHAPTER 7

108 "Artaud is alive at the walls": Hoffman, *Revolution for the Hell of It.*

108 "give us everything that is in crime": Antonin Artaud, *The Theatre and Its Double* (New York: Grove Press, 1958).

109 "Belushi always made active choices": "Belushi: Rock 'n' Roll Actor," MTV, March 5, 1986.

110 "You can always get all the attention": Tim Crouse, "Bill Murray: The Rolling Stone Interview," *Rolling Stone*, August 16, 1984.

110 "John changed Second City": Charles M. Young, "From Samurai Saturday Night Live to Matinee Idol," *Rolling Stone*, August 10, 1978.

111 "a homicidal maniac": ibid.

116 "In your 20s": Lewis Grossberger, "John Belushi, More than Just a Pretty Face," *Rolling Stone*, January 21, 1982.

116 "We came here to off ourselves": "Stage Announcements," *Lemmings* (Blue Thumb Records, 1973).

117 "Dyin' is a high": Paul Jacobs and Sean Kelly, "Megadeath," *Lemmings*.

117 "Shootin' up the highway": Christopher Guest and Sean Kelly, "Highway Toes," *Lemmings*.

117 "We didn't all die": Leo Seligsohn, "They're Putting It to the Rock Generation," *Newsday*, September 6, 1973.

119 "We ran out of things to smoke": Christopher Guest, Tony Hendra, and Sean Kelly, "Colorado," *Lemmings*.

120 "Its strength is in a bitter refusal": Robert Christgau, "Lemmings," *Newsday*, January 23, 1973.

120 "Though some find the humor cruel": Stephen Holden, *Rolling Stone*, quoted in Seligsohn, "They're Putting It to the Rock Generation."

120 "The young in recent years": Ted Kalem, "The Theater: Megadeath by Laughter," *Time*, February 19, 1973.

CHAPTER 8

122 "dredged up a few numbers": Wilmut, *From Fringe to Flying Circus*.

125 "Everything I do is for money": Cindy Lollar, "Can the National Lampoon Still Make Us Laugh?," *Moviegoer*, April 1983.

125 "Is any man as well loved": Trow, *Within the Context of No Context*.

125 "Small wonder that the magazine's staffers": "The Unkindest Cut," *Newsweek*, July 16, 1973.

133 "known around Manhattan": Lynn Hirschberg, "The Grody Bunch," *Rolling Stone*, April 14, 1983.

133 "During the early 70s": Trow, *Within the Context of No Context*.

133 "At some point": "Fall Guy," *Time*, February 2, 1976.

CHAPTER 9

138 "Don't send money": Brian McConnachie, "Public Disservice," *Gold Turkey: National Lampoon Radio Hour/Greatest Hits* (Sony Records, 1975).

138 "I wish I was a Negro": Christopher Guest and Sean Kelly, "Well-Intentioned Blues," *Greatest Hits of the National Lampoon* (Viva Records, 1978).

139 "The Incredulous was making good": Christopher Guest and Doug Kenney, "Flash Bazbo," *Gold Turkey.*

CHAPTER 10

159 "I think we have": Carney, "They Only Laughed When It Hurt."

CHAPTER 11

168 "Our humor is white": DeNeve, "National Lampoon."

170 "The three questions of greatest concern": Fran Lebowitz, *Metropolitan Life* (New York: E. P. Dutton, 1978).

178 "Somewhere I had read": Janis Hirsch, *Anything for a Laugh,* in *Titters,* ed. Anne Beatts and Deanne Stillman (New York: Collier Books, 1976).

178 "Do you know": Anne Beatts, Blanche Boyd, Lee Israel, Judy Jacklin, Trucia Kushner, Cindy Ornsteen, Emily Prager, Rayanna Simons, Deanne Stillman, Tracy Young, *Miz Magazine,* in Beatts and Stillman, *Titters.*

179 "If God had meant": Emily Prager, "Early American Sampler," in Beatts and Stillman, *Titters.*

179 "Know how to do four of the following": Emily Prager, *The Girl Sprout Handbook,* in Beatts and Stillman, *Titters.*

CHAPTER 12

182 "O'Donoghue had the worst timing": Carney, "They Only Laughed When It Hurt."

185 "You sell the products": DeNeve, "National Lampoon."

185 More quantitative demographic research: *National Lampoon* Audit Bureau of Circulations reports, 1970–1980.

190 "I still remember everything": Jeffrey Sweet, *Something Wonderful Right Away* (New York: Limelight Editions, 1978).

190 "My friends would try to get me": Roy Blount, "Gilda," *Rolling Stone,* November 2, 1978.

190 "One thing about working at Second City": Sweet, *Something Wonderful Right Away.*

192 "Good money, a lot of freedom": Carll Tucker, "John Belushi: He Who Laughs First," *Village Voice,* July 26, 1975.

193 "wretched refuse who": John Belushi, Brian Doyle-Murray, Joseph O'Flaherty, Gilda Radner, and Harold Ramis, "The Immigrants," *Gold Turkey.*

193 "football, basketball, swimming": John Belushi and Brian Doyle-Murray, "Alternative Child," *Gold Turkey.*

194 "Jimmy Dugan—a great child": John Belushi and Brian Doyle-Murray, "The Jimmy Dugan Story," *Gold Turkey.*

195 "Several high-ranking members": Henry Beard and Sean Kelly, *National Lampoon Radio Hour,* December 29, 1973.

196 "We are proud, and yet, in a way, humble": Sean Kelly and Bill Murray, "Front Row Center," *Gold Turkey.*

CHAPTER 13

197 "That's too bad": David Felton, "Bill Murray: The New Star of Saturday Night," *Rolling Stone,* April 20, 1978.

201 "there was only one audience's worth": ibid.

201 "I hate clubs. The noise": Tucker, "John Belushi."

201 "bordered on serious squalor": ibid.

207 "There's obviously a large market": Marilyn Stasio, "The National Lampoon Show," *Cue* magazine, April 14, 1975.

207 "just good clever fun": Doug Henning, "The National Lampoon Show," *Playbill,* February 1975.

208 "Gilda—everybody loves her": Timothy White and Mitchell Glazer, "John Belushi," *Rolling Stone,* April 29, 1982.

209 "Nobody considers you legitimate": Tucker, "John Belushi."

CHAPTER 14

211 "What's brown and": Timothy White, "Saturday Night Quarterback," *Rolling Stone,* December 27, 1979.

212 "It was miraculous": Doug Hill and Jeff Weingrad, *Saturday Night: A Backstage History of Saturday Night Live* (New York: Beech Tree, 1986).

213 "offences against the": Wilmut, *From Fringe to Flying Circus.*

213 "Two Nentlemeg": ibid.

215 "very envious": White, "Saturday Night Quarterback."

215 "as if the network had closed down": ibid.

217 "a bop on the head": William Marsano, "TV Goes Underground," *TV Guide,* April 20, 1970.

220 "a function of Media America": Michael Shamberg and Raindance Corporation, *Guerrilla Television* (New York: Holt, Rinehart and Winston, 1971).

220 "no alternate cultural vision": ibid.

221 "whom I have criticized": ibid.

221 "portapack ecology": ibid.

221 "diversity rather than": ibid.

222 "a monument to the rise and fall": Ellin Stein, "Ant Farm," *Boulevards*, September 1980.

223 "The point is that": Shamberg and Raindance, *Guerrilla Television*.

CHAPTER 15

230 "a batch of rhetoric": Hill and Weingrad, *Saturday Night*.

230 "I had a big chip": Young, "From Samurai Saturday Night Live to Matinee Idol."

231 "there was never a moment's doubt": White, "Saturday Night Quarterback."

231 "I believe the phrase": ibid.

233 "the language of kisses blown": Michael Arlen, "On Air," *The New Yorker*, Oct 27, 1975.

234 "Maybe here we can become": Tom Burke, "The Post-Prime Time Follies of NBC's Saturday Night," *Rolling Stone*, July 15, 1976.

235 "The same violent urge": Young, "From Samurai Saturday Night Live to Matinee Idol."

235 "You know, I've always had a problem": ibid.

240 "There's no one performer": Burke, "The Post-Prime Time Follies of NBC's Saturday Night."

241 "This show's good when we're": ibid.

241 "a revolving doorway": Sweet, *Something Wonderful Right Away*.

241 "the tool that lets you": *Saturday Night Live*, April 17, 1976.

CHAPTER 16

246 "much of the humor": Hill and Weingrad, *Saturday Night*.

246 "a snot-nosed kid": ibid.

247 "The revolution will not": Gil Scott-Heron, "The Revolution Will Not Be Televised," *The Revolution Will Not Be Televised* (Flying Dutchman Records, 1974).

248 "pierced his left hand with a": *Saturday Night Live*, November 22, 1975.

249 "the post-Watergate victory party": Hill and Weingrad, *Saturday Night*.

250 "a medium that exists to sell products": Jeff Greenfield, "He's Chevy Chase and You're Not and He's TV's Hot New Comedy Star," *New York* magazine, December 22, 1975.

252 "wanted to force her to eat": Hill and Weingrad, *Saturday Night*.

253 "the liberal code for funny": Greenfield, "He's Chevy Chase and You're Not."

253 "TV's hot new comedy star": ibid.

254 "could be, besides the smartest": Burke, "The Post-Prime Time Follies of NBC's Saturday Night."

254 "Once we bend": ibid.

254 "I sure as hell never discouraged it": ibid.

255 "This show was conceived as": ibid.

CHAPTER 17

257 "It was chilling": Carney, "They Only Laughed When It Hurt."

258 "There could not be a less democratic": Tony Schwartz with Janet Huck, "College Humor Comes Back," *Newsweek*, October 23, 1978.

260 "the finest example": Charles Nicol, "*Ich bin ein* Kefauver Senior," *Harper's*, April 1975.

261 "Here I was": Richard Greene, "Funny Business," *Forbes*, December 22, 1980.

262 "Hardly anybody reads contracts": Carney, "They Only Laughed When It Hurt."

264 "Henry was patient": ibid.

271 "Patronizing indulgence?": Sean Kelly and P. J. O'Rourke, "Owls and Lugers," in *The Best of National Lampoon Number 7* (New York: National Lampoon Magazine, 1977).

272 "How did all this come about?": Tony Hendra and P. J. O'Rourke, "The Tail of Monty Snake," in *The Best of National Lampoon Number 7.*

CHAPTER 18

274 "labor, industry, government": John Weidman, "The System," in *The 199th Birthday Book* (New York: National Lampoon Magazine, 1975).

CHAPTER 20

296 "Haven't we suffered enough?": Richard Belzer, "The 2,105-Year-Old Man," *That's Not Funny, That's Sick* (Label 21, 1977).

296 "Give it to me lover": Sean Kelly, Bill Murray, and Donna Detroit, "Height Report Disco," *That's Not Funny, That's Sick.*

297 "I blew a joke in one of": Crouse, "Bill Murray."

298 "Well, honey": *Saturday Night Live*, May 21, 1977.

299 "Get rid of *all* the old standard characters": Burke, "The Post-Prime Time Follies of NBC's Saturday Night."

300 "artist-businessman": Hill and Weingrad, *Saturday Night.*

300 "I wanted it to be devoid of definition": White, "Saturday Night Quarterback."

302 "They expect you to be around a lot": Felton, "Bill Murray."

303 "Hell, I'd rather be psychotic": David Hirshey, "The Blues Brothers: The Sleazy Comedy of Dan Aykroyd and John Belushi," *New York Daily News Magazine*, January 14, 1979.

304 "the potato eaters, the *lumpenproletariat*": Hill and Weingrad, *Saturday Night.*

305 "This was just after the white heat": David Michaelis, "Dan Aykroyd and John Belushi: The Best of Friends," *Esquire*, December 1982.

306 "He's Mister Careful": Timothy White, "Dan Aykroyd: Messin' with the Kid," *Rolling Stone*, February 22, 1979.

307 "What'd you expect to find": Hirshey, "The Blues Brothers."

307 "everything becomes more heightened": Young, "From Samurai Saturday Night Live to Matinee Idol."

307 "white negro": Norman Mailer, *The White Negro* (San Francisco: City Lights Publishers, 1967).

307 "John and I often discussed": White and Glazer, "John Belushi."

308 "the junkie's cross. Ask any con": Grossberger, "John Belushi."

308 "John wanted to be a rock and roll star": "Belushi: Rock 'n' Roll Actor," MTV, March 5, 1986.

309 "The music just blew me away": Hirshey, "The Blues Brothers."

309 "was our chance to bring back": ibid.

310 "I realized you didn't have to be black": ibid.

310 "The only weakness was the frontmen": "Belushi: Rock 'n' Roll Actor."

311 "the Number One record": Grossberger, "John Belushi."

CHAPTER 21

325 "The first question for Ivan is": Joy Horowitz, "From Slapstick to Yuppie Fantasy," *New York Times Magazine*, June 15, 1986.

CHAPTER 22

328 "a sort of *National Lampoon* that": Richard Schickel, "Cinema: Lightly Browned," *Time*, August 29, 1977.

329 a *Rolling Stone* reporter: White, "Dan Aykroyd."

331 "Doug could have made himself anyone": Anson, "The Life and Death of a Comic Genius."

332 "combination of Harpo Marx and the Cookie Monster": White and Glazer, "John Belushi."

336 "The people who bring you": Eve Drobot, "School for Scandal," *Maclean's*, September 1978.

338 "It's behavioral humor of outrage": Schwartz, "College Humor Comes Back."

339 "A lot of this is a backlash": ibid.

CHAPTER 23

342 "the undeserved audience": Hill and Weingrad, *Saturday Night.*

342 "it was embarrassing. We were the": ibid.

342 "the angel dust crowd": Hirshey, "The Blues Brothers."

343 "After the success of *Animal House*": Stephen Farber and Marc Green, *Outrageous Conduct: Art, Ego and the Twilight Zone Case* (New York: Arbor House / William Morrow & Company, 1988).

343 "a metaphor for America": ibid.

344 "*The Blues Brothers* should have been": ibid.

349 "who raided Chicago's satirical Second City": "The *Lampoon* Goes Hollywood," *Time*, August 14, 1978.

351 "There's a strong right-wing bent": Arthur Lubow, "Screw You Humor," *The New Republic*, October 21, 1978.

352 "Republicans who took drugs": Green, "Last Laughs."

352 "We look like Republicans and": P. J. O'Rourke, *Republican Party Reptile* (New York: Grove/Atlantic, 1987).

352 "Some people are worried": ibid.

352 "ordinary men and women": P. J. O'Rourke, "On Looking into Emily Post's *Etiquette*," *House & Garden*, May 1984.

353 "We take the stance": Schwartz, "College Humor Comes Back."

353 "We are ruling class": "The *Lampoon* Goes Hollywood."

353 "There's more materialism": Ellin Stein, "A 'Rolling Stone' Gathers New Market Demographics," *Adweek*, February 1981.

353 "Like Democrats, we've": P. J. O'Rourke, "Hey, Whatever Works," *National Review*, September 16, 1988.

354 "I read all of Chris Miller's stuff": Mark Matousek, "John Hughes," *Interview*, August 1985.

355 "I don't want to be too cool": ibid.

356 "has marred the vacation plans": P. J. O'Rourke and John Hughes, *Sunday Newspaper Parody* (New York: National Lampoon Magazine, 1978).

357 "perpetuating in spite of myself": Green, "Last Laughs."

357 "Here I was": ibid.

359 "Turning 29 was *really* tough for me": Matousek, "John Hughes."

CHAPTER 24

368 "Sounds as if they emptied": "All the News That's Fun to Print," *Time*, October 23, 1978.

369 "'disco' is a term": "Fall Season Thrown into Confusion by Studio 54 Blaze," *Not the New York Times*, October 1978.

369 "a six-month investigation": "An Exotic Drug, 'Cocaine', Appears Popular," *Not the New York Times*.

369 "Big Bird will show": "TV Listings," *Not the New York Times*.

371 "Ms. Abbie Hoffman": Abbie Hoffman, "Blippie Nation," in *The 80s: A Look Back at the Tumultuous Decade 1980–1989*, ed. Tony Hendra, Peter Elbling, and Christopher Cerf (New York: Workman Publishing Company, 1979).

372 "First National United": Jack Egan, "Futures," in Hendra, Elbling, and Cerf, *The 80s*.

372 "no pregnancy may be terminated": Henry Beard, "The New Bill of Rights," in Hendra, Elbling, and Cerf, *The 80s*.

372 "The redefinition of 'journalism'": Ellis Weiner, "Adieu, Print," in Hendra, Elbling, and Cerf, *The 80s*.

372 "voters repaid Mr. Reagan's patriotic": Peter Elbling, Bruce McCall, Maurice Peterson, George Plimpton, and Harry Shearer, "Where Are They Now '89," in Hendra, Elbling, and Cerf, *The 80s*.

373 "dead, stifling hand of bureaucrats": Jeff Greenfield, "Neo-Irvington," in Hendra, Elbling, and Cerf, *The 80s*.

373 "in the 1970s, we held": Jeff Greenfield, "A Court For Our Time," in Hendra, Elbling, and Cerf, *The 80s*.

376 "Senses dulled by": Christopher Cerf and Henry Beard, *The Pentagon Catalog* (New York: Workman Publishing Company, 1986).

CHAPTER 25

379 "$6 million scholarship to": Anson, "The Life and Death of a Comic Genius."

380 "had any perspective on their lives": Myron Meisel, "Chevy Chase: Mr. Middle Class," *Rolling Stone*, October 13, 1983.

381 "The movie business retains a vague authority": Trow, *Within the Context of No Context*.

391 "to market high-energy, raw-talent artists": Schwartz, "Forever Young."

391 "We know it looks": ibid.

393 "three weeks of recovery": Chevy Chase, "Doug Kenney Dies in Accidental Fall," *Rolling Stone*, October 16, 1980.

393 "Doug was in the midst of making a choice": Anson, "The Life and Death of a Comic Genius."

397 "like an urgent memo from God": Green, "Last Laughs."

398 "exercise of preference": Trow, *Within the Context of No Context.*

INDEX

INDEX